2017
The Supreme Court Review

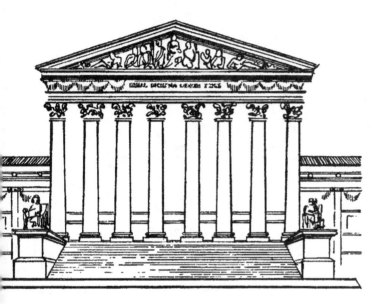

2017
The

"Judges as persons, or courts as institutions, are entitled to no greater immunity from criticism than other persons or institutions . . . [J]udges must be kept mindful of their limitations and of their ultimate public responsibility by a vigorous stream of criticism expressed with candor however blunt."
—*Felix Frankfurter*

". . . while it is proper that people should find fault when their judges fail, it is only reasonable that they should recognize the difficulties. . . . Let them be severely brought to book, when they go wrong, but by those who will take the trouble to understand them."
—*Learned Hand*

THE LAW SCHOOL

THE UNIVERSITY OF CHICAGO

Supreme Court Review

EDITED BY

DENNIS J. HUTCHINSON

DAVID A. STRAUSS

AND GEOFFREY R. STONE

THE UNIVERSITY OF CHICAGO PRESS

CHICAGO AND LONDON

INTERNATIONAL STANDARD BOOK NUMBER: 978-0-226-57685-5

LIBRARY OF CONGRESS CATALOG CARD NUMBER: 60-14353

THE UNIVERSITY OF CHICAGO PRESS, CHICAGO 60637

THE UNIVERSITY OF CHICAGO PRESS, LTD., LONDON

© 2018 BY THE UNIVERSITY OF CHICAGO, ALL RIGHTS RESERVED, PUBLISHED 2018

PRINTED IN THE UNITED STATES OF AMERICA

The paper used in this publication meets the minimum requirements of American National Standard for Information Sciences–Permanence of Paper for Printed Library Materials, ANSI Z39.48-1984. ⊗

TO

DENNIS J. HUTCHINSON

*Nonpareil editor of this journal
for nearly four decades*

CONTENTS

PREFACE

With this volume, Dennis J. Hutchinson retires from editing the *Review* after thirty-seven years. We are delighted that Justin Driver, the Harry N. Wyatt Professor of Law, has agreed to succeed Dennis, and we welcome him. Justin will serve in many of Dennis's roles, as liaison to the University of Chicago Press and as principal contact for authors.

The dedication to this volume reflects, inadequately, our debt to Dennis. His intellectual rigor, commitment to the mission of the *Review*, and deft and graceful writing and editing have made him the heart and soul of the *Review*. *Ave atque vale*, Dennis, but farewell only as our editorial collaborator; we look forward to your company as an academic colleague for many years to come.

DAVID A. STRAUSS
GEOFFREY R. STONE

JEREMY WALDRON

HECKLE: TO DISCONCERT WITH QUESTIONS, CHALLENGES, OR GIBES

Truth, in the great practical concerns of life, is so much a question of the reconciling and combining of opposites, that very few have minds sufficiently capacious and impartial to make the adjustment with an approach to correctness, and it has to be made by the rough process of a struggle between combatants fighting under hostile banners. (John Stuart Mill, *On Liberty*, chapter 2)

I

I would like to consider the case that can be made for permitting, encouraging, and protecting the activity of heckling.[1] Is heckling free speech? (It is certainly speech.)[2] Or is it a violation of free speech

---

Jeremy Waldron is University Professor, New York University Law School.

AUTHOR'S NOTE: Earlier versions of this paper were presented at a "Dangerous Speech" conference at University College, London, in May 2017 and a Faculty Workshop at New York University Law School in July 2017.

[1] I have in mind heckling at political meetings, not at ball games or comedy performances. For sports heckling, see articles like *Knock Me Out at the Old Ball Game*, 56 Or State Bar Bulletin 42 (1996), and cases like *Simmons v Baltimore Orioles Inc.*, 712 F Supp 79, 79 (WD Va 1989). For heckling of comedians, see generally Keith Fields, *How to Handle Hecklers: The Complete Guide to Dealing with Every Performer's Worst Nightmare* (2006).

[2] Thomas Emerson, *The System of Freedom of Expression* (1970), disagrees. He suggests that heckling is like pure noise, and he goes on to observe that "conduct that obstructs or seriously impedes the utterance of another, even though verbal in form, cannot be classified as expression. It has the same effect, in preventing or disrupting communication, as acts of physical force. Consequently it must be deemed action and is not covered by the First Amendment" (id at 338).

(albeit a horizontal violation rather than the sort of vertical violation—violation by government—that the First Amendment seems framed to protect us from).[3] Or is it both—free speech *and* a violation of free speech—to be dealt with under the auspices of an ordered as opposed to an anarchic system of liberty?[4] In this article, I don't want to consider just the threat that heckling poses (or is imagined to pose) to free speech itself. I also want to consider the threat it poses to public order and security, the threat it poses to political choreography, and above all the salutary threat it may pose to forms of political expression that we should not be in the business of trying to nourish and protect.

II

It is not my intention to undertake a First Amendment analysis of heckling. American constitutional doctrine on heckling remains uncertain and unsettled; there are no unequivocal Supreme Court precedents on the matter and state law is mixed.[5] My contribution is intended more as background analysis. It will be relevant to free speech discussions in America certainly, but also in other jurisdictions as well. I want to try to figure out what to say about heckling first, as preparation for thinking about the case that can be made in relation to constitutional or rights norms in some particular system of positive law. Also, I want to engage with the work of Eric Barendt and Timothy Garton Ash in the United Kingdom, who write about free speech but not really about the First Amendment.[6] To the extent that they are interested in constitutional norms, the relevant norm is Article 10 of the European Convention on Human Rights and its counterpart in the United Kingdom's own Human Rights Act. I will be drawing, too, for philosophical background on the work of John Stuart Mill in

---

[3] Alexander Meiklejohn, *Free Speech and Its Relation to Self-Government* 24 (1948), describes the heckler as "a boor, a public nuisance, who must be abated, by force if necessary."

[4] Eve H. Lewin Wagner, *Heckling: A Protected Right or Disorderly Conduct?*, 60 S Cal L Rev 215, 217 (1986), cites the Supreme Court's observation in *Red Lion Broadcasting Co. v FCC*, 395 US 367, 387 (1969), to the effect that "when two people converse face to face, both should not speak at once if either is to be clearly understood."

[5] Compare the California case of *In re Kay*, 1 Cal3d 930 (1970), with Florida's *Carlson v Tallahassee*, 240 So2d 866 (Fla 1970), cert denied, 403 US 910 (1971).

[6] See generally Eric Barendt, *Freedom of Speech* (2007). Timothy Garton Ash, of St. Antony's College, Oxford, is organizer of the website http://freespeechdebate.com/en/ and author of *Free Speech: Ten Principles for a Connected World* (2007). I have profited from many conversations with these scholars at Oxford, the University of London, and elsewhere.

chapter 2 of *On Liberty*. Mill's essay is not presented as legal analysis of any sort; instead he asks about the attitudes toward liberty of expression that should be encouraged in "the intelligent part of the public."[7] That said, some of the discussion in the American case law is instructive for its broad orientation and I shall refer to it and make use of it. I will deploy it, not as authority, but for the persuasive arguments that it might embody. Some remarks of the California Supreme Court in the leading case of *In re Kay* (1970) are, as we shall see, quite helpful.[8]

III

What is heckling? The *Merriam Webster* dictionary offers a helpful definition, which I have adapted for use in the title of this article. It says that to heckle is "to harass and try to disconcert with questions, challenges, or gibes."[9]

"Harass" is not nice, but let's focus on "disconcert." Someone is speaking, all perfectly poised with a well-behaved audience in front of him,[10] and someone else interrupts in order to *disconcert* his performance. "Disconcert"—what does that mean? The same dictionary tells us that to disconcert someone is "to disturb the composure" of that person. (It also says that disconcert can mean "throw into confusion," but that seems a usage associated with disconcerting some *thing* like a plan rather than a person.)

Again, the words are telling. "Composure" need not be confined to self-presentation or control of dress, deportment, or appearance. (I guess someone who throws eggs, tomatoes, or cream pies may disturb a speaker's "composure" in that sense.) Instead, think of composure as a speaker's plan for his address—the strategy he has composed for the thirty minutes or so he will be on stage and communicating with his audience. His composure includes what he plans to say, how he plans to say it, the issues he will raise, the issues he will strive to avoid, and in general the effect he hopes to have on his audience. To heckle

---

[7] John Stuart Mill, *On Liberty*, in John Stuart Mill, *On Liberty and the Subjection of Women* 84 (Alan Ryan, ed, 2006).

[8] *In re Kay*, 1 Cal3d 930 (1970).

[9] *Merriam-Webster Dictionary*. Compare the definition given in the *Oxford English Dictionary*: "Interrupt (a public speaker) with derisive or aggressive comments or abuse."

[10] Pronouns are used inclusively: "him" means "him or her," unless the context clearly indicates otherwise.

is to try to disturb all that—to interrupt the speaker's game plan by shouting out questions he would rather not answer or mentioning facts he would prefer not to talk about (disturbing his strategy for avoiding them), drawing the attention of the audience in directions the speaker does not want it to go.

Back in the day, heckling—in this sense—was a common and accepted feature of political meetings. "The heckling and harassment of public officials and other speakers while making public speeches is as old as American and British politics."[11] I know; I was there. Living in the southernmost cities of New Zealand's South Island, I remember attending political meetings around election time, shouting interjections at crucial points, and sometimes eliciting answers, more often put-downs, from the speaker (who always seemed disconcertingly well equipped to respond to hecklers). It was an accepted part of political life. I had trained for it, in debate team, where interjection and responding to interjections were accepted skills. Our debate coach at Southland Boys' High School was Norman Jones, who later became National Party (conservative) MP for the district.[12] He would sit on stage with Prime Minister Muldoon, as it might be, smiling broadly as his former students locked horns with Muldoon in rough repartee. Sometimes the prime minister would brusquely answer whatever question we had shouted and then proceed with his prepared remarks. Sometimes he would give a brief lecture on the merits of a system that allowed hecklers to speak out (not like the Soviet Union etc.). Sometimes he would respond with an *ad hominem* observation. Very rarely was he lost for words. It wouldn't occur to him to have the hecklers removed. Muldoon was a rough character but he was well equipped to deal with interruptions.[13] Skill with hecklers was an important part of any public speaker's training.[14] Politicians were used to it in Parliament and they expected it on the hustings.

IV

I have the impression those days are gone. In the last election campaign in the United States, I watched on television as people who

---

[11] *In re Kay*, 1 Cal3d 930 (1970).

[12] See generally Norman P. H. Jones, *Jonesy* (1982).

[13] Barry Gustafson, *His Way: A Biography of Robert Muldoon* 101–4 (2000).

[14] See, e.g., John A. Lee, *The Lee Way to Public Speaking* 111–14 (1965) (ch 21: "Interjectors and Questioners").

shouted interjections during speeches by candidate Donald Trump were immediately seized and taken out of the auditorium.[15] And this does not seem a peculiarity of the Trump team's organization, but common across the board. I remember that when Vice President Al Gore gave a commencement speech for Columbia Law School in May 2000, someone in the audience shouted a hostile comment at him during his address. Just one shouted comment. Gore said nothing in response. But we all watched quietly—including Columbia's First Amendment scholars—as the heckler was removed. There was a patter of applause for the security guys as the heckler was led away.[16]

Why is heckling not as tolerated now as it once was, or why is it not tolerated here (in the United States) when it has been tolerated elsewhere? I expect that if you asked those involved—those whose job it is to remove hecklers—they would say it is an issue of public order, security even. Interruption is unruly, it presages disorder. Things might get out of hand. In the midst of disorder, there is always the chance of violence, and this country has had unpleasant experience of political violence over the past fifty years.

There is also a concern about disruption, which is different from disorder. Disruption has to do with throwing out of gear the careful staging of an event. In April 2006, a Falun Gong member interrupted a "solemn" welcome ceremony for the president of China at the White House, shouting "President Bush, make him stop persecuting Falun Gong." Though she was charged with disorderly conduct, it was the disruption of her unwelcome words that was feared. The caption of a photo accompanying the news story I saw about this said: "A Secret Service officer *covers the mouth* of Wenyi Wang, 47, as she is escorted from the camera stand after disrupting President Hu Jintao's speech."[17] Chinese television blacked out the incident and blocked parts of a CNN report that showed it and reported it. The welcome ceremony had been carefully choreographed for television coverage and, as far as possible, Wenyi Wang was not to be permitted to disrupt that choreography. I suspect that the increased importance of political cho-

---

[15] Daniel White, *Donald Trump Tells Crowd to "Knock the Crap Out of" Hecklers*, Time, Feb 1, 2016, available at http://time.com/4203094/donald-trump-hecklers/.

[16] For a somewhat similar case, see *State v Colby*, 185 Vt 464, 472, 972 A2d 197, 204 (2009).

[17] *Heckler Embarrasses Presidents*, The Age (Melbourne), Apr 21, 2006 (my emphasis), available at http://www.theage.com.au/news/world/heckler-embarrasses-presidents/2006/04/21/1145344247214.html.

reography has a great deal to do with our contemporary intolerance for heckling. Campaigns invest an enormous amount of preparation in the events they stage for their candidates: appearances are orchestrated, speeches are drafted by committees of earnest aides and tested in front of focus groups, with every cadence calculated and recalculated, and every applause line carefully positioned. The last thing anyone wants is for these rhythms to be screwed up by importunate hecklers. Heckling—a shouted question, an impudent interjection— means that the audience is not hearing exactly what the speaker wants them to hear in the order he presents it and exactly as he wants them to hear it. He has less control over the event. The prospect of disorder may be cited in defense of the silencing and removal of hecklers, but it's the disruption that matters, and we cannot understand the significance of the disruption without understanding how much is invested in (and expected from) the choreography of political occasions.[18]

V

I will have much more to say about political choreography, but there is another way in which the impact of heckling has changed in recent years. Every week, it seems, we hear of the turmoil that erupts on some college campus when a provocative figure—a clown like Milo Yiannopolouos or a controversial scholar like Charles Murray—is invited to speak.

Sometimes violence erupts beforehand and prevents the speech from taking place: the authorities cancel the speech because of the further disorder they anticipate from hecklers. This is known as the

---

[18] For an example that comes close to political choreography being treated as a First Amendment value, consider this, from *State v Hardin*, 498 NW2d 677, 681 (Iowa 1993):

> Hardin's disruptive conduct occurred in an auditorium filled with persons who had paid for the opportunity to sit and listen to an address by the President of the United States. Although earlier parts of the program involved standing and cheering, the portion interrupted by Hardin was otherwise quiet and respectful. . . . [T]he record reveals that the disruption effectively stopped the meeting, if only for a few minutes, while audience members turned to address the commotion, cameras moved in to focus on the hecklers, and at least one citizen shouted at Hardin while another attempted to physically seat him. There is no dispute in this record that Hardin intended to continue the disruption until forced to cease. . . . We believe that under these circumstances the State proved that Hardin intentionally disrupted this assembly and that his doing so exceeded any authority he might lawfully claim under the free speech provisions of our state and federal Constitutions.

heckler's veto.[19] If the event does take place, opponents infiltrate the audience and use concerted chanting and slow hand-clapping to drown out the speaker for part or all of his address. (This also is known as the heckler's veto, in less sophisticated uses of that term.[20]) One way or another, these tactics are seen as a direct assault on free speech, and the removal and punishment of the chanters, clappers, and taunters, where that is possible, is justified as a defense of free speech values.

These incidents fuel the impression that heckling is inherently intolerant—that it is not itself free speech but something opposed to free speech—and that impression stands alongside the concerns about disorder and disruption that I mentioned in Section IV to justify the demonization of heckling.

When thwarted speakers and embarrassed college authorities call for the identification and punishment of those who interrupt meetings in this way, what they often say is that the hecklers in question have violated the guest's right to free speech. Now, they can't mean this literally in the United States in the sense of a constitutional right, since the First Amendment is framed as a right against the government, not (horizontally) against one's fellow citizens. But in a more expansive sense that we definitely ought to consider in an inquiry of this kind, it is understood that speakers have moral rights of free expression against those of their fellow citizens who attempt to silence them, and that *that* is what is at stake in these incidents. Sometimes this difference is marked by using phrases that are constitutionally noncanonical, like "free intellectual inquiry" or "the free exchange of ideas." Sometimes the principles involved are related to the specific mission of a college or a university.[21]

---

[19] Barendt, *Free Speech* at 297 (cited in note 6): "Although on public order grounds, it makes sense to consider the propensity of the audience to react violently to inflammatory or offensive speech, this has the unfortunate result that it may give aggressive hecklers a veto on what may be said at a public meeting—the hostile audience problem."

[20] The distinction between the two versions of "heckler's veto" is found in the Wikipedia article on the subject. On the one hand, Wikipedia tells us, "In First Amendment law, a heckler's veto is the suppression of speech by the government, because of [the possibility of] a violent reaction by hecklers. It is the government that vetoes the speech, because of the reaction of the heckler." On the other hand, it says that "Heckler's veto is often used outside a strict legal context. One example is an article by Nat Hentoff in which he claims that … everyone has the right to picket a speaker, and to go inside the hall and heckle him or her— but not to drown out the speaker, let alone rush the stage and stop the speech before it starts. That's called the 'heckler's veto.'" (The article cited is from *The Village Voice*, Sept 19, 2007.)

[21] See generally Erwin Chemerinsky and Howard Gillman, *Free Speech on Campus* (2017).

Sometimes in addition, critics of heckling will talk about the rights of the audience, at least those members of the audience who were not involved in the heckling. It is said that they have a right to hear the speaker and not have their hearing of him drowned out by the chanting and cat-calls of the hecklers. This too is a contention worth discussing, again even if it does not fall squarely into First Amendment orthodoxy. I will return to these specific issues about campus disruption and "the heckler's veto" toward the end of the article in Section XIII.

VI

Here's how I want to approach the overall topic. We can think of any given incident, x, of heckling as something located on a spectrum, with the sort of cases I have just mentioned—involving a concerted attempt (maybe even a violent attempt) to shout down someone's speech or drown him out—at one end, and the sort of case I cited proudly in Section III—a brusque but intelligent question shouted out by some smart-ass in the audience—at the other end. I believe it matters not only where x is located on the spectrum, but also from what

```
brusque_____ x_____ shouting
question                                        down
```

end the whole spectrum (and x's location on it) is viewed. Viewed from the right-hand end, any given x is likely to seem like an intimation of violence and intolerance. But viewed from the other end, x might seem quite tolerable, indeed a robust aspect of healthy debate. And there might be things to be said in favor of x, even though some will perceive it to be uncomfortably close to the right-hand end.

I think one of the things that has happened in recent years is that heckling is increasingly viewed through the lens of speech suppression and potential violence. The only mention of heckling in Timothy Garton Ash's free speech materials, for example, is under the heading of "violence": "Violence: *We neither make threats of violence nor accept violent intimidation.*"[22] We don't accept the heckler's veto, says Garton Ash, nor the "assassin's veto."[23] I think it is a mistake to

---

[22] Garton Ash, *Ten Principles* at 129–30 (cited in note 6).

[23] Id.

view heckling only through this lens.[24] We might achieve a more balanced account by viewing it from the other end—the left-hand end—as well. That is what I shall try to do.

VII

So let us begin from the left-hand end. I am of the belief that heckling a speaker—disconcerting him, disturbing the composure he has worked up for the occasion—is often and characteristically a good thing for the exchange of ideas, particularly in the circumstances of modern politics.

Viewed in this light, incidents of heckling have two aims: one is to secure a particular response to the particular comment or question that is shouted out; the other is to ensure that the primary speech is not exactly the poised, planned, calibrated, self-possessed, and precisely choreographed performance that the primary speaker wants it to be. Heckling has (and is intended to have) the effect of making it difficult to proceed with the speech on exactly the primary speaker's own terms. The idea is to make sure that the audience does *not* hear exactly what the primary speaker wants them to hear in the precise order he presents it and exactly as he wants them to hear it. As I said earlier, the primary speaker may want to proceed on the basis that certain awkward facts will not be raised, which might discredit the analysis he is conveying, while the heckler will seek to raise these facts. Or the speaker may want to proceed while minimizing a possible objection to what he is saying, whereas the heckler will try to maximize it, putting in front of the audience's mind what the speaker wishes they could ignore altogether.

Often this is very irksome to the speaker because of the huge investment that has been made in his speech by a committee of his aides and supporters—an investment in precise rhetoric, command of audience, cadences that tend to elicit applause at crucial moments, ceremonious staging, and so on. So he doesn't want to be heckled. But does he have a right not to be heckled? Another way of putting this

---

[24] What I mean is that it's a mistake to use categories like *potential violence* and *heckler's veto* to characterize, for example, the following comment shouted at a speech given by UK Foreign Secretary Boris Johnson in Shildon in the north of England in the days leading up to the 2017 election: "'This is one of the most deprived wards in the United Kingdom,' one activist shouted. That's thanks to Tory austerity" (Jessica Elgot, *Johnson Accuses Corbyn of Siding with UK's Enemies*, The Guardian, June 7, 2017). Such interjections deserve better from the free speech professoriate.

question is: does the primary speaker have a right that the audience hear him *exactly as he wants to be heard* without interruption or distraction?

It is tempting to say "yes." If free speech is about self-expression, then it may seem that what is to be expressed is exactly what the expressing self desires and intends to express: he organizes in his thoughts exactly what he wants to disclose to the audience and his right of free expression is an entitlement to put exactly that into play; otherwise what would be put before them would be something other than what he has determined to express.[25] Of course, the same approach will acknowledge that the exercise of self-expression may fail because the speaker's expressive skills are inadequate. He may be a poor speaker or a poorly organized one, incapable of giving voice to what he wants to say. Like all exercises of freedom, self-expression can face internal obstacles. But his right of free expression is a right only to be free of external obstacles posed by the action and interference of others. It is a negative freedom, not a positive one, and negative freedom at any rate is not affected by lack of internal ability.[26] The speaker's stammer or poor voice projection is one thing. But someone unplugging his microphone or putting a hand over his mouth would amount to an external impediment. And that—according to the approach we are considering—is what disruptive or disconcerting heckling amounts to. It prevents the speaker from giving expression— within the range of his own abilities—to exactly what he wants to express in the way that he wants to express it. For example, what he wants to express is proposition *P* followed immediately by proposition *Q*. But the heckler interrupts the expression of *P* with a blurted comment *X*, which, coming between *P* and *Q*, creates a wholly different impression, even though "*X*" is not spoken by the primary speaker himself. Unlike "*P . . . Q*," which is the speaker's intended sequence, "*P*" followed by "*X*" followed by "*Q*" creates an impression that the primary speaker would go to considerable lengths to avoid if he could.

---

[25] Compare C. Edwin Baker, *Harm, Liberty, and Free Speech*, 70 S Cal L Rev 979, 992 (1997): "Respect for personhood, for agency, or for autonomy, requires that each person must be permitted to be herself and to present herself." I have discussed Baker's approach in Jeremy Waldron, *The Harm in Hate Speech* 161–72 (2012).

[26] Cf Isaiah Berlin, *Two Concepts of Liberty*, in his book *Liberty: Incorporating Four Essays on Liberty* (Henry Hardy, ed, 2002), 166, at 169.

Something like this, I think, is the case that might be made against heckling in the name of freedom of expression.

But the view of self-expression here is way too strong to count as a right. Think of a couple of ways it may fall apart even without a heckler's interruption. First—as before—it may be part of the speaker's intention (creating the impression he wants to create) that he convey Q immediately after conveying P. But if members of his audience are inattentive and miss his saying "P," that impression will not be created. And of course no one wants to say that the right to free expression includes a right to a fully attentive audience. Or secondly: suppose our speaker was preceded on the platform by someone who (unbeknownst to him) managed to convince their common audience that every time they hear P they should associate it with X and resist any unmediated association with Q. (This need not have been directed by the first speaker against the second; it may just have been something the first speaker wanted to convey.) Even so, its effect is to screw things up for the second speaker's presentation. For as soon as he starts going on about P, his audience is going to associate it with X even without the assistance of a heckler, and they will be already inoculated against the unmediated P/Q association that the speaker so fervently wants to convey. But again, no one will say that the second speaker has a right that the first speaker not spoil things for him in this way.[27]

So we cannot predicate any response to heckling on the primary speaker's right of free expression in this strong sense. The primary speaker may have a right to say what he likes. But he does not have a right to this sort of control over the attention or state of mind of his audience. Their reaction is theirs—and theirs in a common world—not his alone to affect and control.[28] Whatever he desires to express and succeeds in expressing, it goes out into a world populated by other speakers and it is heard by a heterogeneous audience. And one simply has to take one's chances with that. The impact of heckling is just a variation on these vicissitudes.

---

[27] Here is a hypothetical example to flesh out the algebra. Theresa May wants to say P: "The Conservatives have always been the party of security," and she wants to follow that immediately with Q: "You should trust us at this time of terrorist threats." But in between P and Q, someone shouts out X: "But, Mrs. May, as Home Secretary you personally were responsible for cutting 20,000 officers from the police force between 2014 and 2016."

[28] Compare the observation in *Payroll Guar. Assn. v Board of Education* (1945), 27 Cal2d 197, 202–3: "Speakers who express their opinions freely must run the risk of attracting opposition; they cannot expect their opponents to be silenced while they continue to speak freely."

It has sometimes been said—and I think said rightly—that a speaker with a right to free speech does not have a right to an audience; he does not have a right that others listen to him when he speaks. He certainly doesn't have a right to the audience he wants, even if there are people willing to listen to him. The members of the audience are independent participants with their own rights. The presence and the actions of a heckler amount to a fragment of the audience asserting itself against the speaker's desire for exactly the sort of audience attention that would serve his purposes. No doubt it is frustrating for the speaker. But the frustration of the speaker's desires is not for that reason a violation of his rights.

VIII

What changes if we look at these interactions from the point of view of the audience—I mean now the rest of the audience apart from the heckler? It is sometimes said,[29] as part of the ethos or principle of free speech, that a willing audience has a right to hear the speaker and that it is this right that the heckler is interfering with.[30] This may be something to consider in the cases—like those set out in Section V—where the effect of heckling is actually to silence the speaker or shut down the occasion. We will consider that again in a moment. But looking at things from the left-hand end of our spectrum in Section VI, how does routine or ordinary heckling affect the rights of the audience?

The first thing to say is that serious contemplation of heckling forces us to disaggregate our talk of "the audience." The presence of a heckler or two shows us that the audience is not homogenous: there are the hecklers, there are the devoted loyalists who really want to hear the speaker, and there are those in between whose experience of the occasion might be affected, pleasantly or unpleasantly, by the interaction. Whose rights are we talking about?

Consider the devoted loyalists. They have come along to hear the speaker; they want the event to be one of unalloyed communication from speaker to audience and hopefully also an event of inspiration

---

[29] I repeat phrases like "It is sometimes said …" because I want to probe and analyze the things that opponents of heckling tend to say in academic discussion (often without thinking).

[30] Cf Note, *Freedom to Hear: A Political Justification of the First Amendment*, 46 Wash L Rev 311, 354–75 (1971).

and galvanization of the audience by the speaker on the speaker's own terms. (Possibly their hopes and expectations also include some non-oppositional heckling—"Lock her up!" etc. I shall put that to one side.) Do the devoted loyalists have a right to hear just what they come expecting to hear and to have their attention seized by the speaker's remarks in just the way that they—and he—want it to be seized?

Again I think the answer is "no," if only because an affirmative answer would mean privileging the interests of some members of the audience over others. In Section VII I implied that the speaker is not entitled to the audience he wants. Now I want to say that no member or faction of the audience has a right that the audience overall be of exactly the kind that they want (to belong to). A member of the audience, who may claim to be aggrieved by heckling, is not entitled to base his grievance on a purported right to be a member of exactly the audience he wants to be a member of. Just as the speaker must take his audience as he finds them, so a given audience member must take his fellow audience members as he finds them. And in a setting like this, his experience of the speech will not be determined by factors solely under his and the speaker's control. The fact that there are some or many in the audience who want to listen passively, with their enthusiastic applause elicited in just the ways that the speaker wants to elicit it, does not give them the right that other audience members should conform to this hyper-receptive paradigm.

I guess for completeness I should add that the heckler usually does not get, and certainly is not entitled to, the audience *he* wants to be a member of either. His shouted remarks may be witty, erudite, and probing. But if the primary speaker comes up with an effective riposte or put-down, the heckler has no legitimate complaint. Nor may he complain if the reaction of the rest of the audience is a roar of disapproval directed at him.[31]

IX

A lot of what I have been saying presupposes what my youthful escapades involved: a political meeting open to the public. How

---

[31] At Michael Oren protest: "Meanwhile, attendees opposed to the hecklers stood up and shouted back, making obscene gestures at those involved in the walkout"—quoted in Andrew Seif, *The University Marketplace of Ideas Under Threat: Why Religious Student Groups on California's Public University Campuses Need to Follow the Rules*, 40 Wash State U L Rev 105, 107 (2012).

much of it changes if we transform the paradigm to a private occasion on private property with a hand-picked audience that the heckler has somehow infiltrated? The speaker may try to secure this by rigging the audience preaching only to an enthusiastic choir, and doing his best or his campaign's best to ensure that dissident and obstreperous choristers are excluded.

The analysis changes in part, but the shift raises other questions too. First, unless the ticket of admission involves an extraordinary degree of contractual constraint, the most that is generated is a right to remove the heckler (or anyone else who proves unwanted, like a parent with a crying baby).[32] This is purely a matter of the exclusionary incident of private property; it has nothing to do with free speech. Maybe there is a liability for trespass if the heckler is there under blatantly false pretenses. But this will not cover the case of the bona fide audience member whose attitudes have been evolving since he received the invitation or, for that matter, since he came into the hall.

Still, it cannot be denied that the privatization of public speaking is one basis on which a speaker and his aides might be entitled to act against hecklers.[33] And commentators talk sometimes of the "the increasing obsolescence of traditional public forums as a meaningful platform for citizen speech."[34] How we should regard such privatization is another matter. Should we think of it as a new paradigm—the new normal—for free political speech? Or should we deplore it as an undermining of free speech values, as indicative in other words of the distortion of free speech values that happens owing to the lengths that speakers now go to ensure a basis for audience control conducive to their choreographic intentions? We cannot rule out this model of privatization—the audience as extras in a scripted performance for TV. But I believe we should not be in the business of certifying or endorsing this as our idealized model of free expression.[35] I have been hinting at that verdict for some time now. But before I face up to it explicitly,

---

[32] Cf Scott Bixby, *"Get the baby out of here": Trump Ejects Crying Infant from Rally*, The Guardian, August 2, 2016.

[33] Kevin Frances O'Neill, *Privatizing Public Forums to Eliminate Dissent*, 75 First Amend L Rev 201 (2000).

[34] Id.

[35] For the value of public meetings, in regard to free speech and political equality, see Emerson, *The System of Freedom of Expression* (cited in note 2), as quoted by Kevin O'Neill and Raymond Vasvari, *Counter-Demonstration as Protected Speech: Finding the Right to Confrontation in Existing First Amendment Law*, 23 Hastings Const L Q 77, 121 (1995).

I want to say something more about the general relation between free speech values and heckling.

X

The arguments given in Sections VII and VIII of this article against the suppression of heckling may seem tricksy and technical—typical philosopher's maneuvering. But I don't think the case is just analytic. I am going to show now that the argument against the suppression of heckling goes to the heart of our free speech commitments.

We value free speech and we give it moral, legal, and constitutional protection for a reason—actually for an array of reasons. No list of reasons will be complete, but here are a few of them.

1. First, there is the account we began to explore in Section VII. We value free speech because it is a means of self-expression—crucial to individual personality in its disclosure of itself to others. This is an autonomy argument, based on the inherent value to each individual of being able to disclose himself to others (to the extent, of course, that they are interested in him and in who he thinks he is). Autonomous self-disclosure may also be an instrumental good as we see what is to be gained in the way of economic and other interaction on the basis of our freedom to give an account of ourselves to others.

2. Connected with this is a strong dignity interest. We say to the government—our government—"How dare you interfere with our speech?!" We are grown-ups and we have opinions of our own, and we will not accept any attempt to silence us, as though our speaking our minds were something to be tolerated only when it suited the purposes of others.

3. A third line of defense looks to the way that spoken interaction with others invigorates thinking and personality, stirring our thoughts and driving us into deeper and more sophisticated understandings. We all have our beliefs, and I guess we can keep them to ourselves if we like. But their free and open expression in the presence of others brings them to life, puts them on their mettle, and by requiring them to defend themselves and to give an account of themselves in public invigorates them and allows them to do the critical work in individual ethical life and moral life among individuals that it is their function to do. Free expression involves the salutary risk of opposition and argument. And that is what brings our beliefs to life and pre-

vents their becoming what John Stuart Mill called a "dull and torpid" encrustation on the mind.[36]

4. A fourth—perhaps the best known—basis on which free speech is defended is its function as a means to the pursuit of truth. False-hoods may live unchallenged where free expression of opposing ideas is not permitted. We value free expression and the freedom to challenge orthodox and heterodox ideas alike, because what is expressed may contribute to truth, or refute falsehood, or may be a necessary means to the filtering of one from the other.

Sometimes the phrase "the marketplace of ideas" is used to capture this third understanding of the value of free speech.[37] Sometimes it is wrongly attributed to Mill. I believe that reference to "the marketplace of ideas" is supposed to be an intimation of the method by which it is thought free expression can contribute to the pursuit of truth. And like all intimations, it is ambiguous. In one understanding, ideas are set out as in an orderly market square—one idea or array of ideas to each stall—and people move from stall to stall in an orderly fashion engaging in quiet and thoughtful comparison shopping. The most popular stall wins the contest (and maybe that's what we should identify as truth). Alternatively, what is envisaged is a more active version of market competition—where ideas are advertised positively and negatively—certainly noisily and often aggressively—like the merits of rival insurance companies on TV, and the claims of their proponents are extolled and denigrated. And we see which ideas can

---

[36] Mill, *On Liberty* at 48 (cited in note 7), speaks of creeds which, in the absence of vigorous opposition, come to be received

> passively, not actively—when the mind is no longer compelled, in the same degree as at first, to exercise its vital powers on the questions which its belief presents to it, there is a progressive tendency to forget all of the belief except the formularies, or to give it a dull and torpid assent, as if accepting it on trust dispensed with the necessity of realizing it in consciousness, or testing it by personal experience; until it almost ceases to connect itself at all with the inner life of the human being. Then are seen the cases, so frequent in this age of the world as almost to form the majority, in which the creed remains as it were outside the mind, encrusting and petrifying it against all other influences addressed to the higher parts of our nature; manifesting its power by not suffering any fresh and living conviction to get in, but itself doing nothing for the mind or heart, except standing sentinel over them to keep them vacant.

[37] The phrase was used by Justice Holmes in *Abrams v US*, 250 US 616, 630 (1919). See generally Vincent Blasi, *Holmes and the Marketplace of Ideas*, 2004 Supreme Court Review 1 (2004).

survive this trial by ordeal. The motto of my article, taken from *On Liberty*, seems to indicate this latter more combative meaning of "the marketplace of ideas," as truth is supposed to emerge (if it does) "by the rough process of a struggle between combatants fighting under hostile banners."[38]

It is not my intention to adjudicate the many possible meanings of "marketplace of ideas" nor to try to figure out how the market analogy is supposed to work. (Markets, we know, are good at delivering some things and not others: is truth supposed to be like efficiency or is it supposed to be like distributive justice?) But the view that the free exchange of ideas is indispensable for progress and the pursuit of truth is an obvious line of defense for free expression and an extraordinarily powerful one.

5. A fifth set of free speech values has to do with political accountability. Those who might suppress speech are most often those who hold political power. Others try to unseat the powerful by calling them to account, denigrating what they are doing with their power, and propounding alternative political agendas. To protect their position, the powerful will suppress these attacks if they can. But we believe in democracy and we will not permit political speech to be suppressed. We value the challenges that might be made against the powerful. And that is why we value free speech.

No doubt there are other lines of defense for free speech besides these. But these five will do. I believe a strong argument can be made—not cast-iron and deductive, but strong—that none of these free speech values requires that people's speaking be uncontaminated by heckling. I will try to make this case. In Section XII, I shall also point to a more ambitious argument: that these free speech values are often actually served by heckling. I also want to return, in that section, to a proposition I have already mentioned—that, from the point of view of these values, we should view with dismay the emergence of a form of "free" speech that consists of a sequence of isolated speech events, each utterly separated from the others, and each under the tightly choreographed control of the respective speakers.

---

[38] Mill, *On Liberty* at 55 (cited in note 7). Cf William J. Brennan, in *Keyishian v Board of Regents*, 385 US 589, at 603 (1967), on the "robust exchange of ideas which discovers truth 'out of a multitude of tongues.'"

XI

So what do these various free speech values imply about heckling? Let's go through the five arguments one by one.

1. The argument about self-expression was already discussed in Section VII. The gist of our discussion there was that self-expression is best not understood as a solipsistic exercise (like giving voice to one's convictions in the shower). It is supposed to be an interactive process, where one gives an account of oneself to a high-spirited audience, whose reactions one is not entitled to control and who are busy also giving an account of *them*selves and giving voice to their reactions to one's own self-disclosure. One may get lucky and find a fascinated and therefore silent audience. But any rule requiring this diminishes self-expression overall by limiting the expressive reactions of the audience and by corralling the self-disclosure of the primary speaker into an artificially controlled environment bereft of the risks and reactions that are a part of the world in which self-disclosure typically takes place.[39] A self-expresser might say (and believe): "You cannot really get who I am unless you listen in silence to the detail of exactly what I say." We all feel like this sometimes in conversation. But it's a plea for a solipsistic mode of self-expression, undermined by the fact that it takes no account of social dynamics. Self-expression is valued when it involves expression *to* an active and moving world of other subjects equally engaged in a similar social exercise.

2. So far as the dignity interest is concerned, we can say a couple of things. One is that there is no affront to individual dignity in an audience having its own voiced reactions to what is said to them and disclosed to them by a dignity-bearing speaker. The audience members are not to be treated like schoolchildren, who have a duty to sit still and silent while they are being harangued. (And we academics should be a little more self-conscious than we are about using the sense of our exalted position as *lecturers*, with students passively vulnerable to our pedagogic authority, as a paradigm for thinking about free speech in general.) Also, as one writer has pointed out, the hecklers have their own dignity: "The goal of protecting an individual's dignity is furthered if each individual is permitted to express his views. Why should

---

[39] Maybe a more moderate line would be to say that self-expression can take a variety of forms. As the Supreme Court said in *In re Kay*, 1 Cal3d 930 (1970), 939: "the Constitution does not require that the effective expression of ideas be restricted to rigid and predetermined patterns." The choice of form cannot be confined to the expresser.

this apply only to the primary speaker? Surely a heckler's dignity will be harmed just as a primary speaker's would be if he were silenced."[40]

3. The connection between the third line of defense—the invigoration of thought and belief—and the prospect of heckling and interruption is pretty clear. Ideas come to life in the rough-and-tumble of active and even disruptive opposition. Those who hold the view that is being presented by the primary speaker, those who interject, and those who hear and watch the interaction get a livelier and more immediate impression of what is at stake in the matter under discussion than they do when the presentation of the primary view is carefully insulated from objection and when everyone has to await another occasion—a future and avoidable occasion—to hear what can be said against it.

4. On the pursuit of truth, it has been well said that "[t]he First Amendment does not merely insure a marketplace of ideas in which there is but one seller."[41] True, as noted earlier, there is at least one version of the "marketplace of ideas" image that involves the presentation of ideas one by one—one at a time—for the purposes of orderly comparison shopping, each separated from any involuntary interaction with the others. This version of the pursuit of truth might require freedom from interruption in the public presentation of each idea. But it is not a particularly attractive conception of the "marketplace of ideas." The immediacy of interjection, which as we just saw contributes to the vigor of debate, may be important too for the comparisons that the intellectual marketplace requires if it is to be successful.[42] Heckling involves the abrupt juxtaposition of a view with one of its rivals, so that the issue between them cannot be avoided. As the California Supreme Court observed in *In re Kay*, "A cogent remark, even though rudely timed or phrased, may 'contribute to the free interchange of ideas and the ascertainment of truth.'"[43] The version of John Stuart Mill's argument about the pursuit of truth intimated in the motto of this article seems to require just such a "rude"

---

[40] Wagner, *Heckling* at 229 (cited in note 4).

[41] *In re Kay*, 1 Cal3d 930, 939 (1970).

[42] For the importance of immediacy, see Emerson, *System of Freedom of Expression* at 286 (cited in note 2), as quoted in O'Neill and Vasvari, *Counter-Demonstration as Protected Speech* at 121–22 (cited in note 35).

[43] *In re Kay*, 1 Cal3d 930, 939 (1970).

confrontation of ideas.[44] Mill uses as an example the "salutary shock" with which

> the paradoxes of Rousseau explode[d] like bombshells ... dislocating the compact mass of one-sided opinion, and forcing its elements to recombine in a better form and with additional ingredients. Not that the current opinions were on the whole farther from the truth than Rousseau's were; on the contrary, they were nearer to it; they contained more of positive truth, and very much less of error. Nevertheless there lay in Rousseau's doctrine, and has floated down the stream of opinion along with it, a considerable amount of exactly those truths which the popular opinion wanted; and these are the deposit which was left behind when the flood subsided.[45]

Someone might answer that these are metaphorical expressions and no one thinks that Rousseau literally heckled the nostrums of polite eighteenth-century society. (Actually I don't know whether that's true or not: Jean-Jacques was certainly a disruptive presence.)[46] In any case, arguments about the "collision of opinions" in books and pamphlets have to be thought through differently. Still it's quite striking that Mill refused an invitation to embrace the (exasperatingly English) view that ideas always have to be expressed politely and moderately.[47] I think he would be much more distressed by contrary ideas being separated politely from one another in a sequence of uninterrupted presentations, each applauded by its own complacent partisans, than he would be by what an American court has referred to as "[t]he happy cacophony of democracy."

5. In the context of political accountability, interruption has proved itself an invaluable device for discomposing the glib evasions of politicians who are being held to account. Think about the cries of "Do your job! Do your job!" that greeted Republican congressmen brave

---

[44] Mill, *On Liberty* at 55 (cited in note 7).

[45] Id at 54–55.

[46] See generally Maurice Cranston, *The Noble Savage: Jean-Jacques Rousseau, 1754–1762* (1991).

[47] See Mill, *On Liberty* at 61 (cited in note 7): "Before quitting the subject of freedom of opinion, it is fit to take notice of those who say, that the free expression of all opinions should be permitted, on condition that the manner be temperate, and do not pass the bounds of fair discussion. Much might be said on the impossibility of fixing where these supposed bounds are to be placed; for if the test be offence to those whose opinion is attacked, I think experience testifies that this offence is given whenever the attack is telling and powerful, and that every opponent who pushes them hard, and whom they find it difficult to answer, appears to them, if he shows any strong feeling on the subject, an intemperate opponent."

enough to hold "town halls" with their constituents during the health care debates of early 2017.[48] A congressman anxious to present his political work in a good light will, if he can, choreograph his meetings with constituents to highlight the good things he has done and evade or mischaracterize his sins of omission and commission. That's understandable. But free speech does not require his constituents to connive at this.[49] And accountability demands much more in the way of interaction and confrontation than the glib presentation and obsequious reception of prepared remarks.[50] As the California Supreme Court observed,

> An unfavorable reception, such as that given [to the Congressman] in the instant case, represents one important method by which an officeholder's constituents can register disapproval of his conduct and seek redress of grievances. . . . Audience response, moreover, may force a speaker to discuss a difficult issue that he may wish to avoid, or to explain some past conduct that he hopes will be forgotten.[51]

The idea that those who raise such inconvenient matters should be silenced and excluded from public meetings of politicians with their constituents is not just unconducive to democratic accountability; it is a direct affront to that idea.[52]

XII

Mostly what I tried to show in Section XI was that free speech values do not require the suppression or elimination of heckling. Of

---

[48] The point is reinforced by reports that many Republican congressmen sought to avoid town halls with their constituents after they observed these audience reactions in their colleagues' town halls. (See, e.g., Amber Phillips, *Republican Town Halls Are Getting Very, Very Nasty*, Wash Post, Feb 10, 2017.)

[49] *Landry v Daley* (ND Ill 1968), 280 F Supp 968, 970: "The happy cacophony of democracy would be stilled if all 'improper noises' in the normal meaning of the term were suppressed."

[50] See generally, Jeremy Waldron, *Accountability and Insolence*, in my collection *Political Theory: Essays on Institutions* (2016).

[51] *In re Kay*, 1 Cal3d 930, 939 (1970).

[52] The political argument for free speech has been taken by some a little further, to suggest that heckling helps level the playing field between outsiders and insiders. In the California case of *In re Kay*, 1 Cal3d 930, 939 (1970), Tobriner J. observed that "[f]or many citizens such participation in public meetings [i.e., heckling], whether supportive or critical of the speaker, may constitute the only manner in which they can express their views to a large number of people." I guess this is a response to what is sometimes said: that the heckler if he wants to express himself can have a meeting of his own, can hire his own hall, can run his own campaign. I'm not convinced, and I want to separate the arguments I am making in the text from

course, some of these points go further. They tend to show also that free speech values are actually *promoted* by heckling—or, as the California Supreme Court said in its constitutional analysis, "[a]udience activities, such as heckling, interrupting, harsh questioning, and booing, even though they may be impolite and discourteous, can nonetheless *advance* the goals of the First Amendment."[53]

Does this mean that free speech might require us to actually enlist the services of noisy interlocutors? John Stuart Mill toyed with an idea along these lines when he suggested that the only way to keep widely accepted beliefs alive might be to arrange artificially for them to be continually challenged:

> The loss of so important an aid to the intelligent and living apprehension of a truth, as is afforded by the necessity of . . . defending it against opponents, though not sufficient to outweigh, is no trifling drawback from, the benefit of its universal recognition. Where this advantage can no longer be had, I confess I should like to see the teachers of mankind endeavoring to provide a substitute for it; some contrivance for making the difficulties of the question as present to the learner's consciousness, as if they were pressed upon him by a dissentient champion, eager for his conversion.[54]

Mill wasn't talking specifically about heckling, though certainly what he wanted was importunate and (from the point of view of a given position) unwelcome challenges. And the logic of his view is the same: if we *do* have the good fortune to have hecklers in our midst, we should not try to suppress them:

> If there are any persons who contest a received opinion, or who will do so if law or opinion will let them, let us thank them for it, open our minds to listen to them, and rejoice that there is some one to do for us what we otherwise ought, if we have any regard for either the certainty or the vitality of our convictions, to do with much greater labor for ourselves.[55]

What this shows more than anything else is that Mill dreaded the emergence of a mode of expression and belief that took pains to insulate each expression of an opinion from any direct and immediate challenge, and to ensure that at the time a given belief was being

---

any reliance on values of political equality connected with hecklers taking a free ride on the opportunity afforded by the scheduled speech of a more powerful politician.

[53] *In re Kay*, 1 Cal3d 930, 939 (1970), my emphasis.

[54] Mill, *On Liberty* at 52 (cited in note 7).

[55] Id at 53.

communicated no hint of any opposition to it should interrupt its expression. That is what Mill dreaded.

And so should we. It puts it a little strongly to say that those who
hope for a political world uncontaminated by heckling are hoping to
minimize confrontation. But the antiheckling mentality comes closer
to this than we ought to be comfortable with. The idea of the antiheckling mentality is that free speech means a laborious succession of
speeches. Each speech will be received passively and respectfully in
silence, and in order to hear an opposing point of view, one will have
to go somewhere else (by which time the detail of any issue or con-
tradiction will be forgotten). Or if that sounds too noiseless to be
plausible, we expect each speech to be responded to, with applause,
just by those whose support for the positions expressed is already well
known and at just the points where applause is most welcome to the
speaker. (The extreme case of this is the privatization of political
meetings that I touched on in Section IX.)

This antiheckling mentality is evinced sometimes also in the way
we deal with protests. A foreign statesman pays a visit and the police
say that protest banners and shouted slogans will be permitted, but
only blocks away from anywhere the foreign statesman will be passing
or his supporters applauding. The protests need never be heard by
those to whom they are directed.

We show it, too, sometimes in Congress with the embarrassing
succession of "special order speeches" delivered every evening usually by individual representatives to an empty chamber after the end
of ordinary business. We are told that "[s]pecial orders provide one of
the few opportunities for non-legislative debate in the House."[56] But
this is nonsense. There is no element of debate or interaction whatsoever. Speeches are delivered one by one. No opponent listens; no
opponent responds.[57]

---

[56] Congressional Research Service, Special Order Speeches: Current House Practices, April 1,
2008, available at http://archives.democrats.rules.house.gov/CRS_Rpt/rl30136.pdf.

[57] It doesn't help that our congressmen are terrible public speakers. See P. J. O'Rourke,
Parliament of Whores: A Lone Humorist Attempts to Explain the Entire U.S. Government 51
(1991):

> The members of the House are, to a man (and twenty-nine women), ridicu-
> lously bad at public speaking. Indeed, they don't speak at all; they read from
> prepared texts and are ridiculously bad at reading. Every clause is an exclamatory

If these are our paradigms of free speech, then that principle is being conceived as *freedom to make a speech* not as *freedom to speak* (in any sense that involves confrontation and engagement).

Of course I exaggerate. A succession of separate speeches, each received in silence or only with the applause that the speaker connives to elicit, can be related to one another dialectically if someone cares to make the effort to bear the first one in mind as he listens to the second and then the third. And sometimes what individual speakers, swimming in their separate lanes, want to do with their receptive audience is precisely to draw attention to the flaws in their opponents' positions. So engagement is not out of the question. Still the suppression of heckling in the name of free speech presages a sad spectacle of lifeless discourse, where we take free speech—*an inherently interactive idea*—and do our best to minimize the lively and immediate confrontation that interactions between speaker and members of the audience used to involve.

I know that some are worried by the noise and unpredictable element of heckling. It leads, they say, to Babel, where everyone is talking across each other and nothing can be heard.[58] Maybe in extreme cases this is true. But projecting the horror of Babel onto any particular episodes of vigorous heckling is, I think, a mistake. People are much better at listening through noises and discerning the true significance of what is at stake in any given confrontation than the antiheckling mentality might suppose. Free speech is and ought to be noisy. And we should not toss around the B-word simply because

---

declaration. Every verb is in the present tense. Every subject is [first] person plural. You can tell, without watching, when a congressman has reached the bottom of a page—there will come a dramatic caesura, a full stop that lasts, no matter its violence to sense, until that page has been turned and the words at the top of the next page kenned.

"We are in a position! To mandate the expenditure! Of great amounts of money! By state and local governments! But we are not! [rustle of paper] Giving them financial aid!"

[58] Dean Erwin Chemerinsky wrote this in response to the heckling of the Israeli ambassador, Michael Oren, on a visit to the UC Irvine campus. He didn't deny that critics of the Israeli government had a right to protest such gatherings, but, he said, once a speaker has begun an invited lecture, "[y]ou have the right—if you disagree with me—to go outside and perform your protest. But you don't get the right to come in when I'm talking and shout me down. Otherwise people can always silence a speaker by heckler's veto, and Babel results." (See David Lumb, *Israel: Interrupted in Irvine*, New University: University of California at Irvine, February 16, 2010.)

the extempore effects of heckling make it impossible for the speaker to have exactly the effect that his choreography requires.

XIII

Let me return finally to the issue we left hanging in Section V—the issue of campus disruption. These are cases in which—typically—an invitation is issued by a conservative campus organization to a speaker who is known to be enormously unpopular among liberals. The unpopularity is usually part of the reason for the invitation: inviting the speaker is a kind of provocation by the conservative group to try to elicit a response by their opponents that will discredit campus liberals and their cause. The speaker's views are already very well known, which is why the liberals are enraged. Still, the speaker welcomes the opportunity to communicate them to a new audience and he accepts the invitation. Liberal students protest and demand that the invitation be withdrawn. The conservative students and some of their professors and college administrators resist this, saying that withdrawing the invitation under pressure would amount to a violation of free speech.[59] They say free speech demands that the speaker, who has accepted the invitation, must now be permitted to come to campus, deliver their speech, and be given a fair hearing. So the speaker comes to campus and is met by a crowd of protestors, some of whom try physically to stop him from entering the venue set up for the speech. Others get inside the venue and heckle the speaker—using an array of techniques ranging from shouted questions, to slow hand-clapping, chanting, and booing. In this cacophony, it is hard to hear much of what the speaker says. After a while, the speaker gives up and goes home, expressing the opinion that the students who drowned out the address are enemies of free speech. This sentiment is echoed by many professors and campus administrators. Desultory attempts are made to identify and punish the worst offenders. Political commentators and writers of op-ed pieces deplore what has happened as evidence of the growing intolerance of young people.

---

[59] This of course is nonsense. Just as the free speech principle does not require or, in itself, provide any reason for issuing any particular invitation, it does not require that an invitation once given should never be withdrawn (by the party who issued it). For the general logic of rights in this regard, see Jeremy Waldron, *A Right to Do Wrong*, 92 Ethics 21 (1981) (rights do not provide reasons or justifications for any particular exercise of the liberties they protect).

What's the best way to analyze incidents of this type? The first thing to say is to say something that everyone agrees about: it is wrong to use or threaten violence against speakers or organizers of the occasion. (It is also wrong to use or threaten violence against hecklers.) It is wrong to break windows, light fires, and damage furniture. These things we should all deplore, in more or less every circumstance in which they take place, whether heckling is involved or not.

But what about heckling itself in these contexts? As I said in Section VII, the term "heckling" comprehends a spectrum of behavior, ranging from the pointed question shouted by a member of the audience to something like a concerted effort by many of them to silence a speaker. I said that it makes a difference from which end of that spectrum one views heckling as a general phenomenon. I don't just mean that my account focuses on cases at one end of the spectrum whereas my opponents (more realistically, as they imagine) focus on cases at the other end. I mean that each of us views cases at the far end through the lens of our starting point. My opponent views even the isolated but unwelcome interruption as an intimation of the sort of disorder I have just described, and I would like to conclude the article by considering the phenomena of chanting, booing, slow hand-clapping, and even shouting down through the lens of the paradigm of heckling that I have outlined already in this essay.

The points made in Section VII about a speaker not having a right to any particular quality of audience applies as much on campus as it applies anywhere. Speakers have to take their chances with whatever audience assembles to listen to them. Sometimes the audience will be compliant and receptive to the speaker's message and willing to play their part in whatever choreography of audience reaction the speaker wants to elicit. Sometimes the audience will be more sullenly passive than that, not applauding where applause seems to be called for and showing by their demeanor, their facial expressions, their whispered asides to one another, or their hissing (by the way, a much under-estimated form of critical audience response) that they are unconvinced and offended by what is being said. And sometimes this discontent will manifest itself more noisily, in shouted comments whose aim is to disconcert a speaker they disapprove of, throwing his calm for the occasion off balance, bringing to the attention of the audience and to those reporting the occasion the untruths that are being peddled or the pertinent facts that are being omitted. The interruptions have this communicative function, but they also have the function of making it clear to the speaker and to his whole audience that at least some of those in the venue know that he is lying to or misleading the audience. The aim is to make the defects in the speech that is being given common knowledge and in this way to embarrass the speaker.

That is the value of heckling. Now, unless one believes that every speaker in every context is entitled to be listened to in respectful silence—a position we showed good reason to reject in Sections VII and XI—there is no basis for objecting to disruptive interventions of this kind when they happen on campus. On the contrary, speakers who accept engagements on campus must expect their audiences there to be more than usually alert to lies, distortions, omissions, and equivocations, and they cannot expect them to be submissively silent about such matters. Audiences on campus will be critical (in the first flush of educated youth) and less jaded—they will have higher expectations—than one might find among audiences generally. College crowds are a hard sell, and rightly so, for students are being trained (if their education is working right) as bullshit-detectors, trained actively to analyze with a critical attitude whatever is put in front of them. Not only that, but (as I said, in the first flush of youth) they are engaged passionately in their own convictions about justice and public policy. We expect them to be so engaged and we ought not to be trying to discipline them out of it with some ethos of passivity and silence.

I say this because recent discussions of free speech on campus always emphasize the special connection between the campus setting, on the one hand, and free speech and open inquiry on the other.[60] The connection is certainly important, but is seldom stated in a way that covers all the bases. Scholars talk about the importance of students being exposed to unfamiliar and unwelcome ideas as part of their education, but they map that on to an ethos of respectful silence rather than active engagement, as though student minds are improved by being required to sit passively while a speaker attempts to manipulate them with fake or distorted ideas. One gets the impression that the impulse sharply to call out when one knows one is being lied to or when obviously relevant material is being omitted or concealed is no part of the mindset we expect intelligent students to display on these occasions. They are not to be permitted to try and make awareness of

---

[60] See, for example, Chemerinsky and Gillman, *Free Speech on Campus* (cited in note 21); Sigal R. Ben-Porath, *Free Speech on Campus* (2017); and John Palfrey, *Safe Spaces, Brave Spaces: Diversity and Free Expression in Education* (2017).

the speaker's distortions common knowledge in the venue at which he is speaking. That is the impression we are given in published discussions of campus speech. I don't buy it. For my money, the noisier disruptive alternative is more realistic and more desirable—certainly more commensurate with the free speech values we considered in Sections X and XI. What is and ought to be special about the campus setting is the sense of intellectual alertness and excitement, with which any visiting speaker is received. Speakers who choose to come to a campus should not think they are coming to a cowed and cloistered environment whose audiences have been pacified and silenced for the sake of exposure to unwelcome ideas. Campuses need to keep faith with the active and disconcerting side of the free speech principle. Speech will elicit a reaction, and that is what campus speakers should be prepared for.

True, no one is requiring that students who disagree with a given speaker must turn up to listen to him. The occasions we are envisaging are not compulsory as a curricular lecture might be. So, someone might ask, why don't those who are disposed to disagree with a speaker just stay away and leave the occasion to an audience that is more receptive to what is going to be said? If people do choose to attend, is it unreasonable to ask that they not spoil the occasion for everyone else? In answering these questions, let's leave aside the implication that an occasion is "spoiled" when the speaker is called out on some lie or distortion. Let's also leave aside the general point developed in Section VIII, that a given set of listeners have no right to be members of exactly the audience they want to be members of, any more than a speaker has a right to exactly the audience he desires. Both points are important, but in addition there are special points to be made about the campus setting. A campus is a sort of intellectual community, and its denizens—the students—are entitled to take an active and critical interest in whatever goes on there. If a notorious liar or racist is invited onto their campus—the campus they share with thousands of fellow students—that is as much an issue for them as it is for the speaker's biggest fans. I mentioned earlier that these invitations are often intended as provocations, by one political faction on campus "in the face" (as it were) of another. Those who are being provoked in this way may welcome the opportunity to go and not only hear but respond to the unwelcome ideas their opponents are trying to upset them with.

(I guess it is possible that a campus gathering may be made into a strictly private affair, tickets only, with an audience vetted for their views and attitudes. This would be a campus version of the sort of privatization of free speech that I talked about in Section IX. I think I would expect my colleagues in the free speech community to be disturbed by this development rather than to welcome it as a new paradigm of campus speech.)

All of this is intended, as I said at the start of this section, as a view of campus unruliness seen from the perspective of one who values the disruption that heckling involves. It is not all that needs to be said. We need also to condemn the violence and vandalism that some of these occasions have involved. But I think the perspective that understands the value of heckling ought to be our first point of reference when we consider how to respond to outbreaks of unruliness at campus speech events. True, that unruliness often involves not just sporadic shouted comments and corrections, but booing, chanting, and general cacophony that makes it difficult for the speaker to be heard. If we approach the prospect of such cacophony with the value of heckling in mind, I think we will deal with it more carefully than if we understand any disruption as a foretaste of violence and intolerance.

I mentioned earlier Dean Erwin Chemerinsky's view that "[y]ou have the right—if you disagree with me—to go outside and perform your protest. But you don't get the right to come in when I'm talking and shout me down. Otherwise people can always silence a speaker by heckler's veto, and Babel results."[61] Chemerinsky posits a stark contrast between shouting a speaker down and making one's protest outside. He does not directly address the intermediate question of interruptions that do not actually prevent the speech being made, but which throw the speaker off balance and establish a different sort of common knowledge in the venue than the one the speaker is attempting to cultivate. But the tenor of Chemerinsky's position seems to be that *any* interruption raises the specter of the speaker being shouted down and that heckling, as such, is ordinarily to be associated with "heckler's veto" and dealt with on that basis. I think hecklers deserve better than that. Heckling should be understood, on campus as elsewhere, as a mode of valued critical engagement, not as something which is inherently likely to get out of hand. If and when it does get out of hand, our response to it ought to be consistent with its value

---

[61] Cited in note 58.

and not predicated on any fundamental right of any speaker to be heard in silence.

XIV

Let me say a word finally about the relation between heckling and cacophony—the difference between a speaker being heckled and a speaker being shouted down. Throughout this article, I have imagined the heckler as a lone individual making a series of telling and unwelcome interventions. But what if there are many hecklers? Even if they are a minority in the audience, there may be twenty or fifty of them and—let us imagine—two or three interventions apiece during a thirty-minute address may use up a lot of the time allocated to the speaker. Does there come a point when heckling has to be suppressed so that the speaker can at least say some of what he wants to say?

Eve Wagner offers the suggestion that heckling is "permissible until it reaches a degree where the audience is unable to hear the primary speaker's message."[62] The suggestion is made in the spirit that I was urging at the end of the previous section: it approaches the problem of cacophony without any assumption that there is something inherently wrong with heckling. But it posits a line that is difficult to draw. If it means that heckling makes it difficult for the primary speaker to convey all that he wants to convey, then that is going to be true of just about any interruption. The point of heckling is to see that the primary speaker cannot convey all that he wants to convey, at least not as he wants to convey it. If the speaker is thrown off balance by several interruptions, if he has to go out of his way to respond to his hecklers, then changes may have to be made to the order and extent of his presentation. We mustn't say that this, in and of itself, means that the heckling has gone too far. On the other hand, if a group of people come to a meeting intent on acting together to make it impossible for the speaker to be heard to say very much at all, then that can be described as simple suppression of speech rather than speaker/heckler engagement. It may not be easy to detect such orchestration of heckling, but if the articulation of a limit is thought necessary in our preaching to students about what free speech requires,

---

[62] Wagner, *Heckling* (cited in note 4).

then that can be treated as beyond the bounds of legitimate intervention.

In the middle are the cases where heckling by many people adds
up to something of a cacophony, even though this is neither orchestrated nor expected by the hecklers. One might approach these middle cases using a metric of fairness: would-be hecklers should limit
their interventions—or those who chair the occasions should limit
them—in a way that is sensitive to how much heckling there is
overall, in order to allow the speaker a fair chance of putting his points
across. That may seem a reasonable approach. But one can imagine
a defense of heckling that is more aggressive than that and that eschews the sort of managerial ethos that the fairness approach involves.
The fact is that we value heckling when we do because it indicates
critical attention and active engagement, a dynamic and interactive
element in the otherwise controlled relation between speaker and
audience. If there are just one or two parts of a speech that elicit interruptions, then the speaker will be largely free of heckling through
most of his address. But if almost everything that is said is controversial, the speaker cannot expect that for the most part his audience
will sit quietly and listen. And we should not be organizing our reaction to heckling around any expectation that much or most of a
speech will be heard in silence, whatever the provocations of its
content.

DANIEL J. HEMEL AND
LISA LARRIMORE OUELLETTE

PUBLIC PERCEPTIONS OF
GOVERNMENT SPEECH

The Supreme Court has stated repeatedly in recent years that the
First Amendment's Free Speech Clause "does not regulate government speech."[1] While in most circumstances the government must
adhere to a requirement of "viewpoint neutrality" in its regulation of
private speech,[2] the government is subject to no such requirement
when it engages in speech of its own. Thus, a public school cannot
prohibit students from expressing antiwar views,[3] but the government
is free to propagate its own messages in support of a war effort.[4] Likewise, a city generally cannot ban neo-Nazis from marching through
its streets,[5] but it can issue its own condemnation of fascism. The rule

Daniel J. Hemel is an Assistant Professor of Law at the University of Chicago Law School.
Lisa Larrimore Ouellette is an Associate Professor of Law at Stanford Law School.

AUTHORS' NOTE: Thanks to Joe Blocher, Doron Dorfman, Amy Kapczynski, Mark Lemley,
Helen Norton, Geoffrey Stone, Lior Strahilevitz, Eugene Volokh, and participants at the
Yale Law School Information Society Project Ideas Lunch for helpful comments.

[1] *Matal v Tam*, 137 S Ct 1744, 1757 (2017); *Pleasant Grove City v Summum*, 555 US 460,
467 (2009); see *Walker v Texas Division, Sons of Confederate Veterans, Inc.*, 135 S Ct 2239, 2255
(2015) ("When government speaks, it is not barred by the Free Speech Clause from determining the content of what it says.").

[2] See, for example, *Rosenberger v Rector & Visitors of the University of Virginia*, 515 US 819,
834 (1995); *Police Department of Chicago v Mosley*, 408 US 92, 95–96 (1972).

[3] See *Tinker v Des Moines Independent Community School District*, 393 US 503 (1968).

[4] See *Matal*, 137 S Ct at 1758.

[5] See *Collin v Smith*, 578 F2d 1197 (7th Cir 1978), cert denied, 439 US 916.

that the government "shall make no law . . . abridging the freedom of speech"[6] does not require the government to remain on the sidelines in public debates.

Although the proposition that the government need not remain viewpoint-neutral in its own speech is clear, the line between "government speech" and private expression is often fuzzy. Consider just a few of the recent cases in which federal courts have wrestled with this question. Does a temporary exhibit on the ground floor of the state capitol constitute government speech or private speech? (A federal district court recently ruled that such exhibits are private speech, and thus Texas could not prohibit a secularist group from displaying a banner inside that state's capitol that declared "[t]here are no gods . . . ."[7]) What about visitors' guides displayed and distributed by a private publisher at highway rest areas operated by a state agency? (The Fourth Circuit recently held that these guides are government speech, and thus the Virginia Department of Transportation could insist on exercising editorial control over the guides.[8]) And does a public university engage in government speech when it permits student organizations to use its trademarked name and logo on T-shirts? (The Eighth Circuit recently answered that question in the negative, holding that Iowa State University could not prevent a student group supporting marijuana legalization from using the school's name and logo on merchandise when it granted such permission to other student organizations.[9])

The stakes of the debate are enormous. In the context of any particular case, the question whether expression constitutes government speech or private speech often will determine the outcome. And over the landscape of First Amendment law, the government-versus-private-speech question looms large. If all government speech were subject to the viewpoint-neutrality requirement, public administration would be paralyzed: a city could not erect a sign saying "STOP" without adding one that says "GO." Yet without some meaningful limit on the government's ability to claim expression as its own, the

[6] US Const, Amend I.

[7] See *Freedom from Religion Foundation, Inc. v Abbott*, 2016 WL 7388401, *2, 4–5 (WD Tex).

[8] See *Vista-Graphics, Inc. v Virginia Department of Transportation*, 682 Fed Appx 231, 236–37 (4th Cir 2017).

[9] See *Gerlich v Leath*, 861 F3d 697, 712–14 (8th Cir 2017).

government speech doctrine could eviscerate the bar on viewpoint discrimination among private speakers.

To draw the line between government speech and private expression, the Supreme Court's early government speech cases looked to whether the speaker is a "traditional" government agency or official[10] and to whether the government exercises "control over the message."[11] In the past decade, however, the Court has placed increasing emphasis on whether members of the public reasonably perceive the relevant expression to be government speech. One Justice has gone so far as to suggest that this factor should be the sole criterion for distinguishing government speech from private expression.[12]

This new emphasis on public perception has manifested itself in the Court's three most recent government speech cases. In 2009, the Court unanimously held in *Pleasant Grove City v Summum* that privately donated monuments in a city park constitute government speech in part because "persons who observe donated monuments routinely—and reasonably—interpret them as conveying some message on the property owner's behalf."[13] Six years later, in *Walker v Texas Division, Sons of Confederate Veterans*, the Court split 5–4 as to whether specialty license plate designs submitted by private organizations qualify as "government speech," with the majority and dissent disagreeing as to whether members of the public would perceive the license plates to convey a message on the state of Texas's behalf.[14] And this past Term, in *Matal v Tam*, the Court held that federal registration of trademarks is not government speech because (among other factors) "there is no evidence that the public associates the contents of trademarks with the Federal Government."[15]

The Supreme Court's turn toward public perception as an often-determinative factor in government speech cases is, we think, a wel-

---

[10] See *Keller v State Bar of California*, 496 US 1, 13 (1990).

[11] See *Johanns v Livestock Marketing Association*, 544 US 550, 561 (2005).

[12] See *Summum*, 555 US at 487 (Souter, J, concurring in the judgment).

[13] 555 US at 471.

[14] Compare *Sons of Confederate Veterans*, 135 S Ct at 2249 ("Texas license plates are, essentially, government IDs. . . . [P]ersons who observe designs on IDs routinely—and reasonably—interpret them as conveying some message on the issuer's behalf." (alterations and quotation marks omitted)), with id at 2255 (Alito, J, dissenting) ("[W]ould you really think that the sentiments reflected in these specialty plates are the views of the State of Texas and not those of the owners of the cars?").

[15] 137 S Ct at 1760.

come development. Government intervention in the marketplace of ideas is especially dangerous when it is nontransparent. In such instances, government officials potentially can launder messages through the mouths of private speakers and escape electoral accountability for that expression. If government officials want to escape the viewpoint-neutrality requirement that is generally applicable to speech regulation, they should—we think—have to claim those messages as their own.

But while there are strong theoretical reasons to draw the line between government speech and private speech on the basis of public perception, the Court has so far failed to develop a reliable method for determining whether the public perceives expression to be government speech. The Court's statement in *Summum* that members of the public "routinely" interpret monuments on government land as government speech rested on nothing more than *ipse dixit*. The majority's conclusion in *Sons of Confederate Veterans* that observers understand specialty license plate designs to be government speech similarly relied on judicial assertion. Most recently, the Court in *Tam* seized on the absence of any evidence that the public associates the content of trademarks with the government but ignored the fact that there was no evidence in the other direction either.

It does not have to be this way. Courts can do better than relying on armchair speculation to determine whether members of the public attribute expression to the government. And in other contexts, courts do. Most notably, courts in trademark infringement cases often consult consumer surveys to determine whether the defendant's use is likely to cause confusion related to the plaintiff's mark[16]—in other words, whether the defendant's use causes consumers to misattribute a product or message to the plaintiff. The acceptance of survey evidence in trademark law reflects a recognition that empirical claims regarding consumer psychology are better supported through quantitative social science than through judicial guesswork.

The argument for resorting to survey evidence applies with similar force in the government speech context. As noted, government speech cases, like trademark infringement cases, often come down to how judges or Justices expect the public to react to certain stimuli. And as in the trademark context, judicial speculation is likely to be

---

[16] J. Thomas McCarthy, 4 *McCarthy on Trademarks and Unfair Competition* §§ 23:1, 32:158 (Thomson Reuters, 5th ed 2017).

biased and inaccurate. If the worry is that members of the public will perceive private speech to be government speech or government speech to be private speech, then it would seem that the best way to resolve the worry is to ask a representative sample of the population. This is not to say that survey results should be dispositive in government speech cases, just as survey results are not dispositive in the trademark infringement context.[17] But as in the trademark infringement context, survey evidence can play an important role in validating and falsifying claims regarding public perceptions as to the source of arguably government speech.

This article lays out the argument for using survey evidence in government speech cases.[18] We supplement our normative argument with a proof of concept: a survey of a nationally representative sample of more than 1,200 respondents whose views on government speech we gauged. Some of the speculative claims made by the Justices in recent government speech cases are borne out by our survey: for example, we find that members of the public do routinely interpret monuments on government land as conveying a message on the government's behalf. In other respects, however, the Justices' speculation proves less accurate: for instance, while the Court in *Tam* says that it is "far-fetched" to suggest that "the federal registration of a trademark makes the mark government speech,"[19] we find that nearly half of respondents hold this "far-fetched" view.

We further find that respondents are somewhat more likely to attribute messages to the government if they agree with those messages themselves. For example, individuals are more likely to attribute pro-choice messages to the government if they hold pro-choice views, and individuals are more likely to attribute atheistic messages to the gov-

---

[17] See id § 32:158.

[18] The idea of using trademark-like consumer surveys in the government speech context is mentioned by Helen Norton, *The Measure of Government Speech: Identifying Expression's Source*, 88 BU L Rev 587, 611–13 (2008). Norton does not, however, explain how the idea might be implemented in practice. She notes the "vexing question of what number or percentage of onlookers need to identify a message's source as governmental," and adds that "[f]ixing the number with any principled specificity poses substantial challenges." Id at 613. Some of these practical issues were addressed by Shari Seidman Diamond and Andrew Koppelman, *Measured Endorsement*, 60 Md L Rev 713 (2001), although their work focused on survey evidence in Establishment Clause cases and predated the general acceptance of online surveys. Building on the insights of these earlier authors, we provide the first empirical demonstration of how a government speech survey might work in practice and address counterarguments beyond the difficulty in implementation.

[19] 137 S Ct at 1748.

ernment if they have positive attitudes toward atheism. One possible interpretation of this finding might be that courts should *not* rely on public perception in government speech cases because doing so will favor already-popular beliefs while disadvantaging minority views. Our interpretation is different. In determining whether expression constitutes government speech, members of the Court as well as members of the public inevitably are affected by both the medium of expression and the content of the message. Survey experiments such as the one we conducted here can be useful in disentangling the effects of medium from the effects of message because the controlled setting allows researchers to vary the message while holding the medium constant. Thus, survey experiments can reduce the risk that government speech doctrine will systematically favor some views over others.

To be sure, the use of survey evidence in government speech cases raises a number of implementation issues that require careful thought. For example, parties might manipulate surveys to support their views, forcing the court to resolve disputes about social science methodologies. But the current approach of armchair speculation is even more manipulable, and courts already evaluate social science methodologies in the trademark survey context as well as many others. Another challenge relates to line-drawing: what percentage of the public must perceive expression to be government speech for it to qualify as such? Rather than proposing a specific numerical threshold, we suggest that the best approach is to compare with controls—that is, to test against expression that any court would (or would not) consider to be government speech. The use of such comparisons can allow courts to assess whether members of the public perceive particular instances of gray-area expression—messages that are arguably but not certainly government speech—more like paradigmatic examples of government speech (e.g., the engravings on the Lincoln Memorial) or more like paradigmatic examples of private expression (e.g., billboards on privately owned property).

We address these and other concerns at further length below. Our reflection on implementation challenges underscores the broader point that government speech doctrine ought not be outsourced to a mechanical test. Using survey evidence to inform government speech doctrine does not obviate the need for judges to apply their own experience and expertise—as well as legal and prudential reasoning—in the context of individual cases. Our more limited claim is that the ability of courts to resolve government speech cases will be aided by more rigorous evidence of how the public actually perceives the kinds of expression at issue.

Our analysis proceeds in three parts. Part I explores the rise of public perception as a factor in government speech cases and considers whether this doctrinal development is a desirable one. We argue that it is, but that the Court's government speech jurisprudence would be enriched by consulting survey evidence as a measure of public perception. Part II explains the structure of our survey—which draws from the facts of *Summum, Sons of Confederate Veterans,* and *Tam*—and presents our results. Part III considers the doctrinal and normative implications of our findings. We conclude that the use of survey evidence can reduce the arbitrariness inherent in the Court's current approach to the public perception factor in government speech cases while also mitigating the pervasive concern that the extension of government speech doctrine to messages produced by private parties will eviscerate First Amendment protections.

I. Relevance of Public Perceptions of Government Speech

We begin with a brief history of the Supreme Court's government speech doctrine and the role of the public perception factor in the Court's cases. We then consider and respond to criticism of the Court's turn toward public perception as a factor distinguishing government speech from private expression. We ultimately conclude that public perception *should* matter—perhaps more than any other factor—in deciding whether expression qualifies as government speech, and that survey evidence can aid the Court in determining whether members of the public perceive speech as coming from the government.

A. DOCTRINAL ROOTS

1. *Origins and purposes of the government speech doctrine.* The phrase "government speech" is nowhere to be found in the first 200 years of Supreme Court opinions. In part this may be attributable to the fact that viewpoint neutrality is itself a relatively young doctrine—only in the mid-1930s did the Court start to take seriously the notion that the First Amendment prevents the government from restricting private expression on the basis of viewpoint.[20] Yet several more de-

---

[20] On the evolution of the Court's viewpoint-neutrality doctrine, see Paul B. Stephan III, *The First Amendment and Content Discrimination*, 68 Va L Rev 203, 215–18 (1982).

cades passed before the Court first made reference to the "so-called 'government speech' doctrine" in the 1990 case of *Keller v State Bar of California*.[21] In that case, a group of California attorneys argued that the State Bar violated their free speech rights by using compulsory dues to finance political and ideological activities with which they disagreed. The Bar responded that—as a government entity speaking on its own behalf—it was exempt from normal Free Speech Clause scrutiny.[22] The Court implicitly accepted the State Bar's argument that government entities are subject to a different Free Speech Clause standard. According to the Court:

> Government officials are expected as a part of the democratic process to represent and to espouse the views of a majority of their constituents. With countless advocates outside of the government seeking to influence its policy, it would be ironic if those charged with making governmental decisions were not free to speak for themselves in the process. If every citizen were to have a right to insist that no one paid by public funds express a view with which he disagreed, debate over issues of great concern to the public would be limited to those in the private sector, and the process of government as we know it radically transformed.[23]

The Court in *Keller* ultimately concluded that the government speech doctrine did not apply in that case because "the very specialized characteristics of the State Bar . . . distinguish it from the role of the typical government official or agency."[24] But in the process of shooting down the State Bar's government speech argument, the Court gave rise to a doctrine that, according to one eminent analyst, would soon threaten "to swallow much of the First Amendment's protections."[25]

---

[21] 496 US 1 (1990). Justices made passing reference to "government speech" in two Establishment Clause cases decided shortly before *Keller*. See *County of Allegheny v ACLU*, 492 US 573, 661, 664 (1989) (Kennedy, J, concurring in the judgment in part and dissenting in part); *Board of Education v Mergens*, 496 US 226, 250 (1990). Justice Stewart arguably anticipated the modern-day government speech doctrine in a footnote to a concurring opinion in *Columbia Broadcasting System, Inc. v Democratic National Committee*, 412 US 94, 132 (1973), but he spoke there only for himself and not for the Court. See id at 139 n 7 (Stewart, J, concurring) ("Government is not restrained by the First Amendment from controlling its own expression.").

[22] *Keller*, 496 US at 10–11.

[23] Id at 12–13.

[24] Id at 12.

[25] Erwin Chemerinsky, *The Roberts Court and Freedom of Speech*, 63 Fed Communications L J 579, 586 (2010); see also Erwin Chemerinsky, *The Troubling Government Speech Doctrine*, ACS Blog (June 19, 2015), https://www.acslaw.org/acsblog/the-troubling-government-speech-doctrine.

As the government speech doctrine has evolved from dicta in *Keller* to *ratio decidendi* in later cases, the Court's rationale for the doctrine has evolved as well. The justification offered in *Keller*—that the doctrine is needed so that government officials can "speak for themselves"—has given way to two other arguments in favor of a Free Speech Clause exemption for government speech.

First, the Justices have said that "it is not easy to imagine how government could function" if government speech were subject to Free Speech Clause scrutiny—and, in particular, the requirement that the government maintain viewpoint neutrality in its regulation of speech.[26] As Justice Scalia observed in *Rust v Sullivan*, a viewpoint-neutrality requirement for government speech would mean that when Congress established the National Endowment for Democracy, it also would have been "constitutionally required to fund a program to encourage competing lines of political philosophy such as communism and fascism."[27] Or as Justice Breyer put the point in *Sons of Confederate Veterans*: "How could a city government create a successful recycling program if officials, when writing householders asking them to recycle cans and bottles, had to include in the letter a long plea from the local trash disposal enterprise demanding the contrary?"[28] And as Justice Alito piled on in *Tam*, a viewpoint-neutrality requirement would suggest that "[d]uring the Second World War," when "the Federal Government produced and distributed millions of posters . . . urging enlistment, the purchase of war bonds, and the conservation of scarce resources," it also needed to "balance the message . . . by producing and distributing posters encouraging Americans to refrain from engaging in these activities."[29] This line of *reductio ad absurdum* argument is meant to establish that the Free Speech Clause's viewpoint-neutrality principle could not possibly apply to the government's own speech.

Second, the Justices have suggested that the government has an interest in disassociating itself from speech that it does not endorse. This interest in disassociation and the avoidance of misattribution appears somewhat obliquely in *Summum*, where Justice Alito notes that it is "not common for property owners to open up their property for the

---

[26] *Summum*, 555 US at 468; *Tam*, 137 S Ct at 1757.

[27] 500 US 173, 194 (1991).

[28] 135 S Ct at 2246.

[29] 137 S Ct at 1758.

installation of permanent monuments that convey a message with which they do not wish to be associated."[30] (Justice Breyer makes essentially the same observation with respect to state-issued license plates in *Sons of Confederate Veterans*.[31]) The point comes through more clearly in several of the Court's earlier cases involving forum doctrine[32] and the regulation of speech in public schools.[33]

The two arguments are related: The government's interest in supporting the spread of democracy and not communism or fascism is based both on a programmatic rationale (equal financing for communism and fascism would undermine the government's pro-democracy objective) and a disassociation rationale (the government does not want communist or fascist views to be attributed to it). And most would agree that both arguments have some merit. Of course the government should be able to say "Get Your Flu Shot" without adding "Beware of Vaccines." Of course it should be able to tell motorists to "Slow for Pedestrians" without adding "Speed Up." The challenge is to delineate the boundaries of the government speech doctrine so as to leave space for nonneutral government speech without at the same time "swallow[ing] much of the First Amendment's protections."[34]

---

[30] 555 US at 471.

[31] 135 S Ct at 2249, quoting id.

[32] See *Lehman v City of Shaker Heights*, 418 US 298, 304 (1974) (interest in "minimiz[ing] . . . the appearance of favoritism" supports city's decision to ban political advertisements on public buses); *Greer v Spock*, 424 US 828, 839 (1976) (ban on speeches and demonstrations of a partisan nature on military base supported by military's interest in being "insulated from both the reality and the appearance of acting as a handmaiden for partisan political causes or candidates"); *Cornelius v NAACP Legal Defense & Education Fund*, 473 US 788, 809 (1985) (interest in avoiding "appearance of favoritism" supports exclusion of legal defense and political advocacy organizations from federal employees' charity drive).

[33] See, for example, *Bethel School District v Fraser*, 478 US 675, 685–86 (1986) ("perfectly appropriate" for high school "to disassociate itself" from student's lewd speech at school assembly—and to suspend student for three days—"to make the point to the pupils that vulgar speech and lewd conduct is wholly inconsistent with the fundamental values of public school education" (quotation marks omitted)); *Hazelwood School District v Kuhlmeier*, 484 US 260, 271 (1988) ("[A] school may in its capacity as publisher of a school newspaper or producer of a school play disassociate itself not only from speech that would substantially interfere with its work or impinge upon the rights of other students, but also from speech that is, for example, ungrammatical, poorly written, inadequately researched, biased or prejudiced, vulgar or profane, or unsuitable for immature audiences" (alterations, citations, and quotation marks omitted)). For an overview, see Abner S. Greene, *(Mis)attribution*, 87 Denver U L Rev 833, 848–53 (2010).

[34] Chemerinsky, 63 Fed Communications L J at 586 (cited in note 25); see also Joseph Blocher, *Viewpoint Neutrality and Government Speech*, 52 BC L Rev 695 (2011) ("Has government speech doctrine undermined the First Amendment's seemingly inviolable viewpoint neutrality requirement?"); Mary-Rose Papandrea, *The Government Brand*, 110 Nw U L Rev

2. *Drawing the line between government and private speech.* In *Keller*, the Justices appear to have assumed that the "so-called 'government speech' doctrine" that they had minted would apply only to the messages of "traditional government agencies and officials."[35] Thus, even though California's highest court had accorded "governmental" status to the State Bar, the Bar's speech was not "government speech" for First Amendment purposes. The Court noted three factors that distinguish the Bar from "most other entities that would be regarded in common parlance as 'government agencies'": its principal funding comes from dues levied on members; all lawyers admitted to practice in California must be members; and the state supreme court rather than the Bar has final authority over admission, suspension, disbarment, and the establishment of ethical codes of conduct.[36]

The *Keller* Court's line between "traditional government agencies and officials," to which the government speech doctrine would apply, and quasi-governmental entities such as the State Bar, to which it would not, did not hold for long. The very next Term, in *Rust v Sullivan*, the Court upheld a regulation that prohibited certain federally funded organizations from using federal dollars to provide abortion-related counseling or otherwise to promote abortion as a method of family planning.[37] The Court did not dwell on the fact that the doctors and nonprofit organizations whose speech was being regulated in *Rust* were not in any sense traditional government agencies or officials. Indeed, the Court did not cite *Keller* at all. Instead, it said "when the Government appropriates public funds to establish a program," it is "entitled"—within broad limits—"to define the limits of that program," including limits on what recipients of program funds can and cannot say.[38]

But the Court would soon come to rethink *Rust*'s sweeping language. In *Legal Services Corporation v Velasquez*,[39] the Court considered the validity of an appropriations provision that barred legal aid attorneys who received federal funding from challenging state wel-

---

1195, 1216 (2016) ("*Walker*'s expensive view of government speech doctrine grants state actors broad authority to restrict private speech.").

[35] *Keller*, 496 US at 13.

[36] See id at 11–12.

[37] 500 US 173 (1991).

[38] Id at 194.

[39] 531 US 533 (2001).

fare laws on federal statutory or constitutional grounds. One might be excused for thinking that this would be an easy case under *Rust*: when the government appropriates public funds to establish a program, it is generally entitled to define the limits of that program. Not so. The Court in *Velasquez* said that a legal aid attorney "is not the government's speaker," and that "[t]he advice from the attorney to the client and the advocacy by the attorney to the courts cannot be classified as governmental speech even under a generous understanding of the concept."[40] The Court failed to explain why a doctor's advice to a patient and an attorney's advice to a client would be classified differently for First Amendment purposes, with the former falling within the government speech doctrine's scope and the latter landing beyond.

The Court's implicit rejection of *Rust* did not, however, signify a return to *Keller*'s "traditional government agencies and officials" standard. Nor would it lead immediately to the Court adopting public perception as a factor in government speech analysis. Indeed, in *Johanns v Livestock Marketing Association*,[41] a 2005 case, a majority of the Court explicitly rejected the notion that public perception had any relevance to whether expression constitutes government speech.

Johanns involved a First Amendment challenge to a federal law requiring beef producers and importers to pay a $1 per head assessment on cattle sales to fund beef promotional campaigns conceived by a twenty-person committee. Half the committee's members were appointed by the Secretary of Agriculture; half were chosen by a beef industry group. Beef producers who objected to the mandatory assessment argued that the per-head assessment compelled them to subsidize private speech with which they disagreed.

The Court—in an opinion by Justice Scalia—rejected the dissident beef producers' argument, holding that the beef promotional campaigns constitute government speech. The Court reached this conclusion notwithstanding the substantial similarities between the twenty-member committee running the beef ad campaigns and the State Bar in *Keller*. In both cases, the organization's principal funding came from assessments on industry participants, who comprised its members.[42] In

[40] Id at 542–43.

[41] 544 US 550 (2005).

[42] Compare *Keller*, 496 US at 11, with *Johanns*, 544 US at 554.

both cases, the organization's actions were subject to the approval of another government actor (in *Keller*, the state Supreme Court; in *Johanns*, the Agriculture Secretary[43]). And yet in *Keller*, these "very specialized characteristics of the State Bar of California . . . served to distinguish it from the role of the typical government official or agency" for First Amendment purposes,[44] whereas the Court in *Johanns* concluded that the ads produced by the twenty-member committee constituted government speech.

What "distinguishes [*Johanns*] from *Keller*," according to the Court, is the "degree of governmental control over the message funded by the [beef] checkoff."[45] Congress described in broad brushstrokes the objective of the promotional efforts, and the Agriculture Secretary "exercises final approval authority over every word used in every promotional campaign."[46] This, in the majority's view, was enough to make the beef ads government speech. "The message set out in the beef promotions is from beginning to end the message established by the Federal Government," Justice Scalia said.[47] This holds true, in the Court's view, notwithstanding the fact that the government "solicits assistance from nongovernmental sources in developing specific messages."[48]

That a message is "from beginning to end" established by the federal government does not, however, appear to be a necessary criterion for classifying expression as government speech. After all, the government does not exercise such control with respect to the doctor-patient communications that came within the scope of the government speech doctrine in *Rust*. It is also doubtful that this degree of government control is a sufficient condition for expression to be classified as government speech: if, for example, the government demanded to see and approve every litigation document produced by a federally funded legal aid lawyer before it was filed, the First Amendment violation in *Legal Services Corporation v Velasquez* would seem more egregious, not less so.

---

[43] Compare *Keller*, 496 US at 11–12, with *Johanns*, 544 US at 563.

[44] *Keller*, 496 US at 12.

[45] 544 US at 561.

[46] See id.

[47] Id at 560.

[48] Id at 562.

Notably, in none of these early government speech cases did the majority ask whether members of the public perceived the messages in question to emanate from the government. Only Justice Souter, dissenting in *Johanns*, suggested that public perception should be relevant to government speech analysis. In his view, the government should not be able to rely on a government speech defense "[u]nless the putative speech appears to be coming from the government."[49] Otherwise, government officials would be able to escape judicial scrutiny for their decisions to support certain expression while at the same time "conceal[ing] their role from the voters with the power to hold them accountable."[50]

Yet a majority of the Court was not yet ready to endorse the idea that public perception should matter to whether expression is classified as government speech. Justice Scalia, writing for the majority in *Johanns*, said that the beef ads at issue in that case constituted government speech "whether or not the reasonable viewer would identify the speech as the government's."[51] The test for the validity of the beef program, according to Justice Scalia, turns "not on whether the ads' audience realizes the Government is speaking, but on the compelled assessment's purported interference with [beef producers'] First Amendment rights."[52]

One-and-a-half decades into the Court's experiment with a special First Amendment exemption for government speech, then, the doctrine was in a state of disarray. The distinction between "traditional" and nontraditional government speeches and agencies had broken down. So too had *Rust*'s bright-line rule allowing the legislature to define the limits of government-funded programs. If any standard could be discerned from *Johanns*, it would be that expression constitutes government speech when "[t]he message . . . is from beginning to end . . . established by the . . . [g]overnment."[53] But the Court

---

[49] Id at 578–79 (Souter, J, dissenting).

[50] Id at 578.

[51] Id at 564 n 7 (majority opinion). "If a viewer would identify the speech as [the beef producers']," according to Justice Scalia, "the analysis would be different." Id. That is, the Free Speech Clause does—under Justice Scalia's view—protect private individuals against the risk that government speech will be misattributed to them. This latter concern fits within the Court's compelled speech framework but is separate from the government speech analysis. See id at 565 n 8.

[52] Id at 564 n 7.

[53] Id at 560.

would quickly pedal back from that "beginning to end" standard as well.

3. *The public perception trilogy.* In the past decade, the Supreme Court has taken a new tack in its government speech cases. The message-control criterion of *Johanns* has given way to a new emphasis on public perception. This jurisprudential trend has manifested itself in three cases so far.

a) Pleasant Grove City v Summum. The Court's 2009 decision in *Pleasant Grove City v Summum* involved a 2.5-acre Pioneer Park in Pleasant Grove City, Utah, that featured fifteen permanent displays, eleven of which were donated by private individuals or organizations. One of those was a Ten Commandments monument donated by the Fraternal Order of Eagles.[54] Summum, a religious organization headquartered in nearby Salt Lake City, sought permission to erect a similarly sized stone monument presenting the "Seven Aphorisms" upon which the Summum religion is based. The city rejected the request. Summum sued, claiming that the city violated its free speech rights by allowing the Ten Commandments monument but rejecting the Seven Aphorisms.[55]

The central question in *Summum* was whether privately donated monuments on display in a public park qualify as government speech. If so, then the city would be free to discriminate between the Ten Commandments and the Seven Aphorisms. All the Justices agreed that monuments in a public park are government speech, and that the city could therefore accept the Ten Commandments while rejecting Summum's contribution.[56]

In explaining how the Court reached this conclusion, Justice Alito, writing for the majority, emphasized the (apparent) fact that "persons who observe donated monuments routinely—and reasonably—interpret them as conveying some message on the property owner's behalf."[57] Thus, Justice Alito saw "little chance that observers will fail

---

[54] 555 US at 465.

[55] See id at 464–66.

[56] The Court noted that there are still restraints on government speech, such as that it "must comport with the Establishment Clause." Id at 468. Establishment Clause issues were not raised in *Summum*, but the concurring opinions disagreed on whether they were settled. Compare id at 482–83 (Scalia, J, concurring) (arguing that there is no Establishment Clause violation), with id at 487 (Breyer, J, concurring) ("It is simply unclear how the relatively new category of government speech will relate to the more traditional categories of Establishment Clause analysis, and this case is not an occasion to speculate.").

[57] Id at 471 (majority opinion).

to appreciate the identity of the speaker."[58] As for why public perception should be a relevant factor in government speech analysis, the only reason offered by Justice Alito was that municipal governments have an interest in controlling the messages they convey internally and externally. "Public parks are often closely identified in the public mind with the government unit that owns the land," he wrote, and selectivity allows a city to "defin[e] the identity that [it] projects to its own residents and the outside world."[59]

Public perception was not the only factor mentioned in the majority opinion: Justice Alito also noted the long history of privately donated monuments on public land[60] as well as the space constraints that might prevent public parks from accommodating all donations.[61] Significantly, though, Justice Alito did not say—as Justice Scalia had in *Johanns*—that the message in question was controlled by the government "from beginning to end." The government's role with respect to privately designed and donated monuments, according to Justice Alito, is one of "selective receptivity"[62] rather than beginning-to-end editorial direction. Indeed, Justice Alito rejected the idea that monuments might convey a discrete message within anyone's control. As he put it, "it frequently is not possible to identify a single 'message' that is conveyed by an object or structure," and "the 'message' conveyed by a monument may change over time."[63]

While the majority in *Summum* placed greater emphasis on public perception than the Court had in the past, Justice Souter went a step further and argued in a concurring opinion that the *sole* test in cases such as *Summum* should be "whether a reasonable and fully informed observer would understand the expression to be government speech."[64] Justice Souter's only explanation for his proposed single-factor test was that it would "serve coherence" by bringing the test for government speech in line with the test employed in Establishment Clause cases "for spotting forbidden governmental endorsement of

---

[58] Id.

[59] Id at 472.

[60] See id at 471.

[61] See id at 480.

[62] Id at 471.

[63] Id at 476–77.

[64] Id at 487 (Souter, J, concurring in the judgment).

religion."[65] Justice Souter also did not explain how a court should determine whether "a reasonable and fully informed observer" would understand privately donated monuments on public land to be government speech—or even how he had reached that conclusion. He simply stated: "Application of this observer test provides the reason I find the monument here to be government expression."[66]

   b) *Walker v Texas Division, Sons of Confederate Veterans*. The public perception factor played an even more prominent role in *Walker v Texas Division, Sons of Confederate Veterans*, which involved a Texas program that allowed private individuals and organizations to propose their own designs for state license plates. The state's Department of Motor Vehicles Board approved hundreds of such designs but rejected a proposal from the Sons of Confederate Veterans for a plate that would feature the group's name and a Confederate battle flag image. The Sons of Confederate Veterans claimed that the rejection of their proposed plate violated their free speech rights.[67]

   In a 5–4 decision, the Court held that specialty license plates are government speech, and that Texas was therefore free to choose which plates it would and would not accept. Writing for the majority, Justice Breyer articulated a three-factor test for distinguishing government speech from private expression. The first factor, "history," looks to whether the relevant medium has been used to communicate government messages in the past.[68] The third factor, selectivity, looks to whether the government "maintains direct control over the messages."[69] The middle factor is public perception: whether "'persons who observe'" the expressions in question "'routinely—and reasonably—interpret them as conveying some message on the [government's] behalf.'"[70]

   But how can a court know whether members of the public perceive speech to be the government's? Justice Breyer listed a number of considerations with variable relevance to the inquiry at hand. For example, he highlighted the fact that Texas law requires vehicle owners to display license plates, which—in Justice Breyer's view—strengthens

---

[65] Id.

[66] Id.

[67] 135 S Ct at 2243–45.

[68] See id at 2248.

[69] See id at 2249.

[70] Id at 2248, quoting *Summum*, 555 US at 471.

the connection that observers will draw between license plates and the state.[71] But Texas also generally requires individuals to wear pants or otherwise to cover their bottoms in public,[72] and this does not mean that pants are perceived to be government speech. Justice Breyer also emphasized that "Texas dictates the manner in which drivers may dispose of unused plates."[73] But Texas also dictates the manner in which tires and untreated infectious waste may be disposed,[74] and those items very obviously do not constitute government speech.

In a stinging dissent, Justice Alito took issue with the majority's application of the public perception factor. "Here is a test," Justice Alito wrote.

> Suppose you sat by the side of a Texas highway and studied the license plates on the vehicles passing by. You would see, in addition to the standard Texas plates, an impressive array of specialty plates. (There are now more than 350 varieties.) You would likely observe plates that honor numerous colleges and universities. You might see plates bearing the name of a high school, a fraternity or sorority, the Masons, the Knights of Columbus, the Daughters of the American Revolution, a realty company, a favorite soft drink, a favorite burger restaurant, and a favorite NASCAR driver. As you sat there watching these plates speed by, would you really think that the sentiments reflected in these specialty plates are the views of the State of Texas and not those of the owners of the cars?[75]

Justice Alito evidently would answer that question in the negative. But it is not entirely clear why. After all, Justice Alito had said in *Summum* that "it frequently is not possible to identify a single 'message' that is conveyed by an object or structure,"[76] and yet the public may perceive that object or structure to be government speech nonetheless. The fact that Texas specialty license plates convey many different messages would not, under the logic of *Summum*, seem to disqualify them from government speech status.

Justice Alito's dissent appears to rest on the strong intuition that the observer on the side of a Texas highway would not perceive spe-

---

[71] Id.

[72] See Tex Penal Code § 21.08.

[73] 135 S Ct at 2248.

[74] See Northeast Recycling Council, *Disposal Bans & Mandatory Recycling in the United States* 134 (May 1, 2017), at https://nerc.org/documents/disposal_bans_mandatory_recycling_united _states.pdf.

[75] 135 S Ct at 2255 (Alito, J, dissenting) (paragraph break omitted).

[76] *Summum*, 555 US at 478.

cialty license plates to be government speech. But one wonders why Justice Alito is so confident in his conclusion. Sitting by the side of a Texas highway and studying the license plates on the vehicles passing by is not—we might surmise—a frequent pastime of any of the Justices (or, for that matter, their clerks). And yet the Court's increasing emphasis on the public perception factor seems to require the Justices to engage in these sorts of imaginative inquiries to determine the Free Speech Clause's scope.

  c) Matal v Tam. The Court's most recent government speech case, *Matal v Tam*, again emphasized public perception as a factor distinguishing government speech from private expression. *Tam* involved a rock band, "The Slants," whose name is a derogatory term for persons of Asian origin. The band's members, who are Asian-American, explained that they sought to "reclaim" the derogatory term. When The Slants' lead singer, Simon Tam, sought to register his band's name as a trademark, the Patent and Trademark Office (PTO) rejected his application on the basis of section 2(a) of the Lanham Act, which prohibits registration of any mark that "may disparage . . . persons, living or dead."[77] Tam sought judicial review of the PTO's decision and argued that the denial of his application violated his free speech rights. The PTO argued in response that federal registration of trademarks is a form of "government speech" exempt from Free Speech Clause scrutiny.[78]

  The Court roundly rejected the PTO's government speech argument. Justice Alito, writing for a unanimous Court on this point, said that it was "far-fetched to suggest that the content of a registered mark is government speech."[79] According to Justice Alito:

> If the federal registration of a trademark makes the mark government speech, the Federal Government is babbling prodigiously and incoherently. It is saying many unseemly things. It is expressing contradictory views. It is unashamedly endorsing a vast array of commercial products and services. And it is providing Delphic advice to the consuming public. For example, if trademarks represent government speech, what does the Government have in mind when it advises Americans to "make.believe" (Sony), "Think different" (Apple), "Just do it" (Nike), or "Have it your way" (Burger King)?

---

[77] 15 USC § 1052(a).

[78] 137 S Ct 1744, 1751–55 (2017).

[79] Id at 1758.

Was the Government warning about a coming disaster when it registered the mark "EndTime Ministries"?[80]

As in *Sons of Confederate Veterans*, Justice Alito seems to believe that the incoherence of the messages conveyed by registered trademarks places these expressions outside the bounds of government speech. And, also as in *Sons of Confederate Veterans*, Justice Alito makes no effort to reconcile this position with *Summum*'s conclusion that incoherence does not disqualify a monument as government speech.

Moreover, while Justice Alito pays lip service to the "history" and "selectivity" factors from *Sons of Confederate Veterans*,[81] it is hard to put much stock in his treatment of either factor. Justice Alito said that "[w]ith the exception of the enforcement of [section 2(a) of the Lanham Act], the viewpoint expressed by a mark has not played a role in the decision whether to place it on the principal register."[82] But that same fact could just as easily support the opposite conclusion: Ever since the Lanham Act was passed, the Patent and Trademark Office has refused to register marks that it deems to be disparaging toward "persons, living or dead."[83] And while one can criticize the Patent and Trademark Office for being insufficiently selective in choosing which marks to register, the PTO does reject approximately a quarter of the marks at the substantive review stage[84]—a figure that would seem to suggest "selective receptivity."

Ultimately, then, Justice Alito's determination that federal registration of trademarks is not government speech seems to come down to his strong intuition—evidently shared by his colleagues—that the public perceives trademarks to be private expression. But his test for what constitutes government speech is no more determinate than Justice Stewart's test for what constitutes obscenity.[85] Lower courts, government officials, and private parties are left to guess how the Court will come out when the question arises in a new context.

---

[80] Id at 1758–59 (footnotes omitted). The Federal Circuit subsequently relied on this conclusion when holding section 2(a)'s ban on "immoral" or "scandalous" marks to be unconstitutional. *In re Brunetti*, 877 F3d 1330, 1351 (Fed Cir 2017).

[81] See id at 1760.

[82] 137 S Ct at 1760.

[83] Act of July 5, 1946, ch 540, § 2(a), 60 Stat 427, 428.

[84] Barton Beebe, *Is the Trademark Office a Rubber Stamp?*, 48 Houston L Rev 751, 770–72 (2011).

[85] See *Jacobellis v Ohio*, 378 US 184, 197 (1964) ("I know it when I see it. . . .").

B. EVALUATING THE ROLE OF PUBLIC PERCEPTION
   IN GOVERNMENT SPEECH ANALYSIS

The Court's government speech jurisprudence is easy to criticize—and the *Summum/Sons of Confederate Veterans/Tam* trilogy is especially vulnerable. One line of attack against the turn toward public perception argues that these perceptions are disconnected from the normative justification for government speech doctrine.[86] A second line of attack focuses on the unpredictability and malleability of the Court's public perception analysis.[87] We address these concerns in turn.

1. *Why should public perception matter?* Recall the reasons given by the Court for exempting government speech from Free Speech Clause scrutiny. The Court in *Keller* argued that the exemption enables government officials to participate in public debates, while subsequent cases emphasize the programmatic importance of government speech as well as the government's interest in avoiding misattribution of private expression to itself. As significant as these interests may be, they do little to justify the use of the government speech doctrine to defeat free speech claims in cases like *Summum* and *Sons of Confederate Veterans*, in which the relevant speech was privately produced.

Consider first the *Keller* Court's argument that allowing government officials to express their positions without violating the Free Speech Clause facilitates the participation of public officials in democratic debate. This seems true enough, and leading academic commentators on government speech doctrine generally agree with the claim.[88] But the argument does not explain why government speech principles ought to extend to cases such as *Johanns*, *Summum*, and *Sons of Confederate Veterans*, in which the relevant expression is pro-

---

[86] See, for example, Case Note, *Walker v. Texas Division, Sons of Confederate Veterans, Inc.*, 129 Harv L Rev 221, 225 (2015) (noting that neither the approach of the majority nor the dissent in *Sons of Confederate Veterans* "aligns with the purported justification for the exemption that regulation of government speech enjoys from the strictures of the First Amendment").

[87] See, for example, Papandrea, 110 Nw U L Rev at 1216 (cited in note 34) ("Because it is not clear who the reasonable observer is and precisely what background knowledge she might have, this test leads to uncertainty and unpredictability.").

[88] See, for example, Mark G. Yudof, *When Governments Speak: Toward a Theory of Government Expression and the First Amendment*, 57 Tex L Rev 863, 865 (1979) ("Government expression is critical to the operation of a democratic polity. . . ."); Steven Shiffrin, *Government Speech*, 27 UCLA L Rev 565, 603 (1980) ("Indeed it is arguably the function, and perhaps the duty, of public officials to speak out on all issues of the day. . . .").

duced in the first instance by nongovernment officials. The *Keller* rationale would instead seem to support something like the following test: expression qualifies as government speech when it is generated by elected or appointed government officials. This, not coincidentally, is quite close to the "traditional government agency or official" standard that the *Keller* Court appeared to embrace.

Consider next the *reductio ad absurdum* argument made by the Court in *Rust, Sons of Confederate Veterans*, and *Tam*: how could the government function if it were required to advocate both sides of every issue or else to stay silent?[89] Again, the argument explains why a viewpoint-neutrality requirement should not apply to every type of government speech: at the very least, the government must be allowed to urge schoolchildren to "Just Say No" to illegal drugs and alcohol without also encouraging them to experiment with depressants, hallucinogens, opiates, and stimulants.[90] But the government could function just fine if Free Speech Clause scrutiny applied to privately designed ad campaigns, monuments, and license plates—it would just have to design those ads, monuments, and license plates itself. While it may be efficient for the government to solicit donations or proposals from private parties under certain circumstances, the need to do so is certainly not existential.[91]

Finally, consider the risk that members of the public will misattribute messages to the government unless the government has the ability to disassociate itself from views with which it disagrees. This interest in avoiding misattribution may be a real one, but it arises only because the government already has begun accepting privately designed monuments, privately designed license plates, and other forms of privately generated expression. If Pleasant Grove City accepted no private donations of monuments, it would not need to disassociate itself from the messages of Summum. If Texas allowed only a "Lone

---

[89] See text at notes 27–29.

[90] On the history and (questionable) efficacy of the Drug Abuse Resistance Education (D.A.R.E.) program, the source of the well-known "Just Say No" slogan, see Wei Pan and Haiyan Bai, *A Multivariate Approach to Meta-Analytic Review of the Effectiveness of the D.A.R.E. Program*, 6 Intl J Envir Res & Pub Health 267 (2009); and Scott O. Lilienfeld and Hal Arkowitz, *Why "Just Say No" Doesn't Work*, Scientific Am (Jan 1, 2014), https://www.scientificamerican.com/article/why-just-say-no-doesnt-work.

[91] Cf. Steven G. Gey, *Why Should the First Amendment Protect Government Speech When the Government Has Nothing to Say?*, 95 Iowa L Rev 1259, 1264 (2010) ("[T]here is no real reason why the government needs to stifle the speech of private persons to get an official government message across.").

Star State" license plate, it would not need to disassociate itself from the Sons of Confederate Veterans. The misattribution problem, in other words, is a problem of the government's own making.

This is not to deny that the government may be justified in rejecting a monument, license plate design, or other form of expression to avoid the risk of misattribution under some circumstances. But before that argument can become a persuasive one, we must first identify a compelling reason or set of reasons why the government should be allowed to solicit private assistance in designing monuments, license plates, and other expression that might then be attributed to it.

Some reasons for allowing the government to reach out for private assistance are relatively obvious but also relatively weak. No doubt there are fiscal benefits to outsourcing certain speech production functions. For example, by accepting privately donated monuments in Pioneer Park, Pleasant Grove City can beautify a public space without bearing the financial cost of designing and producing those structures itself. Private parties also might be more skilled than government officials at designing advertisements, monuments, license plates, and the like. Yet we doubt that these fiscal and aesthetic benefits are so significant as to allow the government to engage in viewpoint discrimination over an ill-defined domain. One might rightly want a more powerful justification before opening this constitutional Pandora's box.

A stronger argument is that private participation in the design of monuments and other items that might be attributed to the government is important to the process of "collective self-definition" that occurs in successful democratic polities.[92] As Justice Alito notes in *Summum*, the Statue of Liberty, the Iwo Jima monument at Arlington National Cemetery, and the Vietnam Veterans Memorial were all privately designed and funded.[93] In each of these cases, the monument or memorial played an important role in articulating shared values or reifying collective memories. Something similar can be said of many other objects with nongovernmental origins. The Ohio state motto was apparently "the brainchild of a Cincinnati schoolboy."[94]

---

[92] See Robert C. Post, *Racist Speech, Democracy, and the First Amendment*, 32 Wm & Mary L Rev 267, 283 (1991).

[93] *Summum*, 555 US at 471.

[94] See *ACLU v Capitol Square Review & Advisory Board*, 243 F3d 289, 318 (6th Cir 2001). The Sixth Circuit rejected an Establishment Clause challenge to the motto "With God, All Things Are Possible." Id.

The drawing of the Roman goddess Diana on the US Postal Service's Breast Cancer Research Stamp was the work of a Baltimore artist.[95] Examples abound.

Applying a viewpoint-neutrality argument to these acts of collective self-definition would, of course, be self-defeating. (Must the Statue of Liberty be paired with a Statue of Tyranny?) And excluding everyone except for "traditional government agencies and officials" from the design of these collective self-expressions would undermine the entire exercise. Citizen involvement in the creation of public monuments, mottoes, stamps, and so on allows individuals from various walks of life—artists, architects, and students, among others—to participate in the process of defining and articulating the values of the polity. Could that task be left entirely to politicians? Perhaps so, but only at a considerable (and not purely financial) cost.

But once we depart from the "traditional government agency or official" standard, several real dangers arise. In addition to the misattribution risk mentioned above (i.e., the risk that individuals will misattribute messages to the government that the government does not endorse), there is the risk of misattribution in the opposite direction: a risk that observers will misattribute the government's message to private parties. Government speech may be more persuasive when it is laundered through the mouths of nongovernmental speakers.[96] For example, the government may seek to free-ride off the credibility of another trusted speaker (e.g., a patient's physician)[97] or may wish to intervene in the marketplace of ideas without its intervention being

---

[95] Rachel Warren, *Stamping Out Breast Cancer, One Envelope at a Time*, Wash Post, July 6, 1998, at C1.

[96] See Gia B. Lee, *Persuasion, Transparency, and Government Speech*, 56 Hastings L J 983, 1009 (2005).

[97] Lawrence Lessig uses the example of *Rust v Sullivan* to illustrate the point:

> There the government required (partially) governmentally funded doctors to say certain things about what methods of family planning were best, and to refrain from giving women any information about abortion as a method of family planning. The clear purpose of these regulations was to steer women away from abortion. But the power of this message was amplified dramatically by its being delivered, without disclaimer, by a doctor. Out of the mouth of a doctor, the antiabortion message had a much more powerful effect than an antiabortion message out of the mouth of Congressman Henry Hyde. . . . In part because it was hidden that it was the government that was speaking, the government's message had a much more powerful effect, if only by deceiving poor women about the source of the message.

Lawrence Lessig, *The Regulation of Social Meaning*, 62 U Chi L Rev 943, 1017 (1995).

discounted as propaganda.[98] In this way, a doctrine meant to facilitate democratic discourse might instead have a distortionary effect.

A related risk is that if individuals do not identify speech as emanating from the government, then government officials might not be held accountable for that expression. This was the concern voiced by Justice Souter in *Johanns*. "Democracy," he wrote, "ensures that government is not untouchable when its speech rubs against the First Amendment interests of those who object to supporting it; if enough voters disagree with what government says, the next election will cancel the message."[99] But this democratic check works only if "the putative speech appears to be coming from the government."[100] Voters are unlikely to punish public officials for speech that they misattribute to a nongovernmental source.

Electoral accountability is, of course, an imperfect check on the abuse of the government speech doctrine. If, for example, a majority of voters in a state are pro-life, then elected officials might be rewarded at the ballot box for allowing a "Choose Life" license plate while rejecting a "Respect Choice" design.[101] More generally, public officials can use the freedom afforded by the government speech doctrine to privilege certain views over others. But while the threat posed by government speech is present even when members of the public perceive the relevant speech to be the government's, the threat is arguably even more acute when members of the public are confused about a message's source.

In any event, whatever apprehensions we might have with regard to public perception as a factor distinguishing government speech from private expression, it is not obvious that there is a better alternative.[102] The focus on history in *Summum*, *Sons of Confederate Vet-*

---

[98] Lessig calls this "the Orwell effect": "when people see that the government or some relatively powerful group is attempting to manipulate social meaning, they react strongly to resist any such manipulation." This, in turn, leads to "a strong incentive for the government to deliver its message of change while hiding the messenger." Id.

[99] *Johanns*, 544 US at 575 (Souter, J, dissenting).

[100] Id at 578.

[101] This example closely tracks the facts of *ACLU v Tennyson*, 815 F3d 183 (4th Cir 2016). In that case, the ACLU sued North Carolina for discriminating between pro-life and pro-choice license plate designs. The Fourth Circuit initially sided with the ACLU but reversed course after the Supreme Court held in *Sons of Confederate Veterans* that specialty license plate designs are government speech. See id at 184.

[102] This is not to say that there is no other possibility for drawing this line. For other proposals, see Blocher, 52 BC L Rev at 751–66 (cited in note 34) (suggesting that govern-

erans, and *Tam* leaves government speech doctrine ill-equipped for technological change. Does, say, a posting on an agency's Facebook page or a retweet from an agency's account qualify as government speech?[103] The fact that no agency posted on Facebook or tweeted before the twenty-first century cannot be dispositive. As noted, the emphasis on selectivity in several of the Court's cases leads to the counterintuitive result that Free Speech Clause scrutiny is relaxed when government exerts *greater* control over the flow of ideas.[104] And the Court's concern regarding space constraints in *Summum* does not translate well to other areas: most of us share the intuition that the Postal Service should be allowed to choose to print Harriet Tubman's face on postage stamps and to choose not to print Adolf Hitler's, even though there is no binding practical constraint that prevents the Postal Service from printing both.

In sum, the public perception factor seems to be consonant with the concerns that underlie the government speech doctrine and applicable—at least in theory—across a wide range of areas.[105] Whether the practical challenges of applying the public perception factor outweigh its abstract appeal is a separate question to which we now turn.

2. *Can public perception be measured?* Even if one agrees that public perception is normatively relevant to the government speech doctrine's scope, one still might doubt whether the public perception factor can be operationalized in a nonarbitrary way. The Court's record on this score is not inspiring. As one commentator appropriately complains, the Court has offered "no meaningful guidance for determining when observers reasonably attribute private expression to the government."[106]

---

ment speech could be limited to when there are adequate alternatives for private expression, or when the government would lack adequate alternatives, or when the government affirmatively offers equal alternatives for discriminated-against viewpoints); Abner S. Greene, *The Concept of the Speech Platform: Walker v. Texas Division*, 68 Ala L Rev 337, 377–92 (2016) (arguing that the government should be able to create and regulate content on "speech platforms").

[103] Cf. Helen Norton and Danielle Keats Citron, *Government Speech 2.0*, 87 Denver U L Rev 899 (2010) (discussing government speech doctrine for new expressive technologies).

[104] See text following note 48.

[105] Of course, speech that passes this test must still satisfy other limitations such as the Establishment Clause. See note 56; see also Nelson Tebbe, *Government Nonendorsement*, 98 Minn L Rev 648, 651 (2013) (arguing that the Constitution also prohibits certain forms of government endorsement, such as "Vote Democrat" or "America is a white nation").

[106] See Papandrea, 110 Nw U L Rev at 1219 (cited in note 34).

Indeterminacy is not, however, an inherent feature of every legal test that relies on public perception. Social science has over the past several decades developed a reasonably reliable—though concededly imperfect—tool for measuring public opinion: the statistical survey.

Courts consult survey evidence in a variety of cases in which public opinion is relevant to the resolution of a legal dispute.[107] In trademark law, litigants routinely introduce survey evidence to show that a defendant's use of a plaintiff's mark is—or is not—"likely to cause confusion" in the minds of consumers.[108] Thus, if the question in *Tam* had not been whether the USPTO could constitutionally reject The Slants' mark for disparaging persons of Asian origin but instead whether the mark was likely to cause confusion with the Boston-based Irish folk band Sláinte,[109] the parties might well have introduced survey evidence to substantiate their claims. Survey evidence also plays an important role in the resolution of false advertising claims. As one court has noted, when "we are asked to determine whether a statement acknowledged to be literally true and grammatically correct nevertheless has a tendency to mislead," the court's own reaction "is at best not determinative and at worst irrelevant."[110] The relevant question in those cases is: "what does the person to whom the advertisement is addressed find to be the message?"[111] Survey evidence is the "customary way of proving significant actual deception" in those cases.[112]

The use of surveys in court is not, however, limited to trademark and false advertising cases. Indeed, courts consult survey evidence in the First Amendment context already. The Supreme Court's three-part test for determining whether speech is obscene—and therefore unprotected by the Free Speech Clause—requires the adjudicator to determine "whether the average person, applying contemporary com-

---

[107] For a comprehensive overview, see Shari Seidman Diamond, *Reference Guide on Survey Research*, in *Reference Manual on Scientific Evidence* 359, 363–67 (National Academies, 3d ed 2011).

[108] 15 USC §§ 1114(1), 1125(a); see *Exxon Corp. v Texas Motor Exchange*, 628 F2d 500, 506 (5th Cir 1980) ("Parties often introduce survey evidence in an effort to demonstrate that there is a likelihood of confusion.").

[109] Sláinte, http://www.slaintetheband.com.

[110] *American Brands, Inc. v R. J. Reynolds Tobacco Co.*, 413 F Supp 1352, 1357 (SDNY 1976).

[111] Id.

[112] *First Health Group Corp. v United Payors & United Providers, Inc.*, 95 F Supp 2d 845, 848 (ND Ill 2000).

munity standards would find that the work, taken as a whole, appeals to the prurient interest."[113] One court has observed that "[e]xpert testimony based on a public opinion poll is uniquely suited to a determination of community standards," and "[p]erhaps no other form of evidence is more helpful or concise."[114]

Survey evidence will not be relevant to every First Amendment question; it is only useful if the legal inquiry focuses on the actual views of members of the public.[115] For example, in deciding whether a regulation of protected speech serves a compelling government interest, survey evidence might be of limited utility because the doctrinal inquiry does not depend on whether members of the public *perceive* the government interest at stake to be compelling. The claim that survey evidence should be consulted in government speech cases is thus contingent on the premise that the distinction between government speech and private expression should depend on the *actual* views of members of the public.

Some have suggested a different yardstick in government speech cases. For example, Justice Souter said in *Summum* that "the best approach that occurs to me is to ask whether a reasonable and fully informed observer would understand the expression to be government speech."[116] If that is the measure of government speech, then surveys of less-than-fully-informed observers would seem to shed little light on doctrinal questions. Yet in our view, Justice Souter's "reasonable and fully informed observer" standard has little to recommend it. The fully

---

[113] *Miller v California*, 413 US 15, 24 (1973).

[114] *Saliba v State*, 475 NE2d 1181, 1185 (Ind Ct App 1985); see also *Commonwealth v Trainor*, 374 NE2d 1216, 1220 (Mass 1978) ("A properly conducted public opinion survey, offered through an expert in conducting such surveys, is admissible in an obscenity case if it tends to show relevant standards in the Commonwealth."). Such surveys can be conducted without themselves falling afoul of obscenity laws by phrasing questions in the abstract, such as whether respondents think it is acceptable for "movie theaters, restricting attendance to adults only, to show films that depict nudity and actual or pretended sexual activities," *Saliba*, 475 NE2d at 1191; see *Trainor*, 374 NE2d at 1222.

[115] This may be true in a number of First Amendment contexts beyond government speech and obscenity cases. See, for example, Diamond and Koppelman, 60 Md L Rev at 716 (cited in note 18) (proposing surveys in Establishment Clause cases); Daniel E. Herz-Roiphe, *Stubborn Things: An Empirical Approach to Facts, Opinions, and the First Amendment*, 113 Mich L Rev First Impressions 47 (2015) (arguing that courts should consult surveys in compelled commercial speech cases to distinguish "fact" from "opinion," and conducting a survey to demonstrate); Robert Post, *Compelled Commercial Speech*, 117 W Va L Rev 867 (2015) (arguing that compelled commercial speech raises no more constitutional concern than government speech based on the empirical claim about public perception that "most members of the public recognize government mandated labels and reports when they see them").

[116] 555 US at 487.

informed observer would never misattribute private speech to the government or vice versa because the observer is, by hypothesis, fully informed about the message's source. Our concern—and, we think, the concern that is normatively relevant to the government speech doctrine—is how a less-than-fully-informed observer might react to a message of muddled origin.

3. *Concerns about the use of survey evidence.* There are, to be sure, several reasons to pause before embracing survey evidence in government speech cases. We canvas those concerns here and explain how some—though not all—can be resolved through real-world demonstrations.

One concern is cost. Our own experience from several such surveys is that nationally representative panels assembled by survey research firms generally cost a few dollars per respondent; a thousand-person sample might thus cost several thousands of dollars (though well below $10,000). This is not a negligible amount for many litigants; moreover, parties to trademark cases sometimes spend even larger sums on surveys (including the cost of survey experts), suggesting that the costs could rise well above the four-digit range.[117] Yet even without the use of surveys, government speech litigation is an expensive enterprise. For example, the religious group Summum requested attorneys' fees of more than $69,000 arising from the district court stage of monument-related litigation parallel to the Pleasant Grove City case in the mid-2000s.[118] More recently, a municipality in California was awarded nearly $230,000 in attorneys' fees and court costs resulting from its (successful) defense against a First Amendment challenge in state court involving government speech issues.[119] That tab only increases at higher levels of appellate review: hourly rates for prominent members of the Supreme Court bar reportedly fall in the $1,100 to $1,800 range.[120] While none of this is meant to trivialize the real costs that parties—especially less affluent parties—would bear in conducting rigorous surveys, it does suggest that insofar as the use of

---

[117] See Lisa Larrimore Ouellette, *The Google Shortcut to Trademark Law*, 102 Cal L Rev 351, 361 & n 53 (2014) (quoting trademark survey expert stating that costs typically fall in the $75,000–$150,000 range).

[118] *Summum v Duchesne City*, 482 F3d 1263, 1276 (10th Cir 2007).

[119] *Vargas v City of Salinas*, 200 Cal App 4th 1331, 1338 (Cal Ct App 2011).

[120] See David Lat, *Top Supreme Court Advocates Charge How Much Per Hour?*, Above the Law (Aug 10, 2015, 4:51 PM), https://abovethelaw.com/2015/08/top-supreme-court-advocates-charge-how-much-per-hour.

survey evidence can reduce uncertainty in government speech cases, the resulting reduction in other litigation costs may make a turn toward survey evidence economical in the long run.

A second concern, and one that is harder to address in the abstract, is whether members of the public can answer questions about government speech in a meaningful way.[121] Asking an ordinary American whether federal registration of a trademark "convey[s] a government message"[122] may be like asking him or her whether the Higgs field has a non-zero constant value in vacuum: the terms of the question are gobbledygook.[123] We defer in-depth discussion of this concern to Part III, where we take stock of the evidence we gather from a survey of a nationally representative sample. As a preview: We think our results suggest that individuals *do* understand these sorts of questions, and that their intuitions about what does and does not constitute government speech are not that far off from the intuitions of the Justices.

A third concern is that even if individuals understand the terms of the question, their answers will be influenced by doctrinally irrelevant factors. For example, individuals may be more likely to ascribe expression to the government if they agree with the message or if they anticipate that politicians will agree with the message. In that case, reliance on public perception in government speech cases may serve to shield popular views from Free Speech Clause scrutiny. To some extent, the government speech doctrine already produces this result because the views expressed by the government are likely to be those that a majority holds. We recognize this as a real concern both with regard to the government speech doctrine in general and with regard to the use of survey evidence specifically, though we will suggest several ways that surveys can mitigate this worry.

A fourth concern is in some respects the flipside of the third: not that individuals will be influenced by doctrinally irrelevant factors, but that individuals will be influenced by the Court's own decisions. If the Supreme Court holds that a particular form of expression constitutes government speech, then individuals who are aware of the Court's decision may update their priors and subsequently say that

---

[121] See Papandrea, 110 Nw U L Rev at 1228 (cited in note 34) (expressing concern that the public perception factor will expand government speech due to mistaken attribution of speech to the government).

[122] *Tam*, 137 S Ct at 1760.

[123] Cf. id at 1759 ("[I]t is unlikely that more than a tiny fraction of the public has any idea what federal registration of a trademark means.").

any similar form of expression also constitutes government speech. This concern is analogous to the "circularity problem" in Fourth Amendment law, where the Court relies on "reasonable expectations of privacy" to determine whether a search has occurred.[124] If an individual's reasonable expectations of privacy are influenced by Fourth Amendment doctrine, then the Court's later decisions may be partly determined by its earlier ones.[125]

We do not think that the circularity concern is fatal to our proposal. As a preliminary matter, it is not clear that circularity—if established—would be a problem for government speech doctrine. As long as individuals identify government speech as such, then the government cannot launder its message through private speakers and government officials cannot escape accountability for government speech. Thus, the checks on government speech that arise when public perceptions are accurate do not depend on whether public perceptions are endogenous to judicial decisions.[126] Moreover, we find little evidence that survey respondents pay close attention to Supreme Court decisions. A majority of respondents reported that they had not heard of *Summum*, *Sons of Confederate Veterans*, and *Tam*, and those that said they had heard about the cases did no better than a coin flip when asked about the results.[127] We also take solace in Matthew Kugler and Lior Strahilevitz's findings regarding circularity in the Fourth Amendment context: they report only a slight and temporary change in public

---

[124] See *Katz v United States*, 389 US 347, 361 (1967) (Harlan, J, concurring).

[125] See Matthew B. Kugler and Lior Jacob Strahilevitz, *The Myth of Fourth Amendment Circularity*, 84 U Chi L Rev 1747 (2017).

[126] To elaborate: Imagine that the Court held that specialty license plate designs were government speech, and that members of the public therefore attributed those designs to the state. Government officials would not be able to disguise their own messages as private expression (because members of the public would understand license plates to be government speech), and they would have to answer to the electorate for those designs. Now imagine instead that the Court held that specialty license plate designs were private speech, and that members of the public therefore did not attribute such designs to the state. Specialty license plate designs would thus be subject to the viewpoint-neutrality rule that is generally applicable to private expression.

[127] Overall, 63% of respondents said they did not know how *Summum* was resolved; 56% said the same about *Sons of Confederate Veterans*; and 59% said that they did not know the result in *Tam*. We asked respondents who claimed that they *did* know how the Court resolved those cases to tell us whether the expression in question was held to be government speech or private speech. Of that group, 48% correctly answered "government speech" in *Summum*; 46% correctly answered "government speech" in *Sons of Confederate Veterans*; and 58% correctly answered "private speech" in *Tam*.

perceptions regarding the privacy of cell phone searches following the Supreme Court's landmark 2014 decision in *Riley v California*.[128]

A fifth concern relates not to the worry that individuals will be influenced by past Supreme Court decisions but that they may be influenced by the upcoming case. If, for example, the citizens of Pleasant Grove City (population 33,509)[129] favor the city's position in *Summum*, and if they understand that identifying statues in Pioneer Park as government speech will advance the city's cause, then reliance on survey evidence drawn from Pleasant Grove City runs the risk of transforming government speech cases into adjudication by Gallup poll. Yet survey designers can take several steps to allay this strategic-response concern. One is to ask potential respondents whether they have heard of the pending case and to exclude those who have. Another is to draw respondents from a larger (perhaps national) pool, where it is less likely that individuals will have heard of a case that is especially salient in a particular jurisdiction. Still another is to vary the facts presented in the survey just enough that the fact pattern is not immediately recognizable: for example, instead of asking whether a privately donated Ten Commandments statue in Pioneer Park is government speech, the survey might ask whether a privately donated statue featuring lyrics of the John Lennon song "Imagine" in New York's Central Park is government speech.[130] Answers to the latter query would still shed light on the public perception question in *Summum*: whether members of the public who observe donated monuments on public land "routinely" interpret them as conveying a message on the government's behalf.[131]

A sixth concern relates to line-drawing: What percentage of respondents must believe that a particular expression is government speech for the speech to qualify as such? A similar question arises in

---

[128] See *Riley v California*, 134 S Ct 2473 (2014) (holding that police cannot search digital information on an arrestee's cell phone without a warrant); Kugler and Strahilevitz, 84 U Chi L Rev at 1781 (cited in note 125) (reporting results from multiwave survey indicating that expectations of privacy with respect to cell phones returned to pre-*Riley* levels within one year after decision).

[129] See US Census Bureau, *Annual Estimates of the Resident Population: April 1, 2010 to July 1, 2016 Population Estimates*, https://factfinder.census.gov/faces/tableservices/jsf/pages/productview .xhtml?src=bkmk. Work by Valerie Hoekstra finds that citizens of the communities from which Supreme Court cases originate "are much more likely to hear about home-grown Court cases than is typically found in national surveys." Valerie J. Hoekstra, *Public Reaction to Supreme Court Decisions* 76 (Cambridge, 2003).

[130] Cf. *Summum*, 555 US at 474–75 (discussing the "Imagine" statue as another example of government speech).

[131] See id at 471.

the trademark confusion context: What percentage of consumers must confuse the defendant's products with the plaintiff's before the defendant will be held liable for trademark infringement? Figures over 25 percent will generally support a likelihood-of-confusion finding, though plaintiffs have prevailed on the basis of much weaker evidence as well.[132] One approach is to use a set of controls: examples of expression that no court would consider to be government speech, as well as examples that virtually any jurist could consider to be government speech. For instance, if members of the public are no more likely to say that federal registration of a trademark constitutes government speech than that a billboard on private property constitutes government speech, then that fact would be powerful evidence in support of the Court's view in *Tam*.[133] By contrast, if members of the public are no less likely to say that trademark registration constitutes government speech than that the text engraved on the Lincoln Memorial does, then that would be equally powerful evidence against the Court's position.[134] The specific threshold courts demand may depend on how they balance the dangers of viewpoint discrimination against the harm of constraining the government's ability to say what it wants. But in any case, we think courts will be aided by rigorous evidence of how public perception of the kind of speech at issue compares with perception of other expression. Resorting to survey evidence does not remove the need for normative judgment in interpreting those results.

Last but certainly not least, the usefulness of survey evidence in any case will depend upon the quality of the survey and its conformance to social-scientific best practices. In federal court, methodological issues generally will be addressed through adjudication of a *Daubert* motion on admissibility.[135] Federal judges routinely (if imperfectly)

---

[132] See McCarthy § 32:188 (cited in note 16).

[133] Diamond and Koppelman offer this suggestion as part of their proposal for using survey evidence in Establishment Clause cases. See Diamond and Koppelman, 60 Md L Rev at 752 (cited in note 18) ("If respondents were also asked precisely the same questions about a display that is widely accepted by the courts as indicating no religious endorsement (e.g., a sign saying 'Welcome to Los Angeles') and twenty percent reported a perception of state endorsement of particular religious views, that twenty percent would properly be attributed to the effects of guessing or the particular wording of the question, and not to the allegedly infringing display.").

[134] This approach would help address the concern of Papandrea, 110 Nw U L Rev at 1226–34 (cited in note 34), that mistaken perceptions will cause an expansion of the government speech defense.

[135] See *Daubert v Merrell Dow Pharmaceuticals, Inc.*, 509 US 579, 593–95 (1993) (court should consider whether evidence relies on falsifiable methodology, whether theory or technique has been subject to peer review, what the likely error rate is, and whether methodology is generally accepted in relevant scientific community).

evaluate the reliability of survey methodologies in the trademark context.[136] We see no reason why the challenge of assessing the reliability of survey methods will be categorically more difficult in the government speech context. Of course, the stakes may be higher when survey evidence will be used to inform a constitutional holding than when used only to resolve a fact-specific dispute in an individual case, and so the risk of manipulation may be more acute. But even this much is not clear—the stakes in cases such as *Summum* and *Sons of Confederate Veterans* are in some respects far greater and in other respects rather paltry compared to a multimillion-dollar trademark battle. Moreover, manipulation is a risk even under the status quo: lawyers and jurists who assert that members of the public do or do not perceive expression to be government speech are no doubt influenced in their claims by their own preferences regarding the case outcome. The use of survey evidence has the virtue of subjecting such claims to falsification. When compared with the current method of assessing public perception—which often entails armchair speculation colored by ideological motivation—we think survey evidence is a substantial improvement.

II. Surveying the Public about Government Speech

Some of the concerns limned above cannot be resolved in the abstract. Most significantly, the concern that individuals will be unable to answer questions about government speech in a coherent fashion can be refuted only by demonstration.[137] To that end, and to provide a first look at how public perception interacts with government speech doctrine, we conducted a proof-of-concept survey based on the scenarios at issue in *Summum*, *Sons of Confederate Veterans*, and *Tam*. Here we describe our survey methodology, followed by the results.

A. METHODOLOGY

The survey was administered online in October 2017 to a nationally representative sample of 1,223 respondents recruited by Survey Sampling International (SSI), as well as in September 2017 to a pilot group

---

[136] See McCarthy § 32:158 (cited in note 16). But see Robert G. Bone, *Enforcement Costs and Trademark Puzzles*, 90 Va L Rev 2099, 2131 (2004) ("Consumer surveys are the best evidence of secondary meaning, but surveys are difficult to design properly and expensive to conduct. . . . Judges also find it difficult to evaluate survey methodology, especially when confronted with competing expert testimony, and this increases the likelihood of error.").

[137] See text at notes 122–23.

of 503 respondents recruited through Amazon's Mechanical Turk (MTurk) platform. Appendix table A1 shows the demographic breakdown of each sample compared with the US population.[138] In this section, we present and discuss only the SSI results; table A3 and figures A1–A5 in the appendix show that the results were similar for the MTurk sample, except that respondents were consistently less likely to view all scenarios as government speech. The survey instrument and datasets are available online.[139]

Each respondent saw four scenarios involving potential instances of government speech: (1) a statue in a city park (as in *Summum*),[140] (2) a specialty state license plate (as in *Sons of Confederate Veterans*),[141] (3) registration of a federal trademark (as in *Tam*),[142] and (4) a private billboard that is visible from a public road (as a control that is clearly not government speech). Each scenario was randomly assigned to a message with a different substantive content: (1) the Ten Commandments (as in *Summum*),[143] (2) either an atheist or Muslim message (as a contrasting religious message), (3) either a pro-life or pro-choice message (as in *ACLU v Tennyson*, a Fourth Circuit decision applying *Sons of Confederate Veterans*),[144] and (4) either a corporate (Mickey Mouse) or patriotic (Abraham Lincoln) message. Thus, for example, one respondent might see the following four scenarios:

1. A city park contains 15 permanent statues. One of the statues is a Ten Commandments monument. Do you think the placement of the monument in the park indicates that the city government endorses the monument's message?
2. Drivers may choose between standard state license plates with the state motto or a variety of specialty license plates. One of the specialty options is a license plate with a Muslim symbol. Do you

---

[138] Table A1 shows that the SSI sample closely matches the US population in terms of gender, age, race, and ethnicity but is somewhat more highly educated. The MTurk sample was more male, young, and white (non-Hispanic) than the national population, and even more highly educated than the SSI sample. For example, the percentage of the population age eighteen and over with a bachelor's degree is 19%, compared with 23% for the SSI sample and 38% for the MTurk sample.

[139] For survey instrument and datasets, see https://dataverse.harvard.edu/dataset.xhtml ?persistentId=doi%3A10.7910%2FDVN%2FDJUALA.

[140] 555 US at 464.

[141] 135 S Ct at 2243–44.

[142] 137 S Ct at 1751.

[143] 555 US at 464.

[144] 815 F3d at 184–85; see note 101 above.

think the availability of this specialty license plate indicates that the state government endorses the license plate design's message?

3. A trademark is a word, phrase, or symbol that identifies brands or products (like Coca-Cola®, Target®, or Nike®). The federal government registers trademarks (as indicated by the ® symbol). One of the trademarks that the government has registered is a trademark for a pro-choice slogan submitted for use on T-shirts. Do you think the registration of this trademark indicates that the government endorses the trademark's message?

4. Disney purchases billboard space from a private company to display a billboard with a picture of Mickey Mouse. Do you think the visibility of this billboard from public roads indicates that the government endorses the billboard's message?

A second respondent might then see a statue with statements supporting atheism, a pro-life specialty license plate, an Abraham Lincoln trademark registration, and a Ten Commandments billboard.

The scenarios also randomly varied in the specific details provided: for the statue, license plate, and trademark conditions, respondents were given (1) the basic fact patterns listed above, (2) additional information about private involvement (i.e., that private organizations donated the statues, designed the license plates, and submitted the trademarks), (3) additional information about government selectivity (i.e., that the government must approve and has rejected park statues, license plate designs, or trademark registrations in the past), or (4) both information about private involvement and government selectivity.

The specific question also randomly varied, with respondents being asked (1) whether the respondent "associate[s]" the message with the government,[145] (2) whether the government's action indicates that it "endorses" the message it issues,[146] or (3) whether the government's action "conveys a message on [its] behalf."[147] These question

---

[145] Cf. id, quoting *Summum*, 555 US at 471 ("[L]icense plates are, essentially, government IDs. And issuers of ID 'typically do not permit' the placement on their IDs of 'message[s] with which they do not wish to be associated.'").

[146] Cf. *Sons of Confederate Veterans*, 135 S Ct at 2249 ("[A] person who displays a message on a Texas license plate likely intends to convey to the public that the State has endorsed that message.").

[147] Cf. id, quoting *Summum*, 555 US at 471 ("'[P]ersons who observe' designs on IDs 'routinely—and reasonably—interpret them as conveying some message on the [issuer's] behalf.'").

forms track the various ways that the Supreme Court has framed the government speech inquiry. For each question form, respondents were given the same four choices: "Definitely not," "Probably not," "Definitely yes," "Probably yes."[148] For example, variations on the fact pattern involving a Ten Commandments statue in a city park included the following:

1. A city park contains 15 permanent statues. One of the statues is a Ten Commandments monument. Do you think the placement of the monument in the park indicates that the city government endorses the monument's message?
2. A city park contains 15 permanent statues, which were donated by private groups or individuals. One of the statues is a Ten Commandments monument donated by a private organization. Do you think the placement of the monument in the park conveys a message on the city government's behalf?
3. A city park contains 15 permanent statues. The city government must approve new statues, and it has rejected proposed statues in the past. One of the approved statues is a Ten Commandments monument. Do you associate the monument's message with the city government?

Table 1 summarizes this variation in scenarios, showing that each scenario will involve one of four mediums, one of seven messages, one of three informational conditions, and one of three question forms.[149] To reiterate, each respondent saw all four mediums (in a random

---

[148] These four responses were then numerically coded as –1.5, –0.5, 0.5, 1.5, so that each jump is 1.0 apart on our "government speech" scale.

[149] The survey contained one additional variation, although the results are not presented below: We wanted to test whether views on trademark registration varied if the trademark at issue was one that might be denied registration under the prohibition on "immoral" or "scandalous" marks in 15 USC § 1052(a), which was at issue in a Federal Circuit case that was decided after our survey was completed. See *In re Brunetti*, 2017 WL 6391161 (Fed Cir, Dec 15, 2017) (holding the bar on immoral or scandalous marks to be unconstitutional). Thus, for the half of respondents whose trademark scenario involved a religious message (Ten Commandments, atheist, or Muslim), these respondents were further randomized into either the normal condition (as above) or a mark that would likely be viewed as "immoral" or "scandalous": "Fuck [the message at issue]." This variation did have large effects on views, but we were averaging over a small number of respondents (fewer than eight for the atheism and Muslim conditions), and the results were not statistically significant. Because there was no parallel to this "scandalous" condition for the billboard, license plate, and statue conditions, or for the pro-life, pro-choice, Mickey Mouse, and Lincoln messages, the results from the scandalous trademark scenarios are omitted from the figures and regressions presented below.

Table 1

Variation in Survey Scenarios

Medium	Content	Added Information	Question Form
1. statue in park (*Summum*)	1. Ten Commandments	1. none	1. associate with government?
2. specialty license plate (*Sons of Confederate Veterans*)	2. atheism	2. private involvement	2. government endorses?
3. trademark registration (*Tam*)	3. Muslim	3. government selectivity	3. conveys a message on government's behalf?
4. private billboard	4. pro-life	4. both	
	5. pro-choice		
	6. Mickey Mouse		
	7. Lincoln		

order), each with a different message. The added information was randomly chosen for each statue, license plate, and trademark registration scenario independently (so one respondent might see information about private involvement for all three of these scenarios, and another might see three different variations). Each respondent always saw the same question form for all four of their scenarios.

Finally, participants were asked for their views on the four messages they saw—the Ten Commandments, atheism or the Muslim religion, abortion, and Disney or Lincoln, and for demographic details.

B. RESULTS

Based on Supreme Court government speech jurisprudence, one would expect the medium of speech to matter significantly to public perceptions, with the expected ordering from most to least likely to be viewed as government speech being: (1) statue in the park, (2) specialty license plate, (3) trademark registration, and (4) private billboard. As discussed in Part I, the Supreme Court unanimously held in *Summum* that the placement of a monument in a city part is government speech.[150] The Court split 5–4 in *Sons of Confederate Veterans*, with Justice Breyer's opinion for the Court holding that specialty license plates are government speech,[151] and Justice Alito's dissent arguing that the public does not in fact associate license plate designs with the state government.[152] In *Tam*, a unanimous Court held that federal registration does not make a trademark government speech.[153] And presumably a private billboard visible from a public highway is an even easier case of purely private speech; Justice Alito's *Sons of Confederate Veterans* dissent gave the example of a *state* selling advertising space on billboards along public highways as an example of the kind of absurd scenario that he thought might be government speech under the majority's logic.[154]

As shown in figure 1, the survey results suggest that the public's actual views roughly accord with the Court's speculations about those

---

[150] 555 US at 464. Justice Souter only concurred in the judgment but agreed that the monument is government speech. Id at 485 (Souter, J, concurring in the judgment).

[151] 135 S Ct at 2253.

[152] Id at 2255 (Alito, J, dissenting).

[153] 137 S Ct at 1760. Other portions of Justice Alito's opinion attracted only a plurality of Justices, but the discussion of government speech in Part IIIA was unanimous.

[154] 135 S Ct at 2256 (Alito, J, dissenting).

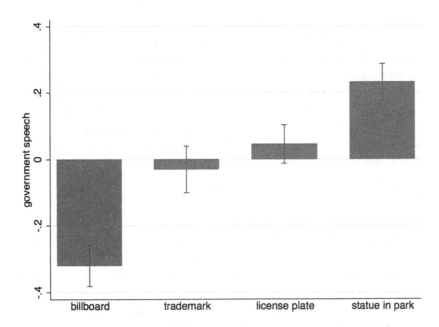

Figure 1. Effect of varying medium of speech on public perception as government speech

views.[155] Respondents were mostly likely to view the statue in the park as government speech—that is, as conveying a message on the government's behalf or indicating endorsement or association—and were least likely to view the private billboard as government speech. In the middle, license plates were more likely to be viewed as government speech than federally registered trademarks, but the difference is small; neither mean is statistically significantly different from zero, although the difference between the means is significant (one-tailed $p = .049$). While the *Sons of Confederate Veterans* and *Tam* majority opinions asserted that the public views the government to be associated with specialty license plates but not registered trademarks,[156] these results suggest that that empirical question is closer than the Court acknowledged.

---

[155] Figure 1 shows the mean of the "government speech" variable, as described above in note 148 (averaging over the three question forms, with the four responses to each question coded as – 1.5, –0.5, 0.5, and 1.5), with error bars representing 95% confidence intervals. The regression results in Table A2, in which the billboard is the omitted medium, show that this effect of variation in medium on public perceptions persists when controlling for other factors.

[156] See text at notes 70–73, 79–80.

As explained in Part I, the Supreme Court has also emphasized the relevance of government *selectivity* in evaluating whether something constitutes government speech. In *Summum*, it was important that cities "have exercised selectivity" and have "select[ed] the monuments that portray what they view as appropriate for the place in question."[157] This became the third factor of the *Sons of Confederate Veterans* test: whether the state "maintains direct control over the messages conveyed."[158]

Figure 2 shows that the public, like the Court, is more likely to view a message as government speech when it is clear that the government is selective in allowing messages of that variety to be conveyed. Evidence that the government is selective in which statues, specialty license plates, or registered trademarks it allows made it more likely that respondents would view the scenario they encountered as conveying a message on the government's behalf or indicating government endorsement of or association with the message. Evidence that these messages were submitted by private parties seemed somewhat less important: it caused a small and statistically insignificant increase in whether respondents viewed the message as government speech, though a larger decrease for the MTurk pilot sample.[159] But information about selectivity, whether combined with information about private involvement or not, caused a large and statistically significant increase in whether the message was viewed as government speech.[160]

While medium and government selectivity are clearly relevant to the government speech question under existing doctrine, the *viewpoint* expressed by the message is not. Indeed, it would be ironic for a Court that generally prohibits viewpoint discrimination to have a doctrine that is viewpoint discriminatory.

But our results show, perhaps unsurprisingly, that the message (as distinct from the medium) does affect perceptions of whether the message is government speech. Figure 3 shows the response across the seven messages we tested, averaging across the other sources of var-

---

[157] 555 US at 471–71.

[158] 135 S Ct at 2249.

[159] Appendix figure A2 shows that for the MTurk sample, information about private involvement decreased the likelihood that the message would be viewed as government speech by just over 0.1, one-tailed $p = .07$.

[160] The difference in the mean government speech outcome variable for respondents who saw information about selectivity versus not was 0.15 ($p < .01$). For the MTurk sample, it was 0.25 ($p < .01$).

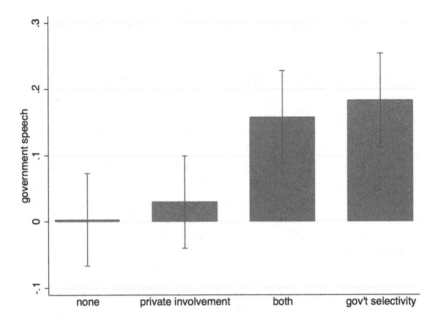

Figure 2. Effect of providing additional information about private involvement or government selectivity for the statue, license plate, and trademark scenarios.

iation. Respondents were most likely to view scenarios as government speech when the message involved Abraham Lincoln, and were least likely to ascribe Mickey Mouse messages to the government. Interestingly, respondents were more likely to credit the government with abortion-related messages—particularly pro-life messages—than religious ones. Among the religious messages, the Ten Commandments was the most likely to be considered government speech, but the difference between it and the atheist messages was significant only at the 10 percent level.

We think there are at least two reasons why the message itself might affect public perceptions. First, it might simply seem more plausible that the government would be endorsing one message over the other. For example, Abraham Lincoln is already the subject of well-known examples of government speech such as the Lincoln Memorial, Mount Rushmore, the five-dollar bill, and—most ubiquitously—the penny. In contrast, it might seem less likely that the government would endorse a corporate message like Disney's Mickey Mouse. And respondents who recall something about separation of church and state from their

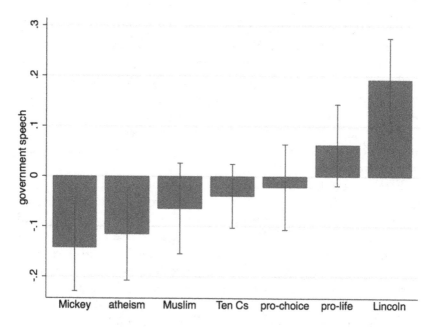

Figure 3. Effect of varying content on public perception as government speech

high school civics classes might be skeptical that religious messages could constitute government speech.

Second, respondents might be more willing to associate messages with the government when they agree with those messages themselves. Lincoln is one of the universally liked US presidents;[161] atheists and Muslims are the religious groups toward which the US public holds the most negative views.[162] To test this second hypothesis, we also asked respondents at the end of the survey for their views on

---

[161] See *Washington, Lincoln Most Popular Presidents: Nixon, Bush Least Popular*, Rasmussen Reports (July 4, 2007), at http://www.rasmussenreports.com/public_content/politics/people2/2007/washington_lincoln_most_popular_presidents_nixon_bush_least_popular (reporting that Lincoln is viewed favorably by 92% of the general public, second only to George Washington at 94%); Robert W. Merry, *America's Greatest President: Abraham Lincoln*, Natl Interest (Feb 16, 2015), http://nationalinterest.org/feature/americas-greatest-president-abraham-lincoln-12957 ("Whenever academics and scholars tickle their fancy by putting forth yet another poll of historians on presidential rankings, there is little doubt about which president will top the list—Abraham Lincoln.").

[162] See *Americans Express Increasingly Warm Feelings Toward Religious Groups*, Pew Research Center (Feb 15, 2017), at http://www.pewforum.org/2017/02/15/americans-express-increasingly-warm-feelings-toward-religious-groups.

the messages at issue in the four scenarios they saw. Appendix table A2 shows that for the nationally representative SSI respondents, this measure of "Agreement" with the message was positively correlated with the assessment of whether it is government speech, and that this correlation is statistically significant at the 1 percent level. This result is driven by respondents who felt the most strongly about the message—those who stated that they had "extremely" or "moderately" negative or positive views—and the results for these respondents are shown in figure 4.[163]

Finally, note that for all of the above results, the responses from our three question forms were combined into one average "government speech" outcome variable. Figure 5 separates the results from the three questions and illustrates that the precise question wording can have a large effect on responses. As explained above, respondents were asked (1) whether they *associate* the message with the government (e.g., "Do you associate the specialty license plate design's message with the state government?"); (2) whether they think the government *endorses* the message (e.g., "Do you think the availability of this specialty license plate indicates that the state government endorses the license plate design's message?"); or (3) whether they think the scenario *conveys a message* on the government's behalf (e.g., "Do you think the availability of this specialty license plate conveys a message on the state government's behalf?").

Figure 5 shows that all else equal, respondents are less likely to say that they associate a given message with the government than that the government endorses the message or that the scenario conveys a message on the government's behalf, an effect that was even stronger for the MTurk sample (as shown in app. fig. A5). We also observed a significant difference between the "conveys a message" and "endorses" responses, but only for the SSI sample. Although the Supreme Court has emphasized the importance of public perception in government speech cases, it has not clarified which (if any) of these phrasings is the relevant question. Our results illustrate, at the very least, that government speech survey designers must pay attention to these differences in wording.

In sum, our survey results support some of the Supreme Court's speculations about public perceptions of government speech, but

---

[163] This effect was not observed for the MTurk respondents.

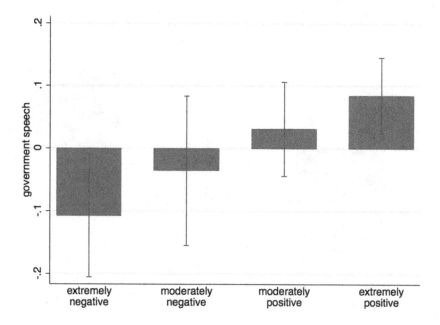

Figure 4. Effect of respondents' views on the message

they also show that the public can be swayed by details that should not matter to the doctrinal outcome, such as the content of the message at issue. As we will discuss further in Part III, we view this as a feature of survey evidence, not a bug: by relying on surveys that isolate the effect of a variable at interest from other distracting details, Justices can prevent government speech doctrine from systematically favoring more sympathetic views.

III. The Promise and Pitfalls of Survey Evidence

What, if anything, can we conclude from these results about the use of survey evidence in government speech cases—or, more generally, about the current state of the Court's government speech jurisprudence? While recognizing that reasonable minds may draw different inferences from the same data, we emerge from this exercise with five key takeaways.

The first, and perhaps most important, is that public perceptions of government speech roughly track the Justices' speculations, except that *Tam* is a closer case from the audience's perspective than it is

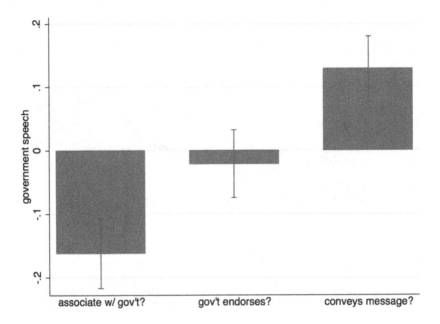

Figure 5. Effect of varying question form

from the Justices'. The ordinal ranking for medium of expression—
with statues in public parks as the most likely to be considered government speech, followed by license plates, followed by federal registration of trademarks—matches the results in *Summum* (9–0), *Sons
of Confederate Veterans* (5–4), and *Tam* (0–8). While we see this as an
encouraging sign that members of the public can answer questions
about government speech in a reasonably coherent way, others might
think this is a strike against our proposal: after all, if the Justices are
already doing a reasonably good job of estimating public perceptions
of government speech based on intuition alone, why do we need
surveys?

Our response is twofold. First, while the Justices' conclusions are
broadly consistent with our survey results, their explanations for those
conclusions are—as emphasized in Part I—rather flimsy. Insofar as
respect for the judiciary depends on well-reasoned opinions, the use
of survey evidence can improve upon judicial *ipse dixit* even if it does
not alter results. Second, while the Justices were unanimous in *Summum* and *Tam*, lower court judges were not: the grant of certiorari

in *Summum* was the outgrowth of a circuit split,[164] and the Federal Circuit's en banc decision below in *Tam* was divided.[165] Likewise, while a slight majority of the Court in *Sons of Confederate Veterans* and a slight majority of our respondents concluded that specialty license plate designs are government speech, six circuits came out the other way,[166] and the issue continues to spark disagreement among lower court judges.[167] The lower courts have also struggled to apply the public perception factor in other cases since *Sons of Confederate Veterans* in contexts ranging from exhibits[168] or rallies[169] on government property to actions by public schools.[170] The question of whether

---

[164] See *Summum v Pleasant Grove City*, 483 F3d 1044 (10th Cir 2007).

[165] See *In re Tam*, 808 F3d 1321, 1375 (Fed Cir 2015) (Dyk, J, concurring in part and dissenting in part) ("[I]t has been questioned whether federal registration imparts the 'imprimatur' of the federal government on a mark, such that registration could be permissibly restricted as government speech. I believe that such action is justified.").

[166] See Papandrea, 110 Nw U L Rev at 1216 n 129 (cited in note 34) (collecting citations).

[167] In *ACLU v Tennyson*, discussed at note 101, the dissenting judge argued that the "specifics" of North Carolina's specialty license plate program "must impact the way the North Carolina public views its specialty plates" and distinguish the resulting perceptions from those in Texas. 815 F3d 183, 188 (4th Cir 2016) (Wynn, J, dissenting). And state supreme courts have disagreed on whether personalized vanity license plates are government speech. Compare *Commissioner of Indiana Bureau of Motor Vehicles v Vawter*, 45 NE3d 1200, 1202, 1205 (Ind 2015) (yes), with *Mitchell v Maryland Motor Vehicle Administration*, 148 A3d 319, 328 (Md 2016) (no).

[168] Compare *Vista-Graphics, Inc. v Virginia Department of Transportation*, 682 Fed Appx 231, 236 (4th Cir 2017) ("[W]e are confident that the public will associate the [informational tourism guides at state rest areas] with the Commonwealth of Virginia, regardless whether the government itself produces the guides."); and *United Veterans Memorial & Patriotic Association of the City of New Rochelle v City of New Rochelle*, 72 F Supp 3d 468, 474–75 (SDNY 2014) ("[I]t is obvious that [a flag flying at a city-owned armory] would be regarded as government speech" because "flags, like monuments, are reasonably interpreted 'as conveying [a] message on the property owner's behalf.'"), aff'd 615 F Appx 693 (2d Cir 2015), with *Freedom from Religion Foundation v Abbott*, 2016 WL 7388401, *5 (WD Tex) ("[A] reasonable person would not find the [Texas State] Capitol exhibits are the voice of the government.").

[169] Compare *A.N.S.W.E.R. Coalition v Jewell*, 153 F Supp 3d 395, 412 (DDC 2016) (holding that government speech doctrine should shield the Trump Presidential Inaugural Committee's exclusive access to areas traditionally used for inaugural protests because "the Inauguration Ceremony and Parade are 'closely identified in the public mind with' the United States government"), aff'd in part on other grounds, *A.N.S.W.E.R. Coalition v Basham*, 845 F3d 1199 (DC Cir 2017), with *Higher Society of Indiana v Tippecanoe County*, 858 F3d 1113, 1118 (7th Cir 2017) ("[R]easonable people would not attribute to the government the views expressed at protests and rallies on government property.").

[170] Compare *Mech v School Board of Palm Beach County*, 806 F3d 1070 (11th Cir 2015) (concluding that observers would believe that a public school had endorsed banners for private businesses hung on its fences on the *Summum* theory that "government property is 'often closely identified in the public mind with the government unit that owns the land'"); and *Cambridge Christian School v Florida High School Athletic Association*, 2017 WL 2458314, *8

members of the public perceive expression to be government speech is not one that can be answered reliably on the basis of judicial intuition. The fact that the Court is 3-for-3, by our accounting, should not be grounds for great confidence in its ability to take the public's pulse.

A second takeaway is that, somewhat to our surprise, the fact that expression is generated by private parties does not seem to reduce the likelihood that members of the public will perceive that expression to be government speech. This finding provides some validation for the Court's decision to jettison the "traditional government agencies and officials" standard from *Keller*. Meanwhile, government selectivity does seem to influence whether members of the public perceive speech to be the government's. This finding suggests a way to harmonize the second and third factors in the three-factor *Sons of Confederate Veterans* test: factor three (whether the government can and does reject messages on the basis of content) is normatively relevant because it feeds into factor two (public perception). Indeed, the three-factor *Sons of Confederate Veterans* test arguably can be boiled down to a single inquiry: whether members of the public have understood and continue to understand the expression in question to be government speech.

A third takeaway is that message matters: members of the public are much more likely to perceive a Lincoln monument, license plate, or mark to be government speech than, say, an otherwise equivalent expression bearing the visage of Mickey Mouse. Somewhat more disconcertingly, members of the public are more likely to perceive speech to be the government's when they approve of that speech personally. The finding that members of the public appear to be influenced by this doctrinally irrelevant factor might be considered a problem for our proposal.

We see the matter differently. Judges, too, are influenced by the message as well as the medium in government speech cases. Consider the license plate controversy. When holding that license plates were government speech meant that the state could exclude a pro-life mes-

---

(MD Fla) (asserting that use of public stadium loudspeaker for a pregame prayer led by a Christian school in the state football playoffs would "be perceived as state endorsement of [the school's] religious message"), with *Gerlich v Leath*, 152 F Supp 3d 1152 (SD Iowa 2016) (dismissing anecdotal evidence that the public associated a student group's marijuana-related T-shirt design with the university "because the record shows almost no reaction to the Article [featuring the T-shirt] from the general public"), aff'd, 861 F3d 697 (8th Cir 2017).

sage, Republican-appointed judges on the Seventh,[171] Eighth,[172] and Ninth Circuits[173] said that license plates were private speech. When holding that license plates were government speech meant that the state could exclude a pro-choice message, Republican-appointed judges on the Sixth Circuit said that license plates were government speech (over the dissent of their Democrat-appointed colleague).[174] When the question came up in the Confederate flag context, every court of appeals judge who was initially appointed to the federal bench by a Democratic president and who weighed in on the question voted in favor of the view that license plates are government speech (in which case the Confederate flag plate could be excluded); all but one of the ten court of appeals judges initially appointed to the bench by a Republican president who weighed in on the question voted in favor of the view that license plates are private speech.[175] The Supreme Court is not immune from ideologically inflected voting patterns on questions of government speech either. With the exception of Justice Thomas, who voted with the majority in *Sons of Confederate Veterans*, the rest of the Court followed the same partisan pattern as the circuits: Democratic-appointed Justices voted for the view that license plates are government speech (and thus that Texas can exclude the Confederate plate), while Republican-appointed Justices took the opposite position.

The fact that ideology influences judicial decision making is nothing new. Yet for those who think that the ideological content of the message should not influence the result in government speech cases, survey evidence provides a promising path. For example, surveys can ask different subsets of respondents about pro-life and pro-choice plates—or about plates featuring the Confederate flags and plates featuring the face of Lincoln—in order to disentangle the effect of medium from the effect of message. And while we are not so naïve as

---

[171] See *Choose Life Illinois, Inc. v White*, 547 F3d 853 (7th Cir 2008). Judge Terrence Evans, a Clinton appointee, joined his co-panelists in *Choose Life Illinois*, marking a departure from the partisan voting pattern observed elsewhere.

[172] See *Roach v Stouffer*, 560 F3d 860 (8th Cir 2009).

[173] See *Arizona Life Coalition Inc. v Stanton*, 515 F3d 956 (9th Cir 2008).

[174] See *ACLU of Tennessee v Bredesen*, 441 F3d 370, 379–80 (6th Cir 2006).

[175] See *Sons of Confederate Veterans, Inc. v Commissioner of the Virginia DMV*, 305 F3d 241 (4th Cir 2002) (denying rehearing *en banc*); *Texas Division, Sons of Confederate Veterans, Inc. v Vandergriff*, 759 F3d 388 (5th Cir 2014), rev'd sub nom, *Sons of Confederate Veterans*, 135 S Ct 2239.

to think that this strategy will mean that government speech cases can be resolved in an ideological vacuum, we think that well-constructed surveys can do some work in counteracting the effect of ideology on government speech decisions.

A fourth takeaway is that the question matters. The Supreme Court toggles among three different versions of the government speech inquiry: whether the public *associates* expression with the government;[176] whether the public understands the government to be *endorsing* expression;[177] and whether expression *conveys* a message on the government's behalf.[178] We find that respondents are more likely to say that the government "conveys" a message than that it "endorses" a message or that they "associate" a message with the government. This might strike some readers as surprising: "endorse" and "convey" are arguably stronger verbs than "associate." On the other hand, we can imagine circumstances in which a speaker might convey a message and yet the listener would not associate the speaker with that message. (Mundanely: If Daniel asks Lisa what time it is, Lisa might "convey" the answer "noon" but Daniel would not therefore "associate" Lisa with the lunch hour.)

Which of these verbs best captures the government speech inquiry depends in part on what interests the government speech doctrine is intended to protect. Insofar as the doctrine serves to shield the government from the risk that it will be associated with messages that it disavows, then asking whether respondents "associate" a message with the government would seem appropriate. Insofar as the doctrine serves to ensure that the government cannot launder its message through the mouths of private speakers, then asking whether the government "conveys" a message via the expression in question might be the better way to frame the inquiry. All of this serves to underscore the point that precision about the normative basis for government speech doctrine will inform the design of surveys.

Fifth and finally, we think our results should allay concerns that reliance on public perception in government speech cases will lead

---

[176] See *Summum*, 555 US at 471 ("associated"); *Sons of Confederate Veterans*, 135 S Ct at 2251 ("associates"); *Tam*, 137 S Ct at 1760 ("associates").

[177] See *Sons of Confederate Veterans*, 135 S Ct at 2249 ("endorsed"); *Tam*, 137 S Ct at 1758 ("endorsing").

[178] See *Summum*, 555 US at 471–72 ("convey"); *Sons of Confederate Veterans*, 135 S Ct at 2246 ("convey"); *Tam*, 137 S Ct at 1760 ("convey").

to a shrinking of First Amendment protections.[179] Members of the public are not systematically more likely than judges to perceive speech as emanating from the government. Moreover, the Court's decisions do not appear to have a profound effect on public perception. Just over two years after the Court held in *Sons of Confederate Veterans* that license plate designs are government speech, our respondents were close to evenly divided on the question. And only three months after the Court held in *Tam* that trademark registration is not government speech, a substantial minority of respondents maintained the opposite view. The fear of a self-reinforcing cycle in which Court decisions drive the public to perceive more and more expression as government speech is not borne out here. While subsequent surveys will be useful in determining whether public perception is consistent across time, our results suggest that members of the public understand the category of government speech to be bounded.

Our results do not, of course, resolve all questions about public perception of government speech, nor do they allay all concerns about the use of survey evidence in government speech cases. We hope this is a first step toward a richer understanding of how the public perceives expression in the gray area between government and private speech, but ours is most certainly not the final word. Among other avenues of inquiry, future research might examine the role of government selectivity in more detail. Does it matter if over 99 percent of messages are approved by the relevant government entity (as for trademark registrations) versus 50 percent or less than 1 percent? Does it matter if the respondents are given a sense of the range of approved messages—such as knowing that the government has approved both pro-life and pro-choice messages—rather than only being asked to evaluate a single message? Future research also might examine whether public perceptions are consistent across jurisdictions and regions. Further data on this question could help parties and courts assess whether the appropriate population for surveys used in litigation is local, regional, or national.

---

[179] See Papandrea, 110 Nw U L Rev at 1234 (cited at note 34) ("Under well-established First Amendment principles, the government is required to support the speech of private speakers. A focus on reasonable observers who erroneously believe this tolerance operates as endorsement threaten the future of free speech rights in this country.").

IV. Conclusion

It has been nearly a decade since a majority of the Court embraced public perception as a factor distinguishing government speech from private expression, and the Justices have yet to offer a justification for that doctrinal turn or a reliable method for determining what public perceptions actually are. This essay has sought to plug both holes. We have argued that a narrower conception of government speech—along the lines of the "traditional government agencies and officials" standard suggested in *Keller*—would fail to capture certain acts of collective self-definition that are important to the development of a democratic community. At the same time, a public perception test serves to police against message laundering while also ensuring that elected officials remain politically accountable for government speech. And although the Court's application of the public perception factor has so far been ad hoc, we have suggested that reliance on survey evidence can channel and constrain the government speech inquiry so that case outcomes are determined by more than judicial guesswork.

As a proof of concept, we have conducted what is to our knowledge the first survey of a nationally representative sample on the subject of government speech. Our results provide a factual basis for certain elements of the Court's government speech jurisprudence. Members of the public are indeed more likely to attribute statues in a public park to the government than to do the same with respect to trademark registration. Moreover, the fact that private parties generated a message does not significantly affect perceptions of government speech, though the fact that the government exercises selectivity with respect to messages does. We also find that members of the public—perhaps no differently than judges—are influenced by the content of messages as well as the medium, and that they are more likely to attribute to the government messages with which they agree.

Our results do not support calls for a revolution in government speech doctrine. More modestly, we suggest that survey evidence can supplant judicial *ipse dixit* in the application of the public perception factor, and that surveys can serve as checks on the government speech doctrine's expansion. To be sure, distinguishing government speech from private expression will remain a difficult line-drawing exercise even with the help of survey data. But at the very least, the use of survey evidence can transform that line-drawing exercise from one that depends on judicial imagination into an empirically grounded inquiry.

APPENDIX

Table A1

Demographic Characteristics

	# in MTurk Sample (N = 503)	% of MTurk Sample	# in SSI Sample (N = 1,223)	% of SSI Sample	% of US Population[a]
Gender:					
Male	278	55	580	47	49
Female	225	45	643	53	51
Age:					
18–24	41	8	196	16	13
25–34	203	40	226	18	18
35–44	107	21	219	18	17
45–54	85	17	226	18	18
55–64	49	10	177	14	16
65+	18	4	179	15	18
Race/ethnicity:					
Non-Hispanic White	394	78	786	64	62
Latino or Hispanic	23	5	173	14	17
Black or African-American	32	6	150	12	12
Asian or Pacific Islander	37	7	55	4	5
Native American	0	0	8	<1	<1
2 or more races or other	17	3	51	4	2
Educational attainment:					
Less than high school	2	<1	20	2	12
High school graduate	52	10	277	23	29
Some college; no degree	122	24	325	27	19
Associate's degree	59	12	129	11	10
Bachelor's degree	191	38	286	23	19
Master's degree	55	11	137	11	8
Doctorate or professional	22	4	49	4	3

[a] See *2011–2015 American Community Survey 5-Year Estimates*, US Census Bureau (2015), at https://factfinder.census.gov/faces/tableservices/jsf/pages/productview.xhtml?pid=ACS_15_5YR_DP05&src=pt (gender, age, and race/ethnicity); *Educational Attainment in the United States: 2016*, US Census Bureau (2016), at https://www.census.gov/data/tables/2016/demo/education-attainment/cps-detailed-tables.html (education).

Table A2

Regression Results for SSI Sample

	1	2	3	4	5
Medium:					
Statue	.551***	.550***	.549***	.550***	.549***
	(.0422)	(.0418)	(.0418)	(.0403)	(.0403)
License plate	.365***	.364***	.364***	.364***	.364***
	(.0429)	(.0426)	(.0426)	(.0411)	(.0411)
Trademark	.290***	.272***	.271***	.267***	.266***
	(.0473)	(.0470)	(.0469)	(.0448)	(.0447)
Content:					
Lincoln		.337***	.326***	.349***	.340***
		(.0599)	(.0598)	(.0577)	(.0576)
Pro-life		.191***	.257***	.195***	.251***
		(.0590)	(.0609)	(.0565)	(.0585)
Pro-choice		.139**	.177***	.148**	.181***
		(.0600)	(.0607)	(.0575)	(.0583)
Ten Cs		.103*	.0970*	.108**	.103**
		(.0535)	(.0534)	(.0510)	(.0509)
Muslim		.0725	.125**	.0768	.122**
		(.0617)	(.0627)	(.0591)	(.0603)
Atheism		.0254	.0969	.0269	.0883
		(.0632)	(.0656)	(.0605)	(.0629)
Question form:					
Convey message		.291***	.286***	.276***	.272***
		(.0376)	(.0375)	(.0362)	(.0361)
Endorse		.138***	.135***	.122***	.119***
		(.0382)	(.0381)	(.0368)	(.0367)

	(1)	(2)	(3)	(4)	(5)
Other:					
Agreement			.0343***		.0294***
			(.00899)		(.00862)
Age				-.0134***	-.0134***
				(.000953)	(.000950)
Female				-.0839***	-.0825***
				(.0309)	(.0309)
Nonwhite				.0887***	.0896***
				(.0331)	(.0330)
Liberal				.0692***	.0673***
				(.00957)	(.00955)
Education				.00981	.00935
				(.0102)	(.0102)
Constant	-.320***	-.584***	-.633***	-.0140	-.0563
	(.0312)	(.0550)	(.0558)	(.0786)	(.0792)
N	4,585	4,585	4,585	4,585	4,585
R^2	.037	.058	.062	.127	.130

Note.—The billboard is the omitted medium, Mickey Mouse is the omitted message, and the association question is the omitted question form. $N = 4{,}585$ because all 1,223 respondents saw four scenarios, and then the 307 respondents who saw a "scandalous" trademark were dropped. Robust standard errors in parentheses.

* $p < .10$
** $p < .05$
*** $p < .01$

Table A3

Regression Results for Mechanical Turk Sample

	1	2	3	4	5
Medium:					
Statue	1.107***	1.102***	1.102***	1.102***	1.102***
	(.0565)	(.0555)	(.0556)	(.0551)	(.0551)
License plate	.738***	.735***	.733***	.735***	.733***
	(.0598)	(.0585)	(.0586)	(.0582)	(.0583)
Trademark	.400***	.402***	.400***	.406***	.404***
	(.0640)	(.0641)	(.0641)	(.0632)	(.0632)
Content:					
Lincoln		.520***	.532***	.539***	.550***
		(.0817)	(.0820)	(.0809)	(.0813)
Pro-life		.410***	.359***	.419***	.373***
		(.0825)	(.0880)	(.0823)	(.0879)
Pro-choice		.307***	.304***	.316***	.313***
		(.0817)	(.0818)	(.0817)	(.0818)
Ten Cs		.352***	.340***	.362***	.351***
		(.0726)	(.0732)	(.0725)	(.0731)
Muslim		.299***	.264***	.314***	.283***
		(.0856)	(.0878)	(.0864)	(.0885)
Atheism		.0699	.0498	.0776	.0597
		(.0827)	(.0829)	(.0829)	(.0830)
Question form:					
Convey message		.226***	.225***	.204***	.203***
		(.0546)	(.0545)	(.0547)	(.0546)
Endorse		.232***	.231***	.217***	.216***
		(.0527)	(.0528)	(.0527)	(.0527)

	(1)	(2)	(3)	(4)
Other:				
Agreement		−.0219*		−.0197
		(.0129)		(.0128)
Age			−.00562***	−.00545***
			(.00186)	(.00186)
Female			.0517	.0529
			(.0447)	(.0447)
Nonwhite			.563	.0565
			(.0549)	(.0551)
Liberal			.0294**	.0295**
			(.0132)	(.0131)
Education			−.0449***	−.0448***
			(.0167)	(.0167)
Constant	−.906***	−1.346***	−1.033***	−1.014***
	(.0377)	(.0673)	(.112)	(.112)
N	1,889	1,889	1,889	1,889
R^2	.161	.197	.210	.211

NOTE.—The billboard is the omitted medium, Mickey Mouse is the omitted message, and the association question is the omitted question form. $N = 1,889$ because all 503 respondents saw four scenarios, and then the 123 respondents who saw a "scandalous" trademark were dropped. Robust standard errors in parentheses.

*** $p < .01$
** $p < .05$
* $p < .10$

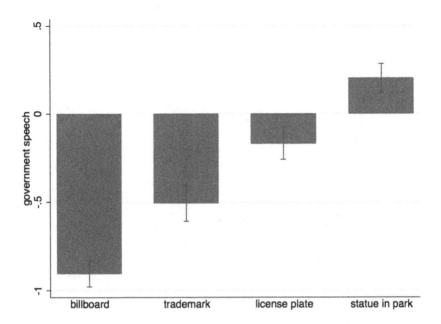

Figure A1. Medium

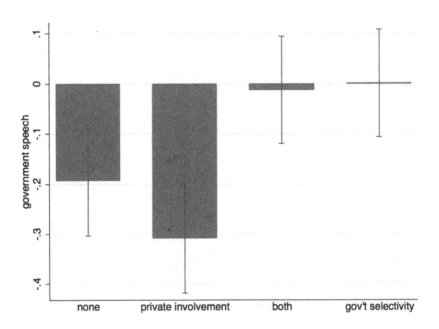

Figure A2. Additional information

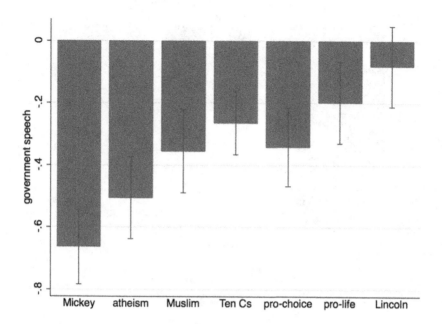

Figure A3. Content

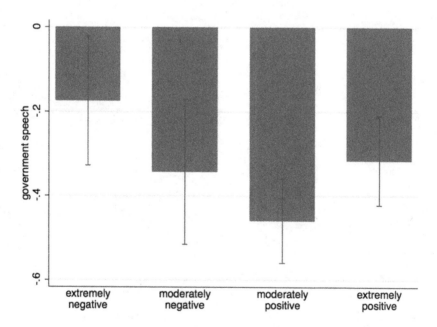

Figure A4. View on the content

91

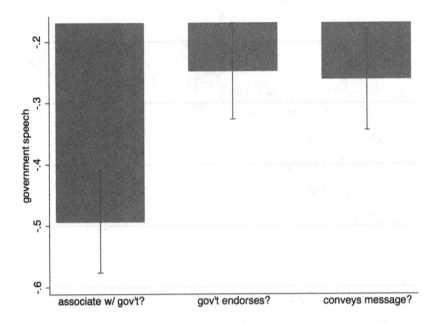

Figure A5. Question form

CASS R. SUNSTEIN

IRREPARABILITY AS IRREVERSIBILITY

I. GONE FOREVER

Some things, people say, are "gone forever." But what exactly does that mean? At a minimum, it suggests that certain losses are final in the sense that they are *irreversible*. Such losses are irreparable in the sense that nothing can be done to restore the status quo ante—or if something can be done, it is not enough (or perhaps outsiders can never know if it is). The experience of grief is usually produced by a sense not only that the loss is large, but also that it cannot be reversed.

Consider some examples. If children are killed, they cannot be brought back to life. If a soldier loses the use of his leg, he cannot grow it back. If a species is lost, it is probably lost forever; the same might well be true of pristine areas. Some people fear that genetically modified organisms might lead to irreversible ecological harm; transgenic crops can impose irreversible losses by increasing pest resistance. In recent decades, the problem of climate change has raised serious concerns about irreversibility. Some greenhouse gases stay in the atmosphere for centuries, and for that reason climate change threatens to be irreversible, at least for all practical purposes. And, of course, genocide may be the most extreme case of irreversible harm.

Cass R. Sunstein is Robert Walmsley University Professor, Harvard University.

AUTHOR'S NOTE: This essay builds on and elaborates a preliminary treatment in Cass R. Sunstein, *Laws of Fear* (Cambridge, 2005), and on some ideas developed elsewhere, with a new focus on irreparable harm and preliminary injunctions. I am grateful to Madeleine Joseph for valuable comments and research assistance.

The idea of irreversibility overlaps with the legal concept of "irreparable harm," a prerequisite for granting preliminary injunctions.[1] In fact some irreparable harms seem to qualify as such precisely because they are irreversible. A standard claim is that some goods have no substitute; consider the loss of companionship with a loved one. A restriction on free speech is usually seen as producing irreparable harm, and violations of constitutional rights are often regarded similarly.[2] It is also standard to emphasize that judges cannot reliably measure or quantify certain harms, such as the loss stemming from unauthorized use of intellectual property; a copyright violation might be found to involve an "irreparable" loss simply because valuation is so uncertain.[3] Judges may be in a poor position to turn certain harms into monetary equivalents (either before or after the fact of loss). On this account, an injury is "irreparable" not because it involves a unique loss, but because of some epistemic deficit faced by the legal system.

But the standard claims raise many puzzles. A loss of companionship with a loved one is, in an intelligible sense, "irreparable," but courts do award compensation for loss of companionship. In that light, the claim cannot be that companionship has infinite value or cannot be turned into some monetary equivalent. A restriction on free speech may be exceedingly difficult to value, but in what sense is it "irreparable"? A loss of the ability to protest for (say) a few weeks might not be worth more than (say) $2 billion. Regulators have established tools for dealing with the problem of uncertainty, and perhaps judges could use such tools as well.[4]

With puzzles of this kind in mind, federal courts, including the Supreme Court, have long debated the meaning of the irreparable harm requirement,[5] often in the context of violations of the National

---

[1] See Douglas Laycock, *The Death of the Irreparable Injury Rule* (Oxford, 1991); Owen Fiss, *The Civil Rights Injunction* (Indiana, 1978); Douglas Lichtman, *Uncertainty and the Standard for Preliminary Relief*, 70 U Chi L Rev 1977 (2003).

[2] See *Elrod v Burns*, 427 US 347, 373 (1976) ("[L]oss of First Amendment freedoms, for even minimal periods of time, unquestionably constitutes irreparable injury.").

[3] See, e.g., *Apple Computer, Inc. v Formula Int'l, Inc.*, 725 F2d 521, 525–26 (9th Cir 1984) (stating that irreparable injury is presumed when copyright is infringed); *Atari, Inc. v North Am. Philips Consumer Electronics Corp.*, 672 F2d 607, 620 (7th Cir 1982) (same); *Wainwright Sec., Inc. v Wall St. Transcript Corp.*, 558 F2d 91, 94 (2d Cir 1977) (same).

[4] See Cass R. Sunstein, *The Limits of Quantification*, 102 Cal L Rev 1369 (2014).

[5] See, for example, *Winter v Natural Resources Defense Council*, 555 US 7 (2008).

Environmental Policy Act (NEPA).[6] As the Court once put it, "[e]nvironmental injury, by its nature, can seldom be adequately remedied by money damages."[7] As it turns out, the question whether and when NEPA violations trigger preliminary injunctions raises deep questions at the intersection of law, economics, ethics, and political philosophy. The potential answers bear on the meaning of irreparable harm more generally.

My goal here is to explore the idea of irreversibility, with particular reference to preliminary injunctions, environmental problems, and some enduring controversies within the Supreme Court. In one sense, any losses are irreversible, simply because time is linear. If Jones plays tennis this afternoon rather than working, the relevant time is lost forever. If Smith fails to say the right words to a loved one, at exactly the right time, the opportunity might be gone forever. If one nation fails to take action to deter the aggressive steps of another, in a particular year, the course of world events might be irretrievably altered. If a project to drill oil in Alaska is delayed for five years, there is an irreversible loss as well: The oil that might have been made available will not be made available when it otherwise would have been. An injunction can prevent irreversible harm; it can also create irreversible harm.

When environmentalists emphasize the importance of irreversibility, I suggest that they have two separate ideas in mind. The first is connected with the idea of option value, and in particular with the view that when information is missing, it is worthwhile to spend resources to maintain future flexibility as knowledge increases. A central goal is to freeze the status quo while new information is obtained—a point that bears on many disputes involving NEPA, where acquisition of such information is the basic point.

The second involves losses of goods that are incommensurable in the sense that they are qualitatively distinctive. It might be possible to translate the value of a pristine area into some monetary equivalent, but (the argument goes) something important is lost in translation. As we shall see, legal (as opposed to philosophical) use of ideas about

---

[6] *Monsanto Co. v Geertson Seed Farms*, 561 US 139 (2010). For general discussion, see Leslye A. Herrmann, Comment, *Injunctions for NEPA Violations: Balancing the Equities*, 59 U Chi L Rev 1263 (1992).

[7] *Amoco Production Co. v Village of Gambell*, 480 US 531, 545 (1987).

incommensurability is best combined with claims about uncertainty about valuation—the epistemic problem faced by judges.

Here, as elsewhere, general propositions do not decide concrete cases, and neither of these ideas, standing by itself, is sufficient to justify a preliminary injunction in environmental cases. But as we shall see, it is much easier to understand the concept of irreparable harm by reference to them.[8] As we shall also see, the exploration of the underlying puzzles bears on a wide range of questions about appropriate precautions, not only in the environmental arena, but in other legal domains, such as constitutional law, and in daily life as well.

II. The Irreversible Harm Precautionary Principle

Concerned about the problem of irreversibility, sensible legal systems might want to adopt a distinctive principle for handling certain kinds of risk: the Irreversible Harm Precautionary Principle. Indeed, some such principle seems to underlie prominent accounts of the Precautionary Principle, which point explicitly to the problem of irreversibility. For example, the United Nations Framework Convention on Climate Change proclaims: "Where there are threats of serious or irreversible damage, lack of full scientific certainty should not be used as a reason for postponing [regulatory] measures, taking into account that policies and measures to deal with climate change should be cost-effective so as to ensure global benefits at the lowest possible cost."[9] Similarly, the Rio Declaration states, "Where there are threats of serious or irreversible damage, lack of full scientific certainty shall not be used as a reason for postponing cost-effective measures to prevent environmental degradation."[10] The idea of irreversibility has become a prominent part of international discussion of the Precautionary Principle and indeed of environmental ethics in general.

---

[8] I am acutely aware that the topic of irreparable harm can be approached from many different angles, and what I am offering here is just one view of the cathedral. Valuable discussions from diverse perspectives can be found in many places, including Laycock, *Death of the Irreparable Injury Rule* (cited in note 1); Fiss, *Civil Rights Injunction* (cited in note 1); John Leubsdorf, *The Standard for Preliminary Injunctions*, 91 Harv L Rev 525 (1978); Thomas R. Lee, *Preliminary Injunctions and the Status Quo*, 58 Wash & Lee L Rev 109 (2001).

[9] See Indur Goklany, *The Precautionary Principle: A Critical Appraisal of Environmental Risk Assessment* 6 (Cato Institute, 2001).

[10] Quoted in Bjorn Lomborg, *The Skeptical Environmentalist* 347 (Cambridge, 2001).

A. FREEZING THE STATUS QUO

The general attitude here is "stop, and then learn," as opposed to the tempting alternative of "keep doing what you have been doing, and then learn." The goal is to freeze the status quo. It is true that for climate change, some people (though increasingly few) continue to believe that research should be our first line of defense. In their view, nations should refuse to commit substantial resources to reducing greenhouse gas emissions until evidence of serious harm is even clearer than it now us. Many people believe that our initial steps should be relatively cautious, increasing in aggressiveness as knowledge accumulates (and the costs of emissions reductions fall).

In this domain, however, there is a large problem with any approach of "keep doing what you have been doing, and then learn." We might want to maintain the status quo while we learn. If precautionary steps are not taken immediately, the results may be irreversible, or at best difficult and expensive to reverse. The claim that greenhouse gas emissions should be cut dramatically, and now, can be seen as a large-scale reflection of the same principles that underlie the issuance of preliminary injunctions.

In American environmental law, related ideas are at work. San Francisco has adopted its own precautionary principle, with an emphasis on irreversibility: "Where threats of serious or irreversible damage to people or nature exist, lack of full scientific certainty about cause and effect shall not be viewed as sufficient reason for the City to postpone cost effective measures to prevent the degradation of the environment or protect the health of its citizens."[11] At the federal level, NEPA requires agencies to discuss "any irreversible and irretrievable commitments of resources which would be involved in the proposed action should it be implemented."[12] Though the law is in flux, some courts have been careful to insist that environmental impact statements should be prepared at a time that permits consideration of environmental effects before irretrievable commitments have been made.[13] A number of other federal statutes, especially in

---

[11] See Precautionary Principle Ordinance, SF Enviro Code § 101 (2018).

[12] 42 USC § 102(c)(5) (2012).

[13] See *Metcalf v Daley*, 214 F3d 1135 (9th Cir 2000); *Scientists' Institute for Public Information v Atomic Energy Commission*, 481 F2d 1079 (DC Cir 1973); *Sierra Club v Marsh*, 976 F2d 763 (1st Cir 1985).

the environmental context, specifically refer to irreversible losses and make their prevention a high priority.[14] Within the federal courts, including the Supreme Court, a special precautionary principle has sometimes seemed to underlie the analysis of preliminary injunctions in cases involving a risk of irreparable environmental harm.[15]

Nonetheless, the Court has squarely rejected a presumption in favor of preliminary injunctions in environmental cases, including those that involve NEPA.[16] That conclusion might be taken to settle long-standing uncertainty about how to think of irreparable harm in the context of NEPA cases.[17] Consider in this regard the fact that NEPA is a purely procedural statute, one that imposes information-gathering duties on agencies *without requiring them to take that information into account*.[18] If courts cannot forbid agencies to act as they choose after producing an adequate environmental impact statement, injunctions might seem an odd remedy in the NEPA setting. But in the most elaborate discussion of the question, one that the Supreme Court has not squarely confronted, then-Circuit Judge Breyer suggested that injunctions are often appropriate in NEPA cases.[19]

B. THE PSYCHOLOGY OF DECISIONMAKERS

Judge Breyer did not contend that a presumption in favor of injunctive relief would be appropriate for environmental cases in general. Instead he argued that NEPA is meant to prevent a particular kind of injury, one that should play a central role in the decision whether to grant an injunction. The purpose of NEPA is to ensure that officials take environmental considerations into account *before*

---

[14] See, for example, 33 USC § 2712(j) (making special exception to planning requirement for use of federal resources "in a situation requiring action to avoid irreversible loss of natural resources"); 42 USC § 9611(i) (same exception for Superfund cleanups); 22 USC § 2151p-1 (c)(2)(A) (requiring President to assist developing countries in a way that responds to "the irreversible losses associated with forest destruction").

[15] See *Amoco Production Co. v Village of Gambell*, 480 US 531 (1987); *Sierra Club v U.S. Dept of Agriculture*, 841 F Supp 349, 358–59 (DDC 2012).

[16] *Winter*, 555 US at 21.

[17] See *New York v Nuclear Regulatory Commission*, 550 F2d 745 (2d Cir 1977); *Conservation Society v Secretary of Transportation*, 508 F2d 927, 933 (2d Cir 1974); *United States v 27.09 Acres of Land*, 737 F Supp 277, 283–84 (SDNY 1990); *Stand Together Against Neighborhood Decay v Board of Estimate*, 690 F Supp 1191 (EDNY 1988); Richard R. W. Brooks and Warren F. Schwartz, *Legal Uncertainty, Economic Efficiency, and the Preliminary Injunction Doctrine*, 58 Stan L Rev 381 (2005).

[18] See *Robertson v Methow Valley Citizens Council*, 490 US 332 (1989).

[19] *Sierra Club v Marsh*, 872 F2d 497 (1st Cir 1989).

they embark on a course of action. "Thus, when a decision to which NEPA obligations attach is made without the informed environmental consideration that NEPA requires, the harm that NEPA intends to prevent has been suffered."[20]

That harm is the increased risk to the environment that arises "when governmental decisionmakers make up their minds without having before them an analysis (with prior public comment) of the likely effects of their decision upon the environment."[21] This is a distinctive NEPA risk, foreign to the common law or indeed to the legal system before the enactment of that statute. The risk involves a failure of ex ante consideration of environmental effects—and a failure to freeze the status quo *before* those effects are considered.

Irreversibility is central here, for it is simply true that administrators are less likely to destroy a nearly completed project than one that has only started. The relevant harm "may well have to do with the psychology of decisionmakers, and perhaps a more deeply rooted psychological instinct not to tear down projects once they are built."[22] Judge Breyer's point, then, is that "the district court should take account of the potentially irreparable nature of this decisionmaking risk to the environment when considering a request for preliminary injunction."[23] This is a point about irreversibility—about how the clock cannot be unwound to restore the status quo ante. As it turns out, that point is connected with a standard view about irreversibility in economics.

III. Uses, Options, and Irreversibility

A. EXISTENCE VALUE, OPTION VALUE

To fix ideas, consider the monetary valuation of an environmental good, such as a pristine area. Some people will be willing to pay to use the area; they may visit it on a regular basis, and they might be very upset at its loss. But others will be willing to pay to preserve it, even if they will not use it. In fact many citizens would be happy to give some money to save a pristine area, perhaps especially if animals can be found there. Hence "existence value" is sometimes included in the

---

[20] Id at 500.

[21] Id.

[22] Id at 504.

[23] Id at 501.

valuation of environmental goods,[24] and indeed federal courts have insisted that agencies pay attention to that value in assessing damages to natural resources.[25] Taken as a group, citizens of many nations would be willing to pay a great deal to preserve an endangered species or to maintain the existence of a remote island and its ecosystem.

But some people are also willing to pay for the *option* to use or to benefit from an environmental amenity in the future, even if they are unsure whether they will exercise that option at any time. Suppose that a pristine area might be developed in a way that ensures its permanent loss. Many people would be willing to pay a significant amount to preserve their option to visit that area. Under federal law, option value must also be considered in the assessment of natural resource damages.[26] Some regulations pay attention to option value in the environmental context.[27] For numerous goods, people are willing to pay and to do a great deal in order to freeze the status quo and ensure that their options are preserved.

Here, then, is a simple sense in which irreversible harm causes a loss that should be considered and that must be included in measures of value. Some skeptics contend that it "is hard to imagine a price for an irreversible loss,"[28] but people certainly do identify prices for such losses, or at least for the risk of such losses. Whether or not we turn that value into some sort of monetary equivalent, it ought to matter.

The idea of option value, as used in the monetary-valuation literature, is closely related to the use of the notion of "options" in the domain that I shall be emphasizing here. The simple claim is that when regulators are dealing with an irreversible loss, and when they are uncertain about the timing, magnitude, and likelihood of that loss, they should be willing to pay a sum—the option value—in order to maintain flexibility for the future. To do that, they freeze the status quo. The option might not be exercised if it turns out that the loss is

---

[24] See David A. Dana, *Existence Value and Federal Preservation Regulation*, 28 Harv Envir L Rev 343, 345 (2004); Charles J. Cicchetti and Louis J. Wilde, *Uniqueness, Irreversibility, and the Theory of Nonuse Values*, 74 Amer J Agric Econ 1121, 1121–22 (1992).

[25] See *Ohio v US Dept of the Interior*, 880 F2d 432, 464 (DC Cir 1989).

[26] Id.

[27] See, e.g., 60 Fed Reg 29914 (1995); 60 Fed Reg 28210, 29914, 29928 (1995); 59 Fed Reg 1062, 1078 (1994). But see 69 Fed Reg 68444 (2004) (doubting whether option value should be recognized as separate from others values).

[28] See Frank Ackerman and Lisa Heinzerling, *Priceless: On Knowing the Price of Everything and the Value of Nothing* 185 (New Press, 2004).

not a serious one. But if the option is purchased, regulators will be in a position to forestall that loss if it turns out to be large.

The concern about irreversibility, and hence the Irreversible Harm Precautionary Principle, is based on the idea that regulators should be willing to buy an option to maintain their own flexibility. This point can easily be linked with Justice Breyer's point about freezing the status quo and psychology in the context of environmental decisions: There is a large difference between making a decision ab initio and making a decision once building has started. (I am using terms that suggest monetary payments, but the basic point holds even if we are skeptical about the use of monetary equivalents; "purchases" can take the form of precautionary steps that do not directly involve money.)

Option theory has countless applications outside of the domain of investments. People would be willing to do, and possibly even to spend, a great deal to preserve their option to have another child—even if they are not at all sure that they really want to have another child. Or consider narrow judicial rulings, of the sort celebrated by judicial minimalists, who want courts to make decisions that are focused on particular details and that leave many questions undecided. Narrow rulings can be understood as a way of "buying" an option, or at least of "paying" a certain amount by imposing decisionmaking burdens on others, in return for future flexibility.

Judges who leave things undecided, and who focus their rulings on the facts of particular cases, are in a sense forcing themselves, and society as a whole, to purchase an option to pay for flexibility in the resolution of subsequent problems. Whether that option is worthwhile depends on its price and the benefits that it provides. Or consider the case of marriage and suppose that because of law or social norms, it is difficult to divorce, so that a decision to marry cannot readily be reversed. If so, prospective spouses might be willing to do a great deal to maintain their flexibility before marrying—far more than they would be willing to do if divorce were much easier.

It should be readily apparent how an understanding of option value can explain the emphasis, in NEPA and other environmental statutes, on irreversible losses. The central point of NEPA is to ensure that government officials give serious consideration to environmental factors before they take action that might threaten the environment. If the government is building a road through a pristine area, or drilling in Alaska, or licensing a nuclear power plant, it must produce an environmental impact statement discussing the environmental effects. The production of these statements can be burdensome and costly. But when potentially irreversible losses are involved, and when officials cannot specify the magnitude or likelihood of such losses, the public, and those involved in making the ultimate decision, ought to know about them.

What needs to be added is that if the (initial) decision is made before the environmental impact statement is issued, the status quo cannot be preserved. The irreversible loss, made relevant by NEPA, is that status quo, so that NEPA can have its desired effect. It is not necessarily a loss to the environment as such (though of course that loss matters); it is a loss of the relevant decisionmaking process. That loss might not be decisive, all things considered. But it counts.

B. OPTIONS, IMPERFECT KNOWLEDGE, AND PRECAUTIONS

It should now be clear how the idea of option value might help support the Irreversible Harm Precautionary Principle. In environmental economics, the seminal analysis comes from Kenneth Arrow and Anthony Fisher, who demonstrate that the ideas of uncertainty and irreversibility have considerable importance to the theory of environmental protection.[29] Arrow and Fisher imagine that the question is whether to preserve a virgin redwood forest for wilderness recreation or instead to open it to clear-cut logging. Assume that if the development option is chosen, the destruction of the forest is effectively irreversible. Arrow and Fisher argue that it matters whether the authorities cannot yet assess the costs or benefits of a proposed development. If development produces "some irreversible transformation of the environment, hence a loss in perpetuity of the benefits from preservation," then it is worth paying something to wait to acquire the missing information. Their suggestion is that "the expected benefits of an irreversible decision should be adjusted to reflect the loss of options it entails."[30] Even if it is costly to wait, that cost might be worth incurring.

Fisher has generalized this argument to suggest that "[w]here a decision problem is characterized by (1) uncertainty about future costs

---

[29] See Kenneth Arrow and Anthony Fischer, *Environmental Preservation, Uncertainty and Irreversibility*, 88 Q J Econ, 312, 313–14 (1974).

[30] Id at 319.

and benefits of the alternatives, (2) prospects for resolving or reducing the uncertainty with the passage of time, and (3) irreversibility of one or more of the alternatives, an extra value, an option value, properly attaches to the reversible alternative(s)."[31] The intuition here is both straightforward and appealing: more steps should be taken to prevent harms that are effectively final than to prevent those that can be easily reversed, and if it is possible to acquire information over time, then it may make sense to wait. When an irreversible harm is on one side and a reversible one on the other, and when decisionmakers are uncertain about future costs and benefits of precautions, an understanding of option value suggests that it is worthwhile to spend a certain amount to preserve future flexibility, by paying a premium to avoid the irreversible harm. A preliminary injunction can be seen as a payment of that premium.

The general point here is that, as in the stock market, those involved in environmental protection are trying to project a stream of good and bad effects over time; the ability to project the stream of effects will improve over time and hence much can be gained from being able to make the decision later in time rather than earlier. If better decisions can be made in the future, then there is a value to putting the decision off to a later date. The key point is that uncertainty and irreversibility should lead to a sequential decisionmaking process. If better information will emerge, regulators might seek an approach that preserves greater flexibility, at least if that approach is not too costly. The extent of the appropriate "irreversibility premium" depends on the situation.

IV. Catastrophe and Sunk Costs

Even under this account, the idea of irreversibility remains ambiguous. Let us consider two possible interpretations. Under the first, an effect is irreversible when restoration to the status quo is impossible or at best extremely costly, at least on a relevant timescale. Literal irreversibility is the extreme case. For example, the "decision not to preserve a rich reservoir of biodiversity such as the 60 million-year-old Korup forest in Nigeria is irreversible. The alteration or

---

[31] See Anthony C. Fisher, *Uncertainty, Irreversibility, and the Timing of Climate Policy* 9 (2001), available at http://citeseerx.ist.psu.edu/viewdoc/download?doi=10.1.1.469.5209&rep =rep1&type=pdf. A valuable discussion is Robert Pindyck, *Irreversibilities and the Timing of Environmental Policy*, 22 Energy and Resource Econ 233 (2000). Pindyck's treatment of "sunk costs" and "sunk benefits" could easily be adapted to the preliminary injunction question in environmental cases; it repays careful study.

destruction of a unique asset of this type has an awesome finality."[32] In other cases, we might be able to reverse the damage, but it would cost a great deal to do so—far more, let us suppose, than it would cost to delay the action that would cause the damage. If this is the appropriate interpretation of irreversibility, then it is an aspect of seriousness. A second interpretation, standard in the economic literature on options, sees irreversibility in terms of sunk costs. The two interpretations lead to different understandings of the problem of irreversibility and the Irreversible Harm Precautionary Principle.

A. IRREVERSIBILITY AND SERIOUSNESS

Under the first interpretation, the question is whether a clear line separates the reversible from the irreversible. Perhaps we have a continuum, not a dichotomy. Outside of the most extreme cases, the question is not whether some effect can be reversed, but instead at what cost. Note that areas that have been developed, or otherwise harmed, can often be returned to their original state, even if at considerable expense. Even lost forests can be restored. But sometimes the cost is high, even prohibitive, and sometimes restoration is literally impossible.

Consider in this regard the mortality effects of certain environmental harms. If air pollution would kill 200 people a year, or if climate change would produce tens of thousands of deaths in India, those losses cannot be recovered. Even biological changes in the human body may not be reversible (whether or not they are associated with immediate or long-term harm). Some kinds of air pollution induce changes that endure for decades. In all of these cases, irreversibility is simply an aspect of seriousness. If 200 people will die from certain levels of pollution, the harm is more serious than if 200 people would merely get sick. If air pollution induces biological changes, everything depends on the magnitude of the harm associated with those changes.

At first glance, these points do not create a serious problem for the Irreversible Harm Precautionary Principle. The extent of the precaution should depend on the size of the harms and the cost and burden associated with preventing or (if possible) reversing them. If climate change cannot be reversed at all, we should take more ag-

---

[32] See Graciela Chichilnisky and Geoffrey Heal, *Global Environmental Risks*, 7 J Econ Persp 65, 76 (1993).

gressive precautions than we would if it can be reversed only at great expense, monetary or otherwise—and if it can be reversed only at great expense, we would take more precautions than we would if it would be easy to reverse it.

But there is a conceptual difficulty here, which is that *whether a particular act is "irreversible" depends on how it is characterized.* Any death, of any living creature, is irreversible, and what is true for living creatures is true for rocks and refrigerators too; if these are destroyed, they are destroyed forever. And because time is linear, every decision is, in an intelligible sense, irreversible. If a couple goes on vacation in Greece in July of a certain year, that decision cannot be reversed, and what else might have been done at that time will have been permanently lost. If government builds a new highway in upstate New York in May, that particular decision will be irreversible; nothing else will be done with that land in May, even though the highway can be later replaced or eliminated. This is the sense in which "irreversibility" depends on how the underlying act is characterized. If we characterize it narrowly, to be and to do precisely what it is and does, any act is irreversible by definition.

Environmentalists who are concerned about irreversibility have something far more particular in mind. They mean something like a large-scale alteration in environmental conditions—one that imposes permanent, or nearly permanent, changes in those conditions. It should be clear that irreversibility in this sense is not a sufficient reason for a highly precautionary approach. At a minimum, the irreversible change has to be for the worse, and it must also rise to a certain level of magnitude. A truly miniscule change in the global temperature, even if permanent, would not justify expensive precautions if it is benign or if it imposes little in the way of harm. For this reason, it is tempting to understand the idea of irreversibility, for environmental purposes, as inseparable from that of seriousness. A loss of a wisdom tooth is irreversible, but not a reason for particular precautions on behalf of wisdom teeth; a loss of an extremely small forest, with no wildlife, hardly justifies an especially aggressive principle, even if that loss cannot be reversed. A loss of a large forest, with a lot of wildlife, is a very different matter.

At first glance, then, irreversibility matters only because of its connection with the magnitude of the harm; irreversibility operates as a kind of amplifier. And if irreversibility in environmental protection is to be analyzed in that way, then an Irreversible Harm Precautionary

Principle is really part of a Catastrophic Harm Precautionary Principle, or at least a Significant Harm Precautionary Principle. If so, the Irreversible Harm Precautionary Principle is important and must be taken into account, and helps illuminate the idea of irreparable harm; but it is not especially distinctive. The principle is also vulnerable, some of the time, to the same objections that apply to the Precautionary Principle as a whole: Significant and even irreversible harms may well be on all sides of risk-related problems, and a focus on one set of risks will give rise to others—perhaps environmental risks as well.

B. IRREVERSIBLE INVESTMENTS

Analysts of real options understand the idea of irreversibility in a different and technical way.[33] Irreversible investments are sunk costs—those that cannot be recovered. Examples include expenditures on advertising and marketing, or even capital investments designed to improve the performance of a factory. In fact the purchase of motor vehicles, computers, and office equipment is not fully reversible, because the purchase cost is usually significantly higher than the resale value. Examples of reversible investments include the opening of bank accounts and the purchase of bonds. The problem with an investment that is irreversible is that those who make it relinquish "the possibility of waiting for new information that might affect the desirability or timing of the expenditure, and this lost option value is an opportunity cost that must be included as part of the investment."[34]

Many people agree that we should characterize, as irreversible harms, environmental effects that are both serious and extremely expensive and time-consuming to reverse. The idea might be in the same family as that of irreversible investments; there may even be an identity here. The key point is that if a highway is built through a park, or if a development project goes forward next to a beach, officials may lack the "information that might affect the desirability or timing of the expenditure," and the lost option value is an opportunity cost. NEPA can be understood as directly responsive to that risk. It does impose a

---

[33] See Avinash Dixit and Robert Pindyck, *Investment under Uncertainty* 6 (Princeton, 1994) ("When a firm makes an irreversible investment expenditure, it exercises, or 'kills,' its option to invest. It gives up the possibility of waiting for new information to arrive that might affect the desirability or timing of the expenditure, and this lost option value is an opportunity cost that must be included as part of the investment.").

[34] Id at 6.

(potentially costly) delay, to be sure, but it freezes the status quo while enabling officials to obtain at least some of that information.

But again, this argument ignores an important point: *Irreversibility, in this sense, might lie on all sides.* We are dealing with irreversibilities, not irreversibility. Regulation that reduces one (irreversible) environmental risk might increase another such risk (environmental or otherwise). Efforts to reduce climate change and other dangers associated with fossil fuel use may lead to increased dependence on nuclear energy, which threatens to produce irreversible harms of its own; in China, nuclear energy has been actively defended as a way of combating climate change.[35] As with the Precautionary Principle in general,[36] so with the Irreversible Harm Precautionary Principle in particular: Measures that the principle requires, on grounds of safety and health, might well be prohibited on exactly those grounds.

There is a more general point. If steps are taken to reduce greenhouse gas emissions, capital costs will be incurred, and they cannot be recouped. Sunk costs are a familiar feature of environmental regulation, in the form of mandates that require technological change. We may well be dealing, then, with irreversibilities, not irreversibility. In some cases that involve requests for a preliminary injunction, that is precisely the problem, as the Supreme Court has recognized.[37]

For some environmental questions, this point complicates the application of the Irreversible Harm Precautionary Principle. As Fisher writes for climate change, "it is not clear whether the conditions of the problem imply that investment in control ought to be slowed or reduced, while waiting for information needed to make a better decision, or that investment should come sooner to preserve the option to protect ourselves from impacts that may be revealed in the future as serious or even catastrophic."[38] It is for this reason that some observers have concluded that the existence of uncertainty and irreversibility argues for *less*, not more, in the way of investments in reducing greenhouse gas emissions. Those investments may themselves turn out to be irreversible. Everything depends on the likelihood and magnitude of the losses on all sides.

---

[35] See, for example, Ling Zhong, Note, *Nuclear Energy: China's Approach Towards Addressing Global Warming*, 12 Georgetown Intl Envir L Rev 493 (2000).

[36] See Cass R. Sunstein, *Laws of Fear* (Cambridge, 2005).

[37] *Winter*, 555 US at 14–15.

[38] Fisher, *Uncertainty* (cited in note 31).

Nothing said here supports the increasingly implausible view that the right approach to climate change is adequately captured in the area of "wait and learn." That approach will not make much sense if we might lose a great deal by virtue of waiting. There is good reason to believe that the irreversible losses associated with climate change do indeed justify the irreversible losses associated with greater investments in emissions reductions, world-wide. In that sense, steps to reduce greenhouse gas emissions, right now, can be understood as motivated by the same principles that sometimes justify the issuance of preliminary injunctions. My conclusion is that if irreversibility is defined in standard economic terms, pointing to the value of preserving flexibility for an uncertain future, it provides a distinctive and plausible understanding of the Irreversible Harm Precautionary Principle. As we will soon see, this understanding also helps explain some of the most important functions of NEPA.

V. Incommensurability and Uncertainty

The discussion thus far misses something important. When people say that the loss of a loved one, a pristine area, or a species is irreversible, they do not merely mean that the loss is grave and that it takes a lot to provide adequate compensation. They mean that what is lost is *incommensurable*—that it is qualitatively distinctive, and that when we lose it, we lose something that is unique. In this regard, John Stuart Mill's objections to Bentham's conception of utlitarianism are worth quoting:[39]

> Nor is it only the moral part of man's nature, in the strict sense of the term—the desire of perfection, or the feeling of an approving or of an accusing conscience—that he overlooks; he but faintly recognizes, as a fact in human nature, the pursuit of any other ideal end for its own sake. The sense of honour, and personal dignity—that feeling of personal exaltation and degradation which acts independently of other people's opinion, or even in defiance of it; the love of beauty, the passion of the artist; the love of order, of congruity, of consistency in all things, and conformity to their end; the love of power, not in the limited form of power over other human beings, but abstract power, the power of making our volitions effectual; the love of action, the thirst for movement and activity, a principle scarcely of less influence in human life than its opposite, the love of ease. . . . Man, that most complex being, is a very simple one in his eyes.

---

[39] See John Stuart Mill, "Bentham," in Alan Ryan, ed, *Utilitarianism and Other Essays* 132 (Penguin, 1987).

For those who emphasize incommensurability, the central claim is that human goods are diverse and that we do violence to our considered judgments about them when we line them up along a single metric.[40] Suppose, for example, that a species of tigers or elephants is lost. People do not value an endangered species in the same way that they value money; it is not as if a species, a beach, a friendship, or a child is indistinguishable from specified monetary sums. If we see species, beaches, friendships, and children as equivalent to one another, or to some amount of money, we will have on odd and even unrecognizable understanding of all of these goods. When people object to the loss of a species or a beach, and contend that the loss is irreversible, they mean to point to its permanence, and to the fact that what has been lost is not valued in the same way, or valued along the same metric, as money.

This claim should not be confused. Some goods have infinite value, in the sense that people would spend all they have to preserve them. At the same time, people are willing to make trade-offs among qualitatively diverse goods, and they do so all the time. We will pay a certain amount, and no more, to be able to protect members of an endangered species or to visit the beach, or to help preserve it in a pristine state; we will not pay an infinite sum to see our friends, or even to maintain our friendships; we will take some precautions, but not others, to protect our children. The emphasis on incommensurability is not meant to deny that trade-offs are made. The point is only that the relevant goods are not fungible. It follows that when a loss is deemed irreversible, one reason is that it is qualitatively distinctive and not fungible with other human goods. Many of those who are concerned about irreversible harms tend to stress this point.

This claim offers a distinctive understanding of what is meant by the idea of irreparable harm. When losses are said to be irreparable, it is sometimes because of the uniqueness of what is lost. Again, the need for trade-offs remains important. A pristine area may be incommensurable with money, and with others things that matter, but we do not attempt to pay an infinite amount to protect it. The claim about irreversibility is not meant to deny this point. What is gained by an understanding of incommensurability is a more vivid appreciation of why certain losses cannot be dismissed as mere "costs." An

---

[40] Good discussions can be found in Elizabeth Anderson, *Value in Ethics and Economics* (Harvard, 1993); Joseph Raz, *The Morality of Freedom* (Oxford, 1985).

Irreversible Harm Precautionary Principle, used in private decisions or democratic arenas, might be implemented with a recognition of the qualitative distinctiveness of many losses—especially when those losses affect future generations.

Here too, however, it is important to see that precautionary steps may themselves impose incommensurable losses, not merely monetary ones. Recall, for example, that environmental protection of one sort may create environmental problems of another sort. If the diverse nature of social goods is to play a part in the implementations of an Irreversible Harm Precautionary Principle, it must attend to the fact that diverse goods may be on all sides.

These are points about how to understand certain problems and debates, and not necessarily about actual practice in law. Because trade-offs are made among qualitatively diverse goods—as, for example, when people pay $X, and no more, to avoid statistical mortality risks—the idea of incommensurability is not sufficient to support preliminary injunctions. That idea is best combined with an emphasis on uncertainty: Courts do not know how to value the relevant loss in monetary terms, and they will not know how to do that ex post. A harm might be irreparable in that sense; consider a preliminary injunction against a restriction on freedom of speech. In actual cases, claims about incommensurability are linked to claims about an epistemic problem faced by courts. They do not have the tools for accurate valuation.[41]

VI. Environmental Injunctions

For many years, some courts of appeals held that when environmental harm was alleged, district courts should adopt a presumption of irreparable damage and indeed a presumption in favor of injunctive relief.[42] In NEPA cases, the result was a likely injunction if the agency had failed to prepare an adequate environmental impact statement: "Irreparable damage is presumed when an agency fails to evaluate thoroughly the environmental impact of a proposed ac-

---

[41] Note in this regard the close connection between the requirement of irreparable injury and the requirement that remedies available at law, such as monetary damages, are inadequate to compensate for the injury. The judgment of the inadequacy of damage remedies may help explain why an injury is irreparable.

[42] See *Thomas v Peterson*, 753 F2d 754, 764 (9th Cir 1985).

tion."[43] But what is the basis for this presumption? And what follows from it? Does it follow, for example, that the United States Navy must be enjoined from conducting weapons-training operations before it has obtained a permit to discharge ordnance into the sea?

In response to the last question, the Supreme Court offered a firm negative answer.[44] Rejecting the idea that environmental violations should give rise to automatic injunctions, the Court in *Weinberger v Romero-Barcelo* said that an injunction is an equitable remedy, subject to traditional balancing, and that it would "not lightly assume that Congress has intended to depart from established principles" permitting district courts to exercise their discretion.[45] Five years later, in *Amoco Production Co. v Village of Gambell*, which involved the Alaska Native Claims Settlement Act, the Court underlined the point and expressly rejected the presumption of irreparable harm in environmental cases.[46] "This presumption is contrary to traditional equitable principles."[47] Nonetheless, the Court stressed that environmental problems raise distinct issues, because "[e]nvironmental injury, by its nature, can seldom be adequately remedied by money damages and is often permanent or at least of long duration, i.e., irreparable."[48] It follows that if an environmental injury is likely, "the balance of harms will usually favor the issuance of an injunction to protect the environment."[49]

When courts of appeals spoke, in the 1980s, in terms of a presumption in favor of injunctive relief, they might be understood as adopting a version of the Irreversible Harm Precautionary Principle— assuming that environmental harm is irreversible in the relevant sense, and requiring a strong showing by those who seek to proceed in the face of that harm. This interpretation helps to explain the simplest exception to the lower courts' presumption: cases in which "irreparable harm *to the environment* would result if such relief were granted."[50] If,

---

[43] *Save Our Ecosystems v Clark*, 747 F2d 1240, 1250 (9th Cir 1984). For general discussion, see Zigmund Plater, *Statutory Violations and Equitable Discretion*, 70 Cal L Rev 524 (1982).

[44] See *Weinberger v Romero-Barcelo*, 456 US 305 (1982).

[45] Id at 313.

[46] *Amoco Production Co.*, 480 US at 544–45.

[47] Id at 544.

[48] Id.

[49] Id.

[50] *People of Village of Gambell v Hodel*, 774 F2d 1414, 1424 (9th Cir 1985) (emphasis in original).

for example, an injunction against the use of a logging road would prevent the removal of diseased trees and hence allow the spread of infection through national forests, no injunction would issue.[51]

Here, then, is a clear recognition of the existence of environment-environment trade-offs, in a way that requires a qualification of any Irreversible Harm Precautionary Principle. And when the Supreme Court rejected the presumption, it did so in favor of traditional equitable balancing, in a way that recognized that serious harms, and perhaps irreversible harms, are on all sides. But even in doing so, the Court endorsed a kind of Irreversible Harm Precautionary Principle through its explicit recognition that environmental injury "is often permanent or at least of long duration." And as noted, Justice Breyer offered a distinctive, NEPA-inflected understanding of the risk, finding irreparable harm not in an injury to the plaintiff or the environment, but in a failure to consider environmental considerations before deciding whether and how to proceed.

In latter cases, the Court has severely qualified these ideas.[52] In one of those cases, *Monsanto Co. v Geertson Seed Farms*,[53] the Court disapproved of decisions that "presume[d] that an injunction is the proper remedy for a NEPA violation except in unusual circumstances."[54] The Court explained that there is nothing in NEPA that allows courts considering injunctive relief to put their "thumb on the scales."[55] The Court emphasized the need for irreparable harm, understood in concrete terms, rather than in terms of abstract risks, and it has not squarely explored the implications, made relevant by NEPA, of a failure to freeze the status quo to allow the requisite consideration.[56] And notwithstanding its seemingly categorical pronouncements, existing doctrine remains in some flux.

In one of the key cases, *Winter v Natural Resources Defense Council*, Justice Breyer wrote separately so as to recapitulate his concerns as a

---

[51] *Alpine Lakes Protection Society v Schlapfer*, 518 F2d 1089 (9th Cir 1975); *Thomas*, 753 F2d at 764 n 8.

[52] See *Winter*, 555 US at 21–32; *Monsanto Co.*, 561 US at 156–66.

[53] 561 US 139, 157 (2010). For an interesting discussion in the context of the Endangered Species Act, where the law remains disputed, see *Cottonwood Environmental Law Center v U.S. Forest Service*, 789 F3d 1075 (2015). The leading case is *TVA v Hill*, 437 US 153 (1978).

[54] *Monsanto Co.*, 561 US at 157.

[55] Id.

[56] See, for example, *Winter*, 555 US at 29–32. In the same vein, see *Sierra Club v U.S. Dept of Agriculture*, 841 F Supp 349, 358–59 (DDC 2012).

court of appeals judge, noting, "NEPA seeks to assure that when Government officials consider taking action that may affect the environment, they do so fully aware of the relevant environmental considerations."[57] It follows that "when a decision to which EIS obligations attach is made without the informed environmental consideration that NEPA requires, much of the harm that NEPA seeks to prevent has already taken place."[58] That means that the "absence of an injunction thereby threatens to cause the very environmental harm" against which NEPA was designed to guard.[59] To date, the Court as a whole has not engaged in Justice Breyer's argument, and for that reason it remains on the table.

Even Justice Breyer agreed that in NEPA cases, preliminary injunctions should not issue as a matter of course; that view would endorse the Irreversible Harm Precautionary Principle in its crudest form. Balancing is required. Sometimes injunctions will themselves impose serious and perhaps irreversible harm, and sometimes the risk to the environment is trivial. But in NEPA cases, it continues to make sense to consider, as a relevant factor, the risk that an inadequately informed decision to proceed will alter the status quo—ensuring that once an environmental impact statement is produced, it will be too late to have a meaningful effect on the outcome. If delay is not exceedingly costly, and if the risk of environmental harm is serious, injunctive relief is appropriate for NEPA violations. An understanding of the risk of irreversibility helps to explain why.

VII. CONCLUSION: ETHICS AND ECONOMICS

There is a coherent and distinctive Irreversible Harm Precautionary Principle, which takes the form of a willingness to pay a premium to freeze the status quo and to maintain flexibility for the future, while new information is acquired. In many settings, it makes sense to pay for an option to avoid a risk of irreversible losses. We can find an implicit understanding of option value in the emphasis on irreversibility in NEPA and other federal statutes, along with many international agreements. We can also obtain new insights into the

---

[57] *Winter*, 555 US at 35.

[58] Id.

[59] Id.

time-honored idea of irreparable harm through the lens of irreversibility, especially in environmental cases.

In some cases, irreparable harm comes in the form of large, qualitatively distinctive injuries, which are exceedingly difficult to turn into monetary equivalents (either before or after the fact). In some cases, irreparable harm is associated with the elimination of option value. Recall the demonstration by Arrow and Fisher that if a project produces "some irreversible transformation of the environment, hence a loss in perpetuity of the benefits from preservation," then it is worth paying something to wait to acquire the missing information. For that reason, "the expected benefits of an irreversible decision should be adjusted to reflect the loss of options it entails."[60]

The issuance of a preliminary injunction can be seen as reflecting such an adjustment. In some cases, it reflects an understanding that the environmental loss is incommensurable with money, not in the sense that it is infinitely valuable, but because it is qualitatively distinct. To be made workable for law, that understanding must be combined with an emphasis on the epistemic problem faced by courts; consider the challenge of valuation stemming from loss of a species or a pristine area.

We have also seen that an emphasis on irreversibility will sometimes argue in favor of delaying, rather than accelerating, environmental protection. There may be irreversible losses, in one or another sense, on both sides. Everything depends on the magnitude and likelihood of the relevant effects. Courts need to assess both of these in order to know how to proceed. But it makes sense to say that in the NEPA context, preservation of the status quo may be necessary to avoid a distinctive risk made relevant by that statute. I speculate that an understanding of this point bears on the meaning of the irreparable harm standard in many contexts, including freedom of speech, privacy, and discrimination on the basis of race and sex.

---

[60] Arrow and Fischer, 88 Q J Econ at 319.

DANIEL A. FARBER

MURR v WISCONSIN AND THE FUTURE OF TAKINGS LAW

Almost a century ago, Justice Holmes famously declared that a regulation becomes a taking of property if it goes too far.[1] Judges and scholars have struggled ever since to give meaning to this test. *Murr v Wisconsin*[2] is the most recent Supreme Court decision wrestling with this issue. This 2017 decision seems to have been something of a sleeper, because it is lacking in dramatic facts or stirring rhetoric. But it actually has broad implications for the rights of property owners and the scope of government regulatory powers.[3] *Murr* sends a strong signal that the property rights crusade led by Justice Antonin Scalia has stalled and that the Court is largely content with the current shape

---

Daniel A. Farber is Sho Sato Professor of Law, University of California, Berkeley.

[1] *Pennsylvania Coal Co. v Mahon*, 260 US 393, 413 (1922).

[2] 137 S Ct 1933 (2017). The Takings Clause, "nor shall private property be taken for public use, without just compensation." US Const, Amend V, cl 5. The language seems plainly to refer to government seizure of possession or title, not to regulation, so *Pennsylvania Coal* was only tenuously supported by the constitutional text. *Chicago Burlington and Quincy RR v City of Chicago*, 166 US 226 (1897), held the clause applicable to the states via the Due Process Clause of the Fourteenth Amendment.

[3] For some recent writing about *Murr*, see Richard A. Epstein, *Will the Supreme Court Clean Up Takings Law in Murr v. Wisconsin?*, 11 NYU L Rev 860, 861–83 (2017); Maureen E. Brady, *Penn Central Square: What the Many Factors of Murr v. Wisconsin Mean for Property Federalism* (2017), online at https://ssrn.com/abstract=3028886; Gavin S. Frisch, *What Is the Relevant Parcel? Clarifying the "Parcel as a Whole" Standard in Murr v. Wisconsin*, 12 Duke J Const L & Pub Pol'y 253 (2017). For an early commentary on the Court's Decision, see Robert H. Thomas, *Restatement (SCOTUS) of Property: What Happened to Use in Murr v. Wisconsin?* (July 22, 2017), online at https://ssrn.com/abstract=3007166.

of takings doctrine.[4] In the dismayed words of one advocate of stronger property rights, *Murr* "further undermined the already enfeebled constitutional rights enjoyed by property owners against regulatory excess."[5]

Murr also has real practical significance. For instance, sea level rise poses an increasing threat to coastal areas.[6] States are experimenting with ways to move existing development back from the shore and limit building in areas that are likely to be at risk in the future.[7] But landowners may claim that it is unconstitutional to require them to abandon existing structures or to prohibit new development or armoring their shorelines.[8] *Murr* does not guarantee government's success against these claims, but it does significantly strengthen the state's hand.[9]

As background for understanding *Murr*, a quick review of takings law may be helpful for the uninitiated. The Supreme Court currently employs three tests to determine whether a regulation should be considered a "taking" of property that requires compensation.[10] First, the Court finds a taking when the government mandates a physical intrusion on private property. Such an intrusion is a taking even if it does not cause any significant harm to the owner.[11] Our focus will be

---

[4] Arguably, the movement has been stalled for at least a decade. Writing in 2006, Richard Lazarus observed that when Clarence Thomas joined Scalia on the bench, "the property rights movement appeared to have the makings of a solid majority on the Court," but that "[n]o such significant legal precedent favoring property rights . . . has resulted." Richard J. Lazarus, *The Measure of a Justice: Justice Scalia and the Faltering of the Property Rights Movement Within the Supreme Court*, 57 Hastings L J 759, 760 (2006). According to Lazarus, Scalia's "penchant for bright line per se tests favorable to takings plaintiffs ultimately had no legs within the Court." Id at 761. Instead, Lazarus argued, Justice Stevens had become the most influential Justice on takings issues, advocating a "more contextual analysis." Id. *Murr*, I will argue, can be seen as cementing in place the more contextual approach.

[5] Nicole Steele Garnett, *From a Muddle to a Mudslide*, 2016–17 Cato Sup Ct Rev 131, 131 (2017).

[6] See Holly Doremus, *Climate Change and the Evolution of Property Rights*, 1 UC Irvine L Rev 1091, 1101–1103 (2011).

[7] Id at 1107.

[8] Id at 1107–10. For another discussion of these issues, see Sean B. Hecht, *Taking Background Principles Seriously in the Context of Sea-Level Rise*, 39 Vt L Rev 781 (2015).

[9] See Part III below.

[10] Eminent domain extends back through the Founding Era, and its roots in legal theory are even older, but regulatory takings doctrine is a relatively modern development. See Joseph L. Sax, *Takings and the Police Power*, 74 Yale L J 36, 38–60 (1964). One constant since Professor Sax wrote fifty years ago is that "the predominant characteristic of this area of law is a welter of confusing and apparently incompatible results." Id at 37.

[11] This per se rule stems from Justice Thurgood Marshall's opinion in *Loretto v Teleprompter Manhattan CSTV Corp.*, 458 US 419 (1982). The "physical-invasion versus use" distinction has

on the remaining two categories. The second category includes so-called "total takings," where the government has eliminated any possible economically beneficial use of the property.[12] With one important but ill-defined exception, such regulations are per se takings under Justice Scalia's opinion in *Lucas v South Carolina Coastal Council*,[13] which is "widely considered the high water mark for the property rights movement."[14] The third category covers all remaining cases. This default category is governed by the *Penn Central* test,[15] which examines whether the government regulation unduly interferes with reasonable, investment-backed expectations. Putting aside the first category (physical intrusions), the other categories both analyze the owner's economic loss due to a regulation. The degree of loss is customarily expressed as a fraction: the decrease in value due to a regulation (the numerator) divided by the property value absent the regulation (the denominator).

The *Murr* litigation involved just such a claim of diminution of value, brought by siblings who owned two adjoining lots on the bank of a scenic river; they claimed that their inability to sell or develop one of the lots separately was a taking.[16] State law and a local zoning ordinance required them to treat both lots as a unit and limited them to a single building on that unit.[17] The central issue in the case was the denominator of the taking fraction. Should the denominator be limited to the preregulation value of the lot they wanted to sell, or should it include the value of both lots? A related question involved the nu-

---

received some justified criticism from various directions. See, e.g., Steven J. Eagle, *The Four-Factor Penn Central Regulatory Takings Test*, 118 Penn State L Rev 602, 627 (2014); Andrea Peterson, *The False Dichotomy Between Physical and Regulatory Takings Analysis: A Critique of Tahoe-Sierra's Distinction Between Physical and Regulatory Takings*, 34 Ecol L Q 381 (2007).

[12] The Court recognized an important exception, allowing an activity to be completely banned when it constitutes a common law nuisance. For discussion of this exception, see Richard Lazarus, *Putting the Correct "Spin" on Lucas*, 45 Stan L Rev 1411 (1993).

[13] 505 US 1003 (1982). Lazarus credits Justice Powell with subtly setting the stage for *Lucas* with dictum in *Agins v City of Tiburon*, 447 US 255, 260 (1980). See Lazarus, 57 Hastings L J at 775 (cited in note 4).

[14] Lazarus, 57 Hastings L J at 775 (cited in note 4).

[15] The test derives from *Penn Central Transportation Co. v New York*, 438 US 104 (1978). In practice, there may be a safe harbor, at least in federal court, for regulations that diminish property values by less than 50 percent. See Justin R. Pidot, *Eroding the Parcel*, 39 Vt L Rev 647, 672 n 133 (2013).

[16] *Murr*, 137 S Ct 1939–41.

[17] Id at 1941.

merator: should the postregulation valuation take into account the benefits of holding both lots as a unit?

In an opinion by Justice Kennedy, the Supreme Court rejected the owners' invitation to adopt a clear rule to address these issues, instead proposing a somewhat open-ended standard that hampers takings claims.[18] Three dissenters, led by Chief Justice Roberts, accepted the owners' argument about the denominator, but pushed back on their arguments regarding the numerator and timing issues.[19] One of the three, Justice Thomas, wrote separately to express discomfort with the whole doctrine built on Justice Holmes's dictum, which has never been persuasively linked with prior case law or with the original understanding.[20]

The article proceeds as follows. Part I explains the evolution of the denominator problem and its resolution in *Murr*. Part II turns to some other issues in takings law that were less central to *Murr* but were clarified by the opinion, including the determination of the nominator of the takings fraction, the relevance of the timing of the owner's acquisition of the property vis-à-vis the enactment of the regulation, and the role of the state's regulatory interest in determining whether a regulation is a taking. Part III is primarily devoted to taking stock of the current state of takings law and the failure of the property-rights movement championed by Justice Scalia on the Court. It also makes a brief foray into assessing the normative desirability of the ad hoc balancing approaches adopted in *Penn Central* and *Murr*.

Because the article is organized topically, *Murr* itself will come on stage, depart, and then return periodically as we investigate different aspects of the opinion. Hopefully the reader will find the resulting clarity worth the sacrifice of narrative flow.

I. MURR AND THE DENOMINATOR PROBLEM

Our first topic will be the denominator of the takings "fraction" discussed in the introduction. In a regulatory takings case, to what extent do the owner's other property interests count in determining the preregulation and postregulation property values?[21] The

---

[18] Id at 1944–47.

[19] Id at 1952–53.

[20] Id at 1957.

[21] A helpful introduction to this issue can be found in John E. Fee, Comment, *Unearthing the Denominator in Regulatory Takings Claims*, 61 U Chi L Rev 1535 (1994).

owner would like to define the relevant property narrowly, as the specific interest the government has impaired, so it can say that it was deprived of a hundred percent of that interest and invoke the *Lucas* total taking rule. The government has the opposite incentive to define the relevant property broadly to include all of the owner's property. This definitional exercise can determine the outcome of the case.[22]

This section will begin with a history of this branch of takings law. It will then turn to the *Murr* litigation, followed by a look at how the issue was analyzed in Justice Kennedy's majority opinion and Justice Roberts's dissent.

A. THE HISTORY OF THE DENOMINATOR PROBLEM

The denominator problem has its roots in the Holmes opinion that this article opened with, in which he said "too much" was taken without ever quite specifying too much of what. For that reason, the denominator problem was present at the creation of regulatory takings doctrine. It received heightened importance with *Penn Central* and later cases that rejected two of the three possible readings of Holmes's opinion. *Murr* is the culmination of this series of cases limiting the ability of owners to define the denominator so as to magnify their perceived loss.

1. *The origin story of regulatory takings law.* Regulatory takings law began with *Pennsylvania Coal Co. v Mahon*,[23] and diminution in value has been central to the law of regulatory takings since then.[24] *Pennsylvania Coal*, an activist decision if there ever was one, rewrote the law of eminent domain. The Fifth Amendment requires compensation when the government takes private property for public purposes. Until *Pennsylvania Coal*, however, the Court had not treated government restrictions on the use of property as takings of property. Justice Holmes's opinion in *Pennsylvania Coal* left much unclear, not least the interpretation of diminution in value.

The holding seems clear enough at first sight. Because coal mines can cause the collapse of structures on the surface, a Pennsylvania statute required mining companies to provide support for mines un-

---

[22] Eagle, 118 Penn State L Rev at 631–32 (cited in note 11). As Richard Lazarus explains, this is especially true in terms of the *Lucas* total taking rule. Lazarus, 57 Hastings L J at 818 (cited in note 4).

[23] 260 US 393 (1922).

[24] Id.

der populated areas, either by leaving pillars of coal in the ground or building support beams. Justice Holmes held the law unconstitutional, not only as to the homeowner who was the plaintiff in the litigation, but as applied to public buildings, streets, and communities above mines. Justice Holmes announced a "general rule that, while property may be regulated to a certain extent, if regulation goes too far it will be recognized as a taking."[25] There are few cases where the Court has made so large a change in doctrine with so little explanation.

Justice Holmes's opinion may have eventually launched a thousand lawsuits, but the opinion itself is enigmatic in key respects, including how much Holmes was actually relying on the Takings Clause, as opposed to the Contract Clause or some more general due process claim.[26] More importantly for our purposes, Holmes's analysis of diminution in value was ambiguous about the denominator—the "property" that was allegedly taken. In terms of the rights of the landowner in the case, Holmes says, the "extent of the taking is great" and "we should think it clear that the statute does not disclose a public interest sufficient to warrant so extensive a destruction of the defendant's constitutionally protected rights."[27] But precisely what right of the mine owner did Holmes think was taken? There are three possible answers to that question.

First, Holmes might have had in mind the "support estate" under Pennsylvania common law. The state's common law treated the right to sue for loss of subterranean support for surface land as a separate interest in property. The coal company had kept the support right when it sold off the surface land. Hence, prior to passage of the statute, it had a common law right to deprive the surface land of support. Holmes remarks at one point that the statute "purports to abolish what is recognized in Pennsylvania as an estate in land—a very valuable estate—and what is declared by the Court below to be a contract hitherto binding the plaintiffs." This language could be interpreted to mean that the "property" which was taken was the support estate. If so, a similar statute in a state without this particular quirk in the common law would be constitutional.

In another key passage, Holmes says that "[t]o make it commercially impracticable to mine certain coal has very nearly the same ef-

---

[25] Id at 415.

[26] Id at 413.

[27] Id at 414.

fect for constitutional purposes as appropriating it or destroying it."[28]
But what did he mean by "certain coal"? He may have been referring
to the specific coal pillars left in place to support existing mines, since
providing other types of bracing was too expensive.[29] Or he may have
been referring to the company's allegation that it would have to close
some mines entirely because of the added expense.[30] If so, the "certain
coal" was all the coal in those mines, not merely the pillars of coal it
would have to leave in place to comply with the statute.[31] The upshot
is that it is unclear just what Holmes was defining as the denominator:
the support estate, the coal pillars, or the closed mines.

Justice Holmes's concise analysis and striking epigrams make for a
welcome contrast to the painful plodding more common among judges
then and now. But these virtues came at a price, the loss of the more
careful elaboration that would help guide future judges and lawyers. In
particular, he established the importance of determining what we now
call the denominator, but gave little indication how to do so. The
Supreme Court made several important efforts to clarify the situation
in the time between *Pennsylvania Coal* and the *Murr* opinion. We begin
with the question of an owner's ability to isolate a particular property
interest for consideration, like the support right in *Pennsylvania Coal*.

2. *The denominator issue in modern takings jurisprudence.* Every journey in modern takings law begins—and many end—with Grand Central Station, the subject of *Penn Central Transportation Co. v City of
New York*.[32] The city designated the station as a historic landmark
and rejected both of the railroad's proposals to expand on the site.[33]
One proposal involved construction of a fifty-five-story office building perched above the terminal; the other involved tearing down part

---

[28] Id.

[29] See id at 398.

[30] See *Pennsylvania Coal*, 260 US at 414, where Holmes remarks that "[w]hat makes the
right to mine coal valuable is that it can be exercised with profit."

[31] The upshot is that we cannot be sure how Holmes would have ruled on an otherwise
identical case from a state that did not distinguish the support estate from the mineral estate
(ownership of the coal). We are also unclear on whether he would find a taking if a mine was
profitable but some coal still had to be left in the ground or if providing mine support had
involved bracing rather than leaving coal in the ground.

[32] 438 US 104 (1976). It is perhaps an unfortunate twist of history that the *Penn Central*
case was not actually about Penn Central Station, to the confusion of generations of law
students.

[33] Id at 107.

of the building to add a fifty-three-story tower.[34] When the company's proposals were predictably rejected, the company claimed the city had taken its property, with particular reference to the airspace above the building.[35]

Justice Brennan's opinion for the Court undertook to synthesize the Court's regulatory takings opinions,[36] which it characterized as engaging in "essentially ad hoc, factual inquiries."[37] The Court first observed that takings were more likely to be found if a regulation amounted to acquisitions of resources rather than merely prohibiting certain uses of land.[38] In cases outside this category, no taking would be found unless the government unduly impaired "interests that were sufficiently bound up with the reasonable expectations of the claimant" or had an insufficient connection to public safety or welfare.[39] No one has ever called this standard a model of clarity, and one commentator has aptly compared it to "a soccer field that changes in size according to the strategy of the players, and where referees apply flexible rules that contract or expand the field, depending on the factual nuances of the latest play."[40]

Directly addressing the denominator interest, the Court rejected the company's argument that the airspace above the existing building constituted a distinct property interest, like the support estate in *Penn-*

---

[34] Id.

[35] Id at 118–19.

[36] Id. A law clerk who worked for Justice Brennan at the time testified that other clerks told him the opinion "shouldn't say too much," and was later told by a clerk in a different chambers that it did not in fact "say anything at all." Eagle, 118 Penn State L Rev at 607 (cited in note 11). For a fuller account of the *Penn Central* Court's decisional process based on the Blackmun Papers, see Lazarus, 57 Hastings L J at 769–71 (cited in note 4). According to Buzz Thompson, another law clerk from the same period who is now a property professor at Stanford, because the *Penn Central* opinion "was written to try to hold together a majority, it sets out a test which is appealing to a large number of judges." Eagle, 118 Penn State L Rev at 608 (cited in note 11). Thus, Thompson continued, "it's not at all surprising that as courts have wrestled with takings issues and found them as difficult as they are, they frequently find themselves coming back to *Penn Central* which appears to offer a refuge for virtually everyone." Id.

[37] Id at 124.

[38] Id at 128.

[39] *Penn Central*, 438 US at 124–25.

[40] Eagle, 118 Penn State L Rev at 632 (cited in note 11). The description may apply even more fittingly to *Murr* than to *Penn Central*. Eagle also complains that the Court "has not provided even general guidance on how to weigh the various factors." Id at 644. To the same effect, see William A. Fischel, *Regulatory Takings: Law, Economics, and Politics* 51 (Harvard, 1995) (adding that the *Penn Central* factors "do not make much economic sense, either.").

sylvania Coal.[41] Inability to use that air space would seemingly deprive it of any economic value, whereas it might have been quite valuable if construction were allowed. The Court held that "'taking jurisprudence' does not divide a single parcel into discrete segments and attempt to determine whether rights in a particular segment have been entirely abrogated."[42]

A decade later, the Court returned to the issue of conceptual severance in *Keystone Bituminous Coal Ass'n v DeBenedictis*,[43] which was in many ways a reprise of *Pennsylvania Coal.* Pennsylvania had passed a newer statute forbidding coal-mining practices causing surface subsidence, which in effect required leaving pillars of coal in place in some locations.[44] In an opinion by Justice Stevens, the Court found the earlier Holmes decision distinguishable partly because of the broader public purpose of the more recent subsidence statute and partly because the new law would not require mine closings.[45]

In terms of the denominator issues, the Court rejected the coal industry's claim that the law was a taking of the specific coal pillars that it would be required to leave in the ground for support.[46] The Court refused to consider coal pillars required for support as a property interest that could be severed from the overall coal mine.[47] The Court also rejected the argument that the newer state statute should be considered a taking of the support estate.[48] In the Court's view, "our takings jurisprudence forecloses reliance on such legalistic distinctions within a bundle of property rights."[49] "In practical terms," the Court added, "the support estate has value only insofar as it protects or enhances the value of the estate [surface or subsurface] with which it is associated."[50] Thus, the denominator consisted of the entire mineral interest owned by the coal company.

---

[41] *Penn Central*, 438 US at 130.

[42] Id.

[43] 480 US 470 (1987).

[44] Id at 474–77.

[45] Id at 487–88.

[46] Id at 498.

[47] Id at 499.

[48] Id at 500.

[49] Id.

[50] Id at 501.

Chief Justice Rehnquist dissented, joined by Justices Powell, O'Connor, and Scalia. The dissenters argued that "there is no need for further analysis where the government by regulation extinguishes the whole bundle of rights in an identifiable segment of property," like the coal that the law required to be left in the ground.[51] Rehnquist also argued that since state law defined the support estate as a separate property interest, federal courts must do so as well.[52]

Justice Stevens again wrote for the Court in *Tahoe-Sierra Preservation Council, Inc. v Tahoe Regional Planning Agency*.[53] The regional planning agency had imposed a building moratorium lasting almost three years while it considered new measures to preserve Lake Tahoe's water quality.[54] The Court sided with the agency, whose position had been argued by John Roberts, the future Chief Justice.[55] In the Court's view, "[t]he starting point for the [lower] court's analysis should have been to ask whether there was a total taking of the entire parcel; if not, then *Penn Central* was the proper framework."[56] The Court continued: "An interest in real property is defined by the metes and bounds that describe its geographic dimensions and the term of years that describes the temporal aspect of the owner's interest."[57] The Court observed that delays of up to a year in processing permits as well as building moratoriums during planning efforts were common aspects of land use planning.[58]

Chief Justice Rehnquist again dissented, joined only by Justices Scalia and Thomas.[59] Rehnquist argued that the government's action was equivalent to seizure of a multiyear lease of the property on its own behalf.[60] In contrast, he contended, "short-term delays attendant

---

[51] Id at 517.

[52] Id at 519–20.

[53] 535 US 302 (2002). This case was considered a major defeat for property rights advocates and their judicial champion, Justice Scalia. Richard J. Lazarus, *Celebrating Tahoe-Sierra*, 33 Envir L 1, 3 (2003).

[54] Id at 306. I am simplifying the facts slightly: there were two moratoria totaling thirty-two months, and also an injunction that Stevens did not count as part of the building pause (though the dissenters did). Id at 306–12.

[55] Id at 305.

[56] Id at 331.

[57] Id at 331–32.

[58] Id at 337.

[59] Id at 343.

[60] Id at 348. This does not appear to be quite accurate. The government had not acquired any right to use the property itself or any right for it or the public to enter the property against the owner's wishes.

to zoning and permit regimes are a long-standing feature of state property law and part of a landowner's reasonable investment-backed expectations."[61] Writing separately, Justice Thomas (joined by Justice Scalia) expressed doubts about the entire "parcel as a whole" doctrine and argued that in any event it should not apply to severance of "temporal slices" of property.[62] Thus, temporary deprivation of the right to use property should always be considered a taking.[63]

As a result of these cases, the Court seemed to have firmly established a rule that the denominator in a takings case constitutes the entire parcel owned by the landowner over the entire time period held by the owner. This rule was established in *Penn Central* and continued to hold majority support despite the Court's continued rightward shift after the mid-seventies. But adherence to the whole-parcel rule only raised the further question: how to define the "parcel" if a landowner owned more than one lot. It was this question that *Murr* addressed.

B. THE MURR LITIGATION

The *Murr* litigation began as a fairly routine zoning dispute. The Murrs were siblings whose parents had given them two adjoining lots on the bank of the St. Croix River,[64] which Congress had designated a protected "wild and scenic river."[65] The parents had first given them a lot containing a cabin (Lot F) and then an adjoining vacant lot (Lot E).[66] The lots contained a 130-foot bluff, with land at the top fronting on a street and land on the bottom next to the river.[67] The Murrs' cabin located on the bottomland frequently flooded, and they wanted to renovate it using funds from selling Lot E.[68] Because of the protected nature of the river, the lots were subject to special zoning restrictions. Their renovation plan required numerous variances to move the cabin away from the river, regrade a protected slope area, construct retaining walls, and build a patio and deck close to the or-

---

[61] Id at 352.

[62] Id at 355.

[63] Id at 356.

[64] See *Murr v St. Croix County Bd of Adjustment*, 796 NW2d 837, 841 (Wis App 2011) (cited as *Board of Adjustment*).

[65] 16 USCA 1274(a)(9).

[66] *Board of Adjustment*, 796 NW2d at 841.

[67] Id.

[68] Id.

dinary high-water mark.[69] The zoning board, with the approval of the Wisconsin courts, rejected the variance requests because the Murrs could instead have flood-proofed the existing cabin or rebuilt in the same place but using fill to raise the building.[70] This left the request for a variance to sell Lot E, which became the central issue in the litigation.

The reason the Murrs needed a variance to sell Lot E separately was that both lots were classified as substandard, being below the minimum buildable area required by the zoning ordinance.[71] If the lots had been owned separately, each of them would be grandfathered in, since they existed before the passage of the building limits, but the grandfather clause did not apply when two adjoining lots were commonly owned.[72] The state court viewed the grandfather clause and its exception as a reasonable accommodation between "property values and the environment,"[73] presumably because it limited building as much as possible while protecting preexisting owners from a wipeout.[74] Moreover, the state appeals court said, the Murrs already knew or should have known about the exception to the grandfather clause when they acquired Lot E from their parents.[75]

Having lost the variance litigation, the Murrs started over again with a takings claim based on the restriction on separate use or sale of Lot E.[76] The Murrs introduced evidence that Lot E was worth only $40,000 separately if the buyer could not build on the site.[77] According to the state's appraiser, Lot F would be worth $373,000 as a separate improved lot, while apparently Lot E would be worth $398,000 on the same basis—yet the value of the two lots as a single buildable unit was $698,000, only about 10 percent below the combined value of two separate buildable lots, because of synergies between the lots.[78]

---

[69] Id.

[70] Id at 846.

[71] Id at 842.

[72] Id.

[73] Id at 844.

[74] Id.

[75] Id.

[76] *Murr*, 137 S Ct at 1940–41.

[77] Id at 1941.

[78] Id. The opinion gives the value for Lot E and the total value of Lots E and F as buildable separate properties; I obtained the value for a buildable Lot F through subtraction. The rea-

The Murrs' petition for certiorari phrased the question presented as the validity of "a rule that two legally distinct, but commonly owned contiguous parcels, must be combined in takings analysis."[79] As we will see, however, the Court did not limit itself to this question in deciding the case.

The parties offered three quite different approaches to the contiguous parcel issue. The Murrs, ably represented by the Pacific Law Foundation (a property rights advocacy group), advocated a rebuttable presumption that diminution in value should be measured in terms of the single lot in question.[80] The burden of proof would be on the government to show instead why "in a particular case, fairness and justice are better achieved by segmentation or aggregation of parcels."[81]

The state of Wisconsin agreed that a clear rule governing the denominator was needed, "[g]iven that regulatory takings analysis already lacks sufficient clarity."[82] The state argued that such clarity could be found by simply following the definition of the relevant property supplied by state law, which in Wisconsin included a merger rule consolidating commonly owned, adjoining tracts when neither lot is separately buildable.[83]

St. Croix County, where the land was located, was separately represented in the Supreme Court by Professor Richard Lazarus of Harvard Law School.[84] Lazarus argued for a multifactor test, involving lot lines, contiguity, ownership history, unity of use, and rules of state law.[85] Lazarus also argued that, regardless of how the denominator

---

son for the synergy is that one lot had more buildable land but the other had more beachfront. Id. As one of the amicus briefs points out, the state's regulation of development along the river probably increased the value of the Murrs' land under all of these scenarios, compared with a situation where greater development resulted in greater water pollution or robbed the view of its aesthetic appeal. See Brief of Carlisle Ford et al as Amici Curiae in Support of Respondents, *Murr v State of Wisconsin* (No 15-214), online at 2016 WL 3398639.

[79] Petition for Certiorari, *Murr v State of Wisconsin* (No 15-214), online at 2015 WL 4932231.

[80] Petitioners' Brief on the Merits, *Murr v State of Wisconsin* (No 15-214) at *12, online at 2016 WL 1459199.

[81] Id.

[82] Brief for Respondent State of Wisconsin, *Murr v State of Wisconsin* (No 15-214) at *35, online at 2016 WL 3227033.

[83] Id at *37–38.

[84] Brief for Respondent St. Croix County, *Murr v State of Wisconsin* (No 15-214), online at 2016 WL 1579483.

[85] Id at *23–24.

was defined, the economic loss to the Murrs was too slight to support a takings claim.[86] He pointed out that lot lines are relatively malleable under Wisconsin law, making them a poor basis for determining the fairness of a government action.[87]

There was also a flurry of amicus briefs, some of which deserve special mention. The United States took a position similar to the county's, but organized the relevant factors into three categories—the geography of the property, its history, and the timing of an owner's acquisition compared with that of the regulation's passage.[88] Libertarian organizations filed briefs reaching varying conclusions. Going further than the Murrs themselves, the Cato Institute argued for a bright-line rule against ever aggregating lots.[89] It argued that the *Penn Central* test had produced a complete mess under which aggrieved owners were almost certain to lose.[90] Allowing aggregation would further muddle the law and make it all the more difficult for mistreated landowners to recover.[91] The Reason Foundation took a similar position to the Murrs, arguing for an ad hoc inquiry with heavy weight given to lot boundaries, subject to revision if the lots are integrated in terms of use or investment plans.[92]

C. THE COURT TACKLES THE DENOMINATOR PROBLEM

In an area as contentious as takings law, it was no surprise that the Court was closely divided or that Justice Kennedy was the swing voter. We begin with Kennedy's majority opinion before turning to the view of the dissenters.

---

[86] Id at *24.

[87] Id at *29.

[88] Brief of the United States as Amicus Curiae Supporting Respondents, *Murr v State of Wisconsin* (No 15-214) at *12–13, online at 2016 WL 3398637.

[89] Brief of the Cato Institute and Owners' Counsel of America as Amici Curiae in Support of Petitioners, *Murr v State of Wisconsin* (No 15-214) at *4, online at 2016 WL 1639712. The complaint that the Takings Clause is muddled is widely shared, and not just by libertarians. See Eduardo Moisés Peñalver, *Regulatory Takings*, 104 Colum L Rev 2182, 2186 n 18 (2004) (citing multiple examples of this complaint).

[90] Cato Brief at *7–12 (cited in note 89).

[91] Id at *19–25.

[92] Brief for Reason Foundation as Amicus Curiae in Support of Petitioners, *Murr v State of Wisconsin* (No 15-214) *3–5, online at 2016 WL 1593411. If libertarian views did not prevail in *Murr*, it was not the fault of the Cato Institute or the Reason Foundation. Speaking as someone who does not share their libertarian perspective, I thought both briefs were excellent.

1. *The majority opinion.* Justice Kennedy's opinion for the Court in *Murr* rejects what he called the "formulaic" rules proposed by the state and the Murrs.[93] By relying exclusively on state law, including the challenged regulation, to define the property, the state might simply "define the relevant parcel in a way that permits it to escape its responsibility to justify regulation in light of legitimate property expectations."[94]

On the other hand, Kennedy said, the Murrs' approach gave too much credence to lot lines, ignoring "the fact that lot lines are themselves creatures of state law, which can be overridden by the State in the reasonable exercise of its power."[95] The merger provision in *Murr* was just such a reasonable exercise of government power: the "merger provision here is likewise a legitimate exercise of government power, as reflected by its consistency with a long history of state and local merger regulations that originated nearly a century ago."[96] Adopting the Murrs' proposed approach "would frustrate municipalities' ability to implement minimum lot size provisions by casting doubt on the many merger provisions that exist nationwide today."[97] Finally, rules regarding lot lines vary between states, making a uniform approach inappropriate.[98]

Rather than what he considered to be these overly rigid approaches, Justice Kennedy articulated a three-factor test for determining the denominator: "the treatment of the land under state and local law, the

---

[93] *Murr*, 137 S Ct at 1946.

[94] Id.

[95] Id at 1947.

[96] Id. The history and prevalence of this practice was documented in an amicus brief. See Brief of Amici Curiae National Association of Counties et al, in *Murr v State of Wisconsin* (No 15-314), online at http://www.scotusblog.com/wp-content/uploads/2016/06/15-214-bsac-National-Association-of-Counties.pdf. As the brief pointed out, "with just a few minutes of research, one can find many periodicals and web pages explaining that the purchaser of a vacant noncomforming lot should be careful to ascertain whether the lot is governed by a merger provision," citing five sources available online.

As it turns out, even a cursory online search would be enough to alert the searcher to merger doctrine. When I googled "purchase of vacant nonconforming lot," the top page of search results contained several mentions of grandfathering and merger either in the name of the source or the brief description displayed on the search page. The source at the top of the list was Kathleen Deegan Dickson, *The Law of Merger*, NY Real Estate J (Nov 11, 2014), online at https://www.forchellilaw.com/nyrej_Nov_KDD_Law%20of%20Merger.pdf. The opening sentence of this post was: "Take caution when purchasing a vacant parcel of land or purchasing a parcel adjacent to one already owned, as the possibility of the merger of lots is a real danger." Id.

[97] *Murr*, 137 S Ct at 1947–48.

[98] Id at 1948.

physical characteristics of the land, and the prospective value of the regulated land"—all with the purpose of determining "whether reasonable expectations about property ownership would lead a landowner to anticipate that his holdings would be treated as one parcel, or, instead, as separate tracts," based on "background customs and the whole of our legal tradition."[99] Kennedy expressed confidence in the ability of lower courts to apply this somewhat amorphous approach, given their "considerable expertise in adjudicating regulatory takings claims."[100]

In elaborating on this test, Justice Kennedy made some notable points that seem to have broader implications for takings law. Regarding the first factor (state law treatment), he said "a use restriction which is triggered only after, or because of, a change in ownership should also guide a court's assessment of reasonable private expectations."[101] This comment is a bit cryptic, since it does not specify whether this should count in favor of or against the validity of the restriction. But in his later discussion of the application of the test, he clearly viewed this factor as undermining the takings claim. In dismissing the argument that the two parcels should be considered separate, he said that "[p]etitioners' land was subject to this regulatory burden, moreover, only because of voluntary conduct in bringing the lots under common ownership after the regulation was enacted."[102]

In terms of the second factor (geography), Kennedy had in mind more than the contiguous nature of the lots or even whether the legal boundary corresponded to some physical feature such as a ravine. Instead, he spoke more broadly of the "physical relationship of any distinguishable tracts, the parcel's topography, and the surrounding human and ecological environment."[103] He emphasized the possibility that "the property is located in an area that is subject to, or likely to become subject to, environmental or other regulation."[104] Thus,

---

[99] Id at 1945.

[100] Id at 1946. There is a reasonable argument that state courts, in particular, are better suited to reviewing land use decisions than the Supreme Court. See Stewart Sterk, *The Federalism Dimension of Takings Jurisprudence*, 114 Yale L J 203, 226–28 (2004). Sterk argued that the dependence of taking claims on the specific details of state law limits the utility of Supreme Court interventions. Id at 226.

[101] *Murr*, 137 S Ct at 1945.

[102] Id at 1948.

[103] Id at 1946.

[104] Id.

in considering the Murrs' lots later in the opinion, he observed that they "could have anticipated public regulation might affect their enjoyment of the property, as the Lower St. Croix was a regulated area under federal, state, and local law long before petitioners possessed the land."[105]

The third factor involves the economic relationship between lots. Diminution in value for one lot "may be tempered if the regulated land adds value to the remaining property, such as by increasing privacy, expanding recreational space, or preserving surrounding natural beauty."[106] For instance, Kennedy says, the market value of the owner's other properties "may well increase . . . if development restraints for one part of the parcel protect the unobstructed skyline views of another part."[107] The Court found this factor particularly easy to apply in the *Murr* case, because the Murrs' loss was "mitigated by the benefits of using the property as an integrated whole, allowing increased privacy and recreational space, plus the optimal location of any improvements."[108] The "special relationship of the lots" was confirmed by the valuation figures, showing that the combined lots are valued far more than "the summed value of the separate regulated lots."[109] While the regulation may have left Lot E with little independent value since it could not be developed separately, merging the lots added considerably to the value that Lot F would have had on its own.[110]

Having concluded that the two lots should be considered as a single unit for takings purposes, Justice Kennedy briskly disposed of the merits of the takings claims. The total taking rule did not apply because of the substantial value of the combined lots.[111] The *Penn Central* test for partial takings cases was also easily satisfied. The appraisal "refutes any claim that the economic impact of the regulation is severe."[112] Furthermore, the Murrs "cannot claim that they reasonably

---

[105] Id at 1948.

[106] Id at 1946.

[107] Id.

[108] Id at 1948.

[109] Id at 1949.

[110] Id.

[111] Id. Stewart Sterk suggests that this reasoning may "signal the beginning of the end for the per se rule invalidating regulations that deny landowners all economically productive use of their land." Stewart E. Sterk, *Dueling Denominators and the Demise of* Lucas *2 (2017), online at https://ssrn.com/abstract=3024093.

[112] Id.

expected to sell or develop their lots separately given the regulations which predated their acquisition of both lots."[113] And, finally, "the government action was a reasonable land use regulation, enacted as part of a coordinated federal, state, and local effort to preserve the river and surrounding land."[114]

2. *The Roberts dissent.* Chief Justice Roberts wrote the primary dissent, which was joined by Justices Alito and Thomas.[115] (The recently appointed Justice Gorsuch did not participate in the case.)[116] Roberts faulted the majority for deviation from "our traditional approach" that state laws defining property boundaries determine the denominator.[117] Roberts cited with approval the *Penn Central* approach of barring landowners from singling out a specific "stick" within the bundle of property rights as the denominator.[118] By the same token, he said, "in all but the most exceptional circumstances," state laws defining the boundaries of a parcel should determine the relevant unit to be considered in takings cases.[119]

I will return later to other aspects of the Roberts dissent and a briefer dissent by Justice Thomas, but the Chief Justice's discussion of the denominator issue deserves attention here. He is clearly correct that the test articulated by the majority for determining the denominator overlaps with the *Penn Central* test for deciding whether the diminution of property is excessive. Roberts is also right that giving the state government the power to define the denominator opens the door to strategic behavior by states and would weaken takings claims in many situations. But in cases like *Murr*, where the challenged regulation effectively merges lots into a single whole, it is hard to see how the definition of the denominator can avoid considering the legitimacy of the state's merger rule, which necessarily overlaps with the test for whether a taking has actually occurred.

Moreover, the assumption that the denominator must automatically coincide with the parcel subject to the regulation overlooks ambiguities in how a state defines parcels and, more importantly, the

---

[113] Id.

[114] Id at 1949–50.

[115] Id at 1950 (Roberts, CJ, dissenting).

[116] Id.

[117] Id.

[118] Id at 1952.

[119] Id at 1953.

purpose of the inquiry. The Court is not, after all, acting as a tax assessor or issuing title insurance. Rather, it is attempting to determine whether it is unfair to leave the owner uncompensated; the denominator is merely a step in that fairness analysis. There is no reason why the determination of the denominator should not reflect the same concern with fairness as the test for determining a taking. While it is true that state law defines the scope of an owner's property rights, determining what set of rights should enter into the takings denominator is a question of federal law. So too is the question of how to measure the value of the relevant property rights after the regulation. Federal law might simply adopt the market value of ownership of the whole parcel as a way of answering both questions, but that is quite distinct from the state law issue of how the regulation modifies the owner's preexisting ownership rights.

One aspect of *Penn Central* that carries into the *Murr* denominator test is circularity, in which the body of existing regulations shapes expectations, thereby saving future regulations from takings challenges.[120] Kennedy seems to maintain a gap between expectations and current state law by indicating that the extent of notice to landowners and their ability to adjust their investments are relevant factors. Thus, the relevant investment expectations may lag changes in state law. The upshot is that abrupt changes, especially when recent, are more likely to be vulnerable to challenge than more evolutionary or venerable ones. We will return to that timing issue later.

II. MURR AND OTHER TAKINGS PUZZLES

The primary focus of the *Murr* litigation was the denominator problem. But because Justice Kennedy not only determined the denominator but also considered the merits of the takings claim, he had to decide two other doctrinal issues (the numerator and timing issues) and touch on a third (the relevance of the state's regulatory interest). The rulings on all three were favorable to the government. This section considers those issues in turn.

---

[120] Eagle, 118 Penn State L Rev at 604 (cited in note 11). As one disgruntled conservative judge complained: "except for a regulation of almost unimaginable abruptness, all regulation will build on prior regulation and hence be said to defeat any expectations. Thus regulation begets regulation." *Dist. Intown Props ITD v District of Columbia*, 198 F3d 874, 887 (DC Cir 1999) (Williams concurring). Speaking of *Penn Central* more generally, Judge Williams also complained that "[f]ew regulations will flunk this nearly vacuous test." Id at 886.

A. THE NUMERATOR PROBLEM

Although the denominator of the takings "fraction" has gotten the most attention, it can also be problematic to identify the numerator for use in determining diminution of value. The problem is that, although the specific property interest subject to regulation might be impaired, this impairment could be offset by other gains. This might happen if the regulation grants the owner an additional property interest or because the owner's other holdings gain value.

Penn Central provides the default test for takings, applicable in the absence of a physical intrusion or a total taking. The case is also significant, however, because it required the Court to consider the extent that benefits outside the affected parcel might be used to offset losses. The Court pointed out that, to the extent the owner of the train station had been denied the right to build above a certain level, "it is not literally accurate to say that they had been denied *all* use of those pre-existing air rights."[121] The ability "to use these rights has not been abrogated; they are made transferable to at least eight parcels in the vicinity," and "the rights afforded are valuable."[122] Thus, "[w]hile those rights may well not have constituted 'just compensation' if a 'taking' had occurred, the rights nevertheless undoubtedly mitigate whatever financial burdens the law has imposed on appellants," and, the Court added, "for that reason, [these transferrable development rights] are to be taken into account in considering the impact of regulation."[123] Thus, the grant of transferrable development rights (TDRs) weighs against finding that a development restriction "takes" private property. In effect, the TDRs were included in the numerator of the takings fraction.

The significance of *Penn Central*'s treatment of TDRs has not been lost on property rights advocates. Justice Scalia called for overruling this aspect of *Penn Central* or limiting it to its facts (involving the owner of contiguous parcels). In his view, transferrable rights are "a clever, albeit transparent, device" that could "render much of our regulatory takings jurisprudence a nullity."[124] Justice Scalia's critique of

---

[121] *Penn Central* at 137.

[122] Id.

[123] Id.

[124] Id at 750.

Penn Central seems misguided, given that TDRs do have legal and economic substance. But the Scalia critique does not seem to have been successful. As a disgruntled commentator conceded, most courts today have "considered TDRs as an economic use existing with the land, thus mitigating the effects of regulation."[125]

In its amicus brief in *Murr*, the federal government cited this part of the *Penn Central* holding[126] and argued that it required taking into account the benefits to the owners of merging the lots in *Murr*: "[a]ny analytically coherent attempt to value what the petitioners have lost in being unable to separately sell or develop Lot E must therefore also account for what they have gained by merging their land into one larger parcel."[127] The government also cited language from *Keystone* indicating that, even if the coal pillar required by the support requirement were considered to be the denominator, the other coal of the owners would be taken into account in determining the economic effect on the owner (the numerator of the takings fraction).[128]

It is unsurprising that the majority opinion included in the numerator the value of utilizing the two lots together, given that it had defined the denominator to include both lots. What is somewhat more surprising is the openness of the dissenters to doing so. In the opening paragraph of the Roberts dissent, he remarks that the majority's rejection of the Murrs' taking claim "does not trouble me; the majority presents a fair case that the Murrs can still make good use of both lots."[129] Then, at the end of the opinion, he mentions that many of the facts relied on by the majority would be relevant to a takings analysis, including that Lot E could still be used "as 'recreational space,' as 'the location for any improvements' [on the combined lots], and as a valuable addition to Lot F."[130] These facts, he says, "could be relevant to whether the 'regulation denies all economically beneficial or productive use' of Lot E."[131]

---

[125] Arthur J. Miller, *Transferable Development Rights in the Constitutional Landscape: Has Penn Central Failed to Weather the Storm?*, 39 Nat Res J 459, 491 (1999).

[126] Amicus Brief of the United States, *30–31 (cited in note 88).

[127] Id at *13.

[128] Id at *24 n 3 (citing *Keystone*, 480 US at 501).

[129] *Murr*, 137 S Ct at 1950.

[130] Id at 1957.

[131] Id.

Roberts seemed to be quite open to considering the synergy between the two property interests in determining the effect of the regulation. In effect, he seemingly countenanced including the regulated lot's enhancement of the adjoining lot's value in the numerator of the takings fraction. If so, his dissent seems to lose much of its practical significance. If there are synergies between the properties, the numerator will increase even under the Roberts approach, making the diminution in value about the same as if both properties were in the denominator.[132] In *Murr* itself, the diminution in value would be 20 percent under the Roberts approach rather than 10 percent under Kennedy's approach, still light years away from the 100 percent loss triggering the *Lucas* "total taking" rule.[133]

Perhaps Roberts would respond to this point by rethinking the issue and excluding from the numerator Lot E's value to someone who also happens to own Lot F. But the federal government's brief seems right about the irrationality of that approach. An economically rational owner of Lot F would be unwilling to sell Lot E for anything under $325,000, the amount by which the value of the owner's combined holdings would be reduced by selling Lot E. To say that Lot E is worth only $40,000 to the Murrs under these circumstances seems completely out of touch with economic reality.[134]

---

[132] For readers who are interested, here's the arithmetic based on *Murr* itself. Recall that, according to the government's appraiser, Lot F is worth $373,000 alone but that the value of being able to build on the combined lots is $698,000. The value of separately developing both lots is $771,000, so the owner has lost the difference, or $73,000, because only combined development is allowed. So if, like Kennedy, we include both lots in the numerator and the denominator, the diminution in value thus is $73,000/$771,000, or about 10 percent. Suppose instead that we include Lot E alone in the denominator, as Roberts advocated. Without the regulation, if it were separately developable, Lot E would apparently be worth $398,000, which would be the denominator. Under Roberts's approach, the numerator is $325,000, the difference between owning only Lot F and owning both lots. (I derived this value by subtracting the separately developed value of Lot F ($373,000) from $698,000, the value of developing the two lots jointly.) Decreasing the denominator makes the diminution of value somewhat larger: with the Murrs retaining $325,000/$398,000, or slightly over 80 percent of the value of a separately developable Lot E.

[133] One way of seeing this is to ask what a rational owner would be willing to accept as a lot E, given the fact that the value of lot F by itself was $325,000 less than the value of holding both lots. The $73,000 is then the difference between their asking price and the value a buyer would be willing to pay for Lot F ($398,000).

[134] Indeed, even if the two lots were in separate hands, the owner of Lot F would be willing to pay up to $325,000 to acquire Lot E in an arms-length transaction. The Murrs' appraiser put a $40,000 value on Lot E, considered in isolation from Lot F, so the parties would have a huge range of bargaining outcomes that would leave them both better off. If they were to split the difference, Lot E would sell for about $182,000. A map suggests that there is another privately owned lot on the other side of Lot E from Lot F. App *28. The possibility of selling to that owner

Thus, it is hard to see how the "total loss" rule could ever apply on any reasonable interpretation of the facts. The most that can be said is that, if Roberts's view on the denominator issue were accepted, the Murrs might have a marginally stronger *Penn Central* claim (retaining only 80 percent rather than 90 percent of the original property value).

Perhaps Roberts is right that this would be a tidier method of analysis, but it seems unlikely to make a difference to whether a taking is actually found. There could conceivably be other cases where this difference would change the outcome, but even the Roberts approach makes it considerably more difficult for a court to find that the owner of contiguous lots had suffered a total taking of one of them. And given the vagueness of the *Penn Central* test, whatever nuanced differences exist between the two approaches seem well inside the test's margin of error anyway.

B. MURR AND THE TIMING PROBLEM

The argument for finding a taking seems stronger when a new regulation unexpectedly impairs an existing investment. But the timing may be different, with the regulation either predating the investment or at least being clearly on the horizon then. How, if at all, should the timing of the regulation vis-à-vis acquisition of the land affect a takings claim? *Murr* also addresses this issue.

The leading authority on this timing issue is *Palazzolo v Rhode Island*.[135] The Palazzolos and others had formed a company to develop land located on the edge of a pond and across the street from dunes and beachfront homes.[136] Palazzolo bought out the other owners and became the direct owner when the corporation was dissolved for failure to pay taxes.[137] Well before the dissolution of the company, however, the state had passed extensive regulation protecting salt mar-

---

might improve the bargaining position of the owner of Lot E vis-à-vis the owner of Lot F if the two lots were owned separately. Of course, the bargain could well be lower, depending on which side had the most willingness to hold out, but it seems clear that Lot E remained a valuable piece of property despite the ordinance and regardless of whether it was held by the owner of Lot F.

[135] 533 US 606 (2001). Although our focus is on the timing issue, *Palazzolo* also rejected the argument made by amici that *Lucas* applies whenever a regulation eliminates any economically viable use of any portion of a piece of property. See Lazarus, 57 Hastings L J at 816 (cited in note 4).

[136] *Palazzolo*, 533 US at 613.

[137] Id at 614.

shes like those on the property from development.[138] Thus, the timing was: (1) Palazzolo made his investments via a corporation, (2) the regulations were enacted, and (3) Palazzolo then acquired title in his own name. The state courts rejected Palazzolo's takings claim, holding that it was necessarily barred because he acquired title after the regulation was in effect.[139]

In an opinion by Justice Kennedy, the Court rejected the state court's per se rule barring a subsequent owner from bringing a takings claim. The Court's strongest argument was that such a rule would sometimes mean no one would ever be in a position to challenge an unconstitutional land regulation. Under ripeness doctrine, an owner cannot bring a takings claim without making a development proposal and having it rejected, which might not happen until the property has changed hands.[140] The Court had "no occasion to consider the precise circumstances when a legislative enactment can be deemed a background principle of state law or whether those circumstances are present here."[141] Rather, it "suffic[ed] to say that a regulation that otherwise would be unconstitutional absent compensation is not transformed into a background principle of the State's law by mere virtue of the passage of time."[142] Thus, "[t]he 'investment-backed expectations' that the law will take into account do not include the assumed validity of a restriction that in fact deprives property of so much of its value as to be unconstitutional."[143]

The concurring opinions debated just how such timing issues should be resolved. Justice Scalia argued that, unless an existing law qualified as a background principle of state law, "the fact that a restriction existed at the time the purchaser took title . . . should have no bearing upon the determination of whether the restriction is so substantial as to constitute a taking."[144] Justice Scalia did not provide any guidance as to how to distinguish between an ordinary rule of law and a background principle. Perhaps, by background principle, he meant a long-standing common law rule, as he seemed to have had in mind in *Lucas*.

---

[138] Id.

[139] Id at 616.

[140] Id at 628.

[141] Id at 629.

[142] Id at 630.

[143] Id.

[144] Id at 373 (Scalia, J).

Yet it surely would seem odd to say that the background principle of water law in some western state is the common law doctrine of riparian rights, even though those rights were replaced over a century ago by a statutory system of water rights, prior appropriation.[145]

Justice O'Connor rejected Scalia's position, stating that "[t]oday's holding does not mean that the timing of the regulation's enactment relative to the acquisition of title is immaterial to the *Penn Central* analysis."[146] "Indeed," she added, "it would be just as much error to expunge this consideration from the takings inquiry as it would be to accord it exclusive significance."[147] Under *Penn Central*, which she said remained the "polestar," a "regulation regime in place at the time the claimant acquires the property at issue helps to shape the reasonableness of those expectations."[148] For "if existing regulations do nothing to inform the analysis, then some property owners may reap windfalls and an important indicia of fairness is lost."[149]

Palazzolo settled one point regarding timing: the fact that property acquisition occurred after a regulation went into effect does not automatically bar a takings claim. But it left open the question whether the timing of the regulation is ever relevant to determining reasonable expectations, as O'Connor thought and Scalia disputed. The theory behind Kennedy's *Palazzolo* opinion was also a bit ambiguous as to whether the current owner's rights are derivative of the prior owner's possible takings claim or whether it is independent. That might matter in situations where the acquisition or other changed circumstances bring the challenged regulation into play or change its practical impact—as in *Murr*, where the exception to the grandfather clause for

---

[145] See Michael C. Blumm and J. B. Ruhl, *Background Principles, Takings, and Libertarian Property: A Reply to Professor Huffman*, 37 Ecol L Q 805, 812 n 27 (2010). Blumm and Ruhl point out that there was a similar switch in the east, from the natural flow doctrine to riparian rights. Id. There have been other changes as well, such as the American abandonment of the English doctrine that improvements on leased land were for the benefit of the landlord, and a contraction of the rights of neighboring landowners under nuisance doctrine. Id at 812, 816. The nineteenth-century expansion of the public trust doctrine from tidelands to other navigable waters could be considered another example. Id at 833. Sax points to other examples of changes in property law, such as limiting rights of dower and curtesy to expand testator freedom and abolishing husbands' property rights in their wives' estates a century before sex discrimination was recognized as a constitutional issue. See Joseph L. Sax, *Property Rights and the Economy of Nature: Understanding Lucas v. South Carolina Coastal Council*, 45 Stan L Rev 1411, 1448 (1993).

[146] *Palazzolo*, 533 US at 633 (O'Connor, J).

[147] Id.

[148] Id.

[149] Id at 635.

adjoining properties was not triggered until the Murr children acquired Lot E after already owning Lot F, which meant that the previous owners had never been subject to the exception themselves.

The parties were well aware of the timing question in *Murr*, and the briefs teed up the issue for the Court. St. Croix County argued that "the distinct treatment of commonly owned, adjacent substandard lots [as effectively merged] is so longstanding and widespread as to be fairly considered part of what Justice Kennedy has described as 'the whole of our legal tradition' upon which 'reasonable expectations must be understood' in defining property rights in land."[150] Thus, the county maintained, "anyone remotely knowledgeable about land use law, including realtors, mortgagees, title companies, builders, and local counsel, knows the implications of owning adjacent, substandard lots."[151]

Similarly, the state argued that "[w]hen Petitioners obtained title to Lot E in 1995, they were 'charged with knowledge' that the Lot was subject to a preexisting merger provision that would trigger if Lot E was brought into common ownership with a contiguous substandard lot."[152] The state read *Palazzolo* narrowly as making the later owner's claim dependent on whether the owners would have had a valid claim if they had been able to get into court when the regulation was passed.[153] Since the previous owners in this case (the Murrs' parents) owned only Lot E in 1976, their only loss was an inability to convey the property without threat of merger to someone who already owned an adjoining lot.[154] The state's view was that only *that* claim of the parents could be brought by the Murrs today.

The Murrs' reply brief took a sharply opposing position. In their view, as in Scalia's, a regulation that is challenged under the Takings Clause can never be considered relevant to determining the owner's reasonable expectations.[155] Among other things, they also quoted language from *Palazzolo* that "[f]uture generations, too, have a right to challenge unreasonable limitations on the use and value of land."[156]

---

[150] St. Croix brief *22 (cited in note 84).

[151] Id at *43.

[152] State brief *36–37 (cited in note 82).

[153] Id at *42.

[154] Id.

[155] Petitioners' Reply Brief, *Murr v State of Wisconsin* (No 15-214), online at 2016 WL 4072806.

[156] Id at *13.

Thus, the Murrs argued, "[u]nder this precedent, the Murr siblings have the same right to seek compensation under the Takings Clause as their parents," given that "the transfer of title from the parents to the children vests the same property interest as was held by the parents."[157] In other words, since a new regulation cannot determine expectations at the time of earlier investments, it remains equally irrelevant no matter how much time goes by or who acquires the property in the meantime.

The Court's opinion clearly rejects the theory that the challenged regulation itself can never become relevant to determining owner expectations. Justice Kennedy observed that the Murrs "could have anticipated public regulation might affect their enjoyment of the property, as the Lower St. Croix was a regulated area under federal, state, and local law long before petitioners possessed the land."[158] While "[a] valid takings claim will not evaporate just because a purchaser took title after the law was enacted," nevertheless "[a] reasonable restriction that predates a landowner's acquisition . . . can be one of the objective factors that most landowners would reasonably consider in forming fair expectations about their property."[159] As noted earlier, the opinion also notes that the merger rule applied only because of the petitioner's voluntary conduct in bringing the land into common ownership after the restriction came into effect. "As a result," Kennedy added, "the valid merger of the lots under state law informs the reasonable expectation they will be treated as a single property."[160]

As with the numerator problem, the Roberts dissent takes only a modestly different course. He notes that the majority relies in part on the fact that the Murrs "could have predicted Lot E would be regulated."[161] This is another fact that he says "could be relevant" to the merits of the takings claim because it would "speak to . . . interference with 'investment-backed expectations.'"[162] While this statement is sufficiently equivocal that the dissenters could justify abandoning it in a later case, it does suggest a lack of much distance between the dissenters and the majority on this issue. There seems little reason to

---

[157] Id.
[158] *Murr*, 137 S Ct at 1948.
[159] Id at 1945.
[160] Id at 1948.
[161] Id at 1957.
[162] Id.

think that the dissenters will support overruling the majority's holding on the timing issue and reverting to Scalia's view.

C. A NOTE ON REGULATORY JUSTIFICATIONS

Even Professor Richard Epstein, arguably the founder of the modern property rights movement, concedes the need for regulation when
the risk level is sufficiently high, as in the 2014 Oso mudslide in
Washington State. As the *New York Times* reported:

> Another prominent libertarian legal thinker, Richard A. Epstein of the
> University of Chicago Law School, said that the case of Oso should be
> simple, however, because of its history of landslides. "The case is a no-
> brainer in favor of extensive government regulation in order to protect
> against imminent perils to life and health," he said. "I'm a property guy, but
> I'm not a madman."[163]

Although it seems clear that regulatory interests are relevant at
some level, the Court has had a great deal of trouble in defining that
role. Justice Scalia's opinion in *Lucas v South Carolina Coastal Commission* argued that only a narrow range of government interests could
be considered in a total takings case. Lucas had purchased two resi-
dential lots on an island in 1986.[164] Two years later, the state had passed
a beachfront management act, which prohibited new construction on
the island because it was in a high-erosion zone.[165] Relying primarily
on dicta in preceding cases, the Court held that "when the owner of
real property has been called upon to sacrifice *all* economically beneficial uses in the name of the common good, that is, to leave his
property economically idle, he has suffered a taking."[166] Thus, while
an owner deprived of 95 percent of the property's use might sometimes
recover nothing, the owner deprived of 100 percent would recover
completely, due to the bright-line nature of the rule.[167] In a footnote,

---

[163] John Schwartz, *No Easy Way to Restrict Construction in Risky Areas*, NY Times (March 28, 2014), online at http://www.nytimes.com/2014/03/29/us/governments-find-it-hard-to-restrict-building-in-risky-areas.html?hpw&rref=us&_r=0. Epstein's libertarian vision of takings law as an instrument to eliminate government regulation is extensively articulated in many writings, including Epstein, 11 NYU L Rev at 883–908 (cited in note 3). Epstein is "widely considered the intellectual fountainhead of the property rights movement." Lazarus, 57 Hastings L J at 799 (cited in note 4).

[164] 505 US 1006.

[165] Id at 1008 & n 1.

[166] Id at 1019.

[167] Id at 1019–20 n 8. *Lucas* was the first time in seventy years that the Court had found a land use rule to be an unconstitutional taking. See Lazarus, 57 Hastings L J at 785 (cited in note 4).

however, Justice Scalia conceded that "[r]egrettably, the rhetorical force of our . . . rule is greater than its precision, since the rule does not make clear the 'property interest' against which the loss of value is to be measured."[168] Thus, what we have called the denominator problem reared its head explicitly for the first time in a footnote, though it had been implicit in takings law since *Pennsylvania Coal*.

Lucas was based on dicta in previous cases,[169] but Justice Scalia marshaled several justifications on behalf of the rule in addition to its long-standing articulation. First, he said, a complete loss of value made it less likely that the rule was simply a matter of the legislature adjusting economic burdens and benefits in a way that on average benefited everyone concerned.[170] Second, total-loss cases were rare enough that requiring compensation would not be a major incursion into the government's ability to function.[171] Third, the fact that a regulation left the owner with no economically viable use of land heightened the risk that the regulation was a disguised condemnation of the property for public benefit.[172]

Announcing the total taking rule did not, however, completely dispose of the case, given that earlier cases had upheld the power of the government to severely regulate property to protect the public.[173] Scalia rejected any distinction between affirmative mandates to provide public benefits and negative restrictions on harmful conduct, though that distinction was articulated by the earlier cases.[174] Instead, he argued that regulations eliminating all economic uses can be upheld only if they "do no more than duplicate the result that could have been achieved in the courts—by adjacent landowners (or other uniquely affected persons) under the State's law of private nuisance, or by the State under its complementary power to abate nuisances that affect the public generally, or otherwise."[175] Scalia gave as two exam-

---

[168] Id at 1016 n 7.

[169] Id at 1015–16.

[170] Id at 1017.

[171] Id at 1018. Of course, the same argument would apply to any rule awarding compensation to any small class of cases, however arbitrarily defined.

[172] Id. Justice Scalia of course provides no support for this empirical assertion. It may be equally likely that such decreases in value occur only in cases where development would be particularly harmful.

[173] Id at 1022.

[174] Id at 1022–24.

[175] Id at 1029. According to Fischel, *Regulatory Takings* at 185 (cited in note 40), William Penn reserved the right to take up to 6 percent of his grantees' land for road-building purposes; the

ples the denial of a permit to engage in landfilling that would flood the lands of neighbors and an order to remove a nuclear plant that is discovered to sit on an earthquake fault.[176] In a concurring opinion, Justice Kennedy argued that Scalia was wrong to limit the permissible justifications to common law doctrines rather than allowing consideration of how statutes might shape reasonable expectations.[177]

The *Lucas* opinion attracted great controversy.[178] But it does at least suggest that background rules of state law, including nuisance law, act as carve-outs from the owner's property rights. State courts were not slow to extend this treatment to other common law rules such as the public trust doctrine. Indeed, in at least one way, *Lucas* weakened the owner's position under the *Penn Central* test. Conduct prohibited by common law nuisance doctrine or the public trust doctrine is now per se ineligible for the *Penn Central* test, because on Scalia's theory, it was never part of the owner's title in the first place. Thus, at least in some cases, state interests embedded in common law doctrines trumped claims of reasonable investment-backed expectations without need for further inquiry.[179]

The role of governmental interests in the takings inquiry has remained unclear in other respects. Dicta predating *Lucas* by a couple of years suggested that one relevant factor was whether a regulation substantially advanced legitimate state interests.[180] In 2005, however, the Court rejected that formulation in *Lingle v Chevron U.S.A.*,[181]

Lucas argument would presumably apply to such a reservation since it was part of the owner's title.

[176] Id.

[177] Id at 1035.

[178] For an incisive critique of *Lucas*, see Sax, 45 Stan L Rev at 1411 (cited in note 145). One of Sax's observations that is especially relevant to this article relates to the evolution of doctrine:

> Of course, predicting future Supreme Court outcomes based on past performance is an uncertain enterprise. The Court is not monolithic; its views change along with its membership. Less obvious, but as important, the Court's views shift as its assumptions regarding the world around it change.

Id at 1431.

[179] Nicole Steele Garnett criticizes *Murr* for "import[ing] public policy considerations into the definition of private property itself." Garnett, 2016–17 Cato Sup Ct Rev at 148 (cited in note 5). But *Lucas* itself did that by making nuisance law a carve-out from the owner's title, given the connection between nuisance law and public policy (particularly in terms of public nuisances).

[180] *Agins v City of Tiburon*, 447 US 255, 260 (1980).

[181] 544 US 528 (2005).

a takings challenge to a rent-control law protecting gas station owners. *Lingle* seemed to downplay any role for regulatory justifications in the takings analysis: "The owner of a property subject to a regulation that *effectively* serves a legitimate state interest may be just as singled out and just as burdened as the owner of a property subject to an *ineffective* regulation."[182] Likewise, the Court continued, "an ineffective regulation may not significantly burden property rights at all, and it may distribute any burden broadly and evenly among property owners."[183]

The primary focus in *Murr* was not on the state's justifications for protecting lands on the St. Croix River. Everyone in the case, even the Murrs, seemed to take those for granted. But Justice Kennedy did indicate that the state's interests were relevant to takings claims. In listing the factors to be considered, he pointed particularly to the possibility that "the property is located in an area that is subject to, or likely to become subject to, environmental or other regulation."[184] He cited his own *Lucas* concurrence, quoting a statement that "[c]oastal property may present such unique concerns for a fragile land system that the State can go further in regulating its development and use than the common law of nuisance might otherwise permit."[185] Thus, it would seem, if the state is pursuing an important goal such as protection of fragile lands, it is more reasonable for property owners to expect regulation and to adjust their "investment-based expectations" accordingly, even when the regulation does not track background principles of state law.

III. Taking Stock of Takings Law

Murr's greatest doctrinal significance was for the denominator problem. But as we have seen, it also had something significant to say about a number of the other issues presented in takings cases. Before we try to think about the larger implications of the decision, it

---

[182] Id at 543.

[183] Id. Other language in *Lingle* suggests that regulatory takings should include only actions functionally equivalent to takings. Id at 539. This standard seems more restrictive than *Penn Central*, but the Court does not seem to have taken notice of the inconsistency. See Andrew W. Schwartz, *No Competing Theory of Constitutional Interpretation Justifies Regulatory Takings Ideology*, 34 Stan Envir L J 247, 286–87 (2015).

[184] *Lingle*, 544 US at 543.

[185] Id at 1946 (quoting *Lucas*, 505 US at 1035).

may be helpful to pull together the doctrinal issues that *Murr* touches upon.

First and foremost, the Court established a multifactored test for the denominator issue, which governed whether adjoining lots should be considered in determining the value of the owner's preregulation holdings. This in itself was a significant defeat for property rights advocates.

The Court also resolved some related issues. It held that in determining the amount of value retained by the owner despite a regulation (the "numerator"), the property's value includes its synergies with the owner's other holdings. The majority found it relevant that the regulation protected an important government interest and that the regulation was in place long before the owners acquired the property. The dissenters seemed willing to entertain these views as well, though stopping short of a full-throated endorsement. Where the majority and dissent came fully together was endorsing the government-friendly *Penn Central* test, living up to an old criticism that the "Court seems to be inordinately proud of the ad hoc nature of its takings opinions."[186]

The overall import of *Murr* is to soften the edges of property rights as barriers to government regulation. This would not have been at all to Justice Scalia's liking, nor is it to the liking of property rights advocates today. We begin by looking at those implications of the decision, before considering its implications for future doctrinal evolution.

A. THE STALLED PROPERTY RIGHTS REVOLUTION

Murr represents a serious blow to efforts to build upon Justice Scalia's opinion in *Lucas*. *Murr*'s approach to the denominator issue obviously reduces the occasions on which an owner will be able to claim a total deprivation of value. Other aspects of *Murr* also help to limit *Lucas*. Justice Kennedy characterized the "nuisance exception" as broadly "recognizing the relevance of state law and land-use customs."[187] Moreover, in discussing the relevance of a property's ecological features, he cited his own *Lucas* concurrence, quoting a statement that "[c]oastal property may present such unique concerns for

---

[186] Susan Rose-Ackerman, *Against Ad Hocery: A Comment on Michelman*, 88 Colum L Rev 1697, 1699 (1988). Rose-Ackerman argues that "[t]he ad hoc nature of the law introduces an element of uncertainty into private investment decisions that could make the coexistence of democracy and private property more, rather than less, difficult." Id at 1702.

[187] *Murr*, 137 S Ct at 1943.

a fragile land system that the State can go further in regulating its development and use than the common law of nuisance might otherwise permit."[188]

During his time on the Court, Justice Scalia championed the cause of property owners. As Peter Byrne puts it, Scalia "advocated for them with characteristic rhetorical vigor that encouraged property rights advocates, terrified regulators and environmentalists, and enriched scholarly debate about constitutional property."[189] Byrne also correctly notes that Scalia "consistently adopted or argued for clear rules without any balancing of interests in his regulatory takings opinions," making sure that any rule "favors private property owners over public regulations."[190] The *Penn Central* test is the epitome of the kind of balancing that Scalia detested. Yet no Justice in *Murr* had a word of criticism of that test.

Murr also reflected a defeat for Justice Scalia's skepticism about the "whole parcel" rule, which was ignored even by the *Murr* dissenters. Instead, Roberts emphasized his support for the whole-parcel view. In Roberts's thinking, the parcel as a whole rule blocks the "strategic" use of individual property interests by owners as the basis of taking claims, which "would undermine the balance struck by our regulatory takings cases."[191] Thus, with the possible exception of Gorsuch, whose view is not yet known, every member of the current Court seems to have endorsed *Penn Central*'s approach, which rejects use of anything less than the whole parcel as the basis for takings claims.

This adherence to the "whole parcel" rule may or may not stick for individual Justices. Roberts, Thomas, and Alito joined a Scalia plurality opinion in *Stop the Beach Renourishment, Inc. v Florida Dept. of Env. Protection*[192] that would have struck out in another direction. The case involved a Florida law limiting the ability of littoral owners to access the sea directly across dry land.[193] The plurality held that a taking would exist whenever a state court eliminates an "established right of property," even if the state court's decision was foreshad-

---

[188] Id at 1946 (quoting *Lucas*, 505 US at 1035).

[189] See J. Peter Byrne, *A Hobbesian Bundle of Lockean Sticks: The Property Rights Legacy of Justice Scalia*, 41 Vt L Rev 741 (2017).

[190] Id at 743.

[191] *Murr*, 137 S Ct at 1954.

[192] 130 S Ct 2592 (2010).

[193] Id at 2598–99.

owed by prior state dicta or holdings.[194] But this plurality opinion was wholly dictum, since a majority of the Court agreed with the plurality that there was actually no established rule of state law establishing the property owners' claim and therefore no possible taking.[195] Whether any of the *Murr* dissenters would be willing to return to this approach in a future case is unclear. All we know is that seven years after *Stop the Beach Renourishment*, Chief Justice Roberts's dissent in *Murr* seemingly endorsed the whole parcel rule, with the support of Alito and Thomas.

Both the majority and the dissenters in *Murr* also seemed quite contented with the ad hoc nature of takings jurisprudence. Writing for the majority, Justice Kennedy observes that the Court has "for the most part refrained from . . . definitive rules" and instead has been prone to "ad hoc, factual inquiries, designed to allow careful examination and weighing of all the relevant circumstances."[196] Thus, he says, "[a] central dynamic of the Court's regulatory takings jurisprudence is its flexibility" as a way of balancing property rights with the public interest in regulating.[197] Chief Justice Roberts's dissent referred to the *Penn Central* test and, a paragraph later, stated that "[d]eciding whether a regulation has gone so far as to constitute a 'taking' of one of those property rights is, properly enough, a fact-intensive task that relies 'as much on the exercise of judgment as on the application of logic.'"[198]

The Justice who might seem most likely to pursue a campaign on behalf of property rights is Justice Thomas, who has long been the most conservative member of the Court. I have delayed discussing Thomas's separate dissent until now, but it suggests that he could actually be moving in the opposite direction. Thomas notes what seems to be common ground—that prior to *Pennsylvania Coal*, "it was generally thought that the Takings Clause reached only a 'direct appropriation' of property . . . or the functional equivalent of a 'practical ouster of [the owner's] possession.'"[199] This is a direct quote from

---

[194] Id at 2608, 2610.

[195] Id at 2612.

[196] *Murr*, 137 S Ct at 1942.

[197] Id at 1943.

[198] Id at 1957 (Roberts, CJ, dissenting).

[199] Id (Thomas, J, dissenting). The consensus among historians seems to be that the Framers understood the Takings Clause to apply only to government expropriation. See John H.

Justice Scalia's opinion in *Lucas*.[200] Although Scalia was an originalist, he seemed unfazed by the historically untethered nature of regulatory takings doctrine. Thomas, who is perhaps a more dedicated adherent to originalism, then suggests that "it would be desirable for us to take a fresh look at our regulatory takings jurisprudence, to see whether it can be grounded in the original public meaning of the Takings Clause of the Fifth Amendment or the Privileges or Immunities Clause of the Fourteenth Amendment."[201]

No doubt the property rights movement will still have its victories from time to time. With a majority of conservatives on the bench, and a malleable approach to takings, property rights owners will surely have their good days. But what seems to be lacking is any great discontent with the legal status quo in a way that would drive the Court toward large-scale doctrinal changes.[202]

B. TAKINGS LAW AFTER MURR

Most of scholarship about takings revolves around the Supreme Court. But the practical significance of the Court's rulings turns on their application by lower courts. As we will see in subsection 1, the Court's ruling in *Murr* is consistent with the overall tenor of takings litigation, which provides spotty protection for landowners. Subsection 2 offers some thoughts about the future direction of takings law. Both *Murr* and lower court decisions are indications of the difficulty of providing more comprehensive protection to property rights given that the existence of a considerable land use regulation has itself become a background principle of property law.

Hart, *Land Use Law in the Early Republic and the Original Meaning of the Takings Clause: Setting the Record Straight*, 1996 Utah L Rev 1099 (2000); William Michael Treanor, *The Original Understanding of the Takings Clause and the Political Process*, 95 Colum L Rev 782 (1995). An early Reconstruction-era opinion does express concern that a ban on liquor might be a violation of the due process rights of owners of existing stocks, see *Batemeyr v Iowa*, 85 US 129, 133–34 (1874). But in *Mugler v Kansas*, 123 US 623 (1887), the Court squarely upheld the validity of a similar law, on the theory that exercises of the state's police power were not equivalent to a taking of property for public use. Id at 662.

[200] 505 US 1014.

[201] Id.

[202] Justice Thomas may be an exception, but his inclination seems to be to exempt the federal government from regulatory takings doctrine based on the original understanding—not a change that would please property rights advocates. He cites an article whose title conveys its thesis: Michael Rappaport, *Originalism and Regulatory Takings: Why the Fifth Amendment May Not Protect Against Regulatory Takings, but the Fourteenth Amendment May*, 15 San Diego L Rev 729 (2008).

1. *Takings law in the lower courts.* Even to the extent that property rights advocates have enjoyed victories in the Supreme Court, it is unclear how much those victories have actually changed land use laws or their applications. The scholarly literature on regulatory takings has focused more on legal theory or doctrinal developments than on the implementation of doctrine. There have been relatively few efforts by legal scholars to examine how lower courts (largely state courts)[203] have been applying the doctrine, or what effects changes in doctrine may be having on actual land use decisions. What information we do have suggests that the Court's rulings may be less momentous than scholars (or perhaps the Justices) believe.

Two of the studies involve an aspect of regulatory takings I have mentioned only briefly: a series of cases on the intersection between takings and unconstitutional conditions doctrine.[204] In such cases, as a condition of approving a development permit, the government demands that the landowner make a concession such as providing free public access or requiring a transfer of property or money to the government. Because these concessions are a condition of obtaining a permit the owner voluntarily sought, these "exactions" are not per se takings. The Court has, however, required such an exaction to have a clear justification as a means to address problems created by the project.

Studies of this rule at different points in its evolution seem to indicate relatively benign effects. The first study involved the impact of the earlier cases on land use planning in California. The researchers concluded that land use planners generally regarded the rule as merely reinforcing good professional practice.[205] Communities with large amounts of development often increased their requirements on developers as a result of reexamining their rules under the new doctrine, although more developed urban areas were more constrained by the doctrine.[206] The second study, involving the most recent expansion of the rule by the Court, found very little effect on litigation in

---

[203] Under *Williamson County v Hamilton Bank*, 473 US 172 (1985), a plaintiff must first seek compensation from the state before a takings claim becomes ripe.

[204] See *Koontz v St. Johns River Water Management Dist.*, 133 S Ct 2586 (2013); *Dolan v City of Tigard*, 512 US 374 (1994); *Nollan v Cal Coastal Comm'n*, 483 US 825 (1987).

[205] Ann E. Carlson and Daniel Pollak, *Takings on the Ground: How the Supreme Court's Takings Jurisprudence Affects Local Land Use Decisions*, 35 UC Davis L Rev 103, 105 (2001).

[206] Id at 105–6.

Virginia.[207] The author speculates that given the repetitive nature of interactions between developers and land use authorities, strategic incentives to reach accommodations outweigh the appeal of litigation despite the availability of compensatory damages and attorney's fees.[208]

Three other studies focus on the diminution-of-value strand of takings doctrine. One of these studies focused specifically on the *Penn Central* and *Lucas* doctrines in federal court.[209] Based on a study of ninety-one federal cases, the author found that the results turned largely on the choice of forum.[210] As of that time, at least, the study found that the Federal Court of Claims was happy to spend the government's money on takings compensation, but that other federal courts took a much different position.[211] In particular, outside of the Court of Claims, application of the *Penn Central* rule meant almost invariably a defeat for the landowner.[212]

Another study by Michael Blumm and Lucas Ritchie found that *Lucas* had the unexpected effect of expanding lower court reliance on background norms to eliminate takings claims.[213] In addition to the nuisance exception articulated in *Lucas*, lower courts had identified a number of other background norms of state law. Perhaps the most obvious additional norm is the public trust doctrine, which traditionally limits the rights of landowners over navigable waters.[214] Some states, however, have applied the public trust doctrine more broadly to include tributaries of navigable waters and dry beach.[215] The federal government has its own protection from takings claims under another background principle: the navigable servitude, which gives it paramount authority over tidal and navigable waters.[216] Courts have also

---

[207] Antonio M. Elias, *Koontz v. St. Johns River Water Management Dist. Was Not a Big Deal*, 34 Va Envir L Rev 457 (2017). For an in-depth analysis of *Koontz* and its implications, see Lee Anne Fennell and Eduardo M. Peñalver, *Exactions Creep*, 2013 Supreme Court Review 287.

[208] Id at 463, 488.

[209] Basil H. Mattingly, *Forum Over Substance: The Empty Ritual of Balancing in Regulatory Takings Jurisprudence*, 36 Willamette L Rev 695 (2000).

[210] Id at 699.

[211] Id at 747.

[212] Id at 743–47.

[213] Michael C. Blumm and Lucas Ritchie, *Lucas's Unlikely Legacy: The Rise of Background Principles as Categorical Takings Defenses*, 29 Harv Envir L Rev 321 (2005).

[214] Id at 341.

[215] Id at 343.

[216] Id at 346–47.

invoked less familiar background principles, including customary rights of beach access,[217] native Hawaiian food-gathering rights (a decision also invoking the "Aloha spirit"),[218] laws protecting in-stream water flows,[219] state ownership of all wildlife under the common law,[220] and Indian treaty rights predating private land ownership.[221]

The final study was by far the most thorough. James Krier and Stewart Sterk examined more than two thousand reported takings decisions from 1979 to 2012.[222] Like Blumm and Ritchie, they found that *Lucas* had an unexpected effect: "After *Lucas*, the success rate for wipeout takings claims dropped precipitously,"[223] from 64 percent to 26 percent.[224] Moreover, few cases raised these claims: under 4 percent of takings claims.[225] Krier and Sterk found that most of the opinions in those cases focused on whether a complete loss of value had occurred.[226] Courts were divided on the issue that would ultimately reach the Court in *Murr* and on situations where inability to use the land was due to a combination of regulation and market forces.[227]

Like the study of federal court decisions discussed above, Krier and Sterk also found that *Penn Central* claims were markedly unsuccessful. Indeed, they said, "courts almost always defer to the regulatory decisions made by government officials, resulting in an almost cate-

---

[217] Id at 347–48.

[218] Id at 349.

[219] Id at 351.

[220] Id at 353.

[221] Id at 354.

[222] James E. Krier and Stewart E. Sterk, *An Empirical Study of Implicit Takings*, 58 Wm & Mary L Rev 35, 39 (2016). The time period was chosen because 1979 was the year after *Penn Central*, and 2012 was the year that their data source, a publication collecting takings cases, ceased publication. Id at 52.

[223] Id at 59.

[224] Id at 60.

[225] Id at 87. An even more recent study found that *Lucas* claims succeed in only 1.6 percent of takings cases that cite *Lucas*. Carol Necole Brown and Dwight H. Merriam, *On the Twenty-Fifth Anniversary of Lucas: Making or Breaking the Takings Claim*, 102 Iowa L Rev 1847 (2017). More specifically, they found only twenty-seven cases in twenty-five years in which *Lucas* claims succeeded. The authors observe that "[e]ven though *Lucas* set out a categorical rule, the rule is so fact-intensive that the gravitational pull is back toward the *Penn Central* weighing." Id at 1892. They conclude: "What does this say about the law? It says that the law is resistant to a categorical rule. It is just as resistant to a compensable taking post-*Lucas* as it was pre-*Lucas*." Id at 1892.

[226] Id at 60–61.

[227] Id.

gorical rule that *Penn Central*-type regulatory actions do not amount to takings."[228] They found that owners won less than 10 percent of *Penn Central* cases and that even this figure exaggerated the level of success, since it included decisions by lower courts that were reversed on appeal.[229]

Taking the sample of cases as a whole, Krier and Sterk found that diminution-of-value claims had only a 5 percent success rate.[230] Claims had higher success when a regulation required out-of-pocket expenses or prohibited an existing property use.[231] Thus, courts seemed to largely take the status quo as the baseline, looking for loss of value compared to current use, rather than taking the property's potential value without regulation as the baseline.

It may be a mistake to read too much into these findings. Nearly all of the studies focus on reported decisions, which are not a random sample of all litigation. Moreover, we still have limited information about how land use planners have responded to the Court's decisions or on how the decisions have affected negotiations between land-owners and regulators. If anything, however, *Murr* should expand the discretion of lower courts, probably further decreasing the likely success of takings claims. After *Murr*, the door is not barred to suc-cessful taking claims, but it appears that relatively few will be able to slip through. The Court, then, seems to have given property rights and the Takings Clause mostly symbolic support, with just enough practical effect so its endorsement of property rights is taken seriously.

2. Prognosis. No one has ever accused the Court's takings decisions of being governed by an excessive obsession with consistency. As Laura Underkuffler has said, "[t]o claim that any particular body of Supreme Court jurisprudence is the most incoherent is to set oneself up for challenge."[232] Still, she continued, "even if proof of the assertion is impossible, as a practical matter, it is—when it comes to takings law—

---

[228] Id at 62.

[229] Id at 64.

[230] Id at 67–68. Claims regarding development exactions were more successful, although litigation was relatively sparse, leading Krier and Sterk to speculate that landowners prefer to agree to the exactions so projects can proceed rather than litigate. Id at 68–69. *Penn Central* claims had higher success when a regulation required out-of-pocket expenses or prohibited an existing property use. Id.

[231] Id at 67–68.

[232] Laura S. Underkuffler, *Property and Change: The Constitutional Conundrum*, 91 Tex L Rev 2015, 2017 (2013).

quite probable."[233] Perhaps this is an overstatement, given the presence of other strong contenders such as the Establishment Clause and standing doctrine. Still, it would be safe to say that the Court has never steered a steady course in the takings domain. Nor does the Court seem to be drifting in any particular direction, having embarked on this journey.

There is a certain paradox to calls for a radical expansion of takings protection. As David Dana points out, "[m]uch of the value of property in land, of investments in land, comes from land use regulation."[234] Whole cities have been built out of desert or farmland, including billions of dollars of private investment, on the assumption that zoning laws apply.[235] A radical expansion of property rights would put much of this legal infrastructure in doubt or invalidate it completely. As the Supreme Court said in a due process case, "[i]t is a purpose of the ancient institution of property to protect those claims upon which people rely in their daily lives, reliance that must not be arbitrarily undermined."[236] As a number of Justices have recognized, land use laws such as zoning are very much now a part of what the Court has called background principles of state law on which everyone relies.[237]

The libertarian program would drastically unsettle those background principles, with tangible impacts on owners. The delight of the owner of any specific piece of property about this newfound freedom would be counterbalanced by fears of what unexpected activities newly empowered neighbors might pursue. It may be all very well to have the option of selling one's house to construct a gas station; it is less pleasant that one's neighbors also have that option.[238]

---

[233] Id.

[234] David A. Dana, *Why Do We Have the Parcel-as-a-Whole Rule?*, 39 Vt L Rev 617, 634 (2015).

[235] See Brief of the American Planning Association and the Wisconsin Chapter of the American Planning Association as Amici Curiae in Support of Respondents, in *Murr v Wisconsin* (No 15-214) *1–4, 13–18 (tracing history of modern land use regulation and of its acceptance by the Court).

[236] *Bd. of Regents of State Colleges v Roth*, 408 US 564, 577 (1972).

[237] See *Palazzolo*, 533 US at 627 (development rights are subject to "valid zoning and land-use restrictions"); *Tahoe-Sierra*, 535 US 302, 352 (Rehnquist, CJ, dissenting, joined by Scalia, J, and Thomas, J) ("zoning and permit regimes are a longstanding feature of state property law").

[238] Pointing to the political backlash against an effort in one state to dramatically expand compensation for the costs of land use regulation, Fennell and Peñalver observe that "once they confront the unpredictability of unregulated land use, owners quickly come to realize the mutually protective value of at least some land use regulation." Fennell and Peñalver, 2013 Supreme

To put it another way, land use laws are equivalent to what property lawyers call negative covenants on the lands of neighbors, and an expansion in takings doctrine would in effect "take" those negative covenants. If, as Carol Rose has said, property rules "encourage individual investment, planning, and effort because actors have a clearer sense of what they are getting,"[239] a radical takings expansion would destabilize those expectations. Paradoxically, a major strengthening of property rights could itself be seen as undermining the purposes of property law. For this reason, it is not surprising that the Court has been so chary of a lunge toward a more libertarian takings jurisprudence. If it is not to unsettle the expectations of property owners, it must take as given most of the existing structure of land use law. That means that the battles will necessarily take place at the margins.[240]

It is tempting to view *Murr* as indicating a new equilibrium in takings law. Certainly the majority, the Chief Justice, and Justice Alito seem content with the *Penn Central* test, and it is hard to see that test being overruled any time soon. But given the number of 5–4 decisions in the area, we might well see smaller movements either because of Justice Kennedy's shifting votes or because of changes in the makeup of the court. So long as Justice Kennedy remains the swing Justice in these cases, doctrinal stability is somewhat dependent on his views, which are not always predictable. If Chief Justice Roberts becomes the swing vote due to a conservative appointee replacing Kennedy or one of the four liberals, we would see other outcomes, but probably not abandonment of the *Penn Central* test or the creation of sweeping new exceptions. Roberts seems largely happy with *Penn Central*. Too much land use regulation is now baked into property law and into the legal system more generally. With due regard for the unpredictability of

---

Court Review at 352 (cited in note 207). There is some recent empirical confirmation of the positive effects of land use planning. In a study of the impact of California's stringent coastal regulations on property values, two economists conclude that the regulatory regime raises property values by 5–8 percent. See Christopher Severen, *Land-Use Regulations, Property Values, and Rents: Decomposing the Effects of the California Coastal Act* (Sept 2017) (Federal Reserve Bank of Philadelphia, Working Paper No 17-33), online at https://www.philadelphiafed.org/-/media/research-and-data/publications/working-papers/2017/wp17-33.pdf.

[239] Carol M. Rose, *The Shadow of the Cathedral*, 106 Yale L J 2175, 2187 (1997).

[240] This kind of incremental intervention is difficult for the Court to oversee effectively. One reason is that none of the Justices are likely to have any expertise in land use law or real estate transactions, making it hard for the Court to assess the impact of its interventions or the need for them. The other is that incremental decisions necessarily leave a great deal of leeway to lower courts, and in the takings area, those are state courts across the nation—a difficult universe for the Court to police effectively on a case-by-case basis.

doctrinal development, especially in an area as muddled as this,[241] it seems likely that *Penn Central* will remain the central fixture of takings law.

It is also significant that the most formidable advocate of property rights, Justice Scalia, is no longer on the Court. His replacement, Neil Gorsuch, may turn out to share his views, but Scalia was an unusually forceful advocate who will be hard to replicate. A decade ago, Richard Lazarus observed that "[t]he Court's analytic framework for regulatory takings analysis remains today, just as it was in 1978, Justice Brennan's opinion for the Court in *Penn Central*."[242] If anything, *Murr* shows that the *Penn Central* test is even more deeply embedded in the law today. If the *Penn Central* test is muddy, the Justices seem happily stuck in the mud.

C. PENN CENTRAL, MURR, AND THE TAKINGS DILEMMA

One reason to expect *Murr* and its elder sibling, the *Penn Central* test, to survive is the difficulty of making the case for a sterner approach to diminution-in-value cases. Subsection 1 argues that the judicial justifications for regulatory takings doctrine are underwhelming and that the best arguments from scholars are also less than compelling. Subsection 2 argues that there is a more fundamental obstacle: a truly strong takings doctrine would resemble a revival of *Lochner*.[243] The Court is not willing to abandon property rights protection, but neither is it willing to embrace this other horn of the dilemma. *Penn Central* and *Murr* allow it to vacillate somewhere in the middle, intervening now and then to protect property without upsetting the regulatory applecart too much.

---

[241] As an example, twenty years ago an astute observer thought that the balancing test was on its way to being supplanted with categorical takings rules, a trend that never eventuated. See Frank Michelman, *Takings, 1987*, 88 Colum L Rev 1621–22 (1988). It is hard to avoid a superstitious fear that any prediction in this area of law is doomed to failure.

[242] Lazarus, 57 Hastings L J at 823 (cited in note 4).

[243] The reference is, of course, to *Lochner v New York*, 198 US 45 (1905) (striking down a maximum-hours law for bakery employees). *Lochner* has become the emblem of an era in which courts defended freedom of contract from regulations they regarded as overreaching. Expansion of regulatory takings doctrine is at least theoretically less intrusive on decisions made through the political process, because the government can save a restriction on property by paying compensation. But given budget constraints, compensation may be more a theoretical than a practical alternative. It probably would have done little to mollify critics of *Lochner* if the Court had allowed the state to impose maximum hours or minimum wages provided the state fully compensated employers.

1. *Possible justifications for regulatory takings doctrine.* In trying to understand takings jurisprudence, it is worth asking what the Justices themselves view as the goals of takings law. Both the majority and the Roberts dissent in *Murr* devote some effort to explaining the normative basis of takings law. As I read them, they present three arguments. Unfortunately, those arguments are all deeply unsatisfactory as a basis for constructing constitutional doctrine. Besides being questionable in their own right, they are also too vague to provide much guidance in structuring constitutional rules.

Justice Kennedy grounds the Takings Clause in individual liberty and fairness. He argues that "[p]roperty rights are necessary to preserve freedom, for property ownership empowers persons to shape and to plan their own destiny in a world where governments are always eager to do so for them."[244] Even if true empirically, this assertion seems tenuously connected with regulatory takings doctrine. If property ownership is necessary to empower people to shape and plan their own destiny, the most pressing problem is that many people do not own property in the first place, not that property is regulated. To the extent Kennedy's assertion is right, it would seem that what people really need for freedom is access to resources— wealth—rather than ownership of any specific piece of property. The remedy would seem to be a major redistribution of wealth, not regulatory takings doctrine.

The second part of Kennedy's assertion ("governments are always eager to do so for them") raises an empirical question—is it true that governments are always eager to control the lives of individuals? Students learn at an early age not to pick an answer with the word "always" on a multiple-choice question, since such statements are rarely true outside of mathematics. Only a student who is completely unaware of current American politics would pick "always" as an answer to the question, "when do governments seek to expand the scope of regulations?" We seem to have no shortage at the moment of legislators and executives whose dearest wish is to eliminate economic regulation.

---

[244] *Murr*, 137 S Ct at 1943. In a similar vein is the suggestion that "the ownership of property gives individuals the security in their homes and businesses that provides the sense of independence necessary for free citizens in a democratic polity," Eagle, 118 Penn State L Rev at 614 (cited in note 11), which seems to relegate to serfdom those who own neither homes nor businesses.

Putting aside the question of the argument's validity, it is unclear where it leads in terms of regulatory takings doctrine.[245] Kennedy agrees that this individual interest in having the material basis for freedom must be balanced against the "government's well-established power to 'adjus[t] rights for the public good.'"[246] Indeed, limiting the property rights of some might be necessary to protect the property rights of others. As to how this balancing is to be accomplished, Kennedy reverts to what he says is "the purpose of the Takings Clause, which is to prevent the government from 'forcing some people alone to bear public burdens which, in all fairness and justice, should be borne by the public as a whole.'"[247] One can hardly quarrel with this premise, but it is hard to see how it provides any traction in deciding an individual case. It is little wonder that the Court has ended up relying on the almost equally vague *Penn Central* test.

Chief Justice Roberts offers his own effort at explaining regulatory takings doctrine. He, too, repeats the formulae about shifting burdens from individuals that the public should bear.[248] But he adds some embellishments. First, he argues (quoting *Pennsylvania Coal*[249]) that if compensation were required for government appropriation of property but not for overregulation, "'the natural tendency of human nature' would be to extend regulations 'until at last private property disappears.'"[250] Alas, that was a silly statement when Holmes made it, and it remains a silly statement a century or so later. Where is the evidence? Was private property on the road to extinction until 1922, when Holmes sprung this new doctrine on the world? Did it disappear

---

[245] To the extent that the concern about singling out property owners to bear burdens does have any implications, it seems to point toward tolerance of broadly applicable property restrictions and greater scrutiny of restrictions that apply only to small groups or individual owners. See Saul Levmore, *Just Compensation and Just Policies*, 22 Conn L Rev 285, 306, 313 (1990). The ad hoc nature of many land use decisions does seem to be an animating force in some takings opinions, but the Court has not clearly articulated this as a part of the takings test. See Fennell and Peñalver, 2013 Supreme Court Review at 313–14 (cited in note 207).

[246] *Murr*, 137 S Ct at 1943.

[247] Id. Justice Kennedy likes this language so much that he repeats it at the end of the opinion. Id at 1949.

[248] Id at 1950 (Roberts, CJ, dissenting). Roberts also finds this mantra worth repeating twice. See id at 1952.

[249] Id at 1951. Holmes's comment seems especially off-center when we remember that he wrote when Harding was in the White House and the government was firmly in Republican hands.

[250] Id at 1951.

in England without the benefit of constitutional protection for property rights?[251] Surely, it is at least as plausible to say that the natural tendency of governments is to leave private property rights alone, because property owners are strongly motivated to resist interference and are more likely than others to be rich and powerful.

Again, putting aside doubts about the validity of Roberts's statement, it suggests at most that governments would use regulation to accomplish the functional equivalent of expropriation. But blocking abuses of this kind would require only a very limited takings doctrine. For instance, courts might find a taking only when property owners lose both the power to exclude others and the right to use the property, since condemnation of property involves both elements.

Roberts also suggests an alternative line of argument. He sees an inherent mismatch between regulatory interests and affected property owners: given that "[r]egulatory takings . . . —by their very nature— pit the common good against the interests of a few," and "[t]he widespread benefits of a regulation will often appear far weightier than the isolated losses suffered by individuals."[252] "[L]ooking at the bigger picture," he says, property rights are likely to be given too little weight because "the overall societal good of an economic system grounded on private property will appear abstract when cast against a concrete regulatory problem."[253]

Empirically, both propositions seem highly contestable. The NIMBY (Not in My Back Yard) phenomenon, as well as the notorious difficulty of passing legislation over the objections of special interests, suggests that adversely affected individuals have all too much ability to block regulations that would be in the public interest. A great deal of public choice theory supports that view. Moreover, it seems dubious as a psychological matter that people will overlook arresting stories of individual unfairness in the pursuit of more abstract public interests.

---

[251] See Byrne, 41 Vt L Rev at 736 n 16 (cited in note 189).

[252] *Murr*, 137 S Ct at 1955.

[253] Id. Once again, however one might feel about these arguments in the abstract, they seem to lead nowhere doctrinally. Roberts's point about the tendency of the political process to overlook harm to individuals seems to have no particular connection with the protection of property as opposed to other individual interests. The need for governments to protect capitalism goes astray in a different direction, for it leads not to regulatory takings doctrine but to *Lochner*. The difficulty that the Court has confronted since the day it decided *Lochner* is the impossibility of finding a nonpolitical standard for determining when regulation has impinged too much on the free market.

Roberts's second proposition seems to come down to the idea that capitalism is in need of judicial assistance in protecting itself against excessive regulation. If so, the Court seems to have administered the cure in *Citizens United*[254] and related cases, ensuring that wealthy and powerful business organizations will have full scope to protect themselves in the political process.

Anyone who was offering these rationales seriously would realize that they at least require justification and refinement to be credible. They are by no means self-evident propositions. Nor is it at all clear how they translate into doctrine. Yet the Justices seem content to repeat them without elaboration. I count at least five repetitions in *Murr* of the language about putting public burdens on individuals. All of this suggests that the language is serving as much a ritualistic as a substantive purpose.

This is not to fault the Court's inability to agree on a usable normative basis for the diminution-of-value standard. It is not easy to formulate such a basis for takings liability based on diminution of value. Because it compensates owners for unexpected losses in market value, it seems akin to an insurance program. In this analogy, takings compensation is like the payout on an insurance policy, while the taxes used to fund compensation are like premiums paid by property owners generally.[255] One of the insurance-like aspects of the system is that only some of the landowners who lose out under a regulation will receive compensation, depending on how severe a diminution of value they suffer. In effect, *Penn Central* establishes something like a deductible in this "insurance program," whereby lower levels of loss are not covered, whereas *Lucas* attempts to ensure compensation to the landowner who has a complete loss.[256] It is unclear, however, why the Constitution should be read to mandate government insurance for this one kind of loss, or why private markets could not do so more efficiently and equitably.[257] Landowners are expected to buy fire in-

---

[254] *Citizens United v Federal Election Commission*, 558 US 310 (2010) (holding that corporations have a First Amendment right to expend unlimited funds to support political candidates).

[255] Lawrence Blue and Daniel L. Rubinfield, *Compensation for Takings: An Economic Analysis*, 72 Cal L Rev 569 (1984).

[256] Susan Rose-Ackerman explains the logic of this insurance-based function of takings compensation. Rose-Ackerman, 88 Colum L Rev at 1705 (cited in note 186).

[257] See Daniel A. Farber, *Public Choice and Just Compensation*, 9 Const Comm 279, 284–85, 287 (1992).

surance, so why not insurance against possible losses due to government regulation?[258]

A related argument is that the prospect of paying compensation forces government to take into account the harm its regulations impose on landowners, which it might otherwise overlook.[259] This rationale is also shaky, because it assumes that the government fully takes into account the benefits of its regulations but systematically overlooks the costs.[260] Public choice theory suggests that the problem will frequently be the opposite: the diffuse public benefits of a regulation will often carry less weight than the opposition of the more concentrated group bearing the costs.[261] Certainly the NIMBY phenomenon supports this perspective. Thus, there's no clear empirical basis for the argument that regulatory bodies overweigh the benefits of regulation over its costs, while both theory and experience suggest that the opposite is as likely to be true.

The Justices' difficulty in articulating a convincing rationale for the diminution-of-value doctrine may help explain the Court's willingness to live with the relatively flaccid *Penn Central* doctrine.[262] The Court's most successful ventures into takings doctrine have taken other directions, such as the blanket rule against permanent physical intrusions or the restrictions on development exactions. These rules avoid relying on the degree of loss. Instead, they prioritize the dignitary harm of nonconsensual intrusions for one rule and concern about unconstitutional conditions for the other.

---

[258] The argument for private insurance is made in Steve P. Calandrillo, *Eminent Domain Economics: Should "Just Compensation" Be Abolished, and Would "Takings Insurance" Work Instead?*, 64 Ohio State L J 451 (2003).

[259] See Michael H. Schill, *Intergovernmental Takings and Just Compensation: A Question of Federalism*, 137 U Pa L Rev 829, 839–60 (1989); William A. Fischel and Perry Shapiro, *Takings, Insurance, and Michaelman: Comments on Economic Interpretations of "Just Compensation" Law*, 17 J Leg Studies 269 (1988).

[260] For a critique of this view, see Peñalver, 104 Colum L Rev at 2216–17 n 160 (cited in note 89). Bethany Berger argues that effects on property taxes provide a better signal to local governments: the beneficial effects of regulation cause property values and therefore tax receipts to go up, while the costs of regulation have the opposite effect. See Bethany R. Berger, *The Illusion of Fiscal Illusion in Regulatory Takings*, 66 Am U L Rev 1 (2016).

[261] Farber, 9 Const Comm at 290 (cited in note 257) .

[262] It may be harsh to say that in takings law, "a 'totality of the circumstances' analysis masks intellectual bankruptcy." Thomas W. Merrill, *The Economics of Public Use*, 72 Cornell L Rev 61, 93 (1986). But such wide-open tests do seem to imply the absence of a clear normative theory behind the test, instead leaving value judgments to be made in the face of specific circumstances.

2. *Defending Penn Central and Murr.* *Penn Central* is a highly contextual, ad hoc analysis. Most lawyers would probably agree that something clearer and easier to apply would be better.[263] Yet, this may be about the best the courts can do. Muddled jurisprudence is often a sign that courts are facing fundamental tensions they are unable to resolve. The Court could escape these tensions by jettisoning the doctrine of regulatory takings, but only Justice Thomas seems willing to even contemplate the slightest possibility of that step. As long as the Court wants to maintain this field of law as more than a hollow shell, however, it will face some very serious problems. As we have seen, one of those problems is that a sweeping assault on land use regulations would destabilize the legal framework in which owners have made countless investment decisions.

Reinforcing this difficulty, and perhaps of greater importance, is the tension between regulatory takings law and the Court's continuing rejection of *Lochner.* The post-*Lochner* era stance of great deference toward economic regulations is in tension with the project of protecting against excessive regulation that is at the heart of regulatory takings doctrine. In this sense, the doctrine might be considered a kind of living fossil from the *Lochner* era. Libertarians have a simple solution: resurrect *Lochner.*[264] But given that the Court is unwilling to do that or to get rid of regulatory takings doctrine, it has to find some way of doing takings law that does not involve reasonableness review and does not present a threat to government regulation at large.[265] This is no easy task.

---

[263] An economist who frequently testifies in takings cases puts the points rather nicely: "Hundred of briefs, decisions and journal articles debating 'how much loss is enough' should be sufficient proof that the *Keystone Bituminous* 'taking fraction' provides poor guidance to decision making in partial taking cases." William W. Wade, *Temporary Takings, Tahoe Sierra, and the Denominator Problems,* 43 Envir L Rep 10189, 10189 (2013).

[264] Fennel and Peñalver explain this as what might be called the *"Lochner* for land-only" approach, Fennel and Peñalver, 2013 Supreme Court Review at 351 (cited in note 207). Not surprisingly, the most prominent academic defender of *Lochner*-era jurisprudence rejects *Murr* and advocates overruling or at least sharply limiting the *Penn Central* test. See Richard A. Epstein, *Disappointed Expectations: How the Supreme Court Failed to Clean up Takings Law in Murr v. Wisconsin,* 11 NYU J L & Liberty 151, 156, 215–17 (2017). Epstein notes ruefully that the Roberts dissent "did not at any point question the soundness of this particular framework, but only disagreed about its application to the parcel-as-a-whole test." Id at 155.

[265] This tension must have posed a particular problem for Justice Scalia, who was both an advocate for property rights and an opponent of active judicial review of economic regulations. See John Echeverria, *Antonin Scalia's Flawed Takings Legacy,* 41 Vt L Rev 689, 708 (2017).

An additional problem is determining just what constitutional value the doctrine is trying to protect, which might give greater direction to efforts to strengthen the doctrine. As we have seen, the Justices have had little success in this regard, but they are not alone. This problem has been the subject of valiant efforts by brilliant scholars, but they have been unable to persuade each other, let alone the judges.[266] On the one hand, one would expect a constitutional value to be something more fundamental than the owner's financial health—thus the impulse to tie the Takings Clause to fundamental theories of property. Yet on the other hand, the compensation portion of the Takings Clause suggests that the clause protects the cash value of property, not the inherent value of property rights.[267]

A final tension stems from the era of legal positivism in which we live. We no longer believe that the shape of property law and the rights of property owners stem from natural law. Rather, they stem from the rules of property law developed by courts and legislatures. This poses a logical problem: if property is created by state law, and state law includes the power to modify property rights, then how can a change in state law be a violation of property rights? Any solution requires adopting the general principle of state control over property rights but nevertheless finding space for exceptions—no easy matter. The concept of background principles seems to address this problem, but the Court has never been able to define the distinction between a background principle and an ordinary rule of law.

The *Penn Central* test is an effort to thread the needle, or perhaps one should say square the circle. Given that it's impossible to square the circle, a lot of hand waving is to be expected and perhaps some ink blots covering part of the argument. Of course, there are ways of escaping the conundrum. The Court could once again embrace *Lochner*. It could efface the compensation part of the clause, just as it has effaced the opening language of the Second Amendment. It could adopt a natural rights approach and impose a nationwide set of property rules, which would almost seem worth trying if only to see what version of the Rule Against Perpetuities the Court discerned in the

---

[266] For a catalogue of the leading theories, which range from Rawles to Nozick, Hegel to law and economics, and much else, see Peñalver, 104 Colum L Rev at 2187 (cited in note 89).

[267] As Peñalver has argued, regulatory takings doctrine is also in severe tension with the government's broad power to acquire money or even tangible forms of property through taxation, creating another intellectual puzzle for takings doctrine. Id at 2183–85.

penumbra of the Takings Clause. Or, at the other extreme, it could abandon the idea of regulatory takings entirely or limit the doctrine to the functional equivalent of the government acquiring title. But it seems the Justices find neither a *Lochner* revival nor blanket approval of regulations to be acceptable.

The Court's reluctance to embrace these more principled, extreme positions is understandable, for either extreme would be unacceptable to a large portion of society. True, it would be more appealing intellectually to embrace one of the extremes—either a libertarian assault on the modern state or complete deference to regulators. But we live in a society that is sharply divided about economic liberty, property rights, and the role of government—and where many are simply ambivalent about the balance. If the Court's regulatory takings doctrine is muddled, the reason may be that our society's values are in disarray.

Given that the best the Court can do is probably to muddle along, something like *Penn Central* is probably about all one should expect. This inevitably leaves the lower courts, and the state courts in particular, to make their own judgments, based on local community practices and norms. When a state seems to have gotten far out of line, the Supreme Court can step in, just as a trial judge can step in when a jury seems to have botched the similar task of defining negligence. Given all the constraints the Court is trying to satisfy, occasional ad hoc interventions may be the best it can do. Certainly, the opinions in *Murr* suggest that most of the Justices have come to that conclusion.

IV. Conclusion

The doctrinal implications of *Murr* may seem subtle, but they have a real impact. Consider state responses to sea-level rise that seek to move development away from the coast, which were discussed in the introduction. As we have seen, both the majority and dissent were agreed in *Murr* that at a minimum the relevant unit of analysis is the lot as a whole and can sometimes include nearby lots of the same owner. *Murr* also shores up *Penn Central*'s holding that the state can give owners transferrable development rights and use those to offset any diminution in value. Moreover, *Murr* indicates that the existence of a restriction on property, especially a long-standing one, can put future coastal owners on notice that their development rights will be limited. Finally, *Murr* observes that coastal lands are fragile, allowing a greater degree of state regulation. All of these features of *Murr* will make it harder for coastal landowners to take advantage of the *Lucas* total takings rule and will count against them in applying the more flexible and less owner-friendly *Penn Central* rule.

In doctrinal terms, *Murr* is revealing for both what was said and what was not said. The Court had been presented with the evidence that, outside of the total takings situation, its balancing test for takings nearly always results in a government victory. No one on the Court bothered mentioning that issue, and the dissenters seemed happy to use the balancing test notwithstanding its friendliness to regulators. In earlier decisions, the dissenters had argued that even a single piece of land was too big a unit to use as the denominator, let alone multiple lots. Instead, they argued, the denominator should be limited to the separate interest at issue, which might be less than the total bundle of property rights to the whole parcel. No one chose to bring up that argument again, and it is incompatible with both the majority opinion[268] and the Roberts dissent.[269] Justice Scalia had also argued that it was irrelevant whether the challenged law was already in effect when the present owner acquired the property. No one on the Court embraced that claim in *Murr*.[270] And in terms of the numerator problem, the majority[271] and dissenters[272] both seemed willing to consider the amount of value added by the vacant lot to the total value of the two lots as offsetting the Murrs' loss from being unable to develop the lot separately. In other words, apart from attracting a minority of the Court on the denominator issue, property rights advocates were rebuffed at every turn.

Justice Scalia had championed a far different vision of takings law, one much closer to the hearts of property rights advocates. In his view, the existence of a taking did not turn on economic loss but rather

---

[268] See id at 1944 (discussing prior holdings prohibiting "conceptual severance").

[269] See id at 1952 (relevant property for Takings Clause purposes is the entire parcel "in all but the most exceptional circumstances").

[270] See id at 1945 (although passage of title after a law is enacted does not automatically extinguish a takings claim, "[a] reasonable restriction that predates a landowner's acquisition . . . can be one of the objective factors that most landowners would reasonably consider in forming fair expectations about their property").

[271] Id at 1949 (plaintiffs have not been deprived of all beneficial use since they can use the vacant tract in conjunction with the other tract to build a house).

[272] Id at 1957 (plaintiffs' ability to use tract in conjunction with adjoining land "would be relevant" to determine the merits of any takings claims for the vacant lot).

on whether the government had impaired any established right of property owners.[273] In describing government land use decisions, he was apt to use terms such as extortion and larceny.[274] Nothing approaching his viewpoint, either substantively or rhetorically, figured in any of the opinions in *Murr*. Perhaps this should not be totally surprising, given that Scalia wrote only two majority opinions on takings during his time at the Court, and none in the last twenty-five years of his tenure.[275] Yet he was always a strong presence in takings cases, if only because of the strength of his rhetoric. That rhetoric was always deployed on the side of the property owner—in his thirty years on the Court, he never wrote in opposition to a takings claim.[276]

Justice Kennedy's majority opinion in *Murr* can easily be seen as the triumph of the *Penn Central* balancing test. That by itself would represent a significant setback for property rights advocates. But what may be equally important in *Murr* is that even the dissenters complacently accept *Penn Central*. Moreover, as I have explained, although they differ from the majority over the narrow issue of how to determine the denominator of the takings fraction, that disagreement has limited significance given the dissenters' seeming accord with the majority on other aspects of *Penn Central*.

As discussed in the previous section, the Court is not in a good position to abandon *Penn Central*. The Justices' own normative arguments are too vague to push strongly toward any particular doctrinal outcome. Indeed, the diminution-in-value test seems hard to ground in any really strong normative justification. And a sharp move away from *Penn Central* would involve either abandoning protection for property owners or else embracing some version of *Lochner*, neither of which is appealing to today's Court.

The Court's embrace of *Penn Central* does not mean the end of takings claims. The Court has carved out exceptions for physical appropriations and for total takings. The total takings category will be narrower after *Murr*, though courts may encounter such regulatory

---

[273] Byrne, 4 Vt L Rev at 744, 750–58 (cited in note 189).

[274] Id at 744, 749, 756.

[275] See Echeverria, 41 Vt L Rev at 692 (cited in note 265). The two majority opinions were *Nollan v Cal. Coastal Comm'n*, 483 US 825 (1987), and *Lucas v South Carolina Coastal Council*, 505 US 1003 (1992). He also wrote a plurality opinion in *Stop the Beach Renourishment, Inc. v Florida Dept of Env. Protection*, 560 US 702 (2010) (stating that a judicial decision overruling a previously established common law property right is a per se taking).

[276] Id at 693.

wipeouts from time to time. Nor would it be surprising if the Court were to identify some other narrow categories of regulation for special treatment, flirting occasionally with the Lochnerian side of takings doctrine. But what does seem clear is that the Court has no stomach for a libertarian campaign to deregulate land use. Nor is it prepared to abandon all protection for property from government regulation. Thus, as we approach the beginning of the second century of regulatory takings doctrine, it seems likely the doctrine's next century will be as muddled as its first.

CARY FRANKLIN

BIOLOGICAL WARFARE: CONSTITUTIONAL CONFLICT OVER "INHERENT DIFFERENCES" BETWEEN THE SEXES

Constitutional sex discrimination law grew out of constitutional race discrimination law and in many ways takes after it. But there are some critical distinctions between the two areas of law, and the most significant involves the Supreme Court's attitude toward biological difference. The Court has explained that once upon a time—indeed not so very long ago—Americans believed there were significant biological differences among the races.[1] The law now recognizes those allegedly biological differences as social constructs: pseudo-scientific assertions about the implications of skin color that masked and legitimated cultural biases and sustained racial hierarchy. As a result, "[s]upposed 'inherent differences' between the races are no longer accepted as a ground for discrimination."[2] The Court tells a different story about

---

Cary Franklin is W. H. Francis, Jr. Professor, University of Texas School of Law.

Author's note: For helpful comments on drafts of this piece, I am thankful to Justin Driver, Joey Fishkin, Serena Mayeri, and Doug NeJaime.

[1] See *United States v Virginia*, 518 US 515, 533 (1996) (citing *Loving v Virginia*, 388 US 1 (1967), in which the trial court upheld a ban on interracial marriage in part because it viewed the different races as akin to different species).

[2] Id.

sex. Where sex is concerned, the Court asserts, it is not pseudo-science all the way down. Unlike the supposed differences between, say, black and white people, "[p]hysical differences between men and women . . . are enduring."[3] Thus, the Court has explained, the law may be more receptive to sex-based state action predicated on "inherent differences" than it is toward race-based state action predicated on those grounds.[4] Of course, that does not mean the state has carte blanche to discriminate on the basis of sex. Inherent differences between the sexes may sometimes justify the use of sex classifications, but such classifications may not be used today, as they once were, to constrain opportunity, to reinforce traditional sex and family roles, or "to create or perpetuate the legal, social, and economic inferiority of women."[5]

Like many constitutional tests of its sort, this test does not automatically resolve the question of what qualifies as permissible state action. It is not always clear when sex classifications help to dismantle sex-based hierarchies and erode conventional sex-role stereotypes and when they do the opposite. Even people committed to gender equality can and do disagree, for instance, about whether it is constitutional for the state to maintain sex-segregated bathrooms or for the military to make sex-based distinctions in its strength and physical fitness requirements. Even more fundamentally, the test raises questions about what counts as an "inherent difference" between the sexes.[6] Many differences between men and women we now understand to be socially constructed were once viewed as biologically based. In the nineteenth century, opponents of higher education for women argued that the sustained contemplation of difficult texts diverted energy from the reproductive organs to the brain and thus

---

[3] Id.

[4] See id (explaining that "[t]he two sexes are not fungible" and that "'[i]nherent differences' between men and women . . . remain cause for celebration").

[5] *Virginia*, 518 US at 534.

[6] Indeed, the Court in *United States v Virginia*, the most important sex discrimination decision since the 1970s, put the phrase "inherent differences" in quotation marks even as it acknowledged the existence of such differences. It is not entirely clear what the Court intended to convey through the use of those quotation marks. I am inclined to believe they reflect the Court's awareness of the long and sorry history of the government's reliance on specious biological distinctions to justify the differential treatment of the sexes and its increasing skepticism toward attempts to justify discrimination on those grounds. For more on this point, see Cary Franklin, *The Anti-Stereotyping Principle in Constitutional Sex Discrimination Law*, 85 NYU L Rev 83, 145–46 & n 133 (2010).

threatened to render women sterile.[7] In the *Lochner* era, the Court itself cited women's lack of stamina and unique physical vulnerability as a reason to uphold sex-based restrictions on their working hours.[8]

Over time—as a result of social movement advocacy and advances in scientific understanding—the list of attributes viewed as "inherent differences" between the sexes has dwindled. Constitutional law today is skeptical of sex-based generalizations and (in theory, at least) will not accept them as a ground for discrimination even if they are true, or believed to be true, of most men and women. In its canonical holding in *United States v Virginia*,[9] the Court rejected the state's claim that women are inherently ill-suited for the Virginia Military Institute's "adversative method" of education, which subjects students to a rigorous series of physical and psychological challenges in order to mold them into "citizen soldiers."[10] Even if it were true that fewer women than men would sign up for, or benefit from, such an ordeal, the Court explained, generalizations "'about the different talents, capacities, or preferences of males and females'" are no longer permissible grounds for discrimination.[11] Under current law, even physical characteristics like height, weight, and upper-body strength

---

[7] See, for example, Edward H. Clarke, *Sex in Education; Or, a Fair Chance for Girls* 62 (J. R. Osgood, 1873) (describing the "numberless pale, weak, neuralgic, dyspeptic, hysterical, menorraghic, dysmenorrhoeic girls and women" among the "classes of our private, common, and normal schools" and "among the female graduates of our colleges"). Clarke, a physician and professor at Harvard Medical School, believed that intensive study diverted blood away from men's reproductive organs as well, but that women were more likely to be rendered sterile through "excessive brain activity" because "the female reproductive apparatus" was larger and more complicated. Id at 137.

[8] See *Muller v Oregon*, 208 US 412 (1908) (upholding a maximum-hour law that applied only to women in part because "[t]he two sexes differ in structure of body, in the functions to be performed by each, in the amount of physical strength, in the capacity for long-continued labor, particularly when done standing, the influence of vigorous health upon the future well-being of the race, the self-reliance which enables one to assert full rights, and in the capacity to maintain the struggle for subsistence"); see also *Bradwell v Illinois*, 83 US 130 (1872) (Bradley, J, concurring) (voting to uphold a law prohibiting women from joining the Illinois bar on the ground that "the civil law, as well as nature herself, has always recognized a wide difference in the respective spheres and destinies of man and woman").

[9] 518 US 515 (1996).

[10] Id at 545 (holding that the goal of creating "citizen-soldiers" is "great enough to accommodate women, who today count as citizens in our American democracy equal in stature to men").

[11] Id at 533 (quoting *Weinberger v Wiesenfeld*, 420 US 636, 643 (1975)); *Virginia*, 518 US at 542 (assuming "for purposes of this decision, that most women would not choose VMI's adversative method," but holding that generalizations about women's interests and preferences cannot justify limiting their opportunities).

cannot justify sex-based limitations on opportunity, for although men and women differ on average with respect to these characteristics, the distinction is hardly absolute: some women are taller and stronger than some men.[12] In fact, the only contexts in which constitutional law today seems to countenance sex-based limitations on individuals' rights and opportunities are those involving reproductive biology—perhaps the sole remaining site of legally cognizable "inherent differences" between the sexes.[13]

Thus, it not surprising that on the two occasions last Term in which the Court called upon the government to justify its use of a sex classification, the government turned to reproductive biology in both instances. In *Pavan v Smith*, Arkansas sought to defend a law that required a birth mother's male spouse to be listed on her child's birth certificate but did not permit a birth mother's female spouse to be listed.[14] The state argued that the differential treatment was justified because men and women are not similarly situated with respect to reproduction: a male spouse almost always has a biological connection to his wife's child, whereas a female spouse never does.[15] In *Sessions v*

---

[12] See Mary Anne Case, *"The Very Stereotype the Law Condemns": Constitutional Sex Discrimination Law as a Quest for Perfect Proxies*, 85 Cornell L Rev 1447, 1449–50 (2000) ("For a sex-respecting rule to withstand constitutional scrutiny . . . it seems to be at least necessary . . . that it embody some perfect proxy. . . . [T]he assumption at the root of the sex-respecting rule must be true of either all women or no women or all men or no men. . . ."); see also *Virginia*, 518 US at 573 (Scalia, J, dissenting) (asserting that under the test the Court developed in *Virginia*, the school's all-male admissions policy would be unconstitutional if even "a single woman [was] willing and able to undertake VMI's program").

[13] The Court has never specified exactly what counts as an "inherent difference" between the sexes. But the only "inherent differences" it has recognized, since it began to accord heightened scrutiny to sex-based state action, have involved reproductive biology. See, for example, *Michael M. v Superior Court of Sonoma County*, 450 US 464, 467 (1981) (upholding a statutory rape law that criminalized sex only with minor females on the ground that "the classification was supported not by mere social convention but by the immutable physiological fact that it is the female exclusively who can become pregnant"); *Nguyen v Immigration and Naturalization Service*, 533 US 53 (2001) (upholding a law requiring unmarried citizen fathers, but not unmarried citizen mothers, to take certain steps before becoming eligible to transmit their citizenship to children born overseas on the ground that pregnancy establishes a biological link between mother and child but not between father and child).

[14] 137 S Ct 2075 (2017).

[15] Brief for the Respondent in Opposition, *Pavan v Smith*, Civil Action No 16-992, *19 (US filed Apr 14, 2017) (available on Westlaw at 2017 WL 1397395) (arguing that the lesbian couples challenging the law "ignore the basic fact that—unlike a husband—a mother's female spouse will *never* be a marital child's biological parent"). In fact, this is not true: there are quite a few women today who have given birth to their female spouse's biological child through the use of in vitro fertilization (a process that allows an embryo made with one woman's egg to be transferred to another woman's uterus). In this scenario, the female spouse of a birth mother is a biological parent of the child in the same way that a male spouse might be. Perhaps the state

Morales-Santana, the federal government sought to defend a portion of the Immigration and Nationality Act (INA) pertaining to the acquisition of U.S. citizenship by children born abroad to one parent who is a U.S. citizen and one who is not.[16] The law placed more onerous restrictions on citizen fathers who wished to transmit their citizenship to such children than it did on citizen mothers.[17] Here too the government turned to reproduction: it argued that giving birth creates a special legal and physical bond between an unmarried mother and her child that an unmarried father—who "enters the scene later, as a second parent"[18]—lacks.[19]

The Court rejected these arguments and ruled in favor of the litigants challenging the laws in both cases. But neither case received much attention. What little press *Pavan* received treated it as an inconsequential derivative of *Obergefell v Hodges*, the landmark 2015 decision in which the Court held that the Constitution affords same-sex couples the right to marry.[20] On this view, *Pavan* simply reiterated what the Court said in *Obergefell*: same-sex couples who marry are entitled to the full complement of obligations and privileges entailed in marriage. *Morales-Santana* attracted a bit more attention than *Pavan*. But when it came down, the nation was embroiled in a vigorous, wide-ranging debate over immigration and citizenship that made the Court's decision look like small potatoes.[21]

What the Court did in *Pavan* and *Morales-Santana* was no small thing, however. In these decisions, the Court genuinely scrutinized the government's ostensibly biological justifications for treating the sexes differently in contexts where it has traditionally declined to do

---

was genuinely unaware of this possibility; or perhaps it elided this possibility in an effort to identify an "inherent difference" between men and women sufficiently universal and absolute to satisfy the high bar the Court has set.

[16] 137 S Ct 1678 (2017).

[17] For a more detailed description of the law, see text accompanying notes 98–99.

[18] *Morales-Santana*, 137 S Ct at 1695 (paraphrasing the government's argument).

[19] More specifically, the government argued that because unmarried mothers are invariably present at a child's birth, and because their parentage is thereby assured, they are recognized at that moment as the child's only legal parent. Because an unmarried father does not prove his paternity through giving birth and has no legal ties to the child's mother, he is not similarly situated—either legally or physically—to an unmarried mother with respect to his child. For more on this argument, see notes 141–43 and accompanying text.

[20] 135 S Ct 2584 (2015).

[21] See, for example, Michael D. Shear and Julie Hirschfeld Davis, *Trump Moves to End DACA and Calls on Congress to Act*, NY Times (Sept 5, 2017); Peter Baker, *Trump Supports Plan to Cut Legal Immigration in Half*, NY Times (Aug 2, 2017).

so. For decades, equal protection law has required the state to adduce "an exceedingly persuasive justification" for classifying individuals on the basis of sex[22] and to show that the differential treatment does not reflect or reinforce traditional sex stereotypes.[23] But there are a few contexts in which courts have pretty consistently declined to apply this kind of heightened scrutiny to laws that classify on the basis of sex, and contexts involving gay people and unmarried fathers are two of the most significant. Historically, courts in these contexts have not asked the kinds of questions that sex classifications are supposed to trigger: they have not asked whether the government's ostensibly biological justifications were devised post-hoc to defend laws actually founded on stereotypes; nor have they required the government to show that it could not achieve its aims using sex-neutral rules.[24] As a result, these areas have become repositories of specious biological justifications for discrimination—not as archaic as the notion that reading renders women sterile, but not completely removed from that species of argument either.

In *Pavan* and *Morales-Santana*, the Court broke with this tradition. It did not give the government a free pass, as it might have in the past, because the litigants challenging the laws were gay, in the case of *Pavan*, and unmarried, in the case of *Morales-Santana*. It carefully examined the government's ostensibly biological justifications for treating the sexes differently and, in so doing, recognized that such justifications can mask traditional stereotypes and limit opportunity where gay people and unwed fathers are concerned, just as they do in cases involving, say, women who wish to attend military institutes. That is a significant development for a number of reasons. *Pavan* and *Morales-Santana* extended sex-based equal protection law beyond the boundaries of the traditional marital family—something the Court has often been loath to do. That is welcome news for gay people, unmarried parents, and others whose families depart from the conventional heterosexual nuclear model. It is also welcome news for pregnant women and mothers, who have not benefited from the Court's ongoing refusal, in

---

[22] *Virginia*, 518 US at 531.

[23] Id at 541–42.

[24] See, for example, *Nguyen*, 533 US at 78 (O'Connor, J, dissenting) (asserting that, in this case, which involved an unmarried father, "[t]he Court recites the governing substantive standard for heightened scrutiny of sex-based classifications, but departs from the guidance of our precedents concerning such classifications in several ways").

some contexts, to scrutinize pregnancy-related justifications for discrimination.

Part I of this article provides some historical context for these developments. It briefly examines the Court's growing skepticism over the past half-century toward justifications for discrimination that rest on "inherent differences" between the sexes. But its central focus is on areas in the law where this skepticism has faltered—most notably, in cases involving pregnancy itself, as well as in cases involving gay people and unwed fathers. It is not a coincidence that the Court has given the government more leeway to discriminate in these areas: they lie at the core of the "separate spheres" ideology the Court has mostly, but never fully, dismantled. The uneven application of heightened scrutiny has resulted in a disjunction between the kinds of biological justifications the Court has continued to accept in these areas and the more narrow set of biological justifications operative elsewhere in the law.

Part II examines *Pavan*. Some scholars may be tempted to dismiss *Pavan* as a mere footnote to *Obergefell*. It is true: Arkansas's refusal to include female spouses of birth mothers on their children's birth certificates while automatically including male spouses was a form of resistance to the Court's landmark ruling.[25] But the Court's rejection of the state's biological justifications for discriminating on the basis of sex in the context of birth certificates—where such justifications were arguably more plausible than in the context of marriage—pressed the point further than the Court had in *Obergefell*. The Court in *Pavan* took a hard look at the state's biological justifications for treating parents of different genders and sexual orientations differently in matters concerning their children. In so doing, it provided an example of what it might look like for courts to scrutinize the sorts of sex classifications that continue to ensnare people who engage in nontraditional means of family formation.

Part III turns to *Morales-Santana*. The Court issued an unusual remedy in this case, which drew a lot of attention.[26] As a result, most

---

[25] See *Smith v Pavan*, 505 SW3d 169 (Ark 2016) (Chief Justice Brill concurring in part and dissenting in part) (quoting Bob Dylan's *The Times They Are A-Changin'* and reminding his colleagues in the majority, who approved the state's discriminatory birth certificate regime, that "[r]egardless of personal values and regardless of a belief that the United States Supreme Court may have wrongfully decided a legal issue, all are bound by the law of the land").

[26] For further discussion of the remedy in *Morales-Santana* and the response to that remedy in the days after the decision came down, see text accompanying notes 150–61.

of the commentary on *Morales-Santana*, at least in the immediate aftermath of the decision, skipped over the momentous move the Court made in this case: it found a sex-based equal protection violation in a case involving an unmarried father. The Court has resisted doing this since the advent of sex-based equal protection law nearly half a century ago. In the first wave of unmarried father cases, the Court almost uniformly declined to engage in any sort of equal protection analysis.[27] It almost always disposed of those cases on due process grounds—and only very rarely in the unmarried fathers' favor. More recently, in cases involving citizenship, the Court has applied equal protection law, but only in a diluted form; it has explicitly and implicitly deferred to the government and upheld laws that discriminate against unmarried fathers.[28] The Court's decision to apply a robust form of equal protection analysis in *Morales-Santana* and to reject the government's ostensibly biological justification for treating unmarried mothers and fathers differently is therefore a significant development. Particularly when coupled with *Pavan*, it opens up possibilities for the extension of genuinely heightened equal protection scrutiny outside the conventional marital family.

Pavan and *Morales-Santana* have attracted much less attention than some other recent developments involving the same areas of law. But, this article argues, the Court did more in these decisions than meets the eye. It extended equal protection into areas it had previously walled off from meaningful constitutional scrutiny. It took a close look at ostensibly biological justifications for discrimination that had previously gone unexamined in cases involving gay people and unmarried fathers. In doing so, it discovered that those justifications were acting as smokescreens, obscuring a set of social judgments inconsistent with contemporary equal protection principles. If the Court abides by this approach, it could have significant ramifications for the rights of gay

---

[27] See Serena Mayeri, *Foundling Fathers: (Non)-Marriage and Parental Rights in the Age of Equality*, 125 Yale L J 2292 (2016) (providing an extensive historical account of the Court's refusal in the 1970s and early 1980s to subject sex classifications to heightened scrutiny in cases involving unmarried fathers).

[28] See Douglas NeJaime, *The Nature of Parenthood*, 126 Yale L J 2260, 2282–85 (2017) (discussing the Court's treatment of unwed fathers in *Nguyen v Immigration and Naturalization Service* and other cases involving citizenship); Kristin Collins, Note, *When Fathers' Rights Are Mothers' Duties: The Failure of Equal Protection in Miller v. Albright*, 109 Yale L J 1669 (2000) (criticizing the Court's failure to apply long-standing equal protection principles in a case involving a citizenship law that discriminated against unwed fathers on the basis of sex).

people and unwed fathers in particular, and more generally for the kind of differential treatment courts consider constitutionally justifiable based on "inherent differences" between the sexes, including in cases involving pregnancy. Whether that will occur, it is too early to say. What is clear is that returning to a regime in which the state may simply cite "inherent differences" between the sexes to justify discrimination against gay people and unmarried fathers would require unseeing much of what *Pavan* and *Morales-Santana* exposed.

I. Constitutional Sex Discrimination Law — and Exceptions to It

For many years, the Eagle Forum, a leader in the conservative "pro-family movement," has maintained on its website a list of the "top ten cases that prove the Equal Rights Amendment (ERA) would have been a disaster."[29] The ERA, which fell three states short of ratification in 1982, would have guaranteed that "[e]quality of rights under the law shall not be denied or abridged by the United States or by any state on account of sex."[30] The Eagle Forum's list, which is designed to illustrate the disastrous consequences a constitutional bar on sex discrimination would have inflicted on American society, is notable for two reasons. The first is the sheer number of cases on the list (an absolute majority) that have to do with the subjects of this article: pregnancy, gay people, and unmarried fathers. The second is that the list underscores the amount of discrimination that still exists with respect to these subjects—despite the fact that the Court over the past half-century has developed a constitutional bar on sex discrimination that functions as a "de facto ERA."[31] It is difficult today

---

[29] Top Ten Cases That Prove the Equal Rights Amendment (ERA) Would Have Been a Disaster, Eagle Forum (2002), at http://www.eagleforum.org/era/2002/top-ten.shtml.

[30] HRJ Res 208, 92d Cong, 1st Sess (1971); SJ Res 8, 92d Cong, 1st Sess (1971). Some classic accounts of the ERA's failure include Mary Frances Berry, *Why ERA Failed* (Indiana, 1986); Jane J. Mansbridge, *Why We Lost the ERA* (Chicago, 1986); and Donald G. Mathews and Jane Sherron De Hart, *Sex, Gender, and the Politics of ERA* (Oxford, 1990).

[31] Michael C. Dorf, *Equal Protection Incorporation*, 88 Va L Rev 951, 985 (2002) ("The social changes that did not quite produce the Equal Rights Amendment produced a de facto ERA in the Court's equal protection jurisprudence."); Reva B. Siegel, *Constitutional Culture, Social Movement Conflict, and Constitutional Change: The Case of the De Facto ERA*, 94 Cal L Rev 1323, 1324 (2006) (observing that "[w]ith energetic countermobilization, the ERA was defeated," but that "[i]n this same period, the Court began to interpret the Fourteenth Amendment in ways that were responsive to the amendment's proponents—so much so that scholars have begun to refer to the resulting body of equal protection case law as a 'de facto ERA'").

"to identify any respect in which constitutional law is different from what it would have been if the ERA had been adopted."[32] Yet a striking number of the regulations the Eagle Forum references—regulations it assumes would automatically be invalidated by a constitutional bar on sex discrimination—either remain good law or were only very recently deemed unconstitutional.

What accounts for the lag? This part shows that the Court has been slower to apply sex-based equal doctrine in certain contexts that strike especially close to the core of "separate spheres" ideology. That ideology, which prevailed for the first two centuries of our nation's history, mandates that women play domestic roles, taking care of hearth and home—and of course children—and that men take charge in the public sphere. As late as 1961, the Court approved a Florida law exempting women from jury service on the ground that the law merely acknowledged the "special responsibilities" that flow from women's natural role as the "center of home and family life."[33] But the 1960s also witnessed the rise of the women's movement, which took aim at stereotyped assumptions about men's and women's roles. Advocates of sex equality argued that much of what looked natural when it came to the sexes was actually socially constructed: it was not biology that required women to serve as the center of home and family life, but rather a vast apparatus of laws and customs that constrained them from straying too far outside those domains.[34] In the 1970s, the Court began to see that this was so. It began to apply heightened scrutiny to laws that discriminated on the basis of sex and, in a very short period of time, invalidated thousands of such laws.

The Court applied its new sex-based equal protection doctrine unevenly, however. Although the Court purported to subject all laws

---

[32] David A. Strauss, *The Irrelevance of Constitutional Amendments*, 114 Harv L Rev 1457, 1476–77 (2001); see also William N. Eskridge, Jr., *Channeling: Identity-Based Social Movements and Public Law*, 150 U Pa L Rev 419, 502 (2001) (asserting that "[b]ecause the women's movement did shift public norms to a relatively anti-discrimination baseline, it was able to do through the Equal Protection Clause virtually everything the ERA would have accomplished had it been ratified and added to the Constitution"); Jeffrey Rosen, *The New Look of Liberalism on the Court*, NY Times § 6 (magazine) at 60 (Oct 5, 1997) (quoting Justice Ruth Bader Ginsburg, who observed: "There is no practical difference between what has evolved and the ERA.").

[33] *Hoyt v Florida*, 368 US 57, 62 (1961). For more on *Hoyt*, see Justin Driver, *The Constitutional Conservatism of the Warren Court*, 100 Cal L Rev 1101, 1114–24 (2012).

[34] For more on the history and development of these denaturalizing arguments, see Franklin, 85 NYU L Rev at 92–106 (cited in note 6).

that classify on the basis of sex to heightened scrutiny, in practice, it carved out an array of exceptions—most notably in cases involving pregnancy, gay people, and single fathers. Sometimes, the Court explicitly exempted discrimination in these areas from heightened scrutiny;[35] other times, it simply applied a rational basis standard without acknowledging the downward departure.[36] The Court's reasons for departing from its general rule regarding sex classifications varied, but the departures themselves reveal a consistent theme. Unmarried fathers and gay people—especially gay people who form couples and/or become parents—present a particularly deep challenge to the separate-spheres ideology, as do pregnant women who do not wish to become mothers and mothers who do not wish to remain at home. As a result, people who fall into these categories have often had to wait longer to benefit from the full protection of constitutional equality law.

Some are still waiting. Around pregnancy, for instance, the Court in the 1970s created a kind of bubble that has insulated various forms of regulation from constitutional review. In 1971, in *Reed v Reed*, the Court—for the first time in American history—invalidated a law on the ground that it discriminated on the basis of sex.[37] Cases involving abortion and pregnancy discrimination soon followed. But the Court did not apply its new, more skeptical equality jurisprudence in either context. Where abortion was concerned, the Court chose to analyze regulations under substantive due process and almost entirely skirted questions about women's equality.[38] Then in 1974, in *Geduldig v Aiello*, it held that pregnancy discrimination is not sex discrimination because it does not differentiate between men and women, but simply

---

[35] See, for example, *Fiallo v Bell*, 430 US 787 (1977) (explicitly applying rational basis review in a case involving discrimination against unwed fathers in the context of citizenship).

[36] See, for example, *Michael M. v Superior Court of Sonoma County*, 450 US 464, 470 (1981) (purporting to apply heightened scrutiny but actually granting "great deference" to the legislature); id at 488–96 (Brennan, J, dissenting) (arguing that the plurality opinion failed to apply heightened scrutiny to the sex classification at issue).

[37] 401 US 934 (1971).

[38] See, for example, *Roe v Wade*, 410 US 113 (1973) (deciding that women have a constitutional right to abortion as a matter of substantive due process); see also Reva B. Siegel, *Reasoning from the Body: A Historical Perspective on Abortion Regulation and Questions of Equal Protection*, 44 Stan L Rev 261, 273 (1992) (observing that "[i]n *Roe*, the Court repeatedly suggests that states should defer to private decisions respecting abortion because they reflect the expertise of a medical professional, not because the community owes any particular deference to women's decisions about whether to assume the obligations of motherhood").

subjects pregnant people to less favorable treatment than nonpregnant people.[39] However, when the government turned around and defended *sex classifications* by reference to pregnancy, the Court changed course and concluded that pregnancy was an "inherent difference" between men and women that could justify their differential treatment.[40] This gave rise to something of a paradox: under the law the Burger Court created, pregnancy discrimination does not count as sex discrimination, yet pregnancy is, in some instances, deemed to be a fundamental difference between the sexes that gives the state a legitimate reason to treat men and women differently. Despite the apparent tension between these approaches, they are consistent in one respect: in both circumstances, the Court steps back and allows the state greater leeway to regulate because pregnancy is involved.

In recent decades, the Court has made several gestures toward limiting this leeway. In 1992, it invalidated an abortion law, which regulated pregnant women, on the ground that it reflected and reinforced a "common-law understanding of woman's role within the family."[41] In 2003, in a case involving the Family and Medical Leave Act, the Court suggested that discrimination against women "when they are mothers or mothers-to-be," that is, pregnant, ought to be treated as a serious constitutional problem.[42] But the Court has never explicitly overruled *Geduldig*; nor has it overruled the decisions in which it effectively applied a lower level of scrutiny when confronted by sex classifications justified by reference to pregnancy. Thus, even if the regulation of pregnancy no longer falls entirely outside the ambit of sex-based equal protection law, there remain substantial questions about how

---

[39] 417 US 484 (1974).

[40] *Michael M. v Superior Court of Sonoma County*, which was decided not too long after *Geduldig*, provides a particularly vivid illustration of this phenomenon. The Court in *Michael M.* upheld a law criminalizing sex with minor females, but not minor males, on the ground that girls, by virtue of their ability to become pregnant, "suffer disproportionately the profound physical, emotional and psychological consequences of sexual activity." *Michael M.*, 450 US at 471.

[41] *Planned Parenthood of Southeastern Pa. v Casey*, 505 US 833, 897 (1992). The law *Casey* invalidated required married women to notify their husbands before terminating a pregnancy. Id at 887.

[42] *Nevada Department of Human Resources v Hibbs*, 538 US 721, 736 (2003) (quotation marks omitted). For more on *Hibbs*'s groundbreaking commentary on the status of pregnancy discrimination under the Equal Protection Clause, see Franklin, 85 NYU L Rev at 149–54 (cited in note 6); Reva B. Siegel, *You've Come a Long Way, Baby: Rehnquist's New Approach to Pregnancy Discrimination in Hibbs*, 58 Stan L Rev 1871 (2006).

closely the Court will scrutinize state action in this area to ensure that it does not perpetuate conventional sex-role stereotypes.

A similar dynamic exists in the domain of sexual orientation. Courts have long shied away from applying heightened scrutiny to laws that facially classify on the basis of sex in cases in which the perceived targets of those laws are sexual minorities.[43] So-called traditional marriage laws are a good example. Such laws explicitly restricted one's choice of partner on the basis of sex. They barred women, but not men, from marrying women (and vice versa). Yet when the first challenge to such a law reached the Court in the early 1970s—after the Court's landmark decision in *Reed*, invalidating a sex classification under equal protection and suggesting that such classifications raise significant constitutional issues—the Court issued a one-sentence order dismissing the lawsuit "for want of a substantial federal question."[44] That 1972 ruling set a powerful precedent: where gay rights are concerned, courts have typically declined to subject facial sex classifications to the same level of scrutiny they apply to such classifications outside that context.

Often, courts in gay rights cases have simply applied rational basis review to laws that classify on the basis of sex without even acknowledging the discrepancy. When courts have supplied a reason for downgrading the level of scrutiny, they generally explain that, although the law at issue facially discriminates on the basis of sex, its real purpose is to regulate homosexuality: the law targets gays and lesbians, not men and women.[45] At this point, there is a substantial academic literature arguing that discrimination against gays and lesbians *is* sex discrimination, not simply because it involves facial sex classifications, but also, more substantively, because it reflects and reinforces traditional

---

[43] See, for example, Suzanne B. Goldberg, *Risky Arguments in Social Justice Litigation: The Case of Sex Discrimination and Marriage Equality*, 114 Colum L Rev 2087 (2014) (discussing courts' hesitancy to apply sex-based equal protection law to the sex classification in marriage).

[44] *Baker v Nelson*, 409 US 810, 810 (1972).

[45] See, for example, *In re Marriage Cases*, 183 P3d 384, 437 (Cal 2008) (declining to apply sex-based equal protection law to the sex classification in marriage because, "in realistic terms, a statute or policy that treats same-sex couples differently from opposite sex couples...does not treat an individual man or an individual woman differently *because of* his or her *gender* but rather accords differential treatment *because of* the individual's *sexual orientation*"); *Hernandez v Robles*, 855 NE2d 1, 11 (NY 2006) (declining to apply sex-based equal protection law because there was no indication that the sex classification in marriage was "designed to subordinate either men to women or women to men as a class").

understandings of men's and women's sex and family roles.[46] There is also a (smaller) literature pushing back against this argument. Martha Nussbaum, for instance, has argued that discrimination against gays and lesbians has less to do with the enforcement of sex stereotypes and more to do with "profound anxieties about bodily penetration and vulnerability" (this argument assumes that "prejudice against gay men ... is really what drives antigay efforts in America").[47]

But even if courts believed that antigay discrimination was driven solely by disgust, and that that disgust had nothing to do with gays' and lesbians' transgression of traditional gender norms, that still does not explain their failure to extend heightened scrutiny to *sex classifications* in this context. The Court has repeatedly and vehemently insisted over the past forty years that equal protection law is anti-classificationist—that it is concerned with regulations that formally classify on forbidden grounds and that the level of constitutional scrutiny does not vary according to subjective judgments about the nature of those classifications. For instance, if a state that assigned white employees to one set of jobs and black employees to another set of jobs were to convince the Court that it did this, not out of racial prejudice, but merely because it wanted wealthier employees in one set of jobs and poorer employees in the other, and race worked as a proxy for this, that would get the state nowhere. All racial classifications, regardless of their purpose, are subject to strict scrutiny.[48] The fact that the government *does* get somewhere when it argues that the real purpose of a sex classification is to prefer heterosexuals to homosexuals suggests that, in fact, the Court exercises considerable judgment in determining

---

[46] See, for example, Suzanne Pharr, *Homophobia: A Weapon of Sexism* (Chardon, 1988); Susan Frelich Appleton, *Missing in Action? Searching for Gender Talk in the Same-Sex Marriage Debate*, 16 Stan L & Pol Rev 97, 125–34 (2005); Mary Anne Case, *What Feminists Have to Lose in Same-Sex Marriage Litigation*, 57 UCLA L Rev 1199 (2010); Cary Franklin, *Inventing the "Traditional Concept" of Sex Discrimination*, 125 Harv L Rev 1307 (2012); Andrew Koppelman, *Why Discrimination Against Lesbians and Gay Men Is Sex Discrimination*, 69 NYU L Rev 197 (1994); Sylvia A. Law, *Homosexuality and the Social Meaning of Gender*, 1988 Wis L Rev 187; Deborah A. Widiss, Elizabeth L. Rosenblatt, and Douglas NeJaime, *Exposing Sex Stereotypes in Recent Same-Sex Marriage Jurisprudence*, 30 Harv J L & Gender 461 (2007).

[47] Martha C. Nussbaum, *From Disgust to Humanity: Sexual Orientation and Constitutional Law* 116 (Oxford, 2010); see also Edward Stein, *Evaluating the Sex Discrimination Argument for Lesbian and Gay Rights*, 49 UCLA L Rev 471 (2001).

[48] *Johnson v California*, 543 US 499, 505 (2005) ("We have insisted on strict scrutiny in every context, even for so-called 'benign' racial classifications...."); *Adarand Constructors, Inc. v Pena*, 515 US 200, 222 (1995) ("[T]he Fourteenth Amendment requires strict scrutiny of all race-based action by state and local governments.").

what counts as a classification for purposes of equal protection law.[49] In the context of gay rights, as in the context of pregnancy, the Court's hesitancy to subject the state's justifications to heightened scrutiny reflects (at least in part) a hesitancy about completely dismantling the sex-role-based structures that have undergirded American society since the time of the founding. The result has been that, in this context too, biological justifications for discrimination have generally gone unchecked.

These same features appear in equal protection cases involving unmarried fathers. Right around the time the Court was beginning to subject laws that discriminate on the basis of sex to heightened scrutiny, unmarried fathers began to bring constitutional challenges to regulations that made it more difficult for them, as opposed to unmarried mothers, to establish legal rights with regard to their children. Many of these cases involved fathers who were contesting the adoption of their children by men married to their children's mothers;[50] others involved child custody[51] or the right to sue for the wrongful death of a child.[52] In all of these instances, the contested laws classified on the basis of sex in ways that saddled unmarried fathers with particular burdens. Unmarried mothers were given the right to consent (or not consent) to the adoption of their children, unmarried fathers were not; unmarried mothers were permitted to bring wrongful death lawsuits when their children were killed, unmarried fathers were not; unmarried mothers automatically retained custody of their children when the fathers of those children died, unmarried fathers did not necessarily retain custody when their children's mothers died.

---

[49] Scholars have written about this phenomenon in the context of race as well. See, for example, Jack M. Balkin and Reva B. Siegel, *The American Civil Rights Tradition: Anticlassification or Antisubordination?*, 58 U Miami L Rev 9, 16–17 (2003) (contrasting cases finding racial classifications when race is considered as one of many factors in the context of affirmative action with cases finding no classification when race is considered as one of many factors in adoption placements and suspect identification); Richard A. Primus, *Equal Protection and Disparate Impact: Round Three*, 117 Harv L Rev 493, 509 (2003) (suggesting that the term "racial classification" may "function[] as a term of art that encompasses a mix of descriptive and normative elements"); Reva B. Siegel, *Equality Talk: Antisubordination and Anticlassification Values in Constitutional Struggles over Brown*, 117 Harv L Rev 1470, 1542–44 (2004) (discussing the indeterminacy of what counts as a racial classification and courts' hesitancy to find racial classifications, and thus apply strict scrutiny, in cases involving, among other things, the collection of racial census data and racial profiling by law enforcement officials).

[50] See, for example, *Lehr v Robertson*, 463 US 248 (1983); *Caban v Mohammed*, 441 US 380 (1979); *Quilloin v Walcott*, 434 US 246 (1978).

[51] See, for example, *Stanley v Illinois*, 405 US 645 (1972).

[52] See, for example, *Parham v Hughes*, 441 US 347 (1979).

Occasionally, unmarried fathers won these cases; more often, they lost. But in almost all of these cases the Court simply sidestepped the equal protection question and resolved the issue on due process grounds.[53] That approach resulted in highly fact-intensive decisions, generally holding that the father in question had not done enough to establish a relationship with his child and had consequently forfeited whatever legal right he was seeking. It also meant that the Court did not engage with the broader constitutional questions about whether laws that discriminate against unmarried fathers reflect or reinforce conventional sex-role stereotypes. When the state sought to justify the differential treatment of unmarried men and women by citing biological differences between the sexes, the Court generally left those justifications unexamined. When the Court did examine such biological justifications, far from drilling down on them in the way that constitutional doctrine by then required, it tended to embrace them. In *Parham v Hughes*, for example, the Court upheld a law that allowed the mother but not the father of a nonmarital child to sue for the child's wrongful death on the ground that "mothers and fathers of illegitimate children are not similarly situated. . . . Unlike the mother of an illegitimate child whose identity will rarely be in doubt, the identity of the father will frequently be unknown."[54] The implications of the Court's decision to give the state a free pass in these cases and to leave unexamined, or even to endorse, biological justifications for discrimination would reverberate through constitutional sex discrimination law for decades to come.

II. Scrutinizing Biological Justifications for Discrimination Against Gay Parents

The ongoing power of biological justifications for sex discrimination was evident in 2016 in the Arkansas Supreme Court's decision

---

[53] Mayeri, 125 Yale L J at 2372 (cited in note 27) (showing that although, in the 1970s and 1980s, "nonmarital fathers achieved some due process protections, they never won a constitutional guarantee of equal treatment based on sex and marital status").

[54] *Parham v Hughes*, 441 US 347, 355 (1979); see also *Caban*, 441 US at 405–06 (Stevens, J, dissenting) (condoning "the differential treatment of the mother and the father in the adoption process" because when a child is born, "the mother and child are together; the mother's identity is known with certainty," whereas the father "may or may not be present; his identity may be unknown," and "[t]hese natural differences between unmarried fathers and mothers make it probable that the mother, and not the father or both parents, will have custody of the newborn infant").

to uphold a law that treated men and women differently with respect to their children's birth certificates.[55] The law required that a man's name be placed on the birth certificate of his wife's newborn child in almost all circumstances, while prohibiting a woman's name from being placed on the birth certificate of her wife's newborn child.[56] A set of married lesbians who had recently become parents challenged the law in the wake of *Obergefell*—which had declared that the Constitution guarantees same-sex couples the right to marry "on the same terms and conditions as opposite-sex couples."[57] The lesbian couples challenging the law argued that it violated this precept and discriminated on the basis of sex and sexual orientation in violation of the Fourteenth Amendment.[58]

The Arkansas Supreme Court disagreed. It endorsed the state's argument that the overarching purpose of its birth certificate system was not to sanctify anyone's marriage but to identify biological ties between parents and children for public health and other purposes.[59] That was an important state interest, the Court held, and it was not discriminatory to treat male and female spouses of birth mothers differently in this context in recognition of the fact that the female spouse "does not have the same biological nexus to the child that the biological mother or the biological father has."[60] In sum, the Court concluded: "It does not violate equal protection to acknowledge basic biological truths."[61]

The Arkansas Court's decision was not an outlier. Indeed, it was indicative of a long-term trend in gay rights law. In 1972, in *Baker v*

---

[55] *Smith v Pavan*, 505 SW3d 169 (Ark 2016).

[56] *Pavan v Smith*, 137 US 2075, 2077 (2017).

[57] 135 S Ct 2584, 2605 (2015). Indeed, the Court in *Obergefell* explicitly cited the placement of one's name on a marital child's birth certificate as one of the "governmental rights, benefits, and responsibilities" traditionally entailed in marriage. Id at 2601.

[58] Appellees' Responsive Brief, *Smith v Pavan*, Civil Action No 15-988, *11–22 (Ark filed May 23, 2016) (available on Westlaw at 2016 WL 7987958).

[59] *Smith*, 505 SW3d at 179–80; see also id at 178 ("[T]he statute centers on the relationship of the biological mother and the biological father to the child, not on the marital relationship of husband and wife.").

[60] Id at 181. The Court accepted the state's assertion that the female spouse of a birth mother will never have a biological relationship to a child of the marriage. Although it did not become central to the United States Supreme Court's holding in *Pavan*, this is, in fact, not true. See note 15, which describes a situation in which a birth mother's female partner is biologically related to her child.

[61] Id.

Nelson, the United States Supreme Court did not even ask the government to justify its discrimination against same-sex couples.[62] Over the next few decades, as constitutional challenges to laws that discriminated against gays and lesbians proliferated, courts began to require that the government provide some sort of justification for the discrimination. At first, the bar for such justifications was exceedingly low. The state could simply argue that homosexuality was immoral and that "[m]any Americans d[id] not want persons who openly engage in homosexual conduct as partners in their business, as scoutmasters for their children, as teachers in their children's schools, or as boarders in their home."[63] Courts in the 1980s and 1990s often sympathized with Americans who viewed antigay laws as a means of "protecting themselves and their families from a lifestyle that they believe to be immoral and destructive."[64] Justice Scalia, who penned the preceding quotations, would have accepted such justifications for sexual-orientation-based discrimination well into the twenty-first century.[65]

But over time, the Court rejected such views. It began to subject laws that discriminate against gays and lesbians to something more than rational basis review and to reject arguments grounded purely in traditional morality.[66] At that point, biological arguments became the coin of the realm in terms of justifying orientation-based state action, particularly in matters relating to family law. Where marriage was

---

[62] See note 44 and accompanying text.

[63] *Lawrence v Texas*, 539 US 558, 602 (2003) (Scalia, J, dissenting).

[64] Id.

[65] Cf. Jeffrey Toobin, *Justice Scalia's Shameful Joke*, New Yorker (Apr 28 2015), available at https://www.newyorker.com/news/daily-comment/on-gay-marriage-its-not-scalias-court (reporting on the oral argument in *Obergefell*, during which Justice Scalia (sort of) joked that a protester's shouted assertion that supporters of gay marriage would "burn in Hell" was "refreshing").

[66] See, for example, *Lawrence*, 539 US at 582 ("This case raises a different issue . . . : whether, under the Equal Protection Clause, moral disapproval is a legitimate state interest to justify by itself a statute that bans homosexual sodomy, but not heterosexual sodomy. It is not."). The Court purported to apply rational basis review in *Lawrence* and *Romer v Evans*, 517 US 620 (1996) (striking down a state constitutional amendment barring all government action designed to protect people on the basis of sexual orientation). Indeed, the Court never explicitly stated, even in *United States v Windsor*, 133 S Ct 2675 (2013) (holding the Defense of Marriage Act unconstitutional), and *Obergefell* that it had heightened the standard of review. But as the dissenting Justices in these cases correctly noted, the Court has clearly departed from traditional rational basis review and now holds laws that discriminate against gays and lesbians to a higher constitutional standard. See, for example, *Windsor*, 133 S Ct at 2706 (Scalia, J, dissenting) (observing that, although the Court does not explicitly state that it has departed from rational basis, it "certainly does not *apply* anything that resembles that deferential framework").

concerned, states began to argue that preserving the sex distinction was essential because only different-sex couples could produce children, and society needed an institution that could bind fathers to their children and to the women who gave birth to those children.[67] When the sex-role stereotypes embedded in that ostensibly biological argument became too apparent to ignore, states stripped it down further, dropping the explicit references to fathers' lack of commitment to their children and arguing simply that marriage was an institution designed to manage the care of children and that only heterosexuals—who often procreated without intending to—were thus in need of it.[68] Proponents of "traditional marriage" argued that allowing same-sex couples to marry would delink the institution from procreation and therefore reduce its efficacy in keeping heterosexuals in check.[69]

It is not surprising that the constitutional argument for excluding gays and lesbians from marriage arrived at this destination. Under the Court's doctrine, biology remains the most promising justification for laws that discriminate on the basis of sex and sexual orientation. In fact, procreation-based justifications for limiting marriage rights to different-sex couples prevailed in lower courts for some years.[70]

Those arguments met their end, however, in *Obergefell*. The Court observed in *Obergefell* that much of what had once seemed "natural" about marriage was subsequently revealed to reflect stereotyped con-

---

[67] See Widiss, Rosenblatt, and NeJaime, 30 Harv J L & Gender 461 (cited in note 46) (describing states' increasing reliance on arguments of this sort).

[68] The best example of this form of the argument appears in Chief Justice Roberts's dissenting opinion in *Obergefell*, 135 S Ct at 2613 (Roberts, CJ, dissenting) ("The human race must procreate to survive. Procreation occurs through sexual relations between a man and a woman. When sexual relations result in the conception of a child, that child's prospects are generally better if the mother and father stay together rather than going their separate ways. Therefore, for the good of children and society, sexual relations that can lead to procreation should occur only between a man and a woman committed to a lasting bond. Society has recognized that bond as marriage."); see also id at 2641 (Alito, J, dissenting) (asserting that states "formalize and promote marriage, unlike other fulfilling human relationships, in order to encourage potentially procreative conduct to take place within a lasting unit that has long been thought to provide the best atmosphere for raising children").

[69] For more on this argument, see Kenji Yoshino, *The Best Argument Against Gay Marriage, and Why It Fails*, Slate (Dec 13, 2010), at http://www.slate.com/articles/news_and_politics/jurisprudence/2010/12/the_best_argument_against_gay_marriage.html.

[70] See Kerry Abrams and Peter Brooks, *Marriage as a Message: Same-Sex Couples and the Rhetoric of Accidental Procreation*, 21 Yale J L & Humanities 1, 3–4 (2009) (describing the emergence and rapid adoption of this argument by courts throughout the country after 2003).

ceptions of men's and women's roles.[71] In the nineteenth century and even into the twentieth, the Court explained, marriage was synonymous with coverture, the system through which a married woman's legal identity was subsumed into that of her husband.[72] Even when coverture receded, "invidious sex-based classifications in marriage remained common."[73] For a long time, those classifications were understood to be justified by men's and women's different talents and capacities—including differences in their reproductive functions. But, in the 1970s and 1980s, it became apparent that lurking underneath the veneer of the government's biological justifications for treating husbands and wives differently was a plethora of social judgments and generalizations incompatible with constitutional liberty and equality guarantees.[74]

Now, the Court held in *Obergefell*, it was time for a similar unmasking in the context of sexual orientation. Upon examination, the biological justifications for limiting marriage to different-sex couples were revealed to be just as socially constructed and constitutionally troublesome as the old arguments in favor of coverture. The Court observed that "[a]n ability, desire, or promise to procreate is not and has not been a prerequisite for a valid marriage in any State."[75] Older people and infertile people have never been barred from marrying, because, in fact, "[t]he constitutional marriage right has many aspects, of which childbearing is only one."[76] Moreover, the Court concluded, it makes no sense to suggest that allowing gay people to marry would "sever the connection between natural procreation and marriage" and thereby cause fewer heterosexuals to marry: "Decisions about whether to marry and raise children are based on many personal, romantic, and practical considerations; and it is unrealistic to conclude that an opposite-sex couple would choose not to marry simply because same-

---

[71] *Obergefell*, 135 S Ct at 2595.

[72] Id.

[73] Id at 2603.

[74] Id at 2603–04 ("These classifications denied the equal dignity of men and women. One State's law, for example, provided in 1971 that 'the husband is the head of the family and the wife is subject to him. . . .' Ga. Code Ann. § 53–501 (1935). Responding to a new awareness, the Court invoked equal protection principles to invalidate laws imposing sex-based inequality on marriage.").

[75] *Obergefell*, 135 S Ct at 2601.

[76] Id.

sex couples may do so."[77] The dissenting Justices pushed back hard on the biological front, insisting that "[f]or millennia, marriage [has been] inextricably linked to the one thing that only an opposite-sex couple can do: procreate."[78] But the Court in *Obergefell* made clear that, although that kind of ostensibly biological justification may have escaped constitutional scrutiny in the past, the law now demanded more.[79]

Just how much more was on display in *Pavan*. If the biological justification for maintaining the sex classification in marriage was always a little shaky, the argument for treating male and female spouses of birth mothers differently with respect to birth certificates seemed, at first glance, more plausible. But once again, the Court declined to defer to the government's proffered biological justifications: it genuinely scrutinized the challenged law to ensure it did not reflect or reinforce illicit social judgments.

Arkansas's birth certificate regime could not withstand such scrutiny. Upon examination, it became clear that there was more at work in the way the state allocated spots on birth certificates than simply biology. For one thing, the automatic inclusion of the birth mother's husband ran directly counter to biology in a range of cases—and intentionally so. The Court observed, for instance, that if the mother used a sperm donor, her husband's name still appeared on the birth certificate as the child's father.[80] Also, the Court noted, if the mother slept with another man and became pregnant that way, the state still mandated that her husband's name be listed on the child's birth certificate, even if he objected to being labeled the father of a child to whom he had no biological ties.[81] The Court pointed to the challeng-

---

[77] Id.

[78] Id at 2641 (Alito, J, dissenting); see also id at 2584 (Roberts, CJ, dissenting).

[79] *Obergefell*, 135 S Ct at 2602 ("The limitation of marriage to opposite-sex couples may long have seemed natural and just, but its inconsistency with the central meaning of the fundamental right to marry is now manifest. With that knowledge must come the recognition that laws excluding same-sex couples from the marriage right impose stigma and injury of the kind prohibited by our basic charter.").

[80] *Pavan*, 137 S Ct at 2077.

[81] Id (noting that one of the very few ways a husband can avoid the inclusion of his name on the birth certificate in these circumstances is if he and "the 'mother' and...'putative father' all file affidavits vouching for the putative father's paternity"). The only other way a husband can avoid being listed on the birth certificate of his wife's newborn child is if a court of competent jurisdiction has determined that he is not the father of the child. See *Smith v Pavan*, 505 SW3d 169, 175 (Ark 2016).

ers' brief for more arguments along these lines[82]—the most striking of which was simply that Arkansas made no effort to ensure that a birth mother's husband actually had biological ties to the child on whose birth certificate he was listed as the father.[83] In fact, biological fathers have traditionally had enormous difficulty obtaining parental rights when their children are born to married women who are not their wives: the marital relationship between husband and wife has generally trumped the genetic relationship between a biological father and his child.[84] Because Arkansas "has … chosen to make its birth certificates more than a mere marker of biological relationships," *Pavan* held, it could not rely on biological justifications to defend its differential treatment of same-sex and different-sex couples.[85]

Pavan was obviously an application of *Obergefell*'s holding that same-sex couples are entitled to civil marriage rights "'on the same terms and conditions as opposite-sex couples.'"[86] But it was not merely a matter of judicial housekeeping—a case in which the Court simply swept away a law that obviously contravened a prior ruling. *Pavan* extended the principles articulated in *Obergefell* even deeper into the family, revealing how normative judgments about gender and sexual orientation can underwrite even the most elementary-seeming "facts" about reproductive biology. The Court's refusal to defer to ostensibly biological reasoning even in *Pavan*, where the state's justifications seemed to be at their most "biological," could have implications for a broad range of cases,[87] particularly in the realm of assisted reproduc-

---

[82] *Pavan*, 137 S Ct at 2078 ("As the petitioners point out, other factual scenarios (beyond those present in this case) similarly show that the State's birth certificates are about more than genetic parentage.").

[83] Reply Brief of Petitioners, *Pavan v Smith*, Civil Action No 16-992, *4–6 (US filed May 1, 2017) (available on Westlaw at 2017 WL 1629334) (pointing out "that a biological relationship with the child is not required for Arkansas to list the male spouse of the birth mother as the child's parent," and that "[n]ot only do [the state's] laws often require the *exclusion* of a child's biological parent from a birth certificate, they permit and sometimes require the *inclusion* of non-biological parents").

[84] See, for example, *Michael H. v Gerald D.*, 491 US 110 (1989) (holding that a biological father's liberty interest in maintaining a relationship with his child did not overcome a statutory presumption that the husband of the child's mother was the child's other parent).

[85] *Pavan*, 137 S Ct at 2078.

[86] Id (quoting that language in *Obergefell*). The Court determined in *Pavan* that inclusion on birth certificates was one of "the constellation of benefits that the States have linked to marriage," and that married same-sex couples could not therefore be treated differently in this regard from married different-sex couples. Id at 2077.

[87] Indeed, a few months after *Pavan* came down, the Arizona Supreme Court relied on it to invalidate that state's differential treatment of male and female spouses of birth mothers in

tive technology (ART)—a method of family formation to which more Americans are turning every year.

Doug NeJaime has extensively chronicled instances in which biological justifications are still being offered—and accepted by courts—for regulations that, in actuality, perpetuate conventional stereotypes about men's and women's sex and family roles and disadvantage gay people.[88] For instance, courts often allow husbands (with no biological relation) to derive parental rights through marriage to a newborn's biological mother, but they do not allow wives (with no biological relation) to derive parental rights through marriage to a newborn's biological father.[89] A woman who relies on a gestational surrogate to carry a child produced with a donor egg and her husband's sperm generally cannot derive parentage by being married to the biological father, whereas if donor sperm is used, a man can derive parental rights by being married to the child's biological mother.[90] This distinction penalizes nonbiological mothers, and it also penalizes gay men. Lesbians can obtain parental rights by being married to a biological mother; gay men cannot obtain parental rights by being married to a biological father. When these distinctions are challenged, judges have cited "actual physiological differences between men and women" as justification for upholding them.[91] But, in fact, from a biological standpoint, nongestational, nongenetic mothers are not situated any differently from nonbiological fathers; lesbians whose wives produce biological children are not situated any differently from gay men whose husbands do.[92]

---

the assignment of legal parentage. See *McLaughlin v McLaughlin*, 401 P3d 492 (Ariz 2017). Prior to this ruling, Arizona presumed that a man was the legal parent of any child to whom his wife gave birth in the course of their marriage, but did not extend the same presumption to female spouses whose wives gave birth. The litigant defending the law argued that the state's sex-differentiated system of parental presumptions simply tracked biology. Id at 498. But the Arizona Supreme Court rejected that argument for reasons similar to those the Court relied on in *Pavan*. See id ("Because the marital paternity presumption does more than just identify biological fathers, Arizona cannot deny same-sex spouses the benefit the presumption affords. See *Pavan*....").

[88] See NeJaime, 126 Yale L J 2260 (cited in note 28).

[89] Id at 2290–2316.

[90] Id.

[91] *In re Parentage of a Child by T.J.S. & A.L.S.*, 54 A3d 263, 264 (NJ 2012) (Hoens concurring) (citation omitted).

[92] The one instance in which there is a difference is when one mother provides the egg and the other gestates the fetus, but courts do not cabin the differential treatment of lesbian mothers and gay fathers to those instances. See NeJaime, 126 Yale L J at 1206–07, 2314–16 (cited in note 28).

The distinction is not a biological one, it is a social one: "[E]ven in an age of sex and sex-orientation equality, courts and legislatures continue to treat *biological mothers* as the parents from whom the *legal family* necessarily springs."[93] If you are a biological mother, or are married to one, your parental rights are likely secure; if not, you are likely to face some problems.

Regulations of this sort, which have the effect of reinforcing traditional sex stereotypes and disadvantaging sexual minorities, are ripe for reconsideration in light of the Court's holding in *Pavan*. Change will not come easily in this area, however. The Court's opinions in *Obergefell* and *Pavan* both triggered vigorous dissents. The dissenting Justices in those cases disavowed the Court's deployment of heightened scrutiny in the context of gay rights; in fact, it is not even clear they entirely accept the use of heightened scrutiny in the context of sex.[94] In both *Obergefell* and *Pavan*, the dissenters would have deferred to the state, allowing it to rely on biological justifications for the challenged discrimination without subjecting those justifications to any real scrutiny.

Indeed, in his dissenting opinion in *Pavan*, Justice Gorsuch—the Court's newest Justice—relied heavily on a case involving an unmarried father in which the Court did just that.[95] In that case, which also involved a sex classification, the Court purported to apply heightened scrutiny, but in fact applied a standard of review akin to rational basis: it accepted a biological justification for discrimination over a strenuous dissenting opinion that exposed the thick layer of stereotypes underlying the state's claims.[96] Justice Gorsuch's dissent likely raised alarm bells for scholars concerned that in the future—especially if more right-leaning Justices are appointed—the Court will cabin its pronouncements about liberty and equality in *Obergefell* to the context of mar-

---

[93] Id at 2314.

[94] See Mary Anne Case, *Missing Sex Talk in the Supreme Court's Same-Sex Marriage Cases*, 84 UMKC L Rev 675 (2016) ("[N]one of the dissenters in *Obergefell* has ever, as far as I can tell, voted in favor of a constitutional sex discrimination claim."). Case observes that when questioned by Senator Joseph Biden during his confirmation hearings, Chief Justice Roberts "did express a commitment to heightened scrutiny for sex distinctions, but in a way that . . . does not quite commit him to upholding, let alone extending, the current settled law of constitutional sex discrimination."). Id at n 64.

[95] *Pavan*, 137 S Ct at 2079 (Gorsuch, J, dissenting) (citing *Nguyen v Immigration and Naturalization Service*, 533 US 53 (2001)).

[96] For further discussion of the Court's holding in *Nguyen* and the dissenting Justices' objections to that holding, see text accompanying notes 122–37.

riage.[97] As the unmarried-father case Justice Gorsuch cited in *Pavan* demonstrates, the Court has long hesitated to apply constitutional principles derived from its decisions striking down sex classifications in cases involving the nonmarital family. What Justice Gorsuch failed to acknowledge in his dissent, however, is that just two weeks prior to *Pavan*, the Court issued a new decision involving unmarried fathers in which it ratcheted up the level of scrutiny and rejected an ostensibly biological justification for treating the sexes differently. It is to that case this article now turns.

III. Extending Sex-Based Equal Protection Outside Marriage

Sessions v Morales-Santana was a case about citizenship—more specifically, the citizenship of children born abroad to unmarried parents, one of whom is a U.S. citizen and the other of whom is not. In these circumstances, the portion of the INA at issue in the case conferred citizenship automatically on the child of a citizen mother, as long as the mother had resided in the United States for at least one year at some point prior to the child's birth.[98] The residency requirements were considerably stiffer for citizen fathers: they could transmit citizenship to their children only if, prior to their children's birth, they had lived in the United States for a total of ten years, five of which occurred after their fourteenth birthday.[99] The child—now a grown man—challenging this law was Luis Morales-Santana. He was born in the Dominican Republic to a Dominican mother and an American father, José Morales.[100] His parents were not married when he was born, although they did marry a few years later.[101] When Morales-Santana was thirteen, the family moved to the Bronx.[102] Years later, he was

---

[97] See, for example, Melissa Murray, *Obergefell v. Hodges and Nonmarriage Inequality*, 104 Cal L Rev 1207 (2016).

[98] Immigration and Nationality Act of 1952, ch 477, § 309(c), 66 Stat 163, 238–39.

[99] Id at §§ 301(a)(7), 309(a). In 1986, the requirement for unmarried citizen fathers was reduced to five years in the United States, two of them after the age of fourteen. Immigration and Nationality Act Amendments of 1986, Pub L No 99-653, § 12, 100 Stat 3655, 3657. This amendment did not help Morales-Santana, however, because he was born prior to the change and it did not apply retrospectively.

[100] *Morales-Santana*, 137 S Ct at 1688.

[101] Id.

[102] Id.

convicted of burglary and attempted murder, and the government sought to deport him after determining he was not a U.S. citizen.[103]

Because Morales-Santana's parents were not married at the time of his birth, he was subject to the portion of the INA governing non-marital children born abroad to mixed-nationality couples. Unfortunately for him, his father had left Puerto Rico for the Dominican Republic at the age of nineteen—twenty days shy of satisfying the residency requirements that would have enabled him to transmit U.S. citizenship to his son.[104] If José Morales had been a woman, he would easily have satisfied the one-year residency requirement and his son would have been a U.S. citizen. But because José was a man, his son was a foreigner. An immigration judge ordered Morales-Santana's removal to the Dominican Republic—and a Supreme Court case was born.[105]

If one knew nothing about the Court's constitutional sex discrimination jurisprudence over the past forty years, it seems unlikely that one would attempt to justify the INA's imposition of different residency requirements on male and female parents by reference to biology. These differential residency requirements are not tied in any obvious way to biological differences between the sexes. It is indicative of how much work "inherent differences" between the sexes continue to perform in justifying discrimination under the Fourteenth Amendment that the government did in fact frame its defense of the differential residency requirements in those terms.

Indeed, constitutional precedents in this area made the government's reliance on biology in *Morales-Santana* a foregone conclusion. About twenty years ago, several different sets of unmarried citizen fathers and their children challenged a closely related provision of the INA having to do with the establishment of parentage.[106] In order to establish parentage, a citizen father of a nonmarital child born abroad to a noncitizen mother was required to "legitimate" or otherwise formally acknowledge paternity of his child before the child turned eigh-

---

[103] Brief for the Petitioner, *Sessions v Morales-Santana*, Civil Action No 15-1191, at *7 (US filed Aug 19, 2016) (available on Westlaw at 2016 WL 4436132).

[104] *Morales-Santana*, 137 S Ct at 1687.

[105] Id at 1688.

[106] See *Nguyen v Immigration and Naturalization Service*, 533 US 53, 78 (2001); *Miller v Albright*, 523 US 420 (1998).

teen.[107] If the father failed to do so, his ability to transmit citizenship to his child evaporated. Citizen mothers were not required to take any equivalent steps. Assuming they satisfied the one-year residency requirement at issue in *Morales-Santana*, their children automatically acquired U.S. citizenship at birth.

The government defended its differential treatment of men and women with respect to the establishment of parentage in two successive constitutional challenges by arguing that the lopsided requirements merely reflected the fact that the sexes are not similarly situated to one another at the moment of a child's birth.[108] Mothers are invariably present at the birth of their children, and, the government asserted, their participation in the birth automatically establishes their parentage and provides them an opportunity to bond with their children. Fathers are not necessarily present at the birth of their children and—especially when they are not married to their children's mother—may not even know those children exist. Thus, the government argued, the law requires fathers to take a series of affirmative steps to establish what the birthing process has already established where mothers are concerned.

There were various problems with this argument, starting with the fact that, in practice, giving birth does not necessarily provide mothers an opportunity to bond with their children.[109] Some children are taken from their mothers at birth and never get to know them. In such cases, children still automatically derive U.S. citizenship from their mothers. Yet fathers who take custody of their children at birth and raise those children in the United States remain powerless to transmit their citizenship unless they formally acknowledge paternity within the legally specified window. Even a DNA test that demonstrates beyond a shadow of a doubt that a man is his child's father is of no avail under the law if he misses that window.[110] But this kind of proof is never required of mothers, even those who long ago lost touch with, or indeed never even met, their children.

---

[107] For a more detailed account of this law, see *Nguyen*, 533 US at 59–60.

[108] For a more fulsome look at the government's arguments, see Brief for the Respondent, *Nguyen v Immigration and Naturalization Service*, Civil Action No 99-2071 (US filed Dec 13, 2000) (available on Westlaw at 2000 WL 1868100).

[109] See *Nguyen*, 533 US at 86–87 (O'Connor, J, dissenting) (discussing situations in which a birth mother may not have an opportunity to develop a relationship with her child).

[110] Id at 80.

Despite these seeming infirmities, and others,[111] the fathers and children in these cases faced an uphill battle: the law they were challenging sat at the intersection of two areas where the Court has traditionally given the government a break under equal protection. As Part I showed, the Court has generally refrained from applying heightened scrutiny to sex-based state action in cases involving unmarried fathers. On top of this, the INA cases involved citizenship—an area where the Court has often deferred to the government under the plenary power doctrine.[112] In 1977, for instance, in *Fiallo v Bell*, the Court heard a challenge to a provision of the INA that granted special immigration preferences to noncitizens who qualify as the "children" or "parents" of U.S. citizens.[113] Unmarried mothers and their children qualified for these preferences; unmarried fathers and their children did not.[114] The Court did not hold in *Fiallo* that the statute was unreviewable,[115] but it applied rational basis review rather than heightened scrutiny in recognition of "the limited scope of judicial inquiry into immigration legislation."[116]

With the plenary power doctrine and judicial precedents involving unmarried fathers in the background, the Court in *Miller v Albright*— the first of the challenges to the INA's sex-differentiated rules regarding the establishment of parentage—left the statute intact.[117] The Court in *Miller* was deeply fractured and did not ultimately resolve the constitutional questions presented.[118] But at least some of the Justices were

---

[111] For more extensive discussion of the imprecise fit between the statute's provisions and the government's stated ends, see id at 78–94.

[112] For more on the Court's deployment of the plenary power doctrine in this context, see Cornelia T. L. Pillard and T. Alexander Aleinikoff, *Skeptical Scrutiny of Plenary Power: Judicial and Executive Branch Decision Making in Miller v Albright*, 1998 Supreme Court Review 1.

[113] 430 US 787 (1977).

[114] Id at 788–89.

[115] Id at 792 (concluding that the question at issue was subject "to narrow judicial review" (quotation marks omitted)).

[116] Id at 791, 795–96 (holding that, because "[o]ur cases have long recognized the power to expel or exclude aliens as a fundamental sovereign attribute exercised by the Government's political departments largely immune from judicial control" (quotation marks omitted), the government had to provide only "a facially legitimate and bona fide reason" for discriminating on the basis of sex in this context).

[117] *Miller v Albright*, 523 US 420 (1998).

[118] Six Justices were in favor of upholding the law in *Miller*. Two of those Justices rejected the sex-based equal protection claim; two others believed there were standing problems; and the final two argued that the Court could not confer citizenship as a remedy in this case even if there were an equal protection violation. The three dissenting Justices would have held that

prepared to accept the government's ostensibly biological justifications for treating men and women differently. In an opinion announcing the judgment of the Court, but joined only by Chief Justice Rehnquist, Justice Stevens concluded that "biological differences between single men and single women provide a relevant basis for differing rules governing their ability to confer citizenship on children born in foreign lands."[119] Only women are necessarily present at their children's births, Justice Stevens explained; men are not, and unmarried men are especially prone to absence. Thus, he reasoned, "the gender equality principle" that generally applies when the state discriminates on the basis of sex "is only indirectly involved" in this case:[120] when it comes to establishing parentage, the differential treatment of the sexes reflects not "'gender stereotypes,'" but real physiological differences.[121]

Three years later, when the Court took up the question again in *Nguyen v Immigration and Naturalization Service*, this proposition gained the assent of a majority of the Court.[122] The petitioner in *Nguyen* was born in Vietnam to an unmarried American citizen father and a noncitizen mother.[123] His father moved him to the United States at an early age and raised him there, his mother having long since left the family. Like Morales-Santana, Nguyen ran into trouble with the immigration authorities after being convicted of a crime. Because his father had not taken the steps the INA required of unmarried men who wish to transmit citizenship to nonmarital children, the government initiated deportation proceedings against him.

Nguyen argued that he was a victim of sex discrimination. If his citizen parent had been female, he would not now be facing deportation to a country he barely remembered. Following in the vein of

---

the differential treatment of male and female parents constituted a sex-based equal protection violation. Id.

[119] Id at 445.

[120] Id at 442.

[121] Id at 443. It is interesting—and revealing—to watch how the Court's placement of quotation marks shifts across different opinions. In the VMI case, the Court placed quotation marks around—and thereby raised ontological doubts about—the phrase "inherent differences." *Virginia*, 518 US at 533. In his lead opinion in *Miller*, Justice Stevens placed quotation marks around the phrase "gender stereotypes" instead. *Miller*, 523 US at 443. In this same vein, it is interesting to consider Justice Alito's placement of quotation marks around the phrase "gender equality" in *Burwell v Hobby Lobby Stores, Inc.*, 134 S Ct 2751, 2779 (2014).

[122] See *Nguyen*, 533 US at 78.

[123] For more on the facts in the case, see id at 57–58.

Justice Stevens's opinion in *Miller*, however, the Court held there was no equal protection violation.[124] The Court explained that "[f]athers and mothers are not similarly situated with regard to the proof of biological parenthood,"[125] and that, "[g]iven the proof of motherhood that is inherent in birth itself, it is unremarkable that Congress did not require the same affirmative steps of mothers" that it required of fathers.[126] Because the mother gives birth, she "knows that the child is in being and is hers and has an initial point of contact with him. There is at least an opportunity for mother and child to develop a real, meaningful relationship."[127] In other words, the Court concluded, birth provides women an opportunity to bond with their children "as a matter of biological inevitability."[128] Fathers do not inevitably have that opportunity. Thus, the Court held, the distinction between unmarried mothers and fathers in these circumstances is not grounded in sex stereotypes, but merely reflects the fact that "[t]he difference between men and women in relation to the birth process is a real one."[129]

The Court in *Nguyen* purported to apply heightened scrutiny,[130] but as the dissenting Justices observed, many of the indicia of that standard of review are missing from its opinion.[131] Sex-based equal protection law, properly applied, requires the government to show that it has "an exceedingly persuasive justification" for discriminating on the basis of sex; cannot reasonably satisfy its important constitutional interests through nondiscriminatory means; and did not develop its justification for the discrimination post-hoc, but actually

---

[124] Id at 73.

[125] Id at 63.

[126] Id at 64.

[127] Id at 65.

[128] Id at 73.

[129] Id. See also id ("To fail to acknowledge even our most basic biological differences—such as the fact that a mother must be present at birth but the father need not be—risks making the guarantee of equal protection superficial, and so disserving it. Mechanistic classification of all our differences as stereotypes would operate to obscure those misconceptions and prejudices that are real.").

[130] *Nguyen*, 533 US at 60–61 (concluding that because the statute at issue in *Nguyen* did not satisfy heightened scrutiny, it was unnecessary to "decide whether some lesser degree of scrutiny pertains because the statute implicates Congress' immigration and naturalization power").

[131] Id at 74 (O'Connor, J, dissenting) ("While the Court invokes heightened scrutiny, the manner in which it explains and applies this standard is a stranger to our precedents.").

relied on that justification at the time it decided to discriminate.[132] The Court in *Nguyen* did not place much of a burden on the government when it came to making these showings. For a start, it was not clear what the discriminatory rule accomplished that a nondiscriminatory rule could not. If the government was interested in ensuring that a child had a biological connection to its American citizen parent before acquiring that parent's citizenship, why wouldn't genetic testing—which the challengers in *Nguyen* had in fact undergone—suffice?[133] Likewise, if the government was interested in ensuring that the child had an actual relationship with its citizen parent, it was unclear why a sex-neutral rule would be inferior to the extant rule.[134] Indeed, a sex-neutral rule would seem to satisfy the government's objectives better because there are certainly cases, like *Nguyen*, in which mothers lack any actual relationship to their children and fathers enjoy a robust one.[135]

Unsurprisingly—given the mismatch between the government's twenty-first-century justifications and the lines the INA draws—history reveals that, in 1940, when Congress enacted the rules governing unmarried citizen parents, it was motivated not by perceived biological differences between men and women, but by stereotyped assumptions about their sex and family roles.[136] Lawmakers in 1940 viewed unmarried mothers as the sole and natural guardians of their children and assumed unmarried fathers would have little to do with their children—especially when those children were born abroad to noncitizen mothers. If the Court had actually scrutinized the law in *Nguyen*, the dissenting Justices argued, the government's biological justifications would have been exposed as post-hoc rationalizations for a

---

[132] Id at 74–78.

[133] Id at 80–81.

[134] Id at 81–83.

[135] As Justice O'Connor's dissenting opinion notes, it is only by reframing the government's proffered interest as an interest in ensuring that a parent has an "opportunity" to bond with his or her child (as opposed to actually bonding with that child) that the biological argument even gets off the ground. Id at 84 ("By focusing on 'opportunity' rather than reality, the majority presumably improves the chances of a sufficient means-end fit. But in doing so, it dilutes significantly the weight of the interest. It is difficult to see how…anyone profits from a 'demonstrated opportunity' for a relationship in the absence of the fruition of an actual tie.").

[136] Id at 91–92.

law that, in practice, perpetuated long-standing and deeply rooted sex-role stereotypes.[137]

Professor, now Judge, Nina Pillard has argued that although the Court did not explicitly advert to plenary power doctrine in *Nguyen* the way it did in *Fiallo*, that doctrine nonetheless informed its decision.[138] Pillard argues that *Nguyen* "took the plenary power doctrine underground"—purporting to apply heightened scrutiny, but actually giving the government a pass in deference to its constitutionally-delegated powers over immigration.[139] That is a plausible contention; it is also true that the Court has historically deferred to the government in Fourteenth Amendment cases involving unmarried fathers.

Whatever combination of factors motivated the Court to slacken the standard of review it actually applied in *Nguyen*, the government was hoping for a reprise of this approach in *Morales-Santana*.[140] Thus, the government focused again on the moment of birth, noting that because unmarried mothers are invariably present at a child's birth, and because their parentage is thereby assured, they are recognized at that moment as the child's only legal parent.[141] Because an unmarried father does not give birth to his child and has no legal relationship to its mother, he "enters the scene later, as a second parent."[142] Accordingly, the government argued, a longer physical connection to the United States is warranted for the unmarried father because he alone will have to contend with the "competing national influence" of the

---

[137] Id at 91–93.

[138] See Nina Pillard, *Plenary Power Underground in Nguyen v. INS: A Response to Professor Spiro*, 16 Georgetown Immig L J 835 (2002).

[139] Id at 836.

[140] Between *Nguyen* and *Morales-Santana*, the Court considered one other sex-based challenge to the rules governing the citizenship of nonmarital children born abroad: *Flores-Villar v United States*, 564 US 210 (2011) (per curiam), affirming by an equally divided Court, 536 F3d 990 (9th Cir 2008). *Flores-Villar* involved the same provision that was at issue in *Morales-Santana*, but Justice Kagan recused herself in the earlier case, which left the Court evenly split on the question of the law's constitutionality. See *Flores-Villar*, 564 US at 210. The Justices did not write in *Flores-Villar*, but simply affirmed by an equally divided Court the Ninth Circuit's decision to uphold the provision. Id. The Ninth Circuit's decision reads much like *Nguyen*. It assumed, without deciding, that heightened scrutiny applies in this context, *Flores-Villar*, 536 F3d at 996 n 2, but did not apply that standard with much rigor.

[141] Brief for the Petitioner, *Sessions v Morales-Santana*, Civil Action No 15-1191, at *28–29, 34 (US filed Aug 19 2016) (available on Westlaw at 2016 WL 4436132) ("*Morales-Santana* Petitioner's Brief").

[142] *Morales-Santana*, 137 S Ct at 1695 (paraphrasing the government's argument).

child's noncitizen mother when trying to impart American values to his child.[143]

Previously, that kind of argument might have prevailed in this context. But the Court in *Morales-Santana* rejected it. The different residency requirements imposed by the INA were not driven by biological differences, the Court held, but rather by the conventional assumption that an unmarried mother will be the guardian of a nonmarital child and the corresponding assumption that an unmarried father will be a secondary parent at best.[144] The Court observed that, until 1934, married women could not transmit their citizenship to children born abroad—only married men could do so.[145] But, the Court observed, "the father-controls tradition never held sway" where unmarried men and women were concerned: "At common law, the mother, and only the mother, was 'bound to maintain [a nonmarital child] as its natural guardian,'" while the father was excused of any responsibility.[146] Echoing the dissenters in *Nguyen*, the Court noted that the officials originally responsible for the sex distinctions in the INA explicitly referenced and endorsed those common-law principles.[147] Indeed, the Court asserted, the only way to make sense of the differential residency requirements for unmarried mothers and fathers was in light of those principles.[148] The government imposed longer residency requirements on unmarried citizen fathers because it assumed they would be absent or negligible presences at best and that their children would be strongly subject to the competing national influence of their noncit-

---

[143] *Morales-Santana* Petitioner's Brief at *9 (cited in note 141). The government also argued that the shortened residency requirement for unmarried citizen mothers was an effort on the part of Congress to reduce the problem of statelessness, as many other countries permit nonmarital children to acquire citizenship only through their mothers. Id at *11. The Court rejected this argument too. See *Morales-Santana*, 137 S Ct at 1696 ("[There is little reason to believe that a statelessness concern prompted the diverse physical-presence requirements. Nor has the Government shown that the risk of statelessness disproportionately endangered the children of unwed mothers."). For more on the statelessness argument, see Brief of Professors of History, Political Science, and Law as Amici Curiae in Support of Respondent, *Sessions v Morales-Santana*, Civil Action No 15-1191, *33–37 (US filed Oct 3, 2016) (available on Westlaw at 2016 WL 5800340).

[144] *Morales-Santana*, 137 S Ct at 1690–93.

[145] Id at 1691; see also id (noting that, through the early twentieth century, the same assumptions motivated a rule that allowed male citizens to confer citizenship on noncitizen wives but barred female citizens from conferring citizenship on their husbands—indeed, subjected women who married noncitizens to expatriation).

[146] Id at 1691.

[147] Id at 1692.

[148] Id.

izen mothers. Of citizen mothers, it assumed the opposite: that they would serve as their children's primary caregivers and thus overwhelm any foreign influence from the paternal side.

The Court was not required to—and did not—overrule *Nguyen* to reach this holding. It distinguished the earlier case on the ground that *Nguyen* involved the establishment of parentage, whereas *Morales-Santana* involved rules regarding the duration of parents' residency in the United States.[149] The nexus between biological differences and the sex distinction in *Nguyen* was arguably closer than the nexus between biological differences and the sex distinction in *Morales-Santana*—but in the same way, I think, that the nexus between biological differences and legal distinctions between the sexes was arguably closer in *Pavan* than it was in *Obergefell*. The sex classification in *Nguyen* passed constitutional muster only because the Court did not actually scrutinize it with much rigor. If the Court had actually applied the same level of scrutiny in *Nguyen* that it applied in *Morales-Santana* (or in *Pavan* and *Obergefell*), it would have detected the fairly substantial gaps between the government's stated ends and its use of a sex discriminatory rule. Thus, although *Morales-Santana* did not overrule *Nguyen*, the Court's decision to scrutinize a citizenship law that discriminated against an unmarried father, rather than to defer to the government in a de facto kind of way, steered the law in a new direction. After *Morales-Santana*, courts and litigants cannot as easily assert or assume that the reach of heightened scrutiny for sex-based state action runs out early, either at the water's edge of citizenship law or when it comes to the rights of unmarried parents.

This is a significant jurisprudential development. But it was obscured in the immediate aftermath of *Morales-Santana* by the controversy that erupted over the Court's choice of remedy. In general, a court has two options when it finds that a law violates equal protection by treating similarly situated groups dissimilarly: while waiting for the legislature to cure the problem, it can either "level up" by extending the benefit to the excluded group or "level down" by removing the benefit from the favored group.[150] Historically, the Court

---

[149] Id at 1694.

[150] For more on the difficult conceptual problems involved in the choice of whether to "level up" or "level down," see Deborah L. Brake, *When Equality Leaves Everyone Worse Off: The Problem of Levelling Down in Equality Law*, 46 Wm & Mary L Rev 513 (2004); Evan H. Caminker, Note, *A Norm-Based Remedial Model for Underinclusive Statutes*, 95 Yale L J 1185,

has almost always concluded that "extension, rather than nullification, is the proper course."[151] In this case, however, the Court took the opposite course: it held that while we wait for Congress to "address the issue and settle on a uniform prescription that neither favors nor disadvantages any person on the basis of gender," the "now-five-year requirement" that applies to children born to unwed U.S.-citizen fathers "should apply, prospectively, to children born to unwed U.S.-citizen mothers."[152] The Court explained that withdrawing, rather than extending, the benefit was appropriate in these circumstances because that is almost certainly what Congress would have wanted.[153] Under the statute at issue in *Morales-Santana*, married men and women and unmarried fathers are all subject to the same residency requirement.[154] The substantially reduced one-year requirement was a special exception to the general rule for unmarried mothers only.[155] Thus, the Court reasoned, it would be strange, as well as constitutionally problematic, to "level up." To extend the special one-year rule to unmarried fathers as well as unmarried mothers would create a new form of discrimination based on marriage—one that would have the odd and almost certainly not-congressionally-approved effect of disadvantaging marital children.[156]

Everyone who has written about *Morales-Santana* has had something to say about this remedy. Some commentators have criticized the Court for a lack of clarity—particularly with regard to children of unmarried citizen mothers who were born prior to the Court's decision but who have not yet had their citizenship adjudicated.[157]

1199–201 (1986); Ruth Bader Ginsburg, Address, *Some Thoughts on Judicial Authority to Repair Unconstitutional Legislation*, 28 Cleve St L Rev 301, 316–19 (1979); Sabina Mariella, Note, *Leveling Up over Plenary Power: Remedying an Impermissible Gender Classification in the Immigration and Nationality Act*, 96 BU L Rev 219, 238–41 (2016).

[151] *Morales-Santana*, 137 S Ct at 1699 (quotation marks omitted).

[152] Id at 1701.

[153] Id at 1699–1701.

[154] Id at 1686–87.

[155] Id at 1699.

[156] See id at 1700 ("Disadvantageous treatment of marital children in comparison to non-marital children is scarcely a purpose one can sensibly attribute to Congress."); id at 1700 n 25 (noting that "[d]istinctions based on parents' marital status ... are subject to the same heightened scrutiny as distinctions based on gender").

[157] See, for example, Kristin Collins, *Equality, Sovereignty, and the Family in Morales-Santana*, 131 Harv L Rev 170, 208–13 (2017); Ian Samuel, *Morales-Santana and the "Mean Remedy*," Take Care (June 12, 2017), available at https://takecareblog.com/blog/morales-santana-and-the-mean-remedy. It is true that the Court does not explicitly address the citizenship status of these

Two things seem clear, however: (1) *Morales-Santana* is unlikely to benefit Morales-Santana himself when it comes to deportation, as the Court's chosen remedy seems to promise only that, going forward, all children born abroad to mixed-nationality couples will be subject to the longer residency requirement; and (2) in the future, nonmarital children born abroad to U.S.-citizen mothers will have a harder time acquiring U.S. citizenship than they would have in the absence of the Court's decision (unless, of course, Congress steps in to change that).

These results have triggered significant criticism. Some commentators have argued that equality came unhinged from justice in *Morales-Santana*.[158] The Second Circuit, examining the same record that was before the Supreme Court, concluded that leveling up was the right course, so it is not as though a case cannot be made for that approach.[159] Some commentators have criticized the opinion's author, Justice Ginsburg, for betraying her feminist principles: standing up for formal equality but issuing a decision that in practice may hurt countless numbers of unwed American women and their children.[160] Some have speculated that the more liberal Justices needed to acquiesce to the stingier remedy in order to garner a majority of votes on the substantive equality question.[161]

---

children. But the suggestion that *Morales-Santana* strips them of their citizenship seems implausible. Prior to the Court's decision, nonmarital children born abroad to citizen mothers and noncitizen fathers became U.S. citizens at birth as long as their mothers satisfied the INA's one-year residency requirement. The Court gave no indication in *Morales-Santana* that it intended to strip these children of their citizenship; indeed, the Court almost certainly applied its remedy "prospectively" precisely in order to avoid stripping people of their citizenship. *Morales-Santana*, 137 S Ct at 1701.

[158] See, for example, Bridget Crawford, *Is Ginsburg's Decision in Sessions v. Morales-Santana Good for Women?*, Feminist Law Professors (June 12, 2017), available at http://www.feministlaw professors.com/2017/06/is-ginsburgs-decision-in-sessions-v-morales-santana-good-for-women/; Ian Millhiser, *The Supreme Court Just Made Our Ugly, Messed-Up Immigration Law Even Uglier*, Think Progress (June 12, 2017), available at https://thinkprogress.org/scotus-immigration-gender -bf65cebccf9d/.

[159] *Morales-Santana v Lynch*, 804 F3d 520, 535–37 (2d Cir 2013) (holding that "the ten-year requirement for fathers and married mothers imposed by Congress in 1940 appears to have represented a significant departure from long-established historical practice," that it is therefore ambiguous what remedy Congress would have preferred, and that "binding precedent . . . cautions us to extend rather than contract benefits in the face of ambiguous congressional intent").

[160] See, for example, Noah Feldman, *Ginsburg's Surprisingly Retro Feminism*, Bloomberg View (June 14, 2017), available at https://www.bloomberg.com/view/articles/2017-06-14/ginsburg-s -surprisingly-retro-feminism.

[161] See, for example, Mark Joseph Stern, *Ruth Bader Ginsburg Affirms the "Equal Dignity" of Mothers and Fathers*, Slate (June 13, 2017), available at http://www.slate.com/articles/news_and _politics/jurisprudence/2017/06/sessions_v_morales_santana_ruth_bader_ginsburg_defends

But the remedy in *Morales-Santana* may also be a product of the subject matter of the case and the times in which we live. Few issues were more hotly contested in the 2016 presidential election than immigration and citizenship. At the time the Court decided *Morales-Santana*, the Republican administration and Republican lawmakers routinely declared themselves committed to the restriction of legal and illegal immigration and the tightening up of lax controls in those areas. Some of the measures the democratic branches of government were taking in pursuit of those ends were already making their way to the Court. Against this backdrop, it is perhaps even less surprising than it might normally be that the Court chose to defer to what it perceived as the will of Congress when devising a remedy—especially in light of the fact that it had already taken the significant step of not deferring on the merits. Given everything else transpiring at the time of *Morales-Santana*, the Court may have been particularly sensitive about the perils of essentially rewriting the INA in a way that it saw no indication Congress—either in 1940 or in 2017—would have preferred. The one thing the Court could be certain about in 2017 was that legal challenges to the government's new policies with respect to immigration and citizenship were heading its way. That knowledge may have influenced, and at least provides some context for, the Court's decision to craft a remedy designed to insulate from criticism—and thereby preserve—the power of judicial review over substantive questions of equal protection in this context.

IV. Conclusion

The exact parameters of the remedy in *Morales-Santana*—and the real reasons the Court adopted it—will likely become clearer in the future. But it is important not to allow the controversy over the Court's decision to "level down" to overshadow its substantive equal protection holding. In the immediate aftermath of *Morales-Santana*, some commentators suggested that there was not much to say about the Court's decision on the merits—that "on the merits," the Court produced "an opinion that is perfectly consonant with what you might predict."[162] Indeed, many commentators skipped right over the Court's

---

_gender_equality.html ("I suspect this compromise was the price of Chief Justice John Roberts' vote, and probably Justice Anthony Kennedy's as well.").

[162] Samuel, *Morales-Santana and the "Mean Remedy"* (cited in note 157).

substantive equal protection holding to address what they perceived as the more interesting and consequential questions of remedy.

In fact, the Court's opinion was not necessarily consonant with what one might predict in a sex-based equal protection case involving unmarried fathers and questions of citizenship. In the past, the Court has not always, or even regularly, scrutinized laws that discriminate on the basis of sex in determining which children of American citizens are citizens themselves. The same analysis holds in the context of gay rights: *Pavan* might have seemed a foregone conclusion in the wake of *Obergefell*, but in light of the Court's past judgments about such matters, its extension of heightened scrutiny to a situation involving the birth certificates of children born to gay parents constitutes a meaningful step. Courts have not historically made a habit of scrutinizing sex classifications for potential injustices when the perceived victims of those classifications are sexual minorities—indeed, the opposite is true.

Thus, *Morales-Santana* and *Pavan* both moved the ball forward in substantial ways where equal protection law is concerned. Both of these decisions raise significant constitutional questions about sex classifications that continue to govern gays and lesbians and unmarried fathers. They both raise questions about the pregnancy-related and other ostensibly biologically based reasons the government continues to offer in these contexts for classifying individuals on the basis of sex. They could both be read to suggest that the days of exempting sex classifications that harm gays and lesbians and unwed fathers from heightened scrutiny are over—and also, more broadly, that constitutional doctrine now takes a harder line toward ostensibly biological justifications for discrimination that in fact provide cover for sex stereotypes. Depending on how energetically the Court chooses to apply the lessons of these cases, they could have particularly significant implications for how the law treats justifications for discrimination rooted in pregnancy.

The new doctrine generated by these cases will not, however, apply itself. The Court could cabin *Pavan* and *Morales-Santana* to their facts. It could unsee what these decisions exposed: that apparently biologically based justifications for discrimination can hide stereotype-reinforcing social judgments even—perhaps especially—where gays and lesbians and unwed fathers are concerned. A generation ago, in *United States v Virginia*, the Court declared that "'[i]nherent differences' between men and women ... remain cause for celebration, but not for denigration of the members of either sex or for artificial constraints on an individual's opportunity."[163] *Pavan* and *Morales-Santana* extended this principle into new territory. In so doing, they struck a blow on behalf of the constitutional equality project that began nearly half a century ago in *Reed v Reed*. It is hard to predict how that project will fare in the future. But these two cases undercut its most persistent and resilient opponent: arguments that build outward from biological foundations to encircle and constrain the scope of men's and women's lives.

---

[163] *Virginia*, 518 US at 533.

JANE S. SCHACTER

PUTTING THE POLITICS OF "JUDICIAL ACTIVISM" IN HISTORICAL PERSPECTIVE

Every student of constitutional law knows the question: If *Lochner*[1] was wrong, can *Roe*[2] (or *Griswold*[3] or *Lawrence*[4] or . . .) be right? Countless discussions in law school classrooms have been launched by a question like this as part of a specific discussion of substantive due process under the Fourteenth Amendment or a more general consideration of judicial discretion in constitutional interpretation. Constitutional law classes aside, anyone who reads Chief Justice Roberts's recent opinion in *Obergefell v Hodges*[5] would be cued to think about the question. In dissenting from the majority's conclusion that same-sex couples have a fundamental right to marry, the Chief Justice cited *Lochner* no fewer than sixteen times.[6] His claim, expressed to the point

Jane S. Schacter is William Nelson Cromwell Professor of Law, Stanford Law School.

AUTHOR'S NOTE: I am grateful for the terrific research assistance of several Stanford Law students at various stages of the project: Minh Nguyen Dang, Sam Dippo, Jon Erwin-Frank, Kate Fetrow, Mary Rock, Michael Skocpol, Steven Spriggs, and, especially, Alex Treiger. I also appreciate the helpful comments of Pat Egan, Dan Ho, Dennis Hutchinson, Nate Persily, and the participants at workshops at the University of Michigan, Stanford, and University of Texas Law Schools.

[1] *Lochner v New York*, 198 US 45 (1905).

[2] *Roe v Wade*, 410 US 113 (1973).

[3] *Griswold v Connecticut*, 381 US 479 (1965).

[4] *Lawrence v Texas*, 539 US 558 (2003).

[5] 576 US ___, 135 S Ct 2584 (2015).

[6] Id at 2612, 2616, 2617, 2618, 2619, 2621, 2622 (Roberts, CJ, dissenting). *Lochner*, of course, struck down a New York law setting maximum hours for bakery employees based on

of exhaustion, was that *Obergefell* was simply a new version of the misguided judicial excesses of the earlier period. His argument repeatedly associated itself with the *Lochner* dissents, quoting Justice Holmes for the proposition that the Constitution "is made for people of fundamentally differing views,"[7] and Justice Harlan for the idea that "courts are not concerned with the wisdom or policy of legislation."[8] Among his many other references to *Lochner* were these:

> the majority's approach has no basis in principle or tradition, except for the unprincipled tradition of judicial policymaking that characterized discredited decisions such as *Lochner v. New York* *** Respecting [the democratic process] requires the Court to be guided by law, not any particular school of social thought. As Judge Henry Friendly once put it, echoing Justice Holmes's dissent in *Lochner*, the Fourteenth Amendment does not enact John Stuart Mill's On Liberty any more than it enacts Herbert Spencer's Social Statics.[9]

The Chief Justice's framing did not escape notice in Justice Kennedy's majority opinion. Kennedy met canon with canon as he countered the invocation of the *Lochner* dissents with well-known language about rights from the flag salute case:

> Of course, the Constitution contemplates that democracy is the appropriate process for change, so long as that process does not abridge fundamental rights. . . . An individual can invoke a right to constitutional protection when he or she is harmed, even if the broader public disagrees and even if the legislature refuses to act. The idea of the Constitution "was to withdraw certain subjects from the vicissitudes of political controversy, to place them beyond the reach of majorities and officials and to establish them as legal principles to be applied by the courts." *West Virginia Bd. of Ed. v. Barnette*, 319 U.S. 624, 638 (1943). This is why "fundamental rights may not be submitted to a vote; they depend on the outcome of no elections."[10]

The basics of this exchange are numbingly familiar in jurisprudential debates in constitutional law. That debate, though, is hardly a rarefied one limited to the pages of opinions or scholarly articles. There is and has long been a parallel debate in the democratic process

---

the principle that the Due Process Clause protects the liberty of contract. Chief Justice Roberts also cited *Dred Scott* for the same point more than once. Id at 2616, 2617.

[7] Id at 2612 (quoting *Lochner*, 198 US at 76 (Holmes, J, dissenting)).

[8] Id (quoting *Lochner*, 198 US at 69 (Harlan, J, dissenting)).

[9] *Obergefell*, 135 S Ct at 2616, 2622 (Roberts, CJ, dissenting).

[10] Id at 2605–06.

itself about the role of courts. In the contemporary period and parlance, that well-worn debate travels under the name of attacks on "judicial activism." Indeed, attacks on judicial activism were a consistent part of the twenty-two-year run-up to *Obergefell*. The decision of the Hawaii Supreme Court that first ignited the same-sex marriage debate in 1993[11] was the prelude to years of backlash measures in the states, the federal Defense of Marriage Act, and proposed federal constitutional amendments to bar same-sex marriage.[12] Throughout these years, the idea that courts had outrageously overstepped their bounds was one of the cornerstones of political attacks. DOMA was justified in 1996 by its proponents as a "preemptive measure to make sure that a handful of judges, in a single state, cannot impose a radical social agenda upon the entire nation."[13] George W. Bush framed his support of a federal constitutional amendment to limit marriage in 2004 as a needed response to " 'activist judges' who sought to redefine marriage,"[14] and the congressional hearings on the proposed Federal Marriage Amendment he supported were given the moniker "Judicial Activism v. Democracy."[15] More recently, congressional measures to limit or overturn the ruling in both *United States v Windsor*[16] and *Obergefell* were likewise framed as responses to "activist court judges overstepping their constitutional authority by legislating from the bench"[17] and as a needed corrective because "the Constitution finds itself under sustained attack from an arrogant judicial elite."[18]

---

[11] *Baehr v Lewin*, 852 P2d 44 (Hawaii 1993).

[12] See Jane S. Schacter, *Courts and the Politics of Backlash: Marriage Equality Litigation, Then and Now*, 82 S Cal L Rev 1153, 1185–87 (2009); Michael J. Klarman, *From the Closet to the Altar: Courts, Backlash, and the Struggle for Same-Sex Marriage* (Oxford, 2012).

[13] Eric Schmitt, *Senators Reject Both Job-Bias Ban and Gay Marriage*, NY Times A1 (Sept 11, 1996) (quoting Senator Trent Lott); see Schacter, 82 S Cal L Rev at 1185, n 199 (cited in note 12).

[14] *Bush Calls for Ban on Same-Sex Marriages*, CNN (Feb 25, 2004) (available at http://www.cnn.com/2004/ALLPOLITICS/02/24/elec04.prez.bush.marriage/).

[15] *Judicial Activism vs. Democracy: What Are the National Implications of the Massachusetts Goodridge Decision and the Judicial Invalidation of Traditional Marriage Laws? Before the Subcommittee on the Constitution of the Committee on the Judiciary*, 108th Cong, 2d Sess 22–23 (2004).

[16] 570 US 744 (2013).

[17] Daniel Wilson, *Lawmakers Want Same-Sex Marriage Laws in State Hands*, Law360 (Feb 11, 2015) (available at https://www.law360.com/tax/articles/620597/lawmakers-want-same-sex-marriage-laws-in-state-hands) (quoting Rep Randy Smith (R-Tex), cosponsor of the post-*Windsor* "State Marriage Defense Act").

[18] Ted Cruz, *Constitutional Remedies to a Lawless Supreme Court*, National Review Online (June 26, 2015) (available at http://www.nationalreview.com/article/420409/constitutional

The Chief Justice did not use the phrase "judicial activism" in his *Obergefell* dissent, but he invoked precisely these ideas. And, he did not offer them up strictly as abstract normative propositions. He also used the *Lochner* analogy to lament particular consequences that he argued would flow from courts going astray. Exhorting his colleagues in the majority to be "attuned to the lessons of history, and what it has meant for the country and Court when Justices have exceeded their proper bounds,"[19] he argued, for example, that the Court's legitimacy depends upon respect for its judgments and that such "respect flows from the perception—and reality—that we exercise humility and restraint in deciding cases according to the Constitution and law."[20] Roberts also emphasized at various points the public resentment caused by aggressive rulings, suggesting that "[t]he Court's accumulation of power does not occur in a vacuum. It comes at the expense of the people. And they know it."[21] Elaborating on this theme, he warned that:

> There will be consequences to shutting down the political process on an issue of such profound public significance. Closing debate tends to close minds. People denied a voice are less likely to accept the ruling of a court on an issue that does not seem to be the sort of thing courts usually decide.[22]

As an empirical matter, the Chief Justice's prediction has thus far been wrong. There has been no sign of minds closing after *Obergefell*. To the contrary, public opinion has grown more supportive of same-sex marriage since the decision, not less.[23] But the deeper flaw in the reasoning goes beyond empirics. The picture of cause and effect drawn by Roberts is strikingly simplistic. It seems to contemplate a straight line of communication from the Court's decisions to the

---

-remedies-lawless-supreme-court-ted-cruz) (online op-ed published the day *Obergefell* was decided).

[19] *Obergefell*, 135 S Ct at 2626 (Roberts, CJ, dissenting).

[20] Id at 2624 (Roberts, CJ, dissenting).

[21] Id.

[22] Id at 2625 (Roberts, CJ, dissenting).

[23] See David Masci, Anna Brown, and Jocelyn Kiley, *Five Facts About Same-Sex Marriage*, Pew Research Center (June 26, 2017) (available at http://www.pewresearch.org/fact-tank /2017/06/26/same-sex-marriage/) (noting new high of 62 percent support for same-sex marriage, compared to 57 percent at time of *Obergefell*); Justin McCarthy, *U.S. Support for Gay Marriage Edges to New High*, Gallup News (May 15, 2017) (available at http://news .gallup.com/poll/210566/support-gay-marriage-edges-new-high.aspx) (noting support rising to 64 percent).

citizenry, unmediated and unbroken. Yet, most citizens do not consume Supreme Court decisions directly, or even at all. Even with the advent of the Internet and instant access to opinions,[24] citizens mostly take their cues about the Court from elites, including elected officials.[25] For this reason, it makes little sense to address the "consequences" of purported judicial activism without accounting for the political forces and factors that surround decisions at particular times in history. Beginning to understand how the public makes sense of judicial actions requires grappling with the political dynamics that surround and will—inevitably—help to give meaning to the Court's decisions.

In this article, I take the Chief Justice's *Lochner* analogy as a point of departure, but pursue the dimension of political context that Roberts ignores. My aim is to explore the *political* history of judicial activism as a rallying cry—both at the time of *Lochner* and today. I take a historical perspective in order to understand similarities and differences in the two contexts, and also to better understand the evolution of the contemporary politics of opposing what is characterized by combatants as judicial activism.

Let me say three things at the outset to frame the inquiry. First, it is, of course, obvious that the political context for attacks on courts *has* changed between the turn into the twentieth century and today. Very little about politics and government has not changed meaningfully in the last century. The interesting question is not whether but *how* the political dynamics shaping attacks on courts have changed. The task of this article is to identify and explore the most relevant differences in the two periods of opposition to courts as activist, and to consider how those dynamics might matter for constitutional law and politics today. It is worth noting, as well, that not everything has changed, and there are similarities in the periods that merit exploration.

---

[24] See generally Jane S. Schacter, *Colloquium on Obergefell: Obergefell's Audiences*, 77 Ohio St L J 1011 (2016) (exploring role of social media and websites in rapidly disseminating information about *Obergefell*).

[25] See Nathaniel Persily, *Introduction*, in Nathaniel Persily, Jack Citrin, and Patrick Egan, eds, *Public Opinion and Constitutional Controversy* 3, 9 (Oxford, 2008) ("The nature of court decisions' effects on public opinion is usually a product of the way elites react to the decision and the messages they send to the mass public concerning the issue adjudicated."); Stephen P. Nicholson and Thomas G. Hansford, *Partisans in Robes: Party Cues and Public Acceptance of Supreme Court Decisions*, 58 Am J Pol Sci 620, 620–23 (2014) (summarizing the literature on cues and public acceptance of the Court's decisions).

Second, I distinguish between political attacks on judicial activism (my focus) and such attacks on judicial supremacy. The latter has been the subject of rich exploration by scholarly proponents of popular constitutionalism and has sometimes been the object of contestation by political antagonists of courts, as well.[26] There are plainly overlaps between the two concepts; both pivot on the claim that judges misunderstand their role and arrogate excessive power to themselves. But the critique of judicial supremacy focuses principally on finality (i.e., that judges wrongly claim final authority to bind other actors, especially other branches of government), while the critique of judicial activism focuses on how courts interpret the law (i.e., that judges inject their substantive preferences and decide questions that ought to be left to political determination).

Third and finally, in labeling political movements as aimed at "judicial activism," I do not mean to imply that the phrase reflects a coherent or readily identifiable concept. I have no disagreement with the common wisdom that the charge of judicial activism can be flung so promiscuously and without principle by critics of different stripes that it often functions as no more than a vacuous statement of disagreement with a ruling.[27] Does the phrase, for example, refer to *any* overturning of legislative or executive action? Only overturning laws in the absence of a Thayerian "clear" doubt about constitutionality? Any embrace of living constitutionalism over originalism? Reversal of precedent? Judicial management of institutions in the context of institutional reform litigation? Something else? Scholars have tried to define and measure it,[28] but the underlying skepticism has persisted—rightly, in my view, if the aim is to convincingly eliminate disagreement about what constitutes activism or to turn it into a precise or conceptually coherent idea.

---

[26] Larry Kramer both reviews historical examples of political opposition to judicial supremacy and presents a scholarly case against it. See Larry Kramer, *The People Themselves* (Oxford, 2004); Larry Kramer, *We the People*, Boston Review (Feb/Mar 2004) (available at http://bostonreview.net/us/larry-kramer-we-people).

[27] See, for example, Frank H. Easterbrook, *Do Liberals and Conservatives Differ in Judicial Activism?*, 73 U Colo L Rev 1401, 1401 (2002) ("'[A]ctivism' just means Judges Behaving Badly—and each person fills in a different definition of 'badly.'").

[28] See, for example, Stefanie Lindquist and Frank B. Cross, *Measuring Judicial Activism* (Oxford, 2009); Lori A. Ringhand, *Judicial Activism: An Empirical Examination of Voting Behavior on the Rehnquist Natural Court*, 24 Const Commen 43, 66 (2007); cf. Thomas M. Keck, *The Most Activist Supreme Court in History: The Road to Modern Judicial Conservatism* (Chicago, 2004) (detailed review and nuanced argument about particular brand of activism pursued by Rehnquist Court).

But the *political* history of judicial activism as a rallying cry to fight the courts can tell a different tale. There is, in fact, an identifiable claim, frequently deployed by opponents of the federal courts in the *Lochner* era and still deployed today, and it is my point of focus. This understanding is one among multiple meanings, but it is one that bridges the two eras and infuses the Roberts dissent in *Obergefell*. It can be stated, roughly, as the claim that unelected judges have usurped the functions of the political branches when they have used legal principles to effectuate their own preferred policy aims. That there is room for debate about whether this claim is fair, apt, or persuasive as applied to particular cases does not diminish its resonance or resilience as a strategy for political organizing and mobilization.

The precise language used to mount this objection has changed somewhat over the years, but there is a common conceptual core. In the *Lochner* era, the term "judicial activism" had not yet been coined, but there were similarly-motivated references to "judicial oligarchy," a term itself traceable to Thomas Jefferson.[29] Progressive lawyer Gilbert Roe's 1912 book challenging the courts used the phrase in its title.[30] In the introduction to the book, Senator Robert LaFollette charged that:

> [B]y usurping the power to declare laws unconstitutional and by presuming to read their own views into statutes without regard to the plain intention of the legislators, they have become in reality the supreme law-making and law-giving institution of government. They have taken to themselves a power it was never intended they should exercise; a power greater than that entrusted to the courts of any other enlightened nation.[31]

Other court critics of the time used the same phrase, including, for example, a Republican senator from Oklahoma who supported instituting a judicial recall;[32] the former governor of Oregon, Sylvester

---

[29] *Letter from Thomas Jefferson to William Charles Jarvis*, in Paul Leicester Ford, ed, 10 *The Writings of Thomas Jefferson* 160, 160 (G. P. Putnam's Sons, 1904–05) ("[T]o consider the judges as the ultimate arbiters of all constitutional questions" would be "a very dangerous doctrine indeed, and one which would place us under the despotism of an oligarchy"); see also Alpheus T. Mason, *Politics and the Supreme Court: President Roosevelt's Proposal*, 85 U Penn L Rev 659, 662 (1937).

[30] Gilbert E. Roe, *Our Judicial Oligarchy* (B. W. Huebsch, 1912).

[31] Id at vi–vii.

[32] See speech by Senator Robert Owen Jr. (D-Okla), *Election and Recall of Federal Judges*, 62nd Cong, 1st Sess, in 3339 Cong Rec (July 31, 1911).

Pennoyer;[33] the chief justice of the North Carolina Supreme Court;[34] LaFollette and other Progressives;[35] Norman Thomas (the head of the Socialist Party);[36] and scholar Alpheus Mason.[37] In the hands of these critics, the term embodied a particular hostility to the hide-bound ways of the law and to the court's perceived protection of rich, propertied classes at the expense of workers.[38] At its heart, though, the term challenged the institutional bona fides of courts to take the actions they did.[39]

Today, the idea that courts are exceeding their legitimate prerog-atives travels under the moniker of judicial activism, a term usually attributed to Arthur Schlesinger's 1947 article in *Fortune Magazine*.[40] The term has become a familiar part of the political vernacular. It appears some 162 times in a search of the *New York Times* from 1896 to the present,[41] with its first use in an October 1962 op-ed by Pro-fessor Alan Westin.[42] Westin's usage seems strikingly anachronistic today. He invoked the term in deploring the criticism then being lobbed by elected officials at the Warren Court and *defended* the Court's action as "in lockstep with the active consensus of this era," which supports "judicial activism on behalf of Negro civil rights and judicial self-restraint in matters of industrial relations and welfare

---

[33] William G. Ross, *A Muted Fury: Populists, Progressives, and Labor Unions Confront the Courts, 1890–1937* at 32 (Princeton, 1994). Pennoyer became better known as the litigant in *Pennoyer v Neff*, 95 US 714 (1878).

[34] Id at 1.

[35] Id at 15.

[36] Laura Weinrib, *The Taming of Free Speech: America's Civil Liberties Compromise* 211 (Harvard, 2016).

[37] Mason, 85 U Penn L Rev at 666 (cited in note 29) (referring to a "rapid conquest by a small but determined judicial oligarchy").

[38] See LaFollette, *Introduction*, in Roe, *Our Judicial Oligarchy* at vi, vii (cited in noted 30) (decrying judicial reverence for "fossilized precedent" and arguing that "because this tre-mendous power has been so generally exercised on the side of the wealthy and powerful, the courts have become at last the strongest bulwark of special privilege").

[39] Indeed, in the recent confirmation hearing of Justice Neil Gorsuch, Senator Mike Crapo referred to the "oligarchy of judges" as a threat to democracy. *Nomination of Neil Gorsuch before the Committee on the Judiciary*, 115th Cong, 1st Sess 24 (2017) (Crapo (R-Idaho)).

[40] See Arthur M. Schlesinger Jr., *The Supreme Court: 1947*, Fortune 73 (Jan 1947).

[41] These were gathered from an August 2017 search of the *New York Times* archives (http://www.nytimes.com/ref/membercenter/nytarchive.html) between January 1986 and July 2017 for articles containing the terms "judicial activist" or "judicial activism." Articles using both terms were counted only once.

[42] Alan Westin, *Also on the Bench: "Dominant Opinion,"* NY Times Magazine 20 (Oct 21, 1962).

programs."[43] Over time, particularly beginning in the late 1960s, the term came to have a negative connotation.[44] More of these articles criticize activism on the left than on the right, but, especially in recent decades, there are numerous examples in the latter category.[45]

The contemporary political attack on judicial activism is probably best captured by the sibling phrase "legislating from the bench."[46] That term showed up in some form fifty-four times in the *New York Times* search,[47] and is almost exclusively used by Republican critics of courts. It was particularly popular among both Presidents Bush and Senator Orrin Hatch.[48] At least as reflected in the *New York Times*, the term is somewhat newer than "judicial activism." It shows up for the first time in 1980.[49]

---

[43] Id at 80.

[44] See, for example, Fred P. Graham, *7-to-2 Ruling Establishes Marriage Privileges Stirs Debate*, NY Times 1, 35 (June 7, 1965) (describing the dissenting Justices in *Griswold* as viewing the decision as an example of judicial activism); Arthur Brock, *History Rewritten on the Bench*, NY Times 265 (Nov 27, 1965) (describing the Court as engaging in judicial activism to advance its notions of equality).

[45] For examples of recent critiques of conservative judicial activism, see Michael D. Shear, *GOP Turns to the Courts to Aid Agenda*, NY Times (Jan 3, 2015) (available at https://www.nytimes.com/2015/01/04/us/politics/gop-turns-to-the-courts-to-aid-agenda.html); Linda Greenhouse, *Actively Engaged*, NY Times (Oct 19, 2011, 9:30 p.m.) (available at https://opinionator.blogs.nytimes.com/2011/10/19/engagement-as-the-new-activism/); Ramesh Ponnuru, *When Judicial Activism Suits the Right*, NY Times (June 23, 2009) (available at http://www.nytimes.com/2009/06/24/opinion/24ponnuru.html).

[46] See, for example, *Comments by President on His Choice of Justice*, NY Times (July 24, 1990) (available at http://www.nytimes.com/1990/07/24/us/comments-by-president-on-his-choice-of-justice.html?pagewanted=1) (President Bush explaining that he selected Justice Souter because he "share[s] a broad view that what he ought to do on the bench is interpret the Constitution and not legislate"); Michael Luo, *G.O.P. Candidates at "Values Voters" Conference*, NY Times (Oct 19, 2007, 8:04 a.m.) (available at https://thecaucus.blogs.nytimes.com/2007/10/19/gop-candidates-at-values-voters-conference/?_r=0) (Mitt Romney promising to appoint judges "who won't legislate from the bench").

[47] The same search described in note 41 was done, but using the term "legislation from the bench" and its cognate verb forms.

[48] See, e.g., Linda Greenhouse, *Brennan, Key Liberal, Quits Supreme Court; Battle for Seat Likely*, NY Times (July 20, 1990) (George H. W. Bush explaining that he hoped to nominate someone "who will be on there not to legislate from the bench but to faithfully interpret the Constitution"); Elisabeth Bumiller, *Bush Vows to Seek Conservative Judges*, NY Times (Mar 29, 2002) (available at http://www.nytimes.com/2002/03/29/us/bush-vows-to-seek-conservative-judges.html) (George W. Bush stating that he wanted "people on the bench who don't try to use their position to legislate from the bench"); Gwen Ifill, *President Is Said to Pick Babbitt for Court Despite Senate Concern*, NY Times (May 11, 1994) (Hatch describing Bruce Babbitt as the kind of judge "who would legislate from the bench laws that the liberal community doesn't have a tinker's chance of getting through the people's elected representatives").

[49] *Carter's Appointees Examined for Clues on Supreme Court Possibilities*, NY Times 20 A20 (Oct 3, 1980).

Thus, while the terminology has changed somewhat over time, there is continuity in the basic claim being made. Whether or not this is a useful, meaningful, or accurate way to look at judicial action is not what this article explores, and I do not offer a normative analysis. I try, instead, to trace the political history of the idea since the *Lochner* era, and to consider the ways it has been used by opponents of judicial actions to shape perceptions and attitudes about the Court. The political dynamics on which I focus involve party politics in elections and in the congressional domain. My aim is to understand how claims of judicial activism in these spheres shape the context in which courts—and especially the Supreme Court—make constitutional law. Although the forces of opposition addressed here can also extend to statutory interpretation and regulatory decisions by courts, my focus is on constitutional law, which is generally the most salient venue for political debates about judicial activism.

The article proceeds as follows. Part I provides a brief narrative to identify and explain the relevant time periods under study—1896–1937 (the period that includes both the embrace of *Lochner* and its undoing) and 1954–present (the period beginning with *Brown* and leading to the present). Part II then looks in more depth at these periods by probing significant dimensions of the respective political attacks on the courts, especially on the Supreme Court. Part III concludes by suggesting some implications of this political history for thinking about constitutional law and politics today.

I. Demarcating the Eras

I briefly set out in this section the periods for comparative analysis,[50] and turn in the next section to the history relevant to my analysis.

A. 1896–1937

I date the first era from 1896–1937. These markers, of course, are not inevitable. The end point is clear enough; it is the New Deal shift

---

[50] The history of this earlier era is probed in detail in Ross, *A Muted Fury* (cited in note 33). The history of the contemporary era is probed in detail in Barry Friedman, *The Will of the People* (Farrar, Straus and Giroux, 2009); Lucas A. Powe Jr., *The Warren Court and American Politics* (Harvard, 2000). On elections and the Supreme Court, see Donald Grier Stephenson Jr., *Campaigns and the Court: The U.S. Supreme Court in Presidential Elections* (Columbia, 1999).

in the Supreme Court's approach to regulation and the ensuing decline in attacks on courts as obstructionist activists. The critical turn was made in *West Coast Hotel v Parrish*[51] (administering the decisive blow to *Lochner v New York*) and, soon after, *NLRB v Jones & Laughlin Steel* (doing the same for the narrow interpretations of the commerce power that had prevailed during the same period).[52]

As to the start date, the history of objecting to courts as arrogating too much power to themselves has, of course, a much longer pedigree. To cite a few examples, such claims stretch back to Thomas Jefferson,[53] appeared with special prominence in attacks on *Dred Scott*,[54] and cropped up in the decade leading up to the 1896 election.[55] Nevertheless, 1896 makes sense as a starting point because it kicked off a new era of political challenges to the Court. A trio of especially controversial Supreme Court decisions in 1895 became politically salient and supplied grist for the presidential contest the next year. All three were decided in favor of protecting private property and business interests. *United States v E. C. Knight Co.*,[56] decided in January of that year, famously distinguished "manufacturing" from "commerce" in adopting a narrow understanding of the commerce power that allowed the so-called sugar trust to operate free of federal regulation. Three months later, the Court struck down the income tax in *Pollock v Farmers Loan and Trust Co.*[57] And a month after that, the

---

[51] 300 US 379 (1937).

[52] 301 US 1 (1937).

[53] See *Letters from Thomas Jefferson to William Charles Jarvis*, in Paul Leicester Ford, ed, 10 *Writings of Thomas Jefferson* at 160 (cited in note 29).

[54] Contemporaneous reactions to *Dred Scott v Sandford*, 60 US 393 (1857), are chronicled in Don E. Fehrenbacher, *The Dred Scott Case: Its Significance in American Law and Politics* 417–48 (Oxford, 1978). Fehrenbacher characterized the decision as "the most striking instance of the Supreme Court's attempting to play the role of *deus ex machina* in a setting of national crisis." Id at 5. Mark Graber notes that "[p]roponents of judicial restraint consistently invoke that ruling to illustrate the dubious results they believe occur whenever Justices attempt to settle those major policy disputes that in our system should be resolved by the elected branches of government." Mark Graber, *Dred Scott as a Centrist Decision*, 83 NC L Rev 1229, 1231 (2005).

[55] See, for example, *Chicago, Milwaukee & St Paul Railway Co. v Minnesota*, 134 US 418 (1890) (decision limiting railroad regulation produced complaints of judicial overreaching). See generally William E. Forbath, *The Shaping of the American Labor Movement*, 102 Harv L Rev 1146 (1989) (on the rise of labor's hostility to courts in the Gilded Age).

[56] 156 US 1 (1895).

[57] 158 US 601, 605–04 (1895).

Court decided *In re Debs*,[58] which upheld the use of injunctions to quash strikes and thus aroused the ire of the growing labor movement. Once decided, this combustible trio of cases promptly became political fodder.[59] William Jennings Bryan, running on both the Democratic and Populist Party tickets in 1896, took aim at the Court.

The years in between 1896 and 1937 included, of course, the *Lochner* era. The Supreme Court decided the case in 1905, striking down a New York law that limited the hours bakers could work. *Lochner* itself, however, did not immediately become a political flashpoint. Indeed, it was not obvious at the time it was decided that it would have the pride of place in the judicial "anticanon" that the *Obergefell* dissent, and so much else, assigns it today.[60] While political objections to judicial invalidation of wage and hour laws were common at the time the Court ruled, the decision's notoriety stemmed more from exaltation of the Holmes dissent—especially by Justice Felix Frankfurter—than from condemnation of the majority holding.[61] After *Lochner*, however, there were a number of cases consistent with the majority's skeptical stance toward regulation that proved to be particular sparks for political controversy—including *Hammer v Dagenhart* in 1918,[62] striking down the first federal statute to restrict child labor; *Truax v Corrigan*,[63] striking down a state statute that would have prohibited injunctions against peaceful picketing; and the 1935–36 cases in which the Supreme Court struck down federal regulatory statutes that were parts of the early New Deal. Cases like *Schechter Poultry Corp. v United States*,[64] *Carter v Carter Coal*,[65] and *United States v Butler*[66] drew tremendous attention to the Court

---

[58] 158 US 564 (1895).

[59] Ross, *A Muted Fury* at 28–29 (cited in note 33).

[60] On *Lochner* as part of the anticanon, see Jamal Greene, *The Anticanon*, 125 Harv L Rev 379, 417–22 (2011).

[61] See id at 446–53; Howard Gillman, *De-Lochnerizing Lochner*, 85 BU L Rev 859, 860 (2005).

[62] 247 US 251 (1918).

[63] 257 US 312 (1921).

[64] 295 US 495 (1935).

[65] 298 US 238 (1936).

[66] 297 US 1 (1936).

and were characterized by FDR as impediments to economic recovery.[67]

The feature that bears emphasis is that this period was not a time of isolated or periodic political disagreement with discrete decisions, but rather one in which there was organized, ongoing opposition to the institutional role of the courts. As I will explore in the next section, the strongest party-based assaults on courts during this period came from Progressives and from Republican candidates running on a Progressive ticket in 1912 (Theodore Roosevelt) and 1924 (Robert LaFollette). Roosevelt and LaFollette both ran on controversial court-curbing proposals that would permit judicial decisions to be overridden and, in LaFollette's case, a move to electing judges to serve with term limits.[68] The repeated charge, in some form or fashion, was that courts had usurped the prerogative of legislatures and had done so in ways that advanced the interests of business and property owners over those of working people. The claims ebbed and flowed in intensity and salience, but once on the political radar in this form, the issue stayed there to some extent until 1937.

Near the end of this era was the most famous court-curbing proposal in American history. After a string of defeats for New Deal programs at the Supreme Court, Franklin Roosevelt announced his court-packing plan in 1937. He first introduced it, misleadingly, as necessitated by the advanced age and associated loss of productivity of several Justices.[69] He was later more candid and, in a Fireside Chat, asserted that his plan was needed because the Supreme Court was "acting not as a judicial body, but as a policymaking body," and indeed as a "super legislature."[70] His language was more muted than those who had provocatively condemned "judicial oligarchy," and some faulted his timidity, but the point was basically the same.

B. 1954–PRESENT

I date the dawn of the new era of political attacks on judicial activism to roughly 1954, early in the Warren Court. The idea (though not the precise phrase) animated the fiery Southern Manifesto in

---

[67] Franklin D. Roosevelt, *Press Conference* (May 31, 1935) (available at http://www.presidency.ucsb.edu/ws/?pid=15065).

[68] Ross, *A Muted Fury* at 255 (cited in note 33).

[69] See Powe Jr., *The Warren Court and American Politics* at 3 (cited in note 50).

[70] Stephenson Jr., *Campaigns and the Court* at 157 (cited in note 50).

protest of *Brown v Board of Education*. The southern members of Congress who issued that statement in 1956 said that *Brown* "is now bearing the fruit always produced when men substitute naked power for established law," and argued that the decision "climaxes a trend in the federal judiciary undertaking to legislate, in derogation of the authority of Congress, and to encroach upon the reserved rights of the States and the people."[71] In 1957, there was also resistance to Warren Court decisions on limiting the government's power to punish communists, including the so-called Red Monday decisions.[72]

The contemporary political campaign against judicial activism started to take shape in a form closer to the one we see today in 1968, when Richard Nixon ran against (among others) the Supreme Court by highlighting the Warren Court's rulings safeguarding the rights of criminal defendants. During the campaign, Nixon often promised that he would "reverse the rule of 'activist judges' and roll back 'crime in the streets.'"[73] His campaign inaugurated a sustained period of Republican attacks on judicial activism. This is one way in which it differed from the Southern Manifesto, which was launched mostly (but not exclusively) by Democrats, but was, in the end, more regional than partisan in its focus. Nixon's 1968 attacks created a prototype for what has been a staple issue for Republicans ever since. As we will see in the next section, Republican challenges to the courts since Nixon have evolved in some ways over the years and could be disaggregated into successive sub-eras of attacks, but the core case against what is frequently branded "liberal judicial activism" has remained largely consistent. That does not mean Democrats have been wholly silent on the issue, but for roughly the last half century, the issue has been a mainstay of the right in a way unmatched on the left.

In some ways, the more continuous and systematic Republican battle cry of "judicial activism" has affinities with the concept of "issue ownership" in political science. That framework posits that the major parties each "own" policy areas as to which the electorate believes

---

[71] *Text of 96 Congressmen's Declaration on Integration*, NY Times 19 (Mar 12, 1956). For more on the Manifesto, see Justin Driver, *Supremacies and the Southern Manifesto*, 92 Tex L Rev 1053 (2014).

[72] The most important of the Red Monday group was *Yates v United States*, 354 US 298 (1957). Other controversial decisions on communism before Red Monday include *Pennsylvania v Nelson*, 350 US 497 (1956) and *Peters v Hobby*, 349 US 331 (1955).

[73] Steven M. Teles, *The Rise of the Conservative Legal Movement: The Battle for Control of the Law* 175 (Princeton, 2008).

that party is most capable of solving problems.[74] The framework, however, is oriented to policy areas in which a broad national consensus exists as to a goal, and the question is which party is viewed as better able to handle the issue.[75] Health care and public safety, for example, are better fits for this framework than judicial behavior, especially because public attitudes about courts are more likely to turn on views of the underlying issues—such as abortion, LGBT rights, or race—than on more abstract institutional questions.[76] Nevertheless, Republicans' pronounced emphasis on activism might be seen as an attempt to frame and own the courts as an issue.

II. Probing the Political Dynamics

In this section, I look at several political dimensions of the early period as they relate to battles against judicial activism. In turn, I consider party polarization; presidential campaigns and platforms involving major and third-party candidates; and activity in Congress, especially the confirmation process. After exploring each one in the context of the earlier period, I consider how the contemporary period compares.

A. PARTY POLARIZATION

A useful place to start is at 30,000 feet. How do the eras compare in terms of political party dynamics? One macro dynamic marks a significant line of distinction between the earlier and the present period. During most of the years between 1896 and 1935, the Republicans had a secure hold on both Houses of Congress. Between 1897 and 1933, Republicans controlled the House for all but six years (1911–17), and the Senate for all but a different six years (1913–19).[77] In addition to having a firm grip on Congress during this period, the

---

[74] For a review of the framework, see John R. Petrocik, William L. Benoit, and Glenn J. Hansen, *Issue Ownership and Presidential Campaigning, 1952–2000*, 118 Pol Sci Quarterly 599, 600 (2003).

[75] See Patrick Egan in *Partisan Priorities: How Issue Ownership Drives and Distorts American Politics* 5 (Cambridge, 2013) (arguing that issue ownership reflects "the long-term positive associations that exist between *individual consensus issues* and America's two political parties") (emphasis added).

[76] See, for example, David Fontana and Donald Braman, *Judicial Backlash? Or Just Backlash? Evidence from a National Experiment*, 112 Colum L Rev 731 (2012).

[77] *Party Divisions of the House of Representatives*, history.house.gov/Institution/Party-Divisions /Party-Divisions/; *Party Division*, https://www.senate.gov/history/partydiv.htm.

Republicans also controlled the White House for most of the time. Woodrow Wilson was the only Democratic president between 1897, when Grover Cleveland left office, and 1933, when Franklin Roosevelt entered office. By contrast, since 1980 (for the Senate) and 1994 (for the House), turnovers of one or both Houses of Congress have occurred more frequently. When the Republicans won control of the Senate in 1980, and the House in 1994, it had been decades since they had held those chambers.[78] The White House has also changed hands more than it had in the earlier era.[79]

Most pertinent for our purposes is the issue of party polarization.[80] In the face of our current political conditions, this has become an area of extensive scholarship for those interested in political parties and their functions (and, increasingly, dysfunctions). The use of roll call voting data to create metrics for assessing polarization permits comparisons across time.[81]

In the earlier period, there were familiar ideological differences between Democrats and Republicans shaped by ideas about the role of government and economic policy. Given that debates about economic regulation were implicated by *Lochner*, judicial approval of labor injunctions, and other high-profile judicial issues of the day, these ideological differences ought to be an important part of the story. And we will see evidence that, as between the major parties, Democrats were, in fact, more likely to be court critics in these areas.

At the macro level, however, much of this period unfolded during a time when the major parties were not as polarized as they are today. Indeed, using a standard measure of polarization that scales legislator voting and facilitates comparisons between different congresses, various scholars have tracked and noted that, beginning roughly with

---

[78] See *Party Division* (cited in note 77); *Party Divisions of the House* (cited in note 77). For reflections on this change, see Frances E. Lee, *Insecure Majorities and the Perpetual Campaign* 18–40 (Chicago, 2016).

[79] See Raymond A. Smith, *Is It That Hard for a Party to Hold Onto the White House for Three Terms?*, The Hill (Apr 15, 2015, 6:00 a.m. EDT) (available at http://thehill.com/blogs /pundits-blog/presidential-campaign/238812-is-it-that-hard-for-a-party-to-hold-the-white -house) (noting that since 1950, neither party has held the White House for three terms with the exception of when George H. W. Bush succeeded Reagan).

[80] I use the term here to mean "ideological convergence within parties and divergence between parties." Nathaniel Persily, *Introduction*, in Nathaniel Persily, ed, *Solutions to Political Polarization in America* 3, 4 (Cambridge, 2015).

[81] See Michael Barber and Nolan McCarty, *Causes and Consequences of Polarization*, in Persily, ed, *Solutions to Political Polarization in America* 15, 17 (cited in note 80).

the turn into the twentieth century, polarization began to decline slowly in both the House and Senate, and it continued to decline until World War II.[82] So the direction of polarization—which was high when the period began—was on the decline for most of these years. It then stayed stable until the mid-1970s, when it began to climb, and has been moving upward ever since.[83]

Moreover, even the high polarization in evidence in the late nineteenth century, which began to drop in the early twentieth, likely did not cleanly reflect *ideological* polarization as we understand it today. In recent work, Frances Lee has argued that the party polarization commonly assumed to have characterized the Gilded Age (1876–96) is not what it might appear to be.[84] Her analysis of roll call voting suggests that, most of the time, Republicans and Democrats in Congress were not clashing about big-picture ideological questions like the role of government or economic redistribution, but instead wrangling over "the distribution of particularized benefits, patronage and control over political office."[85] Indeed, Hans Noel's work suggests, more broadly, that consistent *ideological* polarization as we know it today did not rise until the middle of the twentieth century.[86]

In addition, there was an important factional difference *within* the Republican Party in this era and it pertained directly to attacking the courts as activist. Between the very end of the nineteenth century and about 1915 or so, the Republicans were riven by a conflict between the more conservative, laissez-faire "old guard" and the Progressive faction, epitomized by Theodore Roosevelt and Robert LaFollette.[87]

---

[82] See id for the trend lines. Various graphs can also be seen with updating at *House and Senate Means 1879–2016 (as of October 2016)*, Voteview Blog (Oct 20, 2016) (available at https://voteviewblog.com/2016/10/20/house-and-senate-means-1879-2016-as-of-october -2016/).

[83] Id.

[84] Frances E. Lee, *Patronage, Logrolls, and "Polarization": Congressional Parties of the Gilded Age, 1876–1896*, 30 Studies in Am Pol Dev 116, 118 (Oct 2016).

[85] Id at 126; see also id at 120 ("Questions of regulation and redistribution were hardly on the congressional agendas between 1876 and 1896. Regulatory issues would become more prominent in the national policy agenda during the Progressive Era, but during this period, regulation was a priority for neither major party.").

[86] Hans Noel, *Political Ideologies and Political Parties in America* (Cambridge, 2003) (distinguishing between ideologies and political parties, and arguing that parties have not always been organized around coherent ideologies).

[87] Heather Cox Richardson, *To Make Men Free: A History of the Republican Party* 160 (Basic Books, 2014) (describing the splintering of the Republican Party during the early twentieth century).

LaFollette was part of a bumper crop of other Progressive Republican Senators.[88] He and others were allies of organized labor, a movement deeply aggrieved by judicial rulings of this period.[89] Both Roosevelt and LaFollette were reform-minded and supportive of social and economic regulation in ways that would put them at odds with *Lochner*-friendly courts. That became clearest when each man ran for president as a third-party candidate (discussed below), but even before that, each was skeptical of judicial decisions that constrained reform legislation. Even after the Progressive Party collapsed, LaFollette and some fellow Republican travelers continued to resist Republican orthodoxy and could sometimes marshal significant numbers. Most of the Senate members of the reform-oriented, agrarian Nonpartisan League that became active in 1915, for example, were Republicans.[90]

At roughly the same time Progressivism was beginning to divide Republicans, Democrats were managing internal strains of their own. The more conservative, laissez-faire oriented "Bourbon Democrats" who had supported Grover Cleveland were at odds with the populist forces led by William Jennings Bryan.[91] In his iconic "Cross of Gold" speech at the 1896 Democratic Convention, Bryan criticized the Supreme Court for its *Pollock* decision striking down the income tax. He caustically observed that the tax was not unconstitutional when it was passed or challenged in a prior case, but only when "one of the judges changed his mind."[92] The populist faction was far more likely than the Bourbons to challenge the courts, but this proved a less consequential divide for the Democrats than the Progressive-driven schism was for the Republicans.

This picture of Republicans and Democrats in a phase of declining polarization, and with especially pronounced internal ideological division about courts within the Republican Party, stands in stark

---

[88] Nancy C. Unger, *Fighting Bob La Follette: The Righteous Reformer* 186–88 (UNC, 2000).

[89] Id at 289–90.

[90] On the Nonpartisan League, see Michael J. Lansing, *Insurgent Democracy: The Nonpartisan League in North American Politics* (Chicago, 2015).

[91] On these factions, see Mark Brewer and Jeffrey Stonecash, *Dynamics of American Political Parties* 48–54 (Cambridge, 2009).

[92] William Jennings Bryan, *In The Chicago Convention*, in William Jennings Bryan and Mary Baird Bryan, eds, *Speeches of William Jennings Bryan* 238, 242 (Funk & Wagnalls, 1909).

contrast to the contemporary configuration. Studies of polarization reflect just the opposite dynamic for the Democratic and Republican parties in the relevant period.[93] Since the 1970s, polarization has been steadily increasing. And, as we will see in the Republican platforms, that party's position on courts has grown steadily more conservative and unified over this time period. There are complex (and contested) explanations for rising party polarization.[94] For our purposes, it is worth noting that the increase in polarization began soon after the modern era of anti-judicial activism politics began, and the two rose together. Indeed, the 1968 Nixon campaign, and the partisan-defined "southern strategy" it pursued,[95] used opposition to the Warren Court as means of attracting support from southern whites. Needless to say, the southern strategy paid off handsomely for Republicans and is at least one explanatory piece of the contemporary story of polarization.[96]

Many of the subjects implicated in contemporary debates about judicial activism are issues that reflect strongly polarized partisan attitudes.[97] The racial issues that drove the southern strategy are one central example. The 1968 Nixon campaign's emphasis on "law and order" in relation to the Warren Court was shot through with racial themes.[98] Abortion is another example, and a striking one. As a political issue, opposition to abortion rights was not initially polarized by party. There was, in fact, significant opposition to *Roe* in both parties in the wake of the decision.[99] Over time, however, this changed. Work by Nicole Mellow shows that, by the early 1980s, "between 80 and 100 percent of all abortion-related votes in the House were being cast along party lines."[100] The trend picked up in intensity so that, by the early 1990s, "the average difference between the parties'

---

[93] See Barber and McCarty, *Causes and Consequences of Polarization*, in Persily, ed, *Solutions to Political Polarization in America* at 19 (cited in note 80).

[94] For a good review of these, see id.

[95] Id at 19.

[96] Id at 27 (discussing role of southern realignment in polarization).

[97] See Thomas M. Keck, *Judicial Politics in Polarized Times* 8 (Chicago, 2014).

[98] Kevin J. McMahon, *Nixon's Court* 27 (Chicago, 2011) (discussing rise of Nixon and Wallace campaigns as response to Warren Court).

[99] Nicole Mellow, *The State of Disunion: Regional Sources of Modern American Partisanship* 132–33 (JHU, 2008).

[100] Id at 131.

positions was regularly more than 50 percentage points."[101] Opinion on same-sex marriage has also been subject to stark polarization.[102]

It makes sense that attitudes about polarizing culture war and race issues are likely to be bound up with attitudes and beliefs about courts because constitutional litigation is such a mainstay in these areas. In the face of legislatures that are polarized and sometimes gridlocked on matters of great importance to their political bases, the courts offer a different institutional venue for contesting questions, and both parties have pursued judicial agendas on such issues.[103] The special salience of culture-war litigation may be why, for some, the very phrase "judicial activism" as a political epithet embeds within it the idea of liberal attitudes about disputed issues like these.[104]

B. DYNAMICS IN PRESIDENTIAL CAMPAIGNS

Presidential elections have provided a visible forum for political parties to engage with the issue of judicial activism. In this section, I look principally at party platforms and speeches accepting a presidential nomination. Although not as salient as convention speeches in contemporary times, platforms enable a more detailed explication of party policies and often prefigure policies pursued by elected officials once in office.[105] In different ways, speeches and platforms both offer parties prime opportunities to state positions about the courts.[106]

1. *The earlier period*

a) Major parties. In the earlier period, Republicans were more likely to defend, and Democrats to attack, the courts. But the Dem-

---

[101] Id.

[102] Persily, Citrin, and Egan, *Public Opinion and Constitutional Controversy* at 245–53 (cited in note 25).

[103] See Keck, *Judicial Politics in Polarized Times* at 6–8 (cited in note 97) (identifying abortion, affirmative action, gay rights, and gun rights as "four key culture war issues" that fit this paradigm).

[104] See, for example, David Luban, *The Warren Court and the Concept of a Right*, 34 Harv CR-CL L Rev 7, 9 (1999) ("'[J]udicial activism' has become, in the hands of the politicians, little more than a euphemism for judicial protection and promotion of reverse discrimination, crime on the streets, atheism, and sexual permissiveness while 'judicial restraint' has become a rallying cry for conservative opposition to these so-called policies.").

[105] L. Sandy Meisel, *The Platform-Writing Process: Candidate-Centered Platforms in 1992*, 108 Pol Sci Quarterly 671, 671–72 (1993–94).

[106] See generally John Gerring, *Party Ideologies in America, 1828–1996* 292 (Cambridge, 1998) (despite changes over time in electioneering practices "there is no reason to suppose that the campaign speeches and party platforms of today are any less representative of the view of national party elites that they were in the 1830s").

ocrats were relatively subdued, so the differences between the major parties were less stark than they are today.

The court-related issue that was addressed most frequently in these platforms was the issue of labor injunctions.[107] As industrialization proceeded and unions rose in the Gilded Age, strikes became more frequent and, correspondingly, attempts to enjoin strikes and to punish violators with contempt triggered litigation.[108] The Supreme Court's 1895 decision in *In re Debs* upheld a labor injunction and produced a political response from the AFL and others.[109] Labor sought legislative redress and appealed to allies in both parties. Ultimately, after sustained political efforts, the period was punctuated by passage of two federal bills limiting these injunctions—first, the Clayton Act, passed in 1914, restricting the use of injunctions against labor under antitrust laws, and later the Norris-LaGuardia Act in 1932, closing some of the latitude the Clayton Act had left for such injunctions to continue.[110]

Issues relating to labor injunctions, and contempt remedies for violating such injunctions, may seem like rarefied procedural issues that are distinct from the sort of institutional claims about usurpation that animate the contemporary idea of activism. During this era, however, attacks on injunctions were often paired with larger political critiques and framed as accusations of "government by injunction."[111] For example, in 1896, a year after the *Debs* decision, when William Jennings Bryan ran on a fusion ticket of the Democratic and Populist parties, he strongly opposed labor injunctions. The language in the Democratic platform he ran on was some of the sharpest of the period:

> we especially object to *government by injunction* as a new and highly dangerous form of oppression by which *Federal Judges, in contempt of the laws of the States and rights of citizens, become at once legislators, judges and executioners*; and we approve the bill passed at the last session of the United States Senate, and now pending in the House of Representatives, relative to con-

---

[107] On the centrality of the courts and the injunction question to the labor movement in this era, see Forbath, 102 Harv L Rev at 1186–95 (cited in note 55).

[108] Id.

[109] Ross, *A Muted Fury* at 29 (cited in note 33).

[110] Id at 69, 290.

[111] Forbath, 102 Harv L Rev at 1148 (cited in note 55).

tempts in Federal courts and providing for trials by jury in certain cases of contempt.[112] (Emphasis added.)

Democratic platforms in 1900, 1904, 1908, 1912, 1916, and 1928 all explicitly addressed labor injunctions and called for reform, though none took aim at the courts issuing them quite as sharply as Bryan had.[113] Indeed, the Democrats during this time period were often defensive about their objections to judicial practices.[114] The 1908 platform is instructive. That year, Bryan ran against William Howard Taft (along with Eugene Debs on the Socialist ticket), but the Democratic Party was far more circumspect in its language. The platform made the case for legislating to limit labor injunctions,[115] but even as it did so, it conspicuously disclaimed any disrespect for the courts:

> The courts of justice are the bulwark of our liberties, and we yield to none in our purpose to maintain their dignity. . . . *We resent the attempt of the Republican party to raise a false issue respecting the judiciary. It is an unjust reflection upon a great body of our citizens to assume that they lack respect for the courts.*[116]

In their 1908 platform, Republicans countered with support for mild reform of labor injunctions, but wrapped their position in the kind of language about the sanctity of courts that seemed calculated to put the Democrats on the defensive. The platform asserted that "the rules of procedure in the Federal Courts with respect to the issuance of the writ of injunction should be more accurately defined by statute," and that "no injunction or temporary restraining order should be issued without notice, except where irreparable injury would

---

[112] 1896 Democratic Party Platform (July 7, 1896) (available at http://www.presidency.ucsb .edu/ws/index.php?pid = 29586).

[113] See Ross, *A Muted Fury* at 34–38, 88–89, 119 (cited in note 33).

[114] For example, between Bryan's 1896 run and the New Deal, only two Democratic candidates—Wilson in 1916 (running for re-election) and Al Smith in 1928—made reference to the issue in their acceptance speeches.

[115] See 1908 Democratic Party Platform (July 7, 1908) (available at http://www.presidency .ucsb.edu/ws/index.php?pid = 29589) ("Experience has proved the necessity of a modification of the present law relating to injunctions, and we reiterate the pledge of our national platforms of 1896 and 1904 in favor of the measure . . . which a Republican Congress has . . . refused to enact, relating to contempts in Federal courts and providing for trial by jury in cases of indirect contempt").

[116] Id (emphasis added).

result from delay, in which ease a speedy hearing thereafter should be granted."[117] But that position was hedged by the insistence that:

> The Republican party will uphold at all times the authority and integrity of the courts, State and Federal, and will ever insist that their powers to enforce their process and to protect life, liberty and property shall be preserved inviolate.[118]

In his acceptance speech, moreover, Taft also attacked the Democrats for disrespecting the judiciary. After addressing the injunction issue in a level of detail unimaginable in today's speeches, Taft said of the Democratic proposal that there be a jury trial before imposition of contempt remedies for violating a labor injunction: "Never before in this history of this country has there been such an insidious attack upon the judicial system."[119]

The injunction issue resurfaced in 1912 in the election between Woodrow Wilson, Taft, and Theodore Roosevelt. I address Roosevelt's third-party campaign in more detail below, but the fact that he was in the race and running on a court-curbing platform probably helps to explain what the Republicans did in 1912. The Democrats explicitly incorporated their 1908 language on injunctions in their 1912 document.[120] The Progressive platform addressed favored reform of injunctions, as well.[121] Republicans made no mention of the limited injunction reform they had favored in 1908 and instead hammered even harder the importance of protecting judicial independence and the integrity of the courts. In part, Taft had grown resistant to the AFL's request for stronger injunction reform.[122] But in part, Republicans sought, as they would in later platforms, to gain political advantage by stigmatizing criticism of courts:

---

[117] Republican Party Platform of 1908 (June 16, 1908) (available at http://www.presidency.ucsb.edu/ws/?pid=29632).

[118] Id.

[119] William Howard Taft, *Address Accepting the Republican Presidential Nomination* (July 28, 1908) (available at http://www.presidency.ucsb.edu/ws/index.php?pid=76222).

[120] 1912 Democratic Party Platform (June 25, 1912) (available at http://www.presidency.ucsb.edu/ws/index.php?pid=29590).

[121] Progressive Party Platform of 1912 (Nov 5, 1912) (available at http://www.presidency.ucsb.edu/ws/index.php?pid=29617) (favoring policy of no injunction if none would be granted in a nonlabor case, as well as new restrictions on contempt).

[122] When, in 1910, the AFL supported more forceful pro-labor legislation, Taft criticized the proposal, saying it would "sap the foundations of judicial power." Ross, *A Muted Fury* at 74–75 (cited in note 33).

The Republican party reaffirms its intention to uphold at all times the authority and integrity of the Courts, both State and Federal, and it will ever insist that their powers to enforce their process and to protect life, liberty and property shall be preserved inviolate. An orderly method is provided under our system of government by which the people may, when they choose, alter or amend the constitutional provisions which underlie that government. Until these constitutional provisions are so altered or amended, in orderly fashion, it is the duty of the courts to see to it that when challenged they are enforced.[123]

Taft followed suit in his acceptance speech, sharply attacking both the Democrats and Roosevelt for "promoting the hostility of the people to the courts," and calling Roosevelt's proposals to limit judicial power "grotesque."[124]

After the passage of the Clayton Act in 1914, the subject did not explicitly resurface in platforms again until 1928,[125] when the Democrats supported what would become the Norris LaGuardia Act in 1932 to strengthen protections for labor.[126] In 1928, the Republicans also offered mild support for reform.[127]

Other than supporting injunction reform—for which the Republicans also offered some support twice—the Democrats had surprisingly little to say about the courts. They had criticized the *Pollock* decision on the income tax in the 1896 platform, and in 1912 lamented that "the Sherman anti-trust law [had] received a judicial construction depriving it of much of its efficiency," indicating that they favored "the enactment of legislation which will restore to the statute

---

[123] Republican Party Platform of 1912 (June 18, 1912) (available at http://www.presidency.ucsb.edu/ws/index.php?pid=29633).

[124] William Howard Taft, *The Judiciary and Progress*, repr S Doc 408, 62nd Cong, 2d Sess 9 (March 13, 1912).

[125] The 1920 and 1924 Democratic platforms both asserted that "labor is not a commodity," which was a slogan used in supporting greater protection for labor against injunctions issued under antitrust laws. But these platforms did not explicitly address injunctions. See 1920 Democratic Party Platform (June 28, 1920) (available at http://www.presidency.ucsb.edu/ws/index.php?pid=29592); 1924 Democratic Party Platform (June 24, 1920) (available at http://www.presidency.ucsb.edu/ws/index.php?pid=29593).

[126] The 1928 Democratic platform asserted that "[n]o injunctions should be granted in labor disputes except upon proof of threatened irreparable injury and after notice and hearing and the injunction should be confined to those acts which do directly threaten irreparable injury." 1928 Democratic Party Platform (June 26, 1928) (available at http://www.presidency.ucsb.edu/ws/index.php?pid=29594).

[127] Republican Party Platform of 1928 (June 12, 1928) (available at http://www.presidency.ucsb.edu/ws/index.php?pid=29637) (asserting that "injunctions in labor disputes have in some instances been abused and have given rise to a serious question for legislation.").

the strength of which it has been deprived by such interpretation."[128] Notably, none of their platforms directly addressed *Lochner* or its progeny. They offered support for regulatory legislation of the sort *Lochner* made constitutionally questionable, but did not connect the issue to the courts.

One might have thought that the 1936 election would have finally pushed Democrats to criticize judicial activism more aggressively in their platform. After all, the Supreme Court in 1935 and early 1936 had decided several cases rejecting Roosevelt's New Deal programs, including *Schechter Poultry Corp. v United States*.[129] A few days after *Schechter Poultry* struck down portions of the National Industrial Recovery Act as beyond Congress's commerce power (among its other flaws), Roosevelt held forth on the opinion in a packed and lengthy press conference in which he closely reviewed and analyzed the decision.[130] According to the *New York Times*, he emphasized that the commerce power "constituted the only weapon in the government's hands to fight conditions not even dreamed about 150 years ago," and said the Court was interpreting the clause "in light of the horse-and-buggy days of 1789."[131] Yet, betraying a defensiveness, he was also said in this story to be at pains to "insist[ ] that he was not criticizing the Supreme Court."[132] When the Court later invalidated the Agricultural Adjustment Act in early 1936,[133] Roosevelt, in response, was notably restrained. He pressed the need for agricultural policy change, but did not criticize the Court or parse the decision, as he had done with *Schechter Poultry*.[134]

In the 1936 campaign, the Democratic platform made no mention of the Supreme Court or its decisions striking down New Deal pro-

---

[128] Id.

[129] 295 US 495 (1935).

[130] Charles W. Hurd, *President Says End of NRA Puts Control up to People; Will Act to Halt Deflation*, NY Times 1, 6 (June 1, 1935).

[131] Id.

[132] Id.

[133] *United States v Butler*, 297 US 1 (1936).

[134] Jeff Shesol, *Supreme Power: Franklin Roosevelt vs. The Supreme Court* 147, 197 (W. W. Norton, 2010). Six months later, when the Court struck down New York's minimum-wage law in *Morehad v New York, ex rel Tipaldo*, 298 US 587 (1936), he suggested that the Court had created a "no man's land" in which neither the federal nor state government could legislate. See Franklin D. Roosevelt, *The Three Hundredth Press Conference*, in 5 *Public Papers and Addresses of Franklin D. Roosevelt, The People Approve, 1936* at 191–92 (NY Random House, 1938).

grams. It said only that the party would support any necessary constitutional amendment if it were to be determined that the country's problems "cannot be effectively solved by legislation within the Constitution."[135] At times in the campaign, Roosevelt touted the virtues of a broader interpretation of the federal government's legislative powers, and he was, in general, not reticent about putting forward his own substantive vision of a good constitutional order.[136] But he treaded gingerly around the Court. Some Democrats in Congress were far more willing to condemn the Court directly for its activism,[137] but Roosevelt exercised notable caution. This was also true of his 1936 acceptance speech.[138]

Sensing vulnerability, the Republicans criticized Roosevelt as a radical who did not respect and revere the Constitution. The 1936 Republican platform charged that "[t]he integrity and authority of the Supreme Court have been flouted," and pledged:

> to resist all attempts to impair the authority of the Supreme Court of the United States, the final protector of the rights of our citizens against the arbitrary encroachments of the legislative and executive branches of government. There can be no individual liberty without an independent judiciary.[139]

Republican candidate Alf Landon gave multiple speeches attacking Roosevelt along these lines, claiming that Roosevelt saw Supreme

---

[135] 1936 Democratic Party Platform (June 23, 1936) (available at http://www.presidency .ucsb.edu/ws/?pid=29596) (stating that, if necessary, "we shall seek such clarifying amendment as will assure to the legislatures of the several States and to the Congress of the United States, each within its proper jurisdiction, the power to enact those laws which the State and Federal legislatures, within their respective spheres, shall find necessary, in order adequately to regulate commerce, protect public health and safety and safeguard economic security").

[136] For an account of Roosevelt's concept of "an 'economic constitutional order' . . . essential to protect majorities against the 'enthronement of minorities' and secure a democracy of opportunity," see Joseph Fishkin and William E. Forbath, *The Anti-Oligarchy Constitution*, 94 BU L Rev 669, 689 (2014).

[137] See, for example, Arthur Krock, *A Keynote by Robinson: Republicans Chided on Landon Reservation to Party Platform*, NY Times 13 (June 25, 1936) (quoting Senator Joseph Robinson at Democratic Convention in speech saying "members of the Court are not above the influences of their personal philosophies. . . . The court has undermined itself"); *Senator Barkley's Keynote Speech as Temporary Chairman of the Convention*, NY Times 16 (June 24, 1936) (quoting Senator Alben Barkley at Democratic Convention refuting notion of Court's "infallibility" and its immunity from "criticism").

[138] See Franklin D. Roosevelt, *Acceptance Speech for the Renomination of the Presidency* (June 27, 1936) (available at http://www.presidency.ucsb.edu/ws/?pid=15314).

[139] Republican Party Platform of 1936 (June 9, 1936) (available at http://www.presidency .ucsb.edu/ws/index.php?pid=29639).

Court decisions as mere "barrier[s] to be circumvented,"[140] and accusing his administration of "ridicul[ing] the justices" and him of joining "a shameful attack on these men who were only doing their duty."[141] In this way, the 1936 presidential campaign featured partisan attacks, but for excessive criticism of the Court, *not* for claimed judicial activism by it.

The Democratic caution would lift after the election, as FDR unveiled his court-packing proposal. It hit strong political headwinds and ultimately lost on preliminary votes, but the shift in the Supreme Court's approaches that marked the end of this period mooted the controversial plan.

b) Third parties. Looking at the role of the major parties in the early period gives us only a partial picture of the political dynamics of challenging the courts. Notably, while the Democrats exhibited restraint in criticizing courts during this period, third-party candidates Theodore Roosevelt and Robert LaFollette exhibited no such reticence. The 1912 and 1924 campaigns waged by these insurgent Republicans went hard after courts.

Roosevelt, who had served as president from 1901–1908, had chosen not to seek re-election in 1908 and had yielded that year to Taft, his preferred successor. Unhappy with Taft's conservatism, he came back into the electoral arena with a Progressive fervor a few years later. In the years leading up to the 1912 election, he launched many critiques of the courts as part of an attack on special interests. He began criticizing *Lochner, E. C. Knight,* and other cases in speeches and in print.[142] His sharp rhetoric characterized judges as having "become far more truly the lawgivers than either the executive or legislative bodies."[143] He wrote and spoke in favor of allowing state voters to recall judges, drawing criticism from the *New York Times,* Republican lawmakers, many legal scholars, bar associations, and Taft.[144] He tried to wrest the GOP nomination from Taft, but ulti-

---

[140] *Landon's Speech Warning on New Deal Laws,* Associated Press 21 (Oct 22, 1936).

[141] James A. Hagerty, *Warns Nation on Liberty,* NY Times 1 (Oct 21, 1936).

[142] Ross, *A Muted Fury* at 134–35, 145 (cited in note 33).

[143] Theodore Roosevelt, *Judges and Progress,* The Outlook (Jan 6, 1912); Stephen Stagner, *The Recall of Judicial Decisions and the Due Process Debate,* 24 Am J Legal Hist 257, 257–58 (1980).

[144] Ross, *A Muted Fury* at 134–35 (cited in note 33).

mately lost and chose to run on the Progressive or "Bull Moose" ticket.

In 1912, the controversy about courts was becoming more salient. There was a movement underway around the country to try to institute a judicial recall in states to allow voters to remove a state judge.[145] Lawyer Gilbert Roe, an ally of Senator Robert LaFollette, published *Our Judicial Oligarchy*, a book that pointedly attacked judicial activism. Recall that LaFollette wrote an introduction that excoriated courts.[146] Among other things, he declared that "the judiciary ha[d] grown to be the most powerful institution in our government."[147] In the body of the book, Roe provided several chapters with different answers to the question "Why the People Distrust the Courts," and closed with an endorsement of a judicial recall.

As the candidate of the Progressives, Roosevelt was the driving force in pressing the case against judicial activism in 1912. He was forceful and direct in all the ways the Democrats were not. For the Progressives, skepticism of judicial activism was linked to their sharp, substantive attack on the major parties, which they said had become, "[i]nstead of instruments to promote the general welfare . . . the tools of corrupt interests which use them impartially to serve their selfish purposes."[148] As part of a robust embrace of social welfare legislation and reforms including direct election of senators, nominating primaries, and suffrage for women, their platform pledged to pursue "such restriction of the power of the courts as shall leave to the people the ultimate authority to determine fundamental questions of social welfare and public policy."[149] It then advocated specifically:

> . . . That when an Act, passed under the police power of the State is held unconstitutional under the State Constitution, by the courts, the people, after an ample interval for deliberation, shall have an opportunity to vote on the question whether they desire the Act to become law, notwithstanding such decision.[150]

---

[145] Id at 110–29.

[146] See LaFollette, *Introduction*, in Roe, *Our Judicial Oligarchy* (cited in note 30).

[147] Id at vi.

[148] Progressive Party Platform of 1912 (Nov 5, 1912) (available at http://www.presidency.ucsb.edu/ws/index.php?pid=29617).

[149] Id.

[150] Id.

Roosevelt's advocacy for this recall of judicial decisions met with fierce criticism and claims that his proposals would crush judicial independence. Ultimately, he lost to Woodrow Wilson, but finished ahead of Taft by coming in second and securing 27.4 percent of the popular votes and eighty-eight electoral votes.[151]

The other presidential campaign in the era that squarely engaged questions of judicial activism was 1924, and it was in some ways the most strident of all. Once again, the energy and emphasis came from a Progressive. LaFollette ran against incumbent Calvin Coolidge, the Republican, and lawyer John W. Davis, the Democrat. The Progressive Party of Roosevelt's Bull Moose run had dissolved, so a new Progressive Independent Party was formed to take up the cause. The groundwork for LaFollette's run was set with the creation of the Conference for Progressive Political Action (CPPA), a new coalition of Progressives, unions, and farm leaders formed after the recession of 1921–22. CPPA, the AFL, and LaFollette banded together to focus their efforts on the courts.[152] For the first time in its history, the AFL endorsed a presidential candidate.[153] In a climate of growing political opposition to unions, the AFL found the major parties weak on labor rights and on confronting the judiciary. Indeed, neither major party platform addressed labor issues in 1924.[154]

By contrast, the Progressive Independent Party platform declared that "[t]he great issue before the American people today is the control of government and industry by private monopoly," and condemned the "tyranny" of the judiciary.[155] It denounced the "usurpation in recent years by the federal courts of the power to nullify laws duly enacted by the legislative branch of the government [as] a plain vi-

---

[151] The fourth candidate was Eugene Debs, who ran as a Socialist and garnered 6 percent of the popular vote and no electoral votes. The Election of 1912 (available at http://www.presidency.ucsb.edu/showelection.php?year=1912).

[152] Ross, *A Muted Fury* at 193–94, 201, 215 (cited in note 33); see also Ray P. Orman, *An Introduction to Political Parties and Practical Politics* 55 (Charles Schribner's Sons, 1924).

[153] James Appel, *Labor for Lafollette: The AFL in the 1924 Campaign*, 8 Indust & Labor Rel Forum 101, 101 (1972).

[154] Republican Party Platform of 1924 (June 10, 1924) (available at http://www.presidency.ucsb.edu/ws/index.php?pid=29636); 1924 Democratic Party Platform (June 24, 1924) (available at http://www.presidency.ucsb.edu/ws/index.php?pid=29593).

[155] Progressive Party Platform of 1924 (Nov 4, 1924) (available at http://www.presidency.ucsb.edu/ws/index.php?pid=29618).

olation of the Constitution,"[156] and specifically proposed two dramatic changes:

> We favor submitting to the people, for their considerate judgment, a constitutional amendment providing that Congress may by enacting a statute make it effective over a judicial veto.

> We favor such amendment to the constitution as may be necessary to provide for the election of all Federal Judges, without party designation, for fixed terms not exceeding ten years, by direct vote of the people.[157]

Both Coolidge and Davis criticized LaFollette's position on the courts, with Coolidge and his running mate doing so sharply. Coolidge, for example, characterized the hostility to the Court, and Progressives in general, as being "the heirs of George III and Lenin."[158] Increasingly under attack and finding the public unresponsive, LaFollette then tried to minimize the judicial issue.[159] Coolidge ultimately won in a landslide.

2. *The contemporary period.* The roots of contemporary political attacks on judicial activism can be traced to attacks by southern Democrats on *Brown*,[160] but as this section will demonstrate, the major party platforms began most clearly to engage with the issue of judicial activism in 1968. In the period from 1968 to the present, the major party opposing judicial activism—the Republicans—have been far more consistently critical of courts than the Democrats were in the early period. As alluded to in Part I, there has been a distinctly partisan cast to the charge of judicial activism since the 1968 campaign, with broad-based institutional critiques of the courts as activist asserted principally by the Republican Party. In their own platforms, Democrats, by contrast, have been aggrieved by or supportive of

---

[156] Id. The platform noted that, in his first inaugural address, Lincoln said: "The candid citizen must confess that if the policy of the government, upon vital questions affecting the whole people, is to be irrevocably fixed by decisions of the Supreme Court, the people will have ceased to be their own rulers, having to that extent practically resigned their government into the hands of that eminent tribunal." Id.

[157] Id.

[158] Ross, *A Muted Fury* at 271–72 (cited in note 33).

[159] Id at 276.

[160] See Part I.B. Six years before *Brown*, the platform of the Dixiecrats mentioned opposition to "the usurpation of legislative functions by the executive and judicial departments." Platform of the States Rights Democratic Party (August 14, 1948) (available at http://www.presidency.ucsb.edu/ws/index.php?pid=25851). But race-related battles on judicial activism had not yet been clearly engaged in 1948, and the Dixiecrats did not emphasize that judicial issue at the time. Schacter, 82 S Cal L Rev at 1206–12 (cited in note 12).

particular decisions, but their claims have not been expressed in the register of activism.

The hesitation to harshly criticize courts that we saw in the *Lochner* period was still somewhat operative in Nixon's 1968 challenges to the Supreme Court, but it faded away with subsequent candidates. Indeed, Republican campaign rhetoric about judicial activism can be grouped into three waves: the Nixon campaigns, which were rhetorically restrained but strategically precise; the Reagan campaigns, which newly emphasized abortion and family values, and worked closely with the then-emerging religious right; and the campaigns from Dole's 1996 effort through to the present, which added same-sex marriage to the agenda and escalated the rhetoric.

In 1968, Nixon emphasized law and order. The platform declared that "lawlessness is crumbling the foundations of American society."[161] On the campaign trail, Nixon frequently repeated a favorite line: "some of our courts have gone too far in weakening the peace forces as against the criminal forces."[162] He used the same phrase in his acceptance speech, while also assuring that courts should always be respected.[163] In the platform, the language about appropriate regard for courts was more subtle. It said that the party pledged "a determined effort to rebuild and enhance public respect" for the Supreme Court and other courts.[164]

In one way, 1968 does provide a parallel to the earlier period. This is the only election in the contemporary period where there was a third-party candidate running aggressively against the Supreme Court. George Wallace, who collected forty-six electoral votes and received almost 10 million votes, was far harsher than Nixon about the Court and activism. His American Independent Party Platform said:

> In the period of the past three decades, we have seen the Federal judiciary, primarily the Supreme Court, transgress repeatedly upon the prerogatives

---

[161] Republican Party Platform of 1968 (Aug 5, 1968) (available at http://www.presidency.ucsb.edu/ws/index.php?pid=25841); see McMahon, *Nixon's Court* (cited in note 98).

[162] Stephenson Jr., *Campaigns and the Court* at 181 (cited in note 50).

[163] Richard Nixon, *Address Accepting the Presidential Nomination at the Republican National Convention in Miami Beach, Florida* (Aug 8, 1968) (available at http://www.presidency.ucsb.edu/ws/?pid=25968).

[164] Republican Party Platform of 1968 (cited in note 161). In support of Humphrey, the Democrats' platform said only that crime fighting should not "foster injustice" or come at the expense of the "hard won liberties of all Americans." 1968 Democratic Party Platform (Aug 26, 1968) (available at http://www.presidency.ucsb.edu/ws/index.php?pid=29604).

of the Congress and exceed its authority by enacting judicial legislation, in
the form of decisions based upon political and sociological considerations,
which would never have been enacted by the Congress. We have seen
them, in their solicitude for the criminal and lawless element of our society,
shackle the police and other law enforcement agencies; and, as a result, they
have made it increasingly difficult to protect the law-abiding citizen from
crime and criminals. . . .[165]

The platform went on to propose that federal district judges be made
to face the voters at periodic intervals, and that circuit judges and
Supreme Court Justices be subject to periodic reconfirmation by the
Senate.[166] Wallace did not give a nomination acceptance speech, but
he gave a speech nine days after he launched his campaign that singled out the Supreme Court. Speaking to a crowd of business executives, he said that the Court can "strike down all the acts of your
legislature. I don't want them to have the power over all governors, all
legislatures, and all the people."[167]

In 1972, the Republicans continued their emphasis on crime, with
their platform and Nixon's acceptance speech touting the administration's success in fighting crime and appointing judges with "fi-
delity to the Constitution," who "balance the rights of defendants
with the needs of law enforcement."[168] The platform endorsed "legislation to halt immediately all further court-ordered busing," but did
not challenge judicial activism in any general way.[169]

In 1980, as issues associated with the religious right rose, Republican rhetoric began to emphasize the idea that Democrats had shunted
the family aside and "given its jurisdiction to the courts," along with a
call for judges who "respect the traditional family and the sanctity of
innocent human life."[170] By 1984, when Ronald Reagan ran for re-
election, Republicans offered a more fully elaborated set of institutional ideas about courts, arguing that:

[165] American Independent Party Platform of 1968 (Oct 13, 1968) (available at http://www
.presidency.ucsb.edu/ws/index.php?pid=29570).

[166] Id.

[167] James Strong, *Executives Cheer Talk by Wallace—Hits Actions of High Court*, Chicago
Tribune S1 (Feb 17, 1968).

[168] Republican Party Platform of 1972 (Aug 21, 1972) (available at http://www.presidency
.ucsb.edu/ws/index.php?pid=25842).

[169] Id.

[170] Republican Party Platform of 1980 (July 15, 1980) (available at http://www.presidency
.ucsb.edu/ws/index.php?pid=25844).

judicial power must be exercised with deference towards State and local officials; it must not expand at the expense of our representative institutions. It is not a judicial function to reorder the economic, political, and social priorities of our nation. The intrusion of the courts into such areas undermines the stature of the judiciary and erodes respect for the rule of law. Where appropriate, we support congressional efforts to restrict the jurisdiction of federal courts.[171]

The platform went on to "commend the President for appointing federal judges committed to the rights of law-abiding citizens and traditional family values," "shar[ing] the public's dissatisfaction with an elitist and unresponsive federal judiciary," and calling for judges committed to "judicial restraint."[172]

The language in George H. W. Bush's 1992 acceptance speech marked the appearance of particular language about judicial activism that became common in GOP platforms and speeches thereafter. He said that Bill Clinton would "stock the judiciary with liberal judges who will write laws they can't get approved by the voters."[173] By 1996 and the Dole campaign, the anti-activism rhetoric in Republican platforms was ramping up. At the same time, although no court had yet legalized same-sex marriage, the possibility of that result had been introduced by the Hawaii Supreme Court in a preliminary decision in 1993,[174] and the Republican Party began to fold same-sex marriage into its portfolio of complaints about judicial activism. In 1996, for example, the platform applauded congressional passage of the Defense of Marriage Act, noting that it would prevent "federal judges and bureaucrats from forcing states to recognize other living arrangements as 'marriages.'"[175] Since 1996, references to same-sex marriage in relation to judicial activism have been a mainstay for Republican

---

[171] Republican Party Platform of 1984 (Aug 20, 1984) (available at http://www.presidency.ucsb.edu/ws/index.php?pid=25845). In 1980, Reagan's acceptance speech had not mentioned the abortion issue. In 1984, he referred to the "sacredness of human life" in his speech but did not connect the issue to courts. Ronald Reagan, *Remarks Accepting Presidential Nomination at the Republican National Convention in Dallas, Texas* (Aug 23, 1984) (available at http://www.presidency.ucsb.edu/ws/index.php?pid=40290).

[172] Id.

[173] George Bush, *Remarks Accepting the Presidential Nomination at the Republican National Convention in Houston* (Aug 20, 1992) (available at http://www.presidency.ucsb.edu/ws/index.php?pid=21352).

[174] *Baehr v Lewin*, 852 P2d 44 (Hawaii 1993).

[175] Republican Party Platform of 1996 (Aug 12, 1996) (available at http://www.presidency.ucsb.edu/ws/index.php?pid=25848).

platforms. The 1996 platform also quoted the Tenth Amendment and said "[f]or more than half a century, that solemn compact has been scorned by liberal Democrats and the judicial activism of the judges they have appointed."[176] It admonished that:

> The federal judiciary, including the U.S. Supreme Court, has overstepped its authority under the Constitution. It has usurped the right of citizen legislators and popularly elected executives to make law by declaring duly enacted laws to be "unconstitutional" through the misapplication of the principle of judicial review. [These actions are] fundamentally at odds with our system of government in which the people and their representatives decide issues great and small.[177]

The sharper tone of 1996 has been maintained ever since. Succeeding platforms have argued, for example, that "scores of judges with activist backgrounds in the hard-left now have lifetime tenure" (2000 and 2004);[178] the President should "name only judges who have demonstrated respect for the Constitution and the processes of our republic" (2000);[179] "the sound principle of judicial review has turned into an intolerable presumption of judicial supremacy" (2004);[180] "[j]udicial activism is a grave threat to the rule of law because unaccountable federal judges are usurping democracy, ignoring the Constitution and its separation of powers, and imposing personal opinions upon the public . . ." (2008);[181] "judicial activism" is a "threat to the constitution" and "Republican Senators [must] do all in their power to prevent the elevation of additional leftist ideologues to the courts"

---

[176] Id.

[177] Id. This platform went on to link the problem of activism to the American Bar Association:

> A Republican president will ensure that a process is established to select for the federal judiciary nominees who understand that their task is first and foremost to be faithful to the Constitution and to the intent of those who framed it. In that process, the American Bar Association will no longer have the right to meddle in a way that distorts a nominee's credentials and advances the liberal agenda of litigious lawyers and their allies.

[178] 2004 Republican Party Platform (Aug 30, 2004) (available at http://www.presidency.ucsb.edu/ws/index.php?pid=25850); 2000 Republican Party Platform (July 31, 2000) (available at http://www.presidency.ucsb.edu/ws/?pid=25849).

[179] 2000 Republican Party Platform (July 31, 2000) (cited in note 178).

[180] 2004 Republican Party Platform (Aug 30, 2004) (cited in note 178).

[181] 2008 Republican Party Platform (Sept 1, 2008) (available at http://www.presidency.ucsb.edu/ws/?pid=78545).

(2012);[182] and, most recently, the activist judiciary is a "critical threat to our country's constitutional order," and "only Republican appointments will enable the courts to begin to reverse the long line of activist decisions, including *Roe, Obergefell* and the Obamacare cases," which have "expanded the power of the judiciary at the expense of the people and their elected representatives" (2016).[183]

The Democratic platforms in the contemporary period have typically included one or more of the following: a call for equal rights in various realms;[184] a call for a diverse bench;[185] opposition to jurisdiction-stripping measures;[186] support for abortion rights;[187] and commentary on specific issues or decisions.[188] There is no mention of judicial activism in any of them. The phrase or idea appears neither on defense (as a reply to the GOP's claims) nor on offense (as a way to attack the Supreme Court's rising conservatism over these years). One might

---

[182] 2012 Republican Party Platform (Aug 27, 2012) (available at http://www.presidency .ucsb.edu/ws/?pid=101961).

[183] 2016 Republican Party Platform (July 18, 2016) (available at http://www.presidency .ucsb.edu/ws/index.php?pid=117718). In this time period, several Republican candidates also addressed the activism question in their speeches, some more explicitly than others. See Robert Dole, *Address Accepting the Presidential Nomination at the Republican National Convention in San Diego* (Aug 15, 1996) (available at http://www.presidency.ucsb.edu/ws/index.php ?pid=25960); George W. Bush, *Remarks Accepting the Presidential Nomination at the Republican National Convention in New York City* (Sept 2, 2004) (available at http://www.presidency.ucsb .edu/ws/?pid=25955); John McCain, *Address Accepting the Presidential Nomination at the Republican National Convention in Saint Paul* (Sept 4, 2008) (available at http://www.presidency .ucsb.edu/ws/index.php?pid=78576); Donald J. Trump, *Address Accepting the Presidential Nomination at the Republican National Convention in Cleveland, Ohio* (July 21, 2016) (available at http:// www.presidency.ucsb.edu/ws/index.php?pid=117935).

[184] See, e.g., 1972 Democratic Party Platform (July 10, 1972) (available at http://www .presidency.ucsb.edu/ws/index.php?pid=29605); 1984 Democratic Party Platform (July 16, 1984) (available at http://www.presidency.ucsb.edu/ws/index.php?pid=29608); 2016 Democratic Party Platform (July 21, 2016) (available at http://www.presidency.ucsb.edu/ws/index .php?pid=117717).

[185] See, e.g., 1996 Democratic Party Platform (August 26, 1996) (available at http://www .presidency.ucsb.edu/ws/index.php?pid=29611); 2008 Democratic Party Platform (August 25, 2008) (available at http://www.presidency.ucsb.edu/ws/index.php?pid=78283).

[186] See, e.g., 1984 Democratic Party Platform (July 16, 1984) (cited in note 184); 2000 Democratic Party Platform (August 14, 2000) (available at http://www.presidency.ucsb.edu /ws/index.php?pid=29612).

[187] See, e.g., 1980 Democratic Party Platform (August 11, 1980) (available at http://www .presidency.ucsb.edu/ws/index.php?pid=29607); 2000 Democratic Party Platform (cited in note 186); 2016 Democratic Party Platform (cited in note 184).

[188] See, e.g., 1972 Democratic Party Platform (cited in note 184); 1976 Democratic Party Platform (July 12, 1976) (available at http://www.presidency.ucsb.edu/ws/index.php?pid =29606); 2016 Democratic Party Platform (cited in note 184).

have expected attacks on judicial activism in recent years, given that decisions like *Citizens United v FEC*[189] and *Shelby County v Holder*[190] striking down congressional legislation have provoked outrage from the left. As we will see in the next section, there is some evidence of such claims from Democratic senators in confirmation hearings, but the approach in Democratic platforms has been to criticize these decisions sharply while eschewing more abstract criticism of the institution as activist. For example, the 2012 platform said, "Our opponents have applauded the Supreme Court's decision in *Citizens United* and welcomed the new flow of special interest money with open arms. In stark contrast, we believe we must take immediate action to curb the influence of lobbyists and special interests on our political institutions."[191] In 2016, the platform again attacked *Citizens United* and implicitly criticized *Shelby County* without name checking it. That platform said: "We will fight to end the broken campaign finance system, overturn the disastrous *Citizens United* decision, restore the full power of the Voting Rights Act, and return control of our elections to the American people."[192]

C. DYNAMICS IN CONGRESS

1. *Confirmation in the Senate.* The confirmation process provides another political venue for making claims about judicial activism. But it has changed significantly since the *Lochner* era. Three aspects of that process merit exploration. I will review, in turn, changes to the confirmation process itself, the changing dynamics of voting on nominees, and the changing role of interest groups in the process.

   a) Changes in the confirmation process. The confirmation process of the earlier period looked, for much of that period, very different from the one we see today. First, until the Seventeenth Amendment was ratified in 1913, the Constitution provided for state legislatures to appoint senators. In the absence of popular election, senators were not held directly accountable to voters for confirmation votes, nor typically subject to pressure from voters or interest groups in the

---

[189] 558 US 310 (2010).

[190] 570 US 529 (2013).

[191] 2012 Democratic National Platform (Sept 3, 2012) (available at http://www.presidency.ucsb.edu/ws/index.php?pid=101962).

[192] 2016 Democratic Party Platform (July 21, 2016) (cited in note 184).

same way as they are today. A second difference was that, until 1929, the Senate considered nominations in closed executive session. Thus, both the committee hearing and the vote were typically held out of public view.[193] Third, the nominee did not routinely appear personally before the committee until 1925. All of this means that, for a good deal of the earlier period, confirmation hearings did not afford a robust opportunity to publicly debate judicial activism or the philosophy of nominees poised to take the bench.

Contrast the contemporary process, where hearings are televised and now available for viewing online. Senators on the committee regularly engage in colloquies with nominees and witnesses. Whether or not they get any meaningful answers, they have a chance to raise questions about cases and approaches and thus to communicate with the public about what the Supreme Court is or should (by their lights) be doing. Often, these "questions" take the form of, or are intermingled with, mini-speeches.

Review of the transcript of every confirmation hearing since 1896 shows that, over time, it has become increasingly commonplace for senators to raise the issue of judicial activism, whether phrased in exactly those terms, in related terminology like "legislating from the bench," through a rhetorical antonym like "judicial restraint" or "strict construction," or through questions about approach that are underwritten by concerns about judicial usurpation, such as questions about static versus evolving constitutional meaning and enumerated versus unenumerated rights. As early as William Brennan's hearing in 1957—in the shadow of *Brown*—the nominee was asked about evolving constitutional meaning in skeptical ways. For example, Senator James Eastland of Mississippi asked Brennan: "Do you think the Constitution of the United States could have one meaning this week and another meaning next week?"[194] Other senators responded with a functional defense of evolving meaning.[195]

---

[193] Two relevant exceptions during the earlier period were the nominations of Louis Brandeis (1916) and Harlan Fiske Stone (1925). Michael J. Gerhardt, *The Federal Appointment Process: A Constitutional and Historical Analysis* 67 (Duke, 2003).

[194] *Nomination of William Joseph Brennan Jr. before the Committee on the Judiciary*, 58th Cong, 1st Sess 38 (1957) (Eastland (D-Miss)).

[195] See, for example, id at 43 (Wiley (R-Wis)) ("[W]hen the Constitution was born it was a horse and buggy age. Now we are in the atomic age."); id at 39 (Watkins (R-Utah)) ("[H]uman beings are likely to err. . . . we can't let the first judge who passed on it fix it for all times.").

As far as I can determine, the phrase "judicial activism" itself made its first appearance in the confirmation setting at the 1967 hearing on the nomination of Thurgood Marshall to be Associate Justice. Senator Sam Ervin (D-NC) invoked it, saying:

> My personal opinion is, and I say it with reluctance, but I say, because I believe it to be true, that the road to destruction of constitutional government in the United States is being paved by the good intentions of the judicial activists, who, all too often, constitute a majority of the Supreme Court. *A judicial activist*, in my book, is a man who has good intentions but who is unable to exercise the restraint inherent in the judicial process when it is properly understood and applied, and who is willing to add to the Constitution things that are not in it and subtract from the Constitution things that are in it.[196]

Ervin went on to make comments about activism part of his standard repertoire.[197]

Since 1967, the activism issue, or questions about methodology implicating the issue, have been raised in the confirmation of every Supreme Court nominee, typically by multiple senators. Table 1 reflects the number of senators who have asked questions or made comments about activism at any confirmation hearing for a Supreme Court nominee from 1896 to the present. The compilation in the table distinguishes between questions explicitly employing the term "judicial activism" or a related phrase[198] and those more generally asking about the boundaries of the judicial function, but not using these precise terms.[199] The first general questions appear in 1949. This kind of questioning and commentary has an upward trajectory over time, such that by the late 1960s, multiple senators regularly pursue it.

---

[196] *Nomination of Thurgood Marshall before the Committee on the Judiciary*, 19th Cong, 1st Sess 155–56 (1967) (Ervin (D-NC)).

[197] See, for example, *Nominations of Abe Fortas and Homer Thornberry before the Committee on the Judiciary*, 90th Cong, 2nd 149 (1968) ("The *Harper* case is a plain example of judicial activism at work"); *Nominations of William H. Rehnquist and Lewis F. Powell, Jr. before the Committee on the Judiciary*, 92nd Cong, 1st Sess 22 (1971) ("I think a man who would substitute his personal notions for constitutional principles is not fit to be a member of the Supreme Court.").

[198] Specific terms tracked here are any variant of "judicial activism," "judicial restraint," "legislation from the bench," "strict construction," or references to "usurpation" by the Court.

[199] General terms mean questions or comments about the candidate's judicial or interpretive methodology that do not invoke the specific terms identified above. These questions frequently include references to changing versus static constitutional meanings and, in recent years, living constitutionalism versus originalism.

Notably, in this context, the partisan patterns are different than what we saw in the realm of presidential platforms and acceptance speeches. Recall that, in the contemporary era, the critique of courts-as-activist has been the sole domain of Republicans in that setting, with Democrats defending or criticizing particular decisions, but not launching institutional attacks on the Supreme Court. The picture in confirmation hearings is more bipartisan, but there are nevertheless partisan dimensions of note.

The first movers were southern Democrats (or former southern Democrats, in the case of Strom Thurmond). Even before the explicit references to judicial activism in the 1960s, these senators began to press on issues of method. This pattern is reflected in Senator Eastland's question to nominee Brennan (discussed above), as well as questions from this faction to Potter Stewart in 1959. They asked him about whether "the Constitution has the same meaning today that it had when it was adopted,"[200] whether "you consider yourself what is termed a 'creative judge' or do you consider yourself a judge that follows precedent,"[201] and, as a preface to critiquing *Brown*, "[d]o you agree with me that a judge or court ought not to overrule a prior decision simply because he thinks that it ought to be decided some other way?"[202] As the southern realignment unfolded, though, it gradually became more common for Republicans to press aggressively on the activism issue. Over time, Republicans came to be the most consistent interlocutors on the issue. Standard questions and comments include, for example:

> You have stated that you feel it is personally abhorrent and repugnant, and that it is a legislative matter to deal with it. Do you mean by that we should legally protect the unborn? If so, how, considering the *Roe v. Wade activism* from the judicial branch?[203]

> The role of the judiciary is to interpret the law. However, there have been times when judges have gone beyond their responsibility of interpreting the law and, instead, have exercised their individual will as judicial activists.

---

[200] *Nomination of Potter Stewart before the Committee on the Judiciary*, 86th Cong, 1st Sess 16 (1959) (Eastland (D-Miss)).

[201] Id at 26 (Johnston (D-SC)).

[202] Id at 120 (Ervin (D-NC)).

[203] *Nomination of Sandra Day O'Connor before the Committee on the Judiciary*, 97th Cong, 1st Sess 240 (1981) (Denton (R-Ala)).

Table 1

Number of Senators Asking Supreme Court Nominees Questions About or Related to Judicial Activism at Confirmation Hearings, 1896–Present

Nominee	Year	Republicans Asking Questions with Specific Terms	Democrats Asking Questions with Specific Terms	Republicans Asking Questions with General Terms	Democrats Asking Questions with General Terms
Brandeis	1916	0	0	0	0
Stone	1925	0	0	0	0
Parker	1930	0	0	0	0
Reed	1938	0	0	0	0
Frankfurter	1939	0	0	0	0
Douglas	1939	0	0	0	0
Jackson	1941	0	0	0	0
Stone	1941	0	0	0	0
Vinson	1946	0	0	0	0
Clark	1949	0	0	0	0
Minton	1949	0	0	2	1
Harlan	1954	0	0	0	0
Warren	1955	0	0	0	0
Brennan	1957	0	0	2	1
Whittaker	1957	0	0	0	0
Stewart	1959	0	0	1	5
Goldberg	1962	0	1	0	0
White	1962	0	0	0	1
Fortas (Assoc. J)	1965	0	0	0	1
Marshall	1967	0	2	0	2
Thornberry	1968	1	0	0	0

Table 1 *Continued*

Nominee	Year	Republicans Asking Questions with Specific Terms	Democrats Asking Questions with Specific Terms	Republicans Asking Questions with General Terms	Democrats Asking Questions with General Terms
Fortas (Chief J)	1968	1	2	0	0
Haynsworth	1969	2	2	1	1
Burger	1969	2	2	0	1
Carswell	1970	1	2	0	0
Blackmun	1970	2	4	0	1
Rehnquist (assoc. J)/Powell	1971	0	3	0	3
Stevens	1975	1	1	0	3
O'Connor	1981	4	5	0	0
Scalia	1986	3	0	0	0
Rehnquist (Chief)	1986	3	1	1	0
Bork	1987	5	5	0	0
Kennedy	1987	3	2	0	0
Souter	1990	3	4	0	0
Thomas	1991	4	3	0	0
Ginsburg	1993	4	4	0	0
Breyer	1994	3	1	0	0
Roberts	2005	5	4	0	0
Alito	2006	7	2	0	0
Sotomayor	2009	6	6	0	0
Kagan	2010	6	8	0	0
Gorsuch	2017	4	4	4	3

Would you please briefly describe your views on the topic of judicial activism?[204]

But activism by a growing number of judges threatens our judiciary. And frankly, that is what I am hearing as I talk to my constituents and hear from the American people. Activism is when a judge allows his personal views on a policy issue to infect his judgments. Activist rulings are not based on statutes or the Constitution, but reflect whatever a judge may think is decent or public policy[205]

If [Democrats] had filled [Scalia's] seat, we would have seen a Supreme Court where the will of the people would have been repeatedly cast aside by a new activist Supreme Court majority.[206]

Even while it has been Republicans who have pressed most consistently on this issue, Democratic senators have also engaged with the activism idea in the hearings. This has become especially pronounced since 2010, in the wake of the Supreme Court's decision in *Citizens United*.[207] But Democratic comments and questions are often framed in certain stylized ways. Whereas many Republican questions and comments launch broadsides against judicial activism, Democratic senators often pursue a more narrow and nuanced version of the claim. One common approach is to question the conceptual coherence of judicial activism. Consider these examples:

Judge, as you have just learned, one man's innovative ways is strict construction and another man's application of innovative ways is judiciary running rampant. I think you have found that out by talking to us all up here. Judicial activism is in the eye of the beholder. That seems to me—as the Senator from Utah just pointed out, he knows you will be innovative and if you are innovatively conservative you will be a strict constructionist.[208]

That is why I suggest to everyone watching today that they be a little wary of a phrase that they are hearing at this hearing: "judicial activism." That term really seems to have lost all usefulness, particularly since so many

---

[204] *Nomination of Judge Clarence Thomas before the Committee on the Judiciary*, 102nd Cong, 1st Sess 135 (1991) (Thurmond (R-SC)).

[205] *Confirmation Hearing on the Nomination of John G. Roberts Jr. to be Chief Justice of the United States before the Committee on the Judiciary*, 109th Cong, 1st Sess 30 (Sessions (R-Ala)).

[206] *Nomination of Neil Gorsuch before the Committee on the Judiciary*, 115th Cong, 1st Sess (2017) (Cruz (R-Tex)).

[207] 558 US 310 (2010).

[208] *Nomination of David H. Souter before the Committee on the Judiciary*, 101st Cong, 2nd Sess 314 (1990) (Biden (D-Del)).

rulings of the conservative majority on the Supreme Court can fairly be described as "activist" in their disregard for precedent and their willingness to ignore or override the intent of Congress.[209]

Another common form is to attack Republicans as hypocrites by pointing out examples of what they consider to be conservative activism. Examples include:

Do you think they are activist judges? [referring to Scalia and Thomas] . . . Can you tell me in 30 seconds, so I can just ask one more question, how is it different not to want to characterize Justices Thomas and Scalia but it was okay to characterize Justices Marshall and Brennan as activist?[210]

Many commentators see the *Bush v. Gore* decision as an example of judicial activism, an example of the judiciary improperly injecting itself into a political dispute. Indeed, it appears to many of us who have looked at your record that *Bush v. Gore* seems contrary to so many of the principles that you stand for, that the President has said you stand for when making your nomination in talking about judicial restraint, not legislating from the bench and, of course, respecting the rights of the States.[211]

I think we have heard repeatedly from the other side of the aisle their loyalty to the concept of traditionalism, their opposition to judicial activism. . . . I have two words for them: *Citizens United.* . . . If that is not judicial activism, what is? And it was espoused and sponsored by men who had stood before us under oath and swore they would never engage in judicial activism. That is the reality.[212]

Why is discussion of judicial activism, albeit in different ways, more bipartisan in the context of Senate confirmation hearings than in presidential platforms and speeches? One possible explanation is that the institutional settings are different. Senators on the Judiciary Committee are repeat players, and gain expertise in matters relevant to the Supreme Court. Many serve for long stretches on the committee. Indeed, many senators repeat the same comments or questions in dif-

---

[209] *Confirmation Hearing on the Nomination of the Hon. Sonia Sotomayor before the Committee on the Judiciary,* 111th Cong, 1st Sess 20 (2009) (Feingold (D-Cal)).

[210] *Confirmation Hearing on the Nomination of John G. Roberts Jr. to be Chief Justice of the United States before the Committee on the Judiciary,* 109th Cong, 1st Sess 378 (2005) (Schumer (D-NY)).

[211] *Confirmation Hearing on the Nomination of Samuel A. Alito Jr. before the Committee on the Judiciary,* 109th Cong, 2nd Sess 386 (2006) (Kohl (D-Wis)).

[212] *The Nomination of Elena Kagan before the Committee on the Judiciary,* 111th Cong, 2nd Sess 32 (2010) (Durbin (D-Ill)).

ferent hearings.[213] Relatedly, the senators on the committee are working closely with specialized, knowledgeable interest groups in preparing for the hearings. And, unlike platforms, which cut across multiple topics, Supreme Court confirmation hearings focus in depth on exploring law at the Supreme Court level.

At the macro level, moreover, there may be a larger dynamic at play. Recall that one point of contrast between the more recent and the earlier eras is that control of the Senate has flipped between the two parties more frequently in the contemporary era, at least since 1980 when the Republicans took the Senate for the first time in many years. In her recent book, *Insecure Majorities*, Frances Lee argues that the plausibility of more frequent party shifts has made pursuit of such a shift a more prominent part of congressional operations than it once was.[214] Among other things, these conditions make party leaders eager to capitalize on any issues of electoral benefit,[215] and there are good reasons to place judicial issues in that category. Issues relating to judicial appointments mobilize well organized interests and constituencies on both sides of the aisle, and the intense interest of these groups creates incentives for both Republican and Democratic legislators to use confirmation hearings to engage closely and fiercely with the issue of judicial activism.[216]

b) Changing voting patterns in the Senate. A second difference between the earlier and contemporary periods relates to the dynamics of Senate voting. Between 1896 and 1937, presidents made 23 nom-

---

[213] See, e.g., *Nomination of Ruth Bader Ginsburg before the Committee on the Judiciary*, 103rd Cong, 2nd Sess 5 (1993) (Hatch (R-Utah)); *Nomination of Stephen G. Breyer before the Committee on the Judiciary*, 103rd Cong, 2nd Sess 8 (1994) (Hatch (R-Utah)) (decrying activism and asserting in both hearings that "a Supreme Court Justice should interpret the law and not legislate his or her own policy preferences from the bench" or "impose their own personal views on the American people in the guise of construing the Constitution and Federal statutes"); *Nomination of Judge Clarence Thomas before the Committee on the Judiciary*, 102nd Cong, 1st Sess 212 (1991) (Grassley (R-Iowa)) (*Confirmation Hearing on the Nomination of John G. Roberts Jr. to be Chief Justice of the United States before the Committee on the Judiciary*, 109th Cong, 1st Sess 179 (Grassley (R-Iowa)) (raising the subject of activism and asking nominees in both hearings if they think the "filling of vacuums" by Justices is appropriate).

[214] Lee, *Insecure Majorities* 198 (cited in note 78).

[215] Id.

[216] For an argument that, in the domain of judicial nominations, Republicans are more aggressive in their tactics and dismissive of institutional norms, see David Fontana, *Cooperative Judicial Nominations During the Obama Administration*, 2017 Wis L Rev 285, 288. A broader argument about asymmetric tactics in constitutional politics appears in Joseph Fishkin and David E. Pozen, *Asymmetric Constitutional Hardball*, 118 Colum L Rev (forthcoming 2018) (draft on file with author).

inations to the Supreme Court.[217] Only one—the 1930 nomination of John Parker—was rejected. More strikingly by contemporary standards, two-thirds of them (15 of 22) were approved by voice vote, some within hours of being nominated. Of the seven who were the subject of a roll call vote, more than half won overwhelmingly.[218] The other three won by between 24–26 votes.[219] The closest vote overall was the failed Parker nomination, which went down 39–41.

Overall, then, the vast majority of nominations were not closely contested. A few were, most notably Brandeis (see below), but the picture is very different than today. Contemporary hearings have come to be defined by partisan frames and objectives. There are no voice votes, let alone for two-thirds of the nominees. And the days of 98–0 (Scalia, 1986), 97–0 (Kennedy, 1987), and 96–3 (Ginsburg, 1993) votes would seem to be over, at least for now. The more notable change is the rise of partisanship in voting. Building on work demonstrating the increasing role of ideology in Supreme Court confirmation votes,[220] Charles Shipan has demonstrated that "partisanship has played an increasingly important role over time, with members of the president's party much more likely now than in the past to support his nominee."[221] This should not be surprising because it is simply another facet of the rising polarization in Congress. But it further reinforces that, in contrast to the earlier period, political challenges to

---

[217] The nominees were McKenna, Holmes, Day, Moody, Lurton, Hughes (as Associate Justice), White, Van Devanter, Lamar, Pitney, McReynolds, Brandeis, Clarke, Taft, Sutherland, Butler, Sanford, Stone, Hughes (as Chief Justice), Parker, Roberts, Cardozo, and Black. Denis S. Rukus, Maureen Bearden, and Sam Garrett, *Supreme Court Nominations 1789–2005: Actions (Including Speed) by the Judiciary Committee and the President* 154–57 (Nova, 2007).

[218] Id. The votes were 44–6 (McReynolds (1914)), 61–8 (Butler (1922)), 71–6 (Stone (1925)), and 63–16 (Black (1937)).

[219] Id. The votes were 50–26 (Pitney (1912)), 47–22 (Brandeis (1916)), and 52–26 (Hughes as Chief Justice (1930)).

[220] See Charles Cameron et al, *Senate Voting on Supreme Court Nominees: A Neoinstitutional Model*, 84 Am Pol Sci Rev 525 (1990); Lee Epstein et al, *The Changing Dynamics of Senate Voting on Supreme Court Nominees*, 68 J Pol 296 (2006).

[221] Charles R. Shipan, *Partisanship, Ideology, and Senate Voting on Supreme Court Nominees*, 5 J Empir Legal Studies 55, 72 (2008); see also Scott Basinger and Maxwell Mak, *The Changing Politics of Supreme Court Confirmations*, 40 Am Pol Research 737, 757 (2012) (focusing on internal party cohesion and offering empirical evidence to show that "as partisanship in the Senate has risen, Supreme Court confirmation voting has become more divided along party lines"). For a broader and longer-term historical perspective on partisanship in the confirmation process at the time of Reconstruction, and its decline in ensuing decades, see Richard Friedman, *The Transformation in Senate Response to Supreme Court Nominations: From Reconstruction to the Taft Administration and Beyond*, 5 Cardozo L Rev 1 (1983).

perceived judicial activism today are powerfully shaped by partisan factors.

c) The changing role of interest groups. The third area of contrast is the role of interest groups in the process. For the most part, interest groups were not a major player in judicial confirmations in the earlier period. The closed process gave them limited opportunity to participate, and the attenuated electoral connection between senators and constituents before the Seventeenth Amendment was enacted would have made it more difficult for them to organize and mobilize constituents. Both the hotly contested Brandeis nomination in 1916 and the failed Parker nomination in 1930 were, however, exceptions in the earlier era.

Interest groups pressed their positions as to both Brandeis and Parker, but only the process as it unfolded with Parker bears much resemblance to the process as it exists today. Hoover nominated Parker, a sitting judge on the Fourth Circuit, in 1930. By that time, the Senate had opened to the public its committee proceedings and floor deliberations on confirmations. Parker was done in by two sources of opposition: organized labor, which objected to his opinion in the *Red Jacket* case,[222] in which an employer sought and obtained an injunction enforcing yellow dog contracts; and the NAACP, which objected to racist statements Parker had made discouraging black voting while he was running for governor of North Carolina in 1920. Both William Green, president of the AFL, and Walter White, executive secretary of the NAACP, testified against Parker. Parker defended his *Red Jacket* opinion as compelled by the 1913 Supreme Court ruling in *Hitchman Coal & Coke v Mitchell*,[223] but Green argued—and a majority of the Judiciary Committee seemed ultimately to accept—that his opinion lavished too much approval on labor injunctions and yellow dog contracts. Likewise, Parker tried to explain the 1920 campaign speech in which he had said that "the negro has not yet reached that stage in his development where he can share the burdens and responsibilities of government," and that "the participation of the negro in politics is a source of evil and danger to both races."[224] His

---

[222] *International Union, United Mine Workers of America v Red Jacket Consolidated Coal and Coke Co.*, 18 F2d 839 (4th Cir 1927).

[223] 245 US 229 (1917).

[224] Sondra Kay Wilson, ed, *In Search of Democracy: The NAACP Writings of James Weldon Johnson, Walter White and Roy Wilkins (1920–1977)* 239 (Oxford, 1998).

unsuccessful defense was that he was trying to keep the volatile issue of race out of the campaign. He was ultimately defeated narrowly, with Progressive Republican William Borah one of the leaders against confirmation.

In addition to there being an NAACP-sponsored campaign of intense telephone calls and letter writing, there were other aspects of the process that made it more like contemporary hearings, albeit a very modest form of what happens today. There was some testimony in the record that framed Parker's problems in terms of the concept of judicial activism. Clearest on this was Norman Thomas, the leader of the Socialist Party, whose letter to the committee accused Parker of subscribing to the "reactionary theory of property rights" that the Supreme Court had "virtually legislated," and condemned Parker as embodying "the dead hand of precedent and the live hand of a judicial oligarch."[225] In a similar vein, Green, testifying for the AFL, said that Parker had fatally failed to embrace "legal principles in terms of human rights and needs," was thus "not worthy to sit with a Holmes or a Brandeis," and in following the Supreme Court's decision on injunctions and yellow dog contacts in *Hitchman* had embraced what was "the *Dred Scott* decision to labor."[226] On the opposing side, those favoring the appointment repeated that Parker was "fair and impartial."[227] Ultimately, his supporters and the judge himself blamed "radical Senators" and "quasi-socialistic" groups like the NAACP and organized labor for the failed nomination.[228]

The Brandeis nomination fourteen years earlier also had interest group involvement. Labor, LaFollette, and most Progressives supported Brandeis, who had been nominated by Woodrow Wilson. He was bitterly opposed by business and financial interests, along with the conservative wing of the Republican Party. They claimed that he lacked the necessary temperament[229] and, according to senior Re-

---

[225] *Confirmation of Hon. John J. Parker before the Committee on the Judiciary*, 71st Cong, 2nd Sess 59 (1930). Notably, Thomas's focus on judicial views and method was not the subject of senatorial questioning.

[226] Id at 29, 59.

[227] See, for example, id at 76.

[228] Richard L. Watson Jr., *The Defeat of Judge Parker: A Study in Pressure Groups and Politics*, 50 Miss Hist Rev 213, 233 (Sept 1963).

[229] John A. Maltese, *The Selling of Supreme Court Nominees* 50–51 (JHU, 1998).

publican Elihu Root, was "intellectually acute and morally blind."[230]
In some ways, his nomination functioned as a referendum of sorts on
progressivism, including its attacks on courts. He had given a speech
to the Chicago Bar Association shortly before he was nominated. In
it, he argued that the "struggle for the living law has not been fully
won," and lamented that *Lochner* had not been overruled.[231] One of
his biographers called it "the progressive era's clearest and most cited
critique of the failure to take into account the facts of the real world."[232]
In other ways, though, the opposition was more of a character attack,
one that included plenty of anti-Semitism.[233] The contentious hearings
were held in open session, and they dragged on, but did not feature
testimony by Brandeis and thus could not produce quite the same kind
of public spectacle as we would expect today under the circumstances.

The role of interest groups in contemporary confirmation hearings
has changed dramatically since the earlier period. As the battle against
judicial activism intensified as a Republican political issue, particularly
in the 1980s, so rose a set of interest groups ready to pounce on
nominations, both in support and in opposition. The profile of these
groups grew higher with the televising of Supreme Court confirmations, which began in 1981.[234] Recall that we earlier observed a rise in
the number of senators incorporating the activism issue into their
hearing questions and comments.[235] The introduction of the subject
was, presumably, related to the greater interest in judicial confirmations taken by interest groups.

Over time, both left- and right-leaning groups came to form virtual
standing armies that monitor, organize, and communicate to senators
and the public about nominees. On the left, Alliance for Justice, formed
in 1985, has acted as an umbrella group researching, monitoring, and

---

[230] A. L. Todd, *Justice on Trial: The Case of Louis Brandeis* 128 (McGraw-Hill, 1964).

[231] Louis D. Brandeis, *The Living Law*, 10 U Ill L Rev 461, 467 (1916).

[232] Melvin I. Urofsky, *Louis D. Brandeis: A Life* 431 (Pantheon, 2009).

[233] Id at 438–42.

[234] Maltese, *The Selling of Supreme Court Nominees* at 89 (cited in note 229). The Bork
nomination was a particular turning point, both for its visibility and the intricacy and so-
phistication of the media campaign and strategic efforts waged against Bork. It involved
coordination among many well-known groups. See Gregory A. Caldeira and John Wright,
*Lobbying for Justice: Organized Interests, Supreme Court Nominations, and the United States
Senate*, 42 Am J Pol Sci 499 (1998). After the Bork defeat, however, conservatives became
better organized and centralized.

[235] See Part II.C.1.

messaging about nominees.[236] It has typically worked with a host of left-leaning groups. On the right, umbrella groups like the Judicial Selection Monitoring Project of the Free Congress Foundation (formed in 1987 after the Bork defeat) and the Judicial Crisis Network have played similar roles, working along with right-leaning interest groups and the Federalist Society.[237]

Significantly, over time, these party-loyal interest groups came to be engaged in lower court confirmations as well as Supreme Court nominations.[238] Where such appointments were traditionally matters of patronage, especially appointments to the federal district court, that began to change decisively in the Carter presidency and became institutionalized in the Reagan Administration.[239] The blanket practice of "Senate courtesy," by which home-state senators made choices purely as a matter of patronage, yielded to a more ideologically sensitive practice.[240] In the earlier period, patronage generally reigned and interest groups almost never got involved.

The regular role of interest groups on both sides raises the profile of the judicial activism issue as these groups work to communicate with, attract, and mobilize supporters.[241] Social media is a force-multiplier and makes knowledge about confirmation hearings and debates more easily accessible. The effect of all of this is to widen the sphere of political contestation over nominees and, more generally, judicial activism in ways that were unimaginable in the earlier period.

---

[236] Amy Steigerwalt, *Battle Over the Bench: Senators, Interest Groups, and Lower Court Confirmations* 11 (U Va, 2010).

[237] Id at 12–13. On the role of Leonard Leo of the Federalist Society in the confirmation hearings for Neil Gorsuch, see Eric Lipton and Jeremy W. Peters, *In Gorsuch, Conservative Activist Sees Test Case for Reshaping the Judiciary*, NY Times (Mar 18, 2017) (available at https://www.nytimes.com/2017/03/18/us/politics/neil-gorsuch-supreme-court-conservatives .html).

[238] Steigerwalt, *Battle Over the Bench* at 13–14 (cited in note 236); Nancy Scherer, *Scoring Points: Politicians, Activists, and the Lower Federal Court Appointment Process* 108 (Stanford, 2005).

[239] Roger E. Hartley and Lisa M. Holmes, *Increasing Senate Scrutiny of Lower Federal Court Nominations*, 80 Judicature 274, 277 (1996).

[240] The ideological dimension of lower-court selections is part of what led to the creation of judicial monitoring groups on the left and right. See Steigerwalt, *Battle Over the Bench* at 11 (cited in note 236).

[241] Another arena in which interest groups participate is through the filing of amicus briefs that provide facts to the Justices in ways that can be controversial. See Allison O. Larsen and Neal Devins, *The Amicus Machine*, 102 Va L Rev 1902, 1921, 1944 (2016). This practice has taken off in recent years in a way that had no analogue in the earlier period.

2. *Court-curbing legislation.* Another congressional vehicle for political responses to perceived judicial activism is the proposal of court-curbing legislation. In both the early and the contemporary period, legislators introduced bills designed to modify judicial behavior in various ways. In the early period, bills introduced during heavy periods of court-curbing efforts most frequently addressed matters of procedure, remedy, and jurisdiction.[242] This would be consistent with the controversy surrounding labor injunctions and procedures for adjudicating contempt of such injunctions.[243] In the more recent period, when Congress has been active in proposing curbs on courts, there has been the greatest interest in the composition of the Court, along with jurisdiction, judicial review, and targeting of specific decisions by the court. Social issues have figured prominently.[244]

In *The Limits of Judicial Independence*, Tom Clark offers the most sustained and detailed study of court-curbing.[245] He concludes that bills of this sort, the overwhelming majority of which never see the light of day, are more a means of political communication and "position-taking" than a genuine effort to enact legislation.[246] Most often they are, in other words, symbolic politics, not practical attempts at governance.

Clark compiled a database of bills introduced between 1878 and 2008. I have taken the decades of relevance for present purposes and then added to Clark's data the party identification of the sponsor for each bill in the database. The totals by party are shown in table 2.

The partisan patterns over time are consistent with what we have seen in other areas. The political valence of opposition to courts switches from the liberal side in the early period to the conservative side in the contemporary period. Many bills introduced in the 1950s protested a set of Supreme Court rulings on the rights of communists.[247] These bills tended to come from members of both parties.[248] In the 1960s,

---

[242] Tom S. Clark, *The Limits of Judicial Independence* 45, 52 (Cambridge, 2010).

[243] During the earlier period, there were also some proposals from Progressives to either elect federal judges or limit their terms to a specified number of years. Ross, *Muted Fury* at 95–102 (cited in note 33).

[244] Id at 57.

[245] See Clark, *The Limits of Judicial Independence* (cited in note 242).

[246] Id at 256.

[247] The "Red Monday" cases are cited in note 72; see Clark, *The Limits of Judicial Independence* at 54–55 (cited in note 242).

[248] Clark, *The Limits of Judicial Independence* at 55 (cited in note 242).

Table 2

Jurisdiction-Stripping Bills by Party
of Sponsor, 1896–2008

Decade	Democrats	Republicans	Other
1896–1900	11	5	2 (Populist)
1901–1910	57	37	0
1911–1920	40	14	0
1921–1930	10	12	1 (Farm-Labor)
1931–1940	45	10	5 (Farm-Labor)
1941–1950	4	4	0
1951–1960	39	12	0
1961–1970	91	62	0
1971–1980	74	80	3 (Independents)
1981–1990	25	45	0
1991–2000	15	36	0
2001–2008	9	76	0

the bills took on a more conservative character and reflected hostility to the Warren Court on a number of issues.[249] The partisan makeup of the bills' sponsors in the 1960s, however, reflects that the realignment of southern Democrats had not yet taken root. That partisan turn shows up in this context in the 1970s and 1980s. In the 1980s, bills introduced by Republicans begin to outnumber Democrats and, in recent years, the imbalance has been fairly pronounced.

To take a closer look at contemporary partisan dynamics, I examined the party support for the bills that were introduced between 1980 and 2008 and that were popular enough to draw 10 or more cosponsors. My research finds that there were 49 such bills.[250] They

---

[249] Id at 55–57.

[250] Not all bills have cosponsor information available. My tally is based on bills with records of cosponsorship.

cover an array of issues, mostly social issues, including such familiar ones as abortion, prayer, flag burning, traditional marriage, and the pledge of allegiance, among others. Fully 40 of those 49 bills had more Republican than Democratic cosponsors, and 18 of them had *only* Republican cosponsors. By contrast, bills with only Democratic (or Democratic-leaning independent) cosponsors numbered only three. Two affirmed the primacy of *Roe*, and one expressed the sense of the house that Supreme Court Justices should try to hire more qualified minority law clerks.[251] Not unexpectedly, the partisan patterns we have seen elsewhere hold in connection with bill sponsorship.

III. Implications

What might all of this mean? Let us return to where we began—with an argument that equated the nature and consequences of asserted judicial activism in *Obergefell* with the claimed activism of *Lochner*. As we have seen, there are some broad similarities in how opponents framed their claims of judicial activism in the two eras. And, there are more specific similarities, such as that the party most aggrieved by the courts in each era introduces more court-curbing proposals. Yet, overall, the differences in the prevailing political dynamics far exceed the similarities. Systematic efforts to label and oppose judicial activism in the era of *Obergefell* are marked by key features that were absent in the earlier era, including party polarization and cohesion, the regular use of platforms by one party to condemn the courts as activist, and a confirmation process that serves as a regular venue for airing charges of activism, with a standing army of interest groups on both sides of the aisle poised to do battle regularly over judicial appointees. We have seen the rise of these phenomena from the time of the early Warren Court to the present, and they indicate that Supreme Court decisions in the contemporary era are released into a political ecosystem that is strikingly different from the one that existed in the earlier period.

Moreover, juxtaposing the two eras reveals another difference that is sometimes considered part of contemporary polarization: declining civility on the part of the major political parties, a phenomenon that is

---

[251] HR 5151, 109th Cong, 2nd Sess (Apr 6, 2006) ("Freedom of Choice Act"); S 2593, 109th Cong, 2nd Sess (Apr 6, 2006) ("Freedom of Choice Act"); HR 111, 106th Cong, 1st Sess (Mar 3, 1999) (clerks).

readily apparent in the context of criticizing courts.[252] Contrast the mostly restrained critiques gingerly—and only occasionally—offered up by the Democrats in the earlier period with the more strident language that has been a regular part of Republican platforms of the last few decades. The sense of political caution that held back the major parties from harshly attacking courts in the earlier era has, to put it mildly, receded. Indeed, another thing on display in the *Obergefell* opinions is the extent to which the face of civility on *the Court itself* has been fading, at least in some quarters. In his *Obergefell* dissent, for example, Justice Scalia included a footnote deriding Justice Kennedy's rhetoric that was later characterized by Michael Dorf as "perhaps the most intemperate line in the U.S. Reports."[253] There was, to be sure, incivility of an extreme variety on the Court in the earlier period. Consider, for example, Justice MacReynolds's outrageous racism and anti-Semitism.[254] What is different (not worse, but different) about Scalia's outburst is that it involved the tone he came to take with other Justices in his opinions. The coarseness of the Justices' recent written discourse has sometimes echoed the coarseness in the broader political arena.

One way to summarize all of this change since the earlier period is to say that the judiciary has increasingly come to be seen as a political actor. That is not, of course, entirely new; *Dred Scott* stands as a striking example of critics casting the Court as partisan.[255] But modern in-

---

[252] See Persily, *Introduction*, in Persily, ed, *Solutions to Political Polarization in America* at 9 (cited in note 80). It bears emphasis that I am focused on how the *major political parties* attacked the courts. The earlier era was not one of civility in any broad or categorical sense. In the domain of labor, there were both violent clashes and harshly hostile rhetoric about courts. See Forbath, 102 Harv L Rev at 1141 (cited in note 55); Richard White, *The Republic for Which It Stands* 782 (Oxford, 2017). In addition, as explored earlier, some of the Progressives' rhetoric about the courts was fairly scathing. See Part II.B.1.b.

[253] Michael Dorf, *Symposium: In Defense of Justice Kennedy's Soaring Language*, SCOTUSblog (June 27, 2015, 5:08 p.m.) (available at http://www.scotusblog.com/2015/06/symposium-in-defense-of-justice-kennedys-soaring-language/) (referring to Scalia's assertion that "[i]f, even as the price to be paid for a fifth vote, I ever joined an opinion for the Court that began [in this way], I would hide my head in a bag."). See also *Obergefell*, 135 S Ct at 2612 (Roberts, CJ, dissenting) (suggesting that Justice Kennedy had been "pretentious" and asking "[j]ust who do we think we are?").

[254] David M. O'Brien, *This Time, It's Personal: Justice Scalia's Increasing Incivility*, LA Times (July, 14, 1996) (available at http://articles.latimes.com/1996-07-14/opinion/op-24100_1 _justice-antonin-scalia).

[255] John B. Gates, *The Supreme Court and Partisan Realignment* (Westview, 1992) 36 ("The fact that the [*Dred Scott*] Court was composed of eight Democrats and one Whig only reinforced the partisan debate over the decision").

formation technology has combined with extreme polarization to significantly intensify his phenomenon. The court is most likely to be perceived in frankly partisan terms in high-profile and controversial cases, where public opinion is already polarized by party, such as *Obergefell, NFIB v Sebelius*,[256] *Citizens United*,[257] and *Shelby County*.[258] In such cases, the stakes are high and the Court's decisions are covered by the media like other high-salience political events. This is not to say that the public views the Supreme Court as just another political body, for the evidence suggests that the public sees the Court as both a legal and a political body—as "half-politics-half-law."[259] But it is to say that broad swaths of the public do not see the Court in the simplistic institutional terms that Chief Justice Roberts's propositions about law and legitimacy would suggest.

Indeed, the very assumption that citizens expect judges to decide cases in mechanical or "value-free" ways is not consistent with significant research about how lay citizens view the work of courts. Leading work by James Gibson and Gregory Caldeira argues that citizens are more nuanced than one might think in their perceptions about how judges and courts operate. Based on surveys they fielded, Gibson and Caldeira suggest that nonlawyer citizens believe that judges are not mechanical and do exercise discretion, yet those citizens still retain significant respect for courts:

> The American people know that the justices of the Supreme Court exercise discretion in making their decisions—what better evidence of this is there than the multiple and divided judgments by the group of nine? They are also aware that the justices' discretion is guided to at least some degree by ideological and even partisan considerations. None of these understandings seem to contribute to undermining the legitimacy of the Supreme Court. Instead, legitimacy seems to flow from the view that discretion is being exercised in a principled, rather than strategic, way.[260]

---

[256] 567 US 519 (2012).

[257] *Citizens United v FEC*, 558 US 310 (2010).

[258] *Shelby County, Ala v Holder*, 570 US 529 (2013).

[259] Keith Bybee, *All Judges Are Political—Except When They Are Not: Acceptable Hypocrisies and the Rule of Law* 4 (Stanford, 2010); see Nicholson and Hansford, 58 Am J Pol Sci at 621–22 (cited in note 25) (reviewing literature); see generally James Gibson and Gregory Caldeira, *Has Legal Realism Damaged the Legitimacy of the Supreme Court?*, 45 L & Soc'y Rev 195, 213 (2011).

[260] Gibson and Caldeira, 45 L & Soc'y Rev at 213 (cited in note 259). In the article, they contrast the perceived "sincerity" of courts with what subjects typically see as self-interested, strategic behavior in Congress.

Relatedly, Gibson and various coauthors have long emphasized the difference between specific and diffuse support, suggesting that citizens may object to *specific* decisions in the short term, yet tend to have a reservoir of diffuse institutional support for the Court that is rooted in more general faith in democratic values and institutions.[261] Particularly polarizing decisions, such as *Bush v Gore*, may change the partisan dynamics of even diffuse support to some degree, but there is little evidence that substantive opposition to such decisions translates into long-term threats to the Court's legitimacy.[262]

The picture that Gibson and colleagues draw is one of a public that has a more nuanced perception than the Chief Justice suggests—that is, of citizens perceiving that a mix of rules and discretion guides the Court. One provocative recent analysis went further, suggesting on the basis of experimental research that "a large segment of the public perceives of the court in political terms, and *prefers* that justices be chosen on political ideological bases."[263] There is a debate about whether that view of public perceptions is well-grounded, and it seems premature to go quite that far based on the current state of the research.[264] But it is not controversial to say that, at a minimum, elite cues shape public beliefs about the Court's work, and that these cues are increasingly partisan. Stephen Nicholson and Thomas Hanford, for example, report on an experiment reflecting that "when there is a political party attached to a Court decision, it appears to operate as it might for other political actors, at least in terms of public acceptance of policy outcomes," making it more likely that the public will view

---

[261] See James L. Gibson, Gregory A. Caldeira, and Lester K. Spence, *The Supreme Court and the U.S. Presidential Election of 2000: Wounds, Self-Inflicted or Otherwise?*, 33 Brit J Pol Sci 535, 545 (2003); James L. Gibson and Michael J. Nelson, *The Legitimacy of the U.S. Supreme Court: Conventional Wisdoms and Recent Challenges Thereto*, 10 Annu Rev L Soc Sci 201, 204–05 (2014); Andrea Louise Campbell and Nathaniel Persily, *The Health Care Case in the Public Mind: Opinion on the Supreme Court and Health Reform in a Polarized Era*, in Nathaniel Persily, Gillian E. Metzger, and Trevor W. Morrison, eds, *The Health Care Case: The Supreme Court's Decision and Its Implications* 245, 247–48 (Oxford, 2013).

[262] See Gibson, Caldeira, and Spence, 33 Brit J Pol Sci at 555 (cited in note 261); Manoj Mate and Matthew Wright, *The 2000 Presidential Election Controversy*, in Persily, Citrin, and Egan, eds, *Public Opinion and Constitutional Controversy* at 348–49 (cited in note 25).

[263] Brandon L. Bartels and Christopher D. Johnson, *Political Justice? Perceptions of Politicization and Public Preferences Toward the Supreme Court Appointment Process*, 76 Pub Op Q 105 (2012) (analyzing data from Annenberg Supreme Court Survey). Bartels and Johnson suggest that citizens do not necessarily think it is ideal, but they acknowledge and accept it.

[264] See Gibson and Nelson, 10 Annu Rev L Soc Sci (cited in note 261), responding to Bartels and Johnson, id.

"the Court as a partisan policy maker."[265] This phenomenon was on clear display in the public's reaction to the Roberts's Court decision *upholding* the Affordable Care Act.[266] Notably, even though that case might fit the definition of legitimacy-enhancing judicial restraint suggested in the Chief Justice's *Obergefell* dissent, it engendered sharp, partisan reactions and—at least in the short term—both reduced and further polarized the public's approval of the Court.[267]

The importance of partisan cues about the Court's work intersects with another development of note: evidence of partisan polarization on the Court itself. Neal Devins and Lawrence Baum have found identifiable Democratic and Republican voting blocs among the Justices.[268] They attribute the emergence of this partisan divide to the larger growing polarization among political elites, the fact that presidents have increasingly made ideology central to appointment choices, party-line voting in the Senate, and the fact that legal elites in the two parties have sorted themselves on the basis of ideology.[269] This phenomenon is, of course, at odds with the image of the apolitical Court evoked by the Chief Justice in *Obergefell*. It is also inconsistent with what Roberts has said recently about the increasingly politicized confirmation process. In 2017, for example, he noted that "[w]e don't work as Democrats or Republicans," and lamented that "when you have a sharply political, divisive hearing process, it increases the danger that whoever comes out of it will be viewed in those terms."[270] He is surely right that the confirmation process has become more politicized. But it is misguided to focus on that process in isolation. As we have seen, the confirmation process is part of a much larger and more elaborate political context that surrounds and

---

[265] See Nicholson and Hanford, 58 Am J Pol Sci at 634 (cited in note 25); see generally Persily, Citrin, and Egan, eds, *Public Opinion and Constitutional Controversy* (cited in note 25).

[266] See Campbell and Persily, *The Health Care Case in the Public Mind*, in Persily, Metzger, and Morrison, eds, *The Health Care Case* at 261–65 (cited in note 261).

[267] Id at 265–67.

[268] Neal Devins and Lawrence Baum, *Split Definitive: How Party Polarization Turned the Supreme Court into a Partisan Court* 3 (William & Mary Law School Research Paper No 09-276, 2014) (available at http://papers.ssrn.com/sol3/papers.cfm?abstract_id=2432111); see also Adam Liptak, *The Polarized Court*, NY Times (May 11, 2014) (available at https://www.nytimes.com/2014/05/11/upshot/the-polarized-court.html?_r=0).

[269] Devins and Baum, *Split Definitive* (cited in note 268).

[270] Adam Liptak, *An "Ideological Food Fight" (His Words in 2002) Awaits Neil Gorsuch*, NY Times (Mar 18, 2017) (available at https://www.nytimes.com/2017/03/18/us/politics/neil-gorsuch-supreme-court-trump.html?_r=0).

shapes the Court, and that connects partisanship and law in complex ways.

The dynamics suggested by this body of research on partisanship and judicial decision making were very much on display in the public reactions to *Obergefell*. Indeed, those reactions provide good reasons to doubt the Chief Justice's argument equating public legitimacy with restraint, and suggest that the argument misconceives the contemporary environment in which the Court operates. Given the polarized politics that have surrounded the Court for the last several decades, it is likely that Democrat/Republican or Liberal/Conservative, more than any institutional ideal or legal-methodological commitment, provides the lens through which most citizens, with cues from partisan political and partisan-aligned elites, assess the judiciary and the subset of decisions that capture significant public attention.[271]

Obergefell was among the most salient decisions in recent memory, capturing massive international attention and dominating social media activity the day it was decided. As I have explored elsewhere, in the first hour after *Obergefell* was decided, it spawned 3.8 million posts on Facebook.[272] There were 6.2 million tweets about it, at a pace of 20,000 tweets per minute, in the first four hours after the decision was released. Thousands of people posted excerpts of language from the opinions, which were readily available at scores of news and other websites. Particularly popular on Twitter were Justice Kennedy's closing lines that same-sex couples "ask for equal dignity in the eyes of the law. The Constitution grants them that right."[273] That rights language was countered by many people tweeting language about activism from the dissents, such as Justice Scalia's characterizing the ruling as a "judicial Putsch," the Chief Justice's rhetorical question "Just who do we think we are?," or Roberts's invitation to supporters of marriage equality to relish their victory but not to "celebrate the Constitution. It has nothing to do with it."[274]

Consistent with the high profile of the case, most of the candidates in the 2016 presidential primaries posted rapid reactions to it, with a

---

[271] Nicholson and Hansford, 58 Am J Pol Sci at 634 (cited in note 25); Schacter, 77 Ohio St L J at 1029–31 (cited in note 24) (reviewing partisan reactions to *Obergefell*).

[272] I review this in detail in Schacter, 77 Ohio St L J at 1029–33 (cited in note 24).

[273] Id at 1032.

[274] Id.

clear—and utterly unsurprising—political divide.[275] Hillary Clinton, for example, celebrated the historic victory "from Stonewall to the Supreme Court," while candidate Jeb Bush made a plea for religious liberty protection for opponents of same-sex marriage.[276] Many of the Republican candidates made some version of an activism-based attack, arguing, for example, that "five unelected justices [had] decided to redefine the foundational unit that binds together our society,"[277] and that citizens "must resist and reject judicial tyranny, not retreat."[278] By contrast, President Obama tweeted that "Today is a big step in our march toward equality,"[279] and adopted a rights-based framing in his Rose Garden speech, praising the decision for "reaffirm[ing] that all Americans are entitled to the equal protection of the law. That all people should be treated equally, regardless of who they are or who they love."[280] In the public eye, in other words, the decision unfolded like other high-salience government decisions, with partisan frames and ideologically distinct social media feeds shaping what people saw and learned about the case.

The public criticisms of *Obergefell* from conservative opponents pressed the activism theme as a way of attacking the legitimacy of the ruling and of the "five lawyer" Court itself. But it is not hard to imagine a different kind of legitimacy attack on the Court had the case come out the other way. Let us engage in a thought experiment. Imagine a counterfactual *Obergefell* in which Justice Kennedy cast the deciding vote to affirm the Sixth Circuit. The marriage bans in Kentucky, Tennessee, Michigan, and Ohio were upheld, and other states were thus free to maintain or reinstate bans on same-sex marriage.

---

[275] Id.

[276] Id at 1030.

[277] Jonathan Topaz and Nick Gass, *Republican Presidential Candidates Condemn Gay Marriage Ruling*, Politico (June 26, 2015) (quoting Rick Santorum) (available at http://www.politico.com/story/2015/06/2016-candidates-react-supreme-court-gay-marriage-ruling-119466).

[278] Topaz and Gass, *Republican Presidential Candidates* (cited in note 277) (quoting Mike Huckabee).

[279] President Barack Obama (@POTUS), *Twitter* (June 26, 2015, 7:10 a.m.) (available at https://twitter.com/POTUS/status/614435467120001024).

[280] *Remarks by the President on the Supreme Court Decision on Marriage Equality*, White House Briefing Room (June 26, 2015) (available at https://obamawhitehouse.archives.gov/the-press-office/2015/06/26/remarks-president-supreme-court-decision-marriage-equality).

What would the public reaction have been to this reverse-*Obergefell*? Most likely, with different winners and losers: Praise from social conservatives, condemnation from the left, and a decision at odds with the trajectory of public opinion. What, more specifically, would have been the critique coming from disappointed advocates and elected officials who supported marriage equality?

We can make an informed prediction about the likely critiques that would have greeted this reverse-*Obergefell* based on the reactions to the Sixth Circuit's ruling in *Obergefell* itself. By a 2–1 vote, that court upheld the marriage bans in a case then captioned *DeBoer v Snyder*.[281] Reactions to *DeBoer* are not a perfect parallel because the volume and visibility of reaction was considerably lower than what would have followed a reverse-*Obergefell* ruling.[282] But there are predictable themes and, in truth, neither the media coverage, nor the reaction from marriage-equality supporters to *DeBoer*, should be seen as terribly surprising. Just as the criticisms of the Supreme Court's actual holding in *Obergefell* tracked the dissenters' emphasis on activism, so the criticisms of the *DeBoer* decision tracked the *Obergefell* majority's emphasis on the importance of constitutional equality and judicial independence from politics.

With these caveats, consider the following descriptions of, and commentaries on, the Sixth Circuit's decision. First, mainstream reporters covering the decision identified the writing judges by their party of appointment. The *USA Today* story called Judge Sutton "one of the Republican Party's most esteemed legal thinkers and writers," noted that "fellow GOP nominee Deborah Cook concur[red]," and characterized Judge Martha Craig Daughtrey as "a Democratic appointee" who "delivered a blistering 22-page dissent."[283] The *New York Times* similarly noted that Sutton was "an appointee of George W. Bush," and that the "stinging dissent" was written by Daughtrey,

---

[281] 772 F3d 388 (6th Cir 2014).

[282] And, some of the reaction to the 6th Circuit opinion was shaped by the fact that it was the first federal appellate decision that was decided adversely to same-sex couples after a wave of victories. As such it set up the circuit split that many supporters of marriage equality had hoped for to trigger a certiorari grant.

[283] Richard Wolf, *Gay Marriage Bans in Four States Upheld, Supreme Court Review Likely*, USA Today (Nov 6, 2014) (available at https://www.usatoday.com/story/news/nation/2014/11/06/gay-marriage-appeals-court-ohio-michigan-kentucky-tennessee/15712319/).

"an appointee of Bill Clinton."[284] Just as coverage of *Obergefell* frequently included references to the Supreme Court's "liberal" and "conservative" wings or to the party affiliation of the Justices,[285] so the *DeBoer* decision was framed by national newspapers in terms of the judges' partisan ties.

There were plenty of reactions from those unhappy with Judge Sutton's opinion upholding the marriage bans. Some of those reacting are likely to be the kinds of elites that cue constituencies within the mass public about important decisions. We can begin with a major interest group. The Human Rights Campaign, a leading national LGBT rights group, blasted the opinion with a statement headlined "Shameful Sixth Circuit Decision Upholds Discriminatory Marriage Bans in MI, KY, TN, & OH."[286] The statement included this:

> The legacies of Judges Deborah Cook and Jeffrey Sutton will forever be cemented on the wrong side of history. . . . Gay and lesbian couples in Kentucky, Michigan, Ohio and Tennessee are just as deserving of marriage equality as the rest of America. Now, more than ever before, the Supreme Court of the United States must take up the issue and decide once and for all whether the Constitution allows for such blatant discrimination.[287]

The essential framing here was the accusation of "blatant discrimination," a charge that attacks the court's legitimacy in a different way than the activism charge does. This theme was pursued by some of

---

[284] Eric Eckholm, *Court Upholds Bans in Four States*, NY Times (Nov 6, 2014) (available at https://www.nytimes.com/2014/11/07/us/appeals-court-upholds-same-sex-marriage-ban .html); see also Joshua Berlinger, *Court Upholds 4 Same-Sex Marriage Bans; Will Supreme Court Review?*, CNN (Nov 7, 2014, 8:51 a.m. ET) (available at http://www.cnn.com/2014/11 /07/us/same-sex-marriage-ruling/index.html).

[285] For examples, see Robert Barnes, *The Supreme Court: Too Liberal?*, Wash Post, July 26, 2015 (available at https://www.washingtonpost.com/politics/courts_law/the-supreme-court -too-liberal/2015/07/26/5e31c988-320f-11e5-8353-1215475949f4_story.html?utm_term =.bd0f8cec128d); Lawrence Hurley, *Supreme Court's Landmark Ruling Legalizes Gay Marriage Nationwide*, Reuters, June 27, 2015 (available at https://www.reuters.com/article/us-usa -court-gaymarriage/landmark-u-s-supreme-court-ruling-legalizes-gay-marriage-nationwide -idUSKBN0P61SW20150628). This phenomenon, of course, extends beyond *Obergefell*. See generally Hannah Fairfield and Adam Liptak, *A More Nuanced Breakdown of the Supreme Court*, NY Times, June 26, 2014 (available at https://www.nytimes.com/2014/06/27/upshot /a-more-nuanced-breakdown-of-the-supreme-court.html) (noting that "[t]his is the time of year that the news media rolls out a familiar graphic: nine head shots of Supreme Court justices, arrayed from most liberal to most conservative").

[286] *Shameful Sixth Circuit Decision Upholds Discriminatory Marriage Bans in MI, KY, TN, & OH*, Human Rights Campaign (Nov 6, 2014) (available at https://www.hrc.org/press/shameful-sixth -circuit-decision-upholds-discriminatory-marriage-bans-in-mi).

[287] Id.

the Democratic politicians who got into the act, as well. Consider, for example, this press release from Ohio Senator Sherrod Brown:

> "All Americans should have the same rights," Brown said. "Like so many Ohioans, I'm disappointed in today's ruling that restricts the recognition of lawful marriages regardless of whom they love or where they live. It's time for the courts to join the growing majority of Americans who support full civil rights for our gay and lesbian family, friends, and neighbors."[288]

Representative Dan Kildee, from Michigan's 5th congressional district, alluded in his press release to Michigan Governor Rick Snyder and Attorney General Bill Schuette, saying these partisans had "continue[d] their ideological crusade against loving Michigan families at taxpayer's expense,"[289] and then declared:

> With today's ruling, the U.S. Supreme Court should immediately take up the issue of marriage equality, as I am confident that the U.S. Constitution affords every Michigander and American the right to marry whom they choose. Love is love, and equality will ultimately prevail.[290]

Some commentary from bloggers responded in greater depth and offered more fully elaborated critiques of the Sixth Circuit's ruling. These critiques were likely directed at a politically engaged and aware audience, but are worthy of attention because they spell out ways in which the court's legitimacy, understood beyond the activism/restraint dichotomy, can be questioned. Material of this sort is probably better understood as a source of framing for progressive elites, who might then cue wider audiences, rather than as material likely to be consumed directly by large segments of the public.

Jay Michaelson, columnist for the *Daily Beast*, identified Judge Jeffrey Sutton as a "respected conservative thinker," and a "judge's judge, a consummate professional," and then proceeded to review *seriatim* the multiple arguments in Sutton's opinion.[291] He placed particular emphasis on a normative argument about the role of courts:

---

[288] Senator Sherrod Brown (D-Ohio), *Brown Statement on Sixth Circuit Court Ruling to Uphold Ban on Same-Sex Marriage* (Nov 6, 2014) (available at https://www.brown.senate.gov /newsroom/press/release/brown-statement-on-sixth-circuit-court-ruling-to-uphold-ban-on -same-sex-marriage).

[289] Representative Dan Kildee (D-Mich), *Statement by Congressman Dan Kildee on Sixth Circuit Ruling on Gay Marriage* (Nov 6, 2014) (available at https://dankildee.house.gov/media /press-releases/statement-congressman-dan-kildee-sixth-circuit-ruling-gay-marriage).

[290] Id.

[291] Jay Michaelson, *All The Wrong Reasons to Ban Gay Marriage*, Daily Beast (Nov 7, 2014) (available at https://www.thedailybeast.com/all-the-wrong-reasons-to-ban-gay-unions).

[Sutton] argues that it is better "to allow the democratic processes begun in the states to continue" debating the merits of same-sex marriage, rather than "take a poll of the three judges on this panel." As noted by Judge Martha Craig Daughtrey in dissent, this is an outrageous position. The whole point of courts is to be counter-majoritarian, i.e., to interpret the constitutional principles that constrain majorities from oppressing minorities.[292]

Michaelson then pivoted to considering originalism, noting that Sutton had argued that:

"From the founding of the Republic to 2003, every state defined marriage as a relationship between a man and a woman," and concludes that "the Fourteenth Amendment permits, though it does not require, states to define marriage in that way." Wait, what? From the founding of the Republic until 1967, many states defined marriage as a relationship between two people of the same race. . . .

This is why "originalism" is so beloved of cultural conservatives: All it really means is "keep the status quo."[293]

Note the key claims: Sutton is conservative, majoritarianism in the context of state-sanctioned inequality is outrageous, allowing a ban on same-sex marriage reeks of the bias of segregation, and originalism is a disingenuous form of resisting change. Consider another online writer unhappy with the opinion, Mark Joseph Stern, writing in *Slate*:

Thursday's 2–1 decision by the 6th Circuit upholding four states' gay marriage bans is a deeply obnoxious slog. . . . Its author, Judge Jeffrey Sutton, seems to fundamentally misunderstand the constitutional arguments behind marriage equality. . . . After a while, Sutton's repeated insistence that it's not a federal judge's duty to enforce the constitution makes you want to grab him by the shoulders and ask, *then what in the world were you hired for?*[294]

Stern made a version of Michaelson's core point: This is an indefensible abdication of the judicial role.

The various elements of the attack on the Sixth Circuit were, thus, to emphasize the partisanship of the judges, to accuse the majority of bias, and to argue that the judges have violated their obligation to protect constitutional rights. This sketch suggests that, in the context

---

[292] Id.

[293] Id.

[294] Mark Joseph Stern, *Read the Hilarious, Humane Dissent from the 6th Circuit's Awful Gay Marriage Ruling*, Slate (Nov 7, 2014, 8:30 a.m.) (available at http://www.slate.com/blogs /outward/2014/11/07/the_sixth_circuit_gay_marriage_case_dissent_is_hilarious_and_humane .html).

of sharply polarized parties and divisive issues, there may well be *no* resolution that does not lead one side to react in ways that question the Court's legitimacy. Abdication is a version of a legitimacy argument, though not one that sounds in the logic of activism and restraint. There are undoubtedly others. The Roberts-style plea to leave it to democracy in the name of judicial legitimacy assumes that citizens operate within an activism/restraint dichotomy and assess judges based on it. Yet the dynamics of contemporary politics furnish little reason to believe that is the case.

IV. CONCLUSION

The political dynamics explored here reflect points of sharp contrast between the two eras. The heart of the difference relates to the changes in how the two major parties approach judicial issues and, in a more fundamental sense, how the parties approach one another. As we have seen, the party polarization that has been on the rise for the last four decades is in full force on judicial issues, and is reflected vividly in such settings as confirmation hearings and the identification of party platform positions about courts. Since the 1968 presidential campaign, it has been the Republican Party that has pressed claims of activism and criticized the courts with increasing stridency and vigor. All of this contrasts with the earlier period.

To observe this change over time, however, is not to say that the positions of the parties are immune from further shifts. Indeed, it is not difficult to imagine a progressive faction of Democrats invoking an economic populist case against an increasingly conservative Court it brands as activist. That might make an interesting counterpoint to the *cultural* populist claims that underwrite claims about judicial activism from the right. Both would scorn a set of loathed elites, albeit not the same set. Certainly, some scholars and activists have staked out versions of such a claim.[295] Similarly, the tried-and-true attacks by Republicans on judicial activism may at some point be reframed or abandoned. Already, some on the right wish to retire the idea and

---

[295] See, for example, Ian Milhiser, *Injustices: The Supreme Court's History of Comforting the Comfortable and Afflicting the Afflicted* 229 (Nation Books, 2015) ("the wealthiest Americans, thanks to the Roberts Court, now enjoy an unprecedented ability to corrupt elections. . . . Why bother to rig an election when you can simply buy it?"). Cf. Fishkin and Forbath, 94 BU L Rev (cited in note 136) (de-emphasizing courts and calling for a political movement supporting "constitutional political economy" and an "anti-oligarchy" principle).

rhetoric of activism in favor of what some call "judicial engagement" and "constitutional conservatism."[296] The anchoring principle would be some version of a robust protection of liberty, including economic liberty, and the retreat from presumptive deference to regulatory legislation.

Should the parties refashion their positions in these directions, we would find ourselves in a political moment that looks in some ways more like the *Lochner* era than anything has in a long time. But because of decades of polarization, and the technology of contemporary politics, the political process surrounding the Court will never again look like the one that existed at the time of *Lochner*. Probing these changed political dynamics in the realm of constitutional politics has been the principal task of this article. These changes cast doubt on simple analogies and warnings about the institutional risks of a perceived return to *Lochner* because they do not account for the political dynamics that surround the Court and inevitably shape public perceptions about the Court and the law more generally.

[296] Randy Barnett, *"Judicial Engagement" Is Not the Same as "Judicial Activism,"* The Volokh Conspiracy, Wash Post (Jan 28, 2014) (available at https://www.washingtonpost.com/news /volokh-conspiracy/wp/2014/01/28/judicial-engagement-is-not-the-same-as-judicial-activism /?utm_term=.8309301f74cc) (advocating terms signaling that "judges are restrained to follow the Constitution, whether this leads to upholding or invalidating legislation").

VINCENT BLASI

A READER'S GUIDE TO JOHN MILTON'S *AREOPAGITICA*, THE FOUNDATIONAL ESSAY OF THE FIRST AMENDMENT TRADITION

Fittingly, the most imaginative and densely suggestive of the classic arguments for free speech was written by a poet. Had his career unfolded as he wished, John Milton would never have produced his renowned *Areopagitica* of 1644. It was only with great reluctance that he undertook to engage in prose polemics during the English Civil War, sacrificing his "calm and pleasing solitariness" to "embark in a troubled sea of noises and hoarse disputes."[1] He described pamphleteering as something he did "with the left hand" all the while "knowing myself inferior to myself."[2] Posterity, always a Miltonic concern, has begged to differ with this self-assessment. Wherever the *Areopagitica* ranks on Milton's daunting list of enduring creations, it has proved to be the foundational essay of the Anglo-American free speech tradition.

Vincent Blasi is the Corliss Lamont Professor of Civil Liberties at Columbia Law School.

AUTHOR'S NOTE: Special thanks to Thomas Healy, whose insightful critique at the Yale Free Expression Scholars Conference sent me back to the drawing board.

[1] John Milton, *The Reason of Church Government Against Prelaty* (1642), in Merritt Y. Hughes, ed, *John Milton, Complete Poems and Major Prose* 640, 671 (Macmillan, 1957).

[2] Id at 667.

I. The Setting

Born in 1608, John Milton grew up in a London that was experiencing rapid growth and transformation as a result of the increasing importance of international trade, a redirection of the nation's economy that produced a versatile and politically assertive urban middle class. He was the eldest son of a prosperous scrivener, a profession that entailed the preparation and notarization of financial documents, some money lending and investment counseling, and intermittent contact with legal solicitors. It was assumed that the scrivener's prodigiously talented first son would become a clergyman, the natural career for someone bookishly inclined. (His second son, Christopher, became a distinguished lawyer and judge.)

Events intervened, however. Shortly after Milton completed his studies at Cambridge, the Church of England experienced a theological purge imposed by William Laud, Archbishop of Canterbury in the service of King Charles I. Laud's version of church doctrine and discipline was viewed by Protestant reformers, and especially Puritans, as too devoted to ritual and ecclesiastical hierarchy and too neglectful of preaching, in those respects bearing a suspicious affinity to Catholicism. Milton, whose habit of intense scriptural study and personal interpretation was formed at an early age, realized that he could not serve such a church. The path of preaching thereby blocked, he decided upon a different way to serve his God: writing Christian poetry. To that end, he devoted the better part of the decade of his twenties (living at home at his parents' expense) to the study of ancient and medieval history and literature. He was particularly drawn to the epic poetry of Homer and Virgil. He dreamt of one day writing an English epic.

In 1640 Charles was forced to call the first Parliament in eleven years by his need for money to finance a war with Scottish Covenanters which erupted when he tried to impose the Anglican Prayer Book on a largely Presbyterian populace. The occasion of Parliament assembling brought forth a multitude of grievances against a decade's worth of assertions of royal prerogative that critics claimed were both a threat to the Reformation and a violation of the common law and the Ancient Constitution. Notably, these grievances were aired not only in the houses of Parliament but in the streets of London. Never before had England witnessed so much petitioning, pamphleteering, and mass demonstrating over matters of theology, war, politics, and governance.[3] A gifted writer, in the estimation of others as well as himself, Milton felt a responsibility to do his part. He became a controversialist, a diversion from his poetic calling that would consume the bulk of his writing time for the next twenty years.

He entered the political fray in 1641 writing five pamphlets calling for the complete abolition of the Anglican office of bishop. Eventually, Parliament abolished episcopacy, but not until it had defeated the King after four years of civil war. In the meantime, Milton turned to other subjects: the legitimate grounds for divorce, the reform of education, and the liberty of the press. His polemical efforts during the civil war and its aftermath culminated in six pamphlets defending the Rump Parliament's execution in 1649 of King Charles I. In several, Milton served as the officially-designated spokesperson for his country. These erudite disquisitions, some written in Latin, were addressed not only to the English people but also the political leaders and intellectuals of Europe. He wrote them while going blind.

Despite the importance and ferocity of the continent-wide debate over the regicide, Milton's most stressful experience as a polemicist occurred six years earlier when he produced a bold pamphlet arguing that temperamental or spiritual incompatibility constitutes a legitimate ground for divorce. Torrents of abuse rained down on him for advancing this view. (The conventional understanding was that only infidelity, impotence, or cruelty justifies divorce.)[4] He published his tract in violation of a law that had been passed by Parliament two months before, the Licensing Order of 1643. Apparently, Milton sought to comply with that law's requirement that all publications be approved by a parliamentary committee before being circulated, but he was denied permission. Undeterred, Milton arranged for his pamphlet to be published nevertheless.

The licensing of books and pamphlets was nothing new in England. Immediately upon Gutenberg's new invention crossing the English Channel in 1476, the crown asserted monopoly control over the act of printing, originally restricting the privilege to official printers in London, Oxford, and Cambridge. With the outbreak of the Ref-

---

[3] See David Cressy, *England on Edge: Crisis and Revolution 1640–1642* 290–302 (Oxford, 2007).

[4] See Annabel Patterson, *Milton, Marriage, and Divorce*, in Thomas N. Corns, ed, *A Companion to Milton* 279–80 (Blackwell, 2001).

ormation in the mid-sixteenth century and the growth in literacy that it encouraged and fed off of, administration of the system for licensing books and pamphlets became an important component of statecraft.[5] During Queen Elizabeth's long reign (1559–1603), the power to license religious and political publications was applied rather flexibly in the effort to head off fractious political controversy along religious lines. Although Puritan preachers were denied appointments to livings in the Church of England, they were for the most part permitted to preach freelance, often attracting large followings, and to publish their sermons, a source of income crucial to their support.[6]

Licensing moved to the center of the political stage only during the early seventeenth century, when the Stuart monarchs James I and Charles I, particularly the latter advised by Archbishop Laud, sought to tighten the licensing system in support of royal authority and established theology.[7] When Parliament set about in 1640–43 to challenge royal prerogative on a broad front, two of the casualties were the Court of High Commission and the Star Chamber, both of which had been deeply involved in administering the licensing system. Grievances of other kinds led to the abolition of those two much reviled royal institutions, but an important consequence of their demise was an unaccustomed hiatus in licensing.

Presses were suddenly free. The result was an unprecedented outpouring of unbounded, arguably blasphemous disputation in print that surprised and alarmed the Parliament and much of the nation. It was feared that the venting of political divisions and radical religious nostrums would weaken military resolve and provoke divine displeasure. Such concerns engendered the Licensing Order of 1643. Ironically, the only precedent available to Parliament for how to construct and administer a licensing regime was the old royal system. Enforcement was placed in the hands of parliamentary committees and their staffs rather than Church of England bureaucrats, but other than that the previous practices were more or less reinstated. Specialized licensers were appointed to examine writings in specified categories.

---

[5] See Fredrick Seaton Siebert, *Freedom of the Press in England 1476–1776* 21–37, 64–87 (Illinois, 1952).

[6] On Elizabethan regulation of dissident writing, see generally Cyndia Susan Clegg, *Press Censorship in Elizabethan England* (Cambridge, 1997).

[7] See generally Cyndia Susan Clegg, *Press Censorship in Jacobean England* (Cambridge, 2001); Cyndia Susan Clegg, *Press Censorship in Caroline England* (Cambridge, 2008).

Four censors were named, for example, to scrutinize law books, three for books of philosophy and history, one for "mathematics, almanacks, and prognostications." Not only miscreant authors and their printers but also licensers who had been too permissive were subject to imprisonment.[8]

Milton thought the Order was a dispiriting and disillusioning relapse by Parliament. He had imagined that free thought within the Protestant community in the service of completing the Reformation was part of what Parliament and its supporters were fighting for in risking their lives and fortunes to challenge the King. Friends and political allies importuned him to lend his polemical talents to their cause of persuading Parliament to repeal the Licensing Order. Milton obliged. On November 23, 1644, he published *Areopagitica; A Speech of Mr. John Milton for the Liberty of Unlicensed Printing, to the Parlament of England*. The pamphlet appeared on the streets of London without the required imprimatur but with the author's name (though not his printer's) in bold letters, as if in ostentatious defiance of the licensing requirement. So far as posterity is concerned, he needn't have bothered. Nobody else, then or later, could possibly have written this pamphlet or anything like it.

II. Framing

The title alludes to a written speech of the Greek orator Isocrates presented in 355 B.C. to the Athenian Ecclesia, which set a precedent of an ordinary citizen submitting a written petition to a lawmaker.[9] Such presumption we take for granted today, but it was not so in Milton's day. Citizens petitioning Parliament, often in huge crowds, was both common in the 1640s and also widely condemned. It was a much-mooted question whether this is a legitimate form of political participation.[10]

The reference to the Areopagus, a knoll on the Acropolis, may also refer to a passage in the Book of Acts in which Saint Paul recounts the respectful hearing he received, the openness to new ideas he observed, and the converts he made on the Areopagus when he criticized the

---

[8] See Siebert, *Freedom of the Press* at 187–90 (cited in note 5).

[9] See Eric Nelson, *"True Liberty": Isocrates and Milton's Areopagitica*, 40 Milton Studies 201 (2001).

[10] See Cressy, *England on Edge* 5, 110–26 (cited in note 3).

Athenians for being too superstitious in their religion.[11] He compares Athens favorably to other locations where he was not so well received.

Finally, Milton's choice of title may have been meant to signal his belief that the issue of whether printing should be licensed must be examined by drawing upon a broad range of sources and reasons. In other words, Milton here might be broadcasting his intellectual debt to Renaissance humanism even as he explores how his country can best protect and complete the Protestant Reformation.

Superbly educated in classical rhetoric, Milton begins his "speech" by announcing the four divisions of his argument. First, he will identify the inventors of the practice of licensing writings, "those whom ye will be loath to own." Second, he will discuss "what is to be thought in general of reading, whatever sort the books be." Third, he will contend that "this Order avails nothing to the suppressing of scandalous, seditious, and libelous books, which were mainly intended to be suppressed." Fourth, he will argue that the principal effect of licensing books and pamphlets will be "the discouragement of all learning, and the stop of truth."[12] This phrase, "the *stop* of truth," is revealing. It captures one of the most important elements of his overall argument: his deep commitment to the notion that truth is in essence dynamic. Truth's dynamic essence operates "both in religious and civil wisdom." It is important to note how explicit he is at the outset that he is addressing civil concerns such as sedition, libel, and military effectiveness no less than religious concerns such as blasphemy, idolatry, heresy, and Christian charity.

III. The Argument from Association

The first part of Milton's argument consists of a quick tour across the centuries "to show what hath been done by ancient and famous commonwealths against this disorder" of free writing.[13]

Milton reports that in Athens, "where books and wits were ever busier than in any other part of Greece," the magistrate "cared to take notice" only of writings that were blasphemous and atheistical or else

---

[11] Acts 17:16–18.

[12] John Milton, *Areopagitica* (1644), in Hughes, ed, *John Milton* at 720 (cited in note 1).

[13] Id. Calling free writing a "disorder" is Milton's characteristically sardonic way of introducing a pamphlet designed to prove precisely the opposite.

libelous. Works "tending to voluptuousness," "denying of divine Providence," or expressing "Cynic impudence" were left alone.[14]

Like the Athenians, the Romans of the republican period punished libel and blasphemy of their gods but left unregulated Lucretius's Epicurean philosophy regarding the mortality of the soul and much "satirical sharpness." Octavius Caesar failed to suppress a history that extolled the part played by his rival Pompey.

During the middle ages, although "the Popes of Rome, engrossing what they pleased of political rule into their own hands, extended their dominion over men's eyes," they were "sparing in their censures."[15] Only with the fear engendered in the late fourteenth and early fifteenth centuries by the writings of John Wyckliffe and Jan Huss, precursors of Luther, were individual readers excommunicated for violating the Church's injunctions. When the Reformation broke out in the sixteenth century, prohibitions and punishments became widespread, "until the Council of Trent and the Spanish Inquisition engendering together brought forth, or perfected, those Catalogues and expurging Indexes, that rake through the entrails of many a good old author, with a violation worse than any could be offered to his tomb." Wielders of the power to censor grew increasingly arbitrary: "Nor did they stay in matters heretical, but any subject that was not to their palate, they either condemned in a Prohibition, or had it straight into the new purgatory of an index."[16]

At every turn, Milton emphasizes the Roman Catholic pedigree of the practice of licensing. His characterization of Catholic censors is indelible:

> To fill up the measure of encroachment, their last invention was to ordain that no book, pamphlet, or paper should be printed (as if St. Peter had bequeathed them the keys of the press also out of Paradise) unless it were approved and licensed under the hands of two or three glutton friars. . . . Sometimes five Imprimaturs are seen together dialoguewise in the piazza of one titlepage, complimenting and ducking each to other with their shaven reverences, whether the author, who stands by in perplexity at the foot of his epistle, shall to the press or to the sponge.[17]

---

[14] Id at 720–21.

[15] Id at 723–24.

[16] Milton, *Areopagitica* at 724 (cited in note 12).

[17] Id.

Milton describes the Licensing Order's requirement of an imprimatur authorizing publication as "apishly Romanizing."

Milton ends his first part by specifying the point of his selective history lesson. He concedes that "though the inventors were bad, the thing for all that may be good." He counters that "if that thing be no such deep invention, but obvious, and easy for any man to light on, and yet best and wisest commonwealths through all ages and occasions have forborne to use it, and falsest seducers and oppressors of men were first who took it up, and to no other purpose but to obstruct and hinder the first approach of Reformation," it would take an act of alchemy "to sublimate any good use out of such an invention."

IV. The Argument from Inseparability

The second part of Milton's four-part argument he vaguely labels "what is to be thought in general of reading books, whatever sort they may be, and whether be more the benefit or the harm that thence proceeds."[18] He tries to demonstrate that the vices and dangers that would-be regulators fear from unlicensed printing are inseparable from qualities of persons and effects of their activities that no member of his audience can possibly wish to sacrifice or discourage, in no small part due to shared religious understandings.

Milton builds his argument around a passage from Paul's Epistle to Titus: "To the pure, all things are pure."[19] Knowledge, he says, whether of good or evil, "cannot defile, nor consequently the books, if the will and conscience be not defiled."[20] He notes how the Bible preaches the virtue of temperance. "Yet God commits the managing of so great a trust, without particular law or prescription, wholly to the demeanor of every grown man."[21] Likewise for ideas. Rather than relegating man "under a perpetual childhood of prescription," God "trusts him with the gift of reason to be his own chooser." Indeed, "there were but little work left for preaching, if law and compulsion should grow so fast upon those things which heretofore were governed only by exhortation."[22]

---

[18] Id.

[19] Titus 1:15.

[20] Milton, *Areopagitica* at 727 (cited in note 12).

[21] Id.

[22] Id.

This argument is rhetorically ingenious in several respects. It responds to several of the chief concerns of those who might be tempted to support the Licensing Order. The fear that all the free thinking in the pamphlet literature was risking God's wrath is answered by scriptural evidence of the value of free reading, even of bad theology, as a preparation for choosing, if only "to discover, confute, forewarn, or illustrate."[23] The worry about backsliding in the project of advancing the Reformation is assuaged by an argument that ascribes a crucial role to preachers. The perception that the proliferation of sectarian theologies that ensued after the royal licensing system was abolished represents a form of disorder is addressed by Milton's description of a supervening divine order. A few pages later he returns to this point, commenting on "the high providence of God, who, though he command us temperance, justice, continence, yet pours out before us, even to a profuseness, all desirable things, and gives us minds that can wander beyond all limit and satiety."[24] Why, asks Milton, "should we then affect a rigor contrary to the manner of God and of nature, by abridging or scanting those means, which books freely permitted are, both to the trial of virtue and the exercise of truth."[25]

Next Milton turns to his argument from inseparability, introducing a theme he was to explore years later to great effect in *Paradise Lost*:

> Good and evil we know in the field of this world grow up together almost inseparably. . . . It was from out the rind of one apple tasted, that the knowledge of good and evil, as two twins cleaving together, leaped forth into the world. And perhaps this is that doom which Adam fell into of knowing good and evil, that is to say of knowing good by evil.[26]

Free reading, even of false and dangerous ideas, indeed especially of false and dangerous ideas, is integral to the experience of purification by means of resisting the pervasive temptations of a fallen world: "He that can apprehend and consider vice with all her baits and seeming

---

[23] Id.

[24] Milton, *Areopagitica* at 727 (cited in note 12).

[25] Id.

[26] Id at 728. For an argument that this passage represents an important moment in the evolution of Milton's "muscular postlapsarianism" that would eventuate in *Paradise Lost*, see William Poole, *Milton and the Idea of the Fall* 138–40 (Cambridge, 2005).

pleasures, and yet abstain, and yet distinguish, and yet prefer what is truly better, he is the true warfaring Christian."[27]

Recall that one of the main arguments against leaving unregulated the recent explosion of sectarian speculation was the fear that it was weakening antiroyalist military prospects both by risking divine displeasure and stirring up theological divisiveness within the parliamentary coalition. Milton calls free reading a "warfaring" activity, then develops an extended military metaphor in the effort to turn the argument around:

> I cannot praise a fugitive and cloistered virtue, unexercised and unbreathed, that never sallies out and sees her adversary but slinks out of the race, where that immortal garland is to be run for, not without dust and heat. . . . Since therefore the knowledge and survey of vice is in this world so necessary to the constituting of human virtue, and the scanning of error to the confirmation of truth, how can we more safely, and with less danger, scout into the regions of sin and falsity than by reading all manner of tractates and hearing all manner of reason? And this is the benefit which may be had of books promiscuously read.[28]

Having asserted the inseparability of good and evil in the postlapsarian world and having explained the consequent duty of fallen man to scout into the regions of sin and falsity, Milton identifies three types of harm that his adversaries assert might follow from such free inquiry. The first is "infection that may spread."[29] He responds to this danger by suggesting it proves too much: "the Bible itself" he notes "oftimes relates blasphemy not nicely, it describes the carnal sense of wicked men not unelegantly, it brings in holiest men passionately murmuring against Providence through all the arguments of Epicurus; in other great disputes it answers dubiously and darkly to the common reader."[30] Not only the Bible but "all the heathen writers of greatest infection," thinkers "with whom is bound up with the life of human learning," would be at risk if this concern were to justify the licensing of books.

The second and third feared harms from evil books and pamphlets get short shrift. One such harm is distraction, the worry that readers might "employ our time in vain things." The other is temptation.

---

[27] Milton, *Areopagitica* at 728 (cited in note 12).

[28] Id at 728–29.

[29] Id at 729.

[30] Id.

Both harms Milton dismisses on the ground of inseparability: "to all men such books are not temptations, nor vanities, but useful drugs and materials wherewith to temper and compose effective and strong medicines."[31]

V. The Argument from Futility

Milton's third part is the most practical, and in that way perhaps the most applicable to modern controversies about the freedom of speech. He stresses the need for realism and common sense. He asserts that in practice regulatory reach will far exceed the bounds of any acknowledged justification due to factors such as frustration, incompetence, personal antipathy, inertia, and delay. Despite such arbitrary overreach, he maintains that licensing will be "easily eluded."[32]

The reason that licensing cannot tame intellectual and theological disorder, Milton argues citing Plato as authority, is that the true sources of order are the "unwritten, or at least unconstraining, laws of virtuous education, religious and civil nurture."[33] Voluntary constraints that flow from commitment, responsibility, self-discipline, and loyalty are the "bonds and ligaments of the commonwealth, the pillars and sustainers of every written statute." He concedes that disorder is disastrous: "Impunity and remissness, for certain, are the bane of a commonwealth." That is not in dispute. But practically speaking, "here the great art lies, to discern in what the law is to bid restraint and punishment, and in what things persuasion only is to work."[34]

"Persuasion only" has a large role in creating and preserving order, according to Milton, because to a great degree order stems from virtue, both civic and religious. And virtue is best nurtured by trust: "If every action, which is good or evil in man at ripe years, were to be under pittance and prescription and compulsion, what were virtue but a name, what praise could then be due to well-doing, what gramercy to be sober, just, or continent."[35] Order must penetrate to the inner person. Persuasion does that better than law.

---

[31] Milton, *Areopagitica* at 731 (cited in note 12).

[32] Id at 733.

[33] Id.

[34] Id.

[35] Milton, *Areopagitica* at 733 (cited in note 12).

Milton returns repeatedly to his futility argument, likening licensing to "the exploit of that gallant man who thought to pound up the crows by shutting his park gate"[36] and commenting on how the inevitable evasions "will make us all both ridiculous and weary, and yet frustrate."[37] He notes how porous any licensing scheme is bound to be, given that it cannot practically call in writings already in circulation and cannot prevent the initial production and distribution of works of foreign origin.

He asks the reader to "consider the quality which ought to be in every licenser," and compares that to the drudgery of being "made the perpetual reader of unchosen books and pamphlets, oftimes huge volumes." "[W]e can easily foresee," Milton says, "what kind of licensors we are to expect hereafter, either ignorant, imperious, and remiss, or basely pecuniary."[38]

In sum, a host of practical considerations suggests that any attempt to bring order to the thought of a nation by means of the exercise of bureaucratic authority is destined to be futile. The objective is absurdly ambitious, the opportunities for both evasion and regulatory abuse are ever present, and the human resources available to execute the project are unimpressive.

VI. The Argument from Design

The fourth and final part of *Areopagitica* takes up nearly half the tract. It is more passionate, peripatetic, eloquent, and aspirational than the preceding parts—and that is no mean trick. Milton really lets loose. Several of his figures of speech are unforgettable. It is also true that this is the part in which he does the most to establish his case, but only by means of assertions and proofs that are out of the ordinary and difficult to evaluate by conventional standards.

The first several pages of Part Four are devoted to a series of characterizations that illustrate how much the licensing of books and pamphlets reflects distrust of authors, readers, the preachers who guide them, in effect all persons and institutions that make up the social and religious order. Milton describes this distrust as "an undervaluing and vilifying of the whole nation."[39] But his frame of reference is not ex-

---

[36] Id at 730.

[37] Id at 733.

[38] Id at 734.

[39] Milton, *Areopagitica* at 736 (cited in note 12).

clusively the collective. At the personal level, licensing is an under-valuing that cuts deeply: "so far to distrust the judgment and the honesty of one who hath but a common repute in learning, and never yet offended, as to not count him fit to print his mind without a tutor and examiner, lest he should drop a schism, or something of a corruption, is the greatest displeasure and indignity to a free and knowing spirit that can be put upon him."[40]

One of the first questions to ask about any justification for the freedom of speech is whether at bottom the argument rests on a claim about collective consequences or individual entitlement. Not every argument is easily classified in these terms; many can be read either way. Moreover, an argument can be "individual-centered" in the sense that it rests on a notion of how persons deserve respect or develop qua individuals, and still maintain that such respect or development is important mainly for the collective benefits that members of the community generate by virtue of their individuality. In my view, the *Areopagitica* is best understood as making a hybrid argument of this sort. Milton speaks often of the Reformation, posterity, collective energy, the divine order, and the unique place in history of the English people. He also discusses dignity, charity, the inner person, and the centrality of choice. His repeated invocation of the religious and civic benefits of trust is an example of his integration of individual and collective units of reference.

Milton is scathing in the way he describes the inherent paternalism of licensing. "What advantage," he asks, "is it to be a man, over it is to be a boy at school . . . if serious and elaborate writings, as if they were no more than the theme of a grammar-lad under his pedagogue, must not be uttered without the cursory eyes of a temporizing and extemporizing licenser?"[41] Moreover, if revisions occur to the author while the licensed book is in production, he must "trudge to his leave-giver"[42] to get them validated. The cost is not only in personal respect but also authorial authority, and hence impact:

> And how can a man teach with authority, which is the life of teaching; how can he be a doctor in his book as he ought to be, or else had better be silent, whenas all he teaches, all he delivers, is but under the tuition, under

---

[40] Id at 735.

[41] Id.

[42] Id.

the correction of his patriarchal licenser to blot or alter what precisely
accords not with the hidebound humour which he calls his judgment.[43]

This is no way to persuade. "[E]very acute reader," Milton complains,
will think "I hate a pupil teacher. I endure not an instructor that comes
to me under the wardship of an overseeing fist."[44]

An "acute reader" may distrust authors under a licensing regime,
but the regime itself distrusts the bulk of readers, whom it assumes to
be anything but acute:

> Nor is it to the common people less than a reproach; for if we be so
> jealous over them, as that we dare not trust them with an English pam-
> phlet, what do we but censure them for a giddy, vicious and ungrounded
> people; in such sick and weak state of faith and discretion, as to be able to
> take nothing down but through the pipe of a licenser?[45]

The corrosive distrust is not even confined to authors and readers:

> [I]t reflects to the disrepute of our ministers also, of whose labors we
> should hope better . . . than that after all this . . . continual preaching,
> they should still be frequented with such an unprincipled, unedified and
> laic rabble, as that the whiff of every new pamphlet should stagger them out
> of their catechism and Christian walking.[46]

Such an assumption of the weakness of the English people contrasts mightily with Milton's admiring account of fortified London
during the Civil War:

> Behold now this vast city: a city of refuge, the mansion house of liberty,
> encompassed and surrounded with his protection; the shop of war hath not
> more anvils and hammers waking, to fashion out the plates and instru-
> ments of armed justice in defense of beleaguered truth, than there be pens
> and heads there, sitting by their studious lamps, musing, searching, re-
> volving new notions and ideas wherewith to present, as with their hom-
> age and their fealty, the approaching Reformation: others as fast reading,
> trying all things, assenting to the force of reason and convincement. What
> could a man require more from a nation so pliant and so prone to seek after
> knowledge?
>
> Where there is much desire to learn, there of necessity will be much
> arguing, much writing, many opinions, for opinion in good men is but
> knowledge in the making.[47]

---

[43] Milton, *Areopagitica* at 735–36 (cited in note 12).

[44] Id at 736.

[45] Id at 737.

[46] Id.

[47] Milton, *Areopagitica* at 743–44 (cited in note 12).

This pivotal passage captures not only Milton's shameless appeal to national pride, but also three of the most striking ideas in the *Areopagitica*: (1) the importance of an energizing environment to the quest for knowledge, (2) the dynamic character of truth and understanding, and (3) the order that can subsist in the collective project of persons trying to think independently about "the solidest and sublimest points of controversy and new invention."[48]

In intellectual and spiritual matters, for all his years of solitary study, for all the focus on individual choice and responsibility in his various prose works and later epic poetry, Milton is an environmentalist in the sense that he thinks the surrounding atmosphere, the collective energy of an age and place, really matters. This is one reason why he was less troubled by radical sectarian thinking about matters divine than were most of his compatriots. Ideas beyond the pale, emanating from strange creatures, contribute to the collective quest, even if only by functioning as "dust and cinders" which "serve to polish and brighten the armory of Truth."[49] In that way, even the wild nostrums of the sectaries can be part of "knowledge in the making."[50]

"Knowledge in the making" is a double entendre. It refers both to a quest destined never to be completed till "the end of mortal things,"[51] and to the fact that understanding and believing are as much a function of *how* as of *what*. Both meanings speak of dynamism. Regarding the first, Milton says: "The light which we have gained was given us, not to be ever staring on, but by it to discover onward things more remote from our knowledge."[52] Milton would be nobody's favorite in a humility contest. That said, it is notable how much his argument depends on his view of the limits of human understanding: "he who thinks we are to pitch our tent here, and have attained the utmost prospect of reformation that the mortal glass wherein we contemplate can show us, till we come to beatific vision, that man by this very opinion declares that he is yet far short of truth."[53]

---

[48] Id at 745.

[49] Id at 748.

[50] Id at 743.

[51] Milton, *Areopagitica* at 747 (cited in note 12).

[52] Id at 742.

[53] Id at 741.

The perpetual dynamism of truth suggests the difficulty of domesticating it for the purpose of regulation: "Truth and understanding are not such wares as to be monopolized and traded in by tickets and statutes and standards. We must not think to make a staple commodity of all the knowledge in the land, to mark and license it like our broadcloth and our woolpacks."[54] Precisely because truth is "our richest merchandise,"[55] it would be self-defeating to "set an oligarchy of twenty engrossers over it, to bring a famine upon our minds again, when we shall know nothing but what is measured to us by their bushel."[56]

A reader of Milton might wonder how his economic metaphor here compares to a later economic metaphor introduced by Justice Holmes, the "marketplace of ideas," which has come to play a large and persistent role in modern First Amendment analysis.[57] Blair Hoxby, an important Milton scholar, has shown how the struggle for liberty of the press in the seventeenth century was part of a larger controversy over free trade, and that Milton wrote *Areopagitica* in part at the behest of journeymen printers aggrieved by crown, and later parliamentary, patents restricting profitable printing to a privileged few master printers.[58] Recall also that Milton's father, with whom he was close, was an enterprising businessman who raised his son in the heart of the City of London, then and now the concentrated financial district of the greater metropolis. So is Milton contending for the freedom to print on the analogy to the freedom to buy and sell?

Some of his arguments relating to inevitable regulatory inefficiency, incompetence, corruption, and perverse consequences might suggest as much, but there is a big difference between how Milton and Holmes deploy their economic metaphors. Holmes's point arguably, and the point of later exponents of the marketplace metaphor

---

[54] Id at 736–37.

[55] Milton, *Areopagitica* at 741 (cited in note 12).

[56] Id at 745.

[57] See *Abrams v United States*, 250 US 616, 630 (1919) (Holmes, J, dissenting); Vincent Blasi, *Holmes and the Marketplace of Ideas*, 2004 Supreme Court Review 1 (2004).

[58] See Blair Hoxby, *The Trade of Truth Advanced: Areopagitica, Economic Discourse and Libertarian Reform*, 36 Milton Studies 177 (1998).

more explicitly, is that speech should be left free to be governed by market forces because ideas do not warrant special treatment: they embody arbitrary preferences derived from adventitious experiences and thus can be likened to commodities.[59] Persons aggrieved by what they take to be excessive regulation of transactions regarding commodities therefore should be concerned also about excessive regulation of speakers. Milton's point is the opposite: because speech is uniquely important ("our richest merchandise"), it should *not* be subject to the same types of regulation, including licensing, that in his day (more than a century before Adam Smith) comprehensively governed the production and sale of commodities.

The second meaning of the double entendre "knowledge in the making" is that truth is only valuable if it is earned and held in the right way:

> [O]ur faith and knowledge thrives by exercise, as well as our limbs and complexion. Truth is compared in Scripture to a streaming fountain; if her waters flow not in a perpetual progression, they sicken into a muddy pool of conformity and tradition. A man may be a heretic in the truth; and if he believe things only because his pastor says so, or the Assembly so determines, without knowing other reason, though his belief be true, yet the very truth he holds becomes his heresy.[60]

The concept of "perpetual progression" is central to Milton's argument. Not only in the nation as a whole but within each individual must there be a perpetual progression of inquiry. Milton makes that clear with his concept of a "heretic in the truth."

With the assistance of licensing, heresy in the truth can occur "among the clergy themselves." An "easily inclinable" cleric ensconced in "a warm benefice" may be able to fulfill his "weekly charge of sermoning" with small effort, "forming and transforming, joining and disjoining" the "gatherings and savings of a sober graduateship" supplemented by additional cribs such as published breviaries and synopses.[61] However, "if his back door be not secured by the rigid licenser, but that a bold book may now and then issue forth and give the assault to some of his old collections in their trenches, it will

---

[59] See Oliver Wendell Holmes Jr., *Natural Law*, 32 Harv L Rev 40, 41 (1918).

[60] Milton, *Areopagitica* at 739 (cited in note 12).

[61] Id at 740.

concern him then to set good guards and sentinels about his received opinions."[62] Our comfortable clergyman may not be frightened into a perpetual progression of ceaseless inquiry, but at least he will need to make a start in the direction of active understanding in order to pass muster with his flock.

The third of Milton's key claims that are embedded in his extended image of embattled, energetic, inquisitive London relates to the concern about order that contributed to Parliament's decision to reinstitute licensing. To turn free thinkers into soldiers of the Reformation manning the city's defenses with their pens and lamps is to transmute perceived anarchy into order and perceived military weakness into strength. Later he turns the argument of his adversaries around a second time, upping the religious stakes to assert a divine order that is being served by the wide-ranging theological speculation:

> Under these fantastic terrors of sect and schism, we wrong the earnest and zealous thirst after knowledge and understanding which God hath stirred up in this city. What some lament of, we rather should rejoice of, should rather praise this pious forwardness among men, to reassume the ill-deputed care of their religion into their own hands again.[63]

Defenders of licensing make too much of the proliferation of new ideas and distinctive sects, he argues: "They fret, and out of their own weakness are in agony, lest these divisions and subdivisions will undo us. . . . Fool! He sees not the firm root, out of which we all grow, though into branches."[64]

Probably Milton's most effective response to the fear of disorder is his recounting an Egyptian myth regarding Isis and Osiris, derived from Plutarch's *Lives* and adapted to appeal to the religious sensibilities of his audience:

> Truth indeed came once into the world with her divine Master, and was a perfect shape most glorious to look on: but when he ascended, and his Apostles after him were laid asleep, then straight arose a wicked race of deceivers, who . . . took the virgin Truth, hewed her lovely form into a thousand pieces, and scattered them to the four winds. From that time ever since, the sad friends of Truth, such as durst appear, imitating the careful search that Isis made for the mangled body of Osiris, went up and down

---

[62] Id at 741.

[63] Id at 743–44.

[64] Milton, *Areopagitica* at 744 (cited in note 12).

gathering up limb by limb, still as they could find them. We have not yet found them all, Lords and Commons, nor ever shall do, till her Master's second coming; he shall bring together every joint and member, and shall mould them into an immortal feature of loveliness and perfection.[65]

The brilliance of this move lies not so much in its religious resonance generally but in its description of fallen men, in the form of bold inquirers like the sectaries, laboriously and perpetually doing God's work by piecing together the scattered fragments of a once perfect truth that cannot be fully reassembled "in mortal time" but which needs to be sought as a precondition for the Second Coming.[66] In other words, free thinking is not a destructive activity that breaks apart the understandings that hold a community together but rather a constructive activity that paves the way for the true order of redemption through divine grace. Those threatening radicals are actually builders.

Never one to let pass the opportunity to turn an adversary's argument around, Milton accuses the licensers themselves of sowing the seeds of disorder: "They are the troublers, they are the dividers of unity, who neglect and permit not others to unite those dissevered pieces which are yet wanting to the body of truth." Failing to "recover any enthralled piece of truth out of the grip of custom" retards the project of reassembly. It keeps "truth separated from truth, which is the fiercest rent and disunion of all."[67] In contrast, Milton's unity consists of "still searching what we know not by what we know, still closing up truth to truth as we find it. . . . not the forced and outward union of cold, and neutral, and inwardly divided minds."[68]

This terse description of what true order is *not*, contained in less than a sentence, might be the most pregnant passage in the entire *Areopagitica*. In it Milton weaves together no fewer than five of the figurative dichotomies that drive his overall argument: (1) forced vs. free (law vs. persuasion, authority vs. reason); (2) outward vs. inward

---

[65] Id at 741–42.

[66] For an account of Milton's millenarianism, including its role in *Areopagitica*, see Barbara K. Lewalski, *Milton and the Millennium*, in Juliet Cummins, ed, *Milton and the Ends of Time* 13, 18 (Cambridge, 2003). ("His core belief, sometimes intimated, sometimes stated explicitly, is that the millennium will come when the English and presumably others have become virtuous and free, rejecting all the forces that promote servility, be they popes or bishops or kings or any other such idols.")

[67] Milton, *Areopagitica* at 747 (cited in note 12).

[68] Id at 742.

(Catholic vs. Protestant, ritual vs. conscience); (3) cold vs. warm (frozen vs. fluid, inert vs. energetic, static vs. dynamic); (4) neutral vs. committed (passive vs. active, obedient vs. independent); and (5) divided vs. united (partial vs. whole).

Milton cares as much about order as he does about virtue, indeed he finds each integral to the other, as can be seen by tracing how these five dichotomies serve his argument in tandem. More remains to be said to capture the full measure of his understanding of virtue and order, but a key point to make at this stage is that Milton's argument for free printing has little in common with later arguments that treat the freedoms of thought and speech as instances of a general right to be free of unnecessary restraint or tutelage or a general right to express or exercise one's individuality. Milton is no libertarian, and only in the broadest sense of the term verging on the meaningless can he be labeled a liberal. Neither is he a pluralist. And he certainly is not a moral skeptic, nor much of an epistemic one. Regarding the latter, his belief that God's method is to "deal out by degrees his beam, so as our earthly eyes may best sustain it"[69] and his admonition not to "pitch our tent here"[70] marry the limits of human understanding to the possibility of epistemic progress. The *Areopagitica* is an argument from design for free printing as a means to the end of serving a demanding God, albeit a God whose demands center on individual choice, effort, curiosity, and discipline.

An argument from design is bounded in its coverage by its rationale, as are arguments of other sorts such as those from necessity, experience, commitment, or predicted consequences. If certain activities do not perform a function in the design, they are not covered by the argument, unless there exists a strategic reason to cover them in order to protect other activities that do serve such a function. Milton announces at the end of the tract that his thirty-plus pages of riveting, imaginative, overflowing, visionary argumentation apply only to differences within bounds, not disagreement over basics. His adversaries "stumble and are impatient at the least dividing of one visible congregation from another, though it be not in fundamentals." In calling for free printing, Milton reassures his reader that "neighboring differences, or rather indifferences, are what I speak of,

---

[69] Id at 748.

[70] Id at 741.

whether in some point of doctrine or of discipline, which though they be many, yet need not interrupt the unity of spirit."[71]

To the chagrin of his modern admirers, Milton gives examples of ways of thinking that lie beyond the bounds of his unity of spirit, and thus do not serve the theological/moral/political order his proposed regime is meant to enable. "I mean not tolerated popery," he says, "and open superstition, which as it extirpates all religions and civil supremacies, so itself should be extirpate." He goes on to exclude "that also which is impious or evil absolutely either against faith or manners." "[N]o law can possibly permit" such writings, Milton says, "that intends not to unlaw itself."[72] His argument, he makes clear, is not about toleration as a first principle or free-standing individual right. Rather, it is about the understanding that can result from vigorous contestation among members of a faith community who "all cannot be of one mind—as who looks they should be?"[73] and who are regrettably prone to generate "subdichotomies of petty schisms,"[74] but who nonetheless share sufficient common ground as to be eligible to experience the Pauline "unity of spirit"[75] that is the essence of Christian Liberty.

In short, Milton's theology, and the political theory he derives therefrom, is informed by how much he and his compatriots need continually to learn—and also how much they stand to gain by trying to learn—even as ultimate knowledge is beyond the reach of fallen man. Inquiry, he maintains, is the key to God's order. Such inquiry requires "the liberty to know, to utter, and to argue freely according to conscience."[76] It also requires spiritual qualities that some would-be speakers and writers do not possess.

VII. IMPLICATIONS BEYOND LICENSING

Perhaps the most basic interpretative question presented by the *Areopagitica* is whether the tract has anything to say about efforts to regulate speech by means other than licensing. When Milton

---

[71] Milton, *Areopagitica* at 747 (cited in note 12).

[72] Id at 747.

[73] Id at 735.

[74] Id.

[75] Milton, *Areopagitica* at 735 (cited in note 12).

[76] Id at 746.

specifies the targets of his criticism, usually he chooses terms that suggest he is talking only about a comprehensive requirement that all writings be submitted to an administrative censor before publication. For example, the paternalism he objects to consists of distrust, supplication, certification, and loss of control over timing that characterizes administrative censorship to a much greater degree than other forms of regulation. An author who is prosecuted after publication, or enjoined, or made to pay civil damages for causing personal injury with his words, does not suffer the indignity of being made to "trudge to his leave-giver."[77] Such an author does not have his serious work, the product of "the hardest labor in the deep mines of knowledge,"[78] judged by "the cursory eyes of temporizing or extemporizing licenser."[79] His regulators do not "keep a narrow bridge of licensing where the challenger should pass."[80] His audiences are not considered to be "in such a sick and weak state of faith and discretion, as to be able to take nothing down but through the pipe of a licenser."[81]

Moreover, Milton's repeated arguments from futility, among his most powerful to a modern reader, have greater purchase as applied to licensing compared to other forms of regulation. Regulation by means of criminal punishment, tort damages, or injunction is designed to be selective. The initiative lies with the regulators. The need for prioritization lowers the bar for measuring efficacy. The comprehensiveness of a licensing regime makes it not only intrusive, expensive, and unwieldy, but also destined to suffer endemic evasions.

Still another reason to read *Areopagitica* as tailored to the specific characteristics of licensing is the emphasis Milton places on the disputational environment. Like most early proponents of free speech, he operates at the level of the society as a whole. He seeks a highly energized, dynamic, fearless collective quest for understanding. Think of the perpetually flowing fountain,[82] the army of "true warfaring" Christians scouting "into the regions of sin and falsity" by means of "books promiscuously read,"[83] the "much writing, much arguing,

---

[77] Id at 735.

[78] Id at 746.

[79] Milton, *Areopagitica* at 735 (cited in note 12).

[80] Id at 747.

[81] Id at 737.

[82] Id at 739.

[83] Milton, *Areopagitica* at 728–29 (cited in note 12).

many opinions" of "knowledge in the making."[84] All regulation of speech threatens to slow down and take the edge off of these energizing activities, but especially licensing with its comprehensive reach, placement of the burden of inertia, built-in delays, distrust, predictable administrative rigidity and mediocrity, and escalating severity born of futility.

On the other hand, there are some important specific features of Milton's argument, features he emphasizes, that surely carry over to the regulation of speech by means other than licensing. Among the most important is the positive value he sees in confronting evil and dangerous ideas. By the logic of his argument, the search for understanding would be much worse off were those ideas not to be available as foils and provocations and were authors and readers not seasoned by the experience of engaging them. It is true that licensing more than other means of regulation threatens to suppress ideas to the point of making them unavailable, but the difference is only in degree. One objective of criminal sanctions is to deter future transgressions. There is every reason to believe that a regime that eschews licensing but systematically punishes authors after publication for lines crossed or harms done will on that account lose much of the writing that Milton values, both because some authors will steer far wide of the danger zone of prosecution and many who don't and are prosecuted will alter their ways going forward. Although his concern for the discursive environment might suggest that Milton should be especially hostile to licensing, his emphasis on the disputational energy level of the society should also make him more sensitive than most advocates of free speech to the chilling effects of criminal and civil liability postpublication.

Furthermore, Milton claims that "the best and surest suppressing" is not subsequent punishment but rather the confuting of falsehood.[85] He says there "would be little work left for preaching if law and compulsion should grow so fast upon those things which heretofore were governed only by exhortation."[86] These arguments from divine design apply to any form of legal regulation of printing.

Milton's arguments from the value of confronting falsehood, from the dynamic nature of truth and the consequent value of an ener-

---

[84] Id at 743.

[85] Id at 746.

[86] Id at 727.

gizing environment of collective inquiry, from the comparative efficacy of controlling evil ideas by means of refutation, and from the role in the divine plan of free choosing by fallen man all have application not only to licensing but also to other means of regulating writing. In that respect, his arguments cannot be cabined in the narrow (in modern times) domain of comprehensive administrative licensing, even as, like a good lawyer, Milton in *Areopagitica* takes care to shape his presentation to the case at hand, leaving more wide-ranging implications to be teased out by his readers.

VIII. ASYMMETRIC TREATMENT OF CONSEQUENCES

Milton makes a variety of strong claims regarding how unlicensed printing can advance both English republicanism and the "reforming of Reformation itself"[87] by virtue of how readers are enlightened, challenged, tempted, corrected, energized, and inspired by the bold, conscientious writing that is the subject of the tract. His argument depends on the proposition that ideas can be powerful, capable of penetrating to the inner person and altering the reader's understanding, character, and motivation to act. However, the causal link that Milton perceives between writer and reader seems to be stronger when he is waxing eloquent about the potential good effects of his proposed regime for republicanism and religion than when he is minimizing the harms of infection, temptation, and distraction that can follow from free printing. In this regard, is the argument of *Areopagitica* internally inconsistent? If ideas have the power to "spring up armed men,"[88] why should we assume that those men will be disproportionately soldiers of an enlightened rather than misguided religious or political order—or no order at all?

There can be no need to demonstrate how numerous, various, profound, and enduring are the salutary effects upon readers that Milton believes will ensue from trusting authors with "the liberty to know, to utter, and to argue freely according to conscience."[89] The fourth and final part of the *Areopagitica*—the longest and most eloquent part—is a veritable catalog of such posited good effects. The key question, so far as Milton's consistency is concerned, is why he

---

[87] Milton, *Areopagitica* at 743 (cited in note 12).

[88] Id at 720.

[89] Id at 746.

does not deploy his extraordinary gift for imaginative description to impress upon the reader the multifarious ways that false teachers, left unregulated, can harm gullible readers and vulnerable third parties. His discussion of "infection" does not deny or minimize the phenomenon but neither does he elaborate upon the scope or severity of the danger. Rather, Milton argues that any attempt to root out infection will threaten "the fall of learning and of all ability in disputation."[90] The harms of temptation and distraction ("vain things") are double-edged, he asserts, in that they present opportunities for self-control. These are clever responses, not without some validity, but they lead one to wonder whether Milton doubts the power of bad ideas, at least those generated by persons arguing freely according to conscience, to spread and thereby cause serious harm.

His belief in divine providence might suggest as much. Shortly after he observes that Truth "needs no policies, nor stratagems, nor licensings to make her victorious,"[91] Milton explains that when false teachers are "busiest in seducing" God then "raises to his own work men of rare abilities" to set things right. However, what is most notable about this passage is that under the providential dispensation that Milton embraces, human agency plays an important role, hence the saving work of the "men of rare abilities" and the danger posed by ill-conceived laws like the Licensing Order of 1643.[92] Even if the ultimate triumph of good over evil is preordained under "the Angels' ministry at the end of mortal things,"[93] it is imperative that fallen man "ordain wisely as in this world of evil, in the midst whereof God hath placed us unavoidably."[94] In this respect, the potency and resilience of bad ideas, as well as their susceptibility to human containment by noncoercive means, is something that Milton needs to consider. Faith in divine providence does not free him from this obligation. But his belief in the intervention of divine providence in the present, as "the state of man now is,"[95] informs his assessment of the net damage that evil ideas can cause. And that intervention, as he understands it, is to

---

[90] Id at 730.

[91] Milton, *Areopagitica* at 747 (cited in note 12).

[92] See Lewalski, *Milton and the Millennium* at 18 (cited in note 66).

[93] Milton, *Areopagitica* at 747 (cited in note 12).

[94] Id at 733.

[95] Id at 728.

make divine Truth "strong, next to the Almighty" when apprehended by fallen mortals reading and arguing with the requisite "unity of spirit."[96] So strong, it seems, that false teachings, even when widely disseminated in the absence of licensing, are no match.

The point is that Milton's unbalanced treatment of the consequences of free printing, his disproportionate attention to the good effects, derives from his transcendent faith in the power of good ideas, a faith which is the product of his particular theological commitments. *Areopagitica* disappoints the modern reader with its inattention to the risks and costs of unlicensed printing, but that is no mark against Milton because the logic of his argument does not depend on the claim that evil ideas will not achieve wide dissemination and considerable impact in the absence of regulation. Even if many bad consequences were to occur as a result of unlicensed printing, he would consider the cost to be acceptable. His twin causes of republicanism and Reformation, both of which he views as dependent in an elemental way on free inquiry and communication, would take priority.

In this view, his case for free inquiry and critical argumentation "according to conscience,"[97] if not necessarily for all manner of free expression, does not turn on how much harm it causes. However much that harm is, it is dwarfed by the fundamental, generative, perpetually-renewing good of "knowledge in the making."[98]

IX. Enduring Ideas

One way to read Milton is with an eye to his possible impact on subsequent thought about the freedom of speech. His argument in *Areopagitica* is notable for its reliance on the high value of free writing rather than doubt about the capacity of ideas to cause harm; its recognition that not every form or act of writing embodies that high value; its thesis that exposure to bad ideas can lead to a deeper understanding of and stronger commitment to good ideas; its claim that "confuting is the best and surest suppressing";[99] its derivation of freedoms from duties; its focus on audience interests rather than

---

[96] Id at 747.

[97] Milton, *Areopagitica* at 746 (cited in note 12).

[98] Id at 743.

[99] Id at 746.

those of speakers; its synthesis of dynamic, contingent phenomena and perdurable, foundational commitments; its attention to individual character and communal spirit, and more generally its view of individual freedom as instrumental to collective achievement; and its premise that freedom of (disciplined) thought is the transcendent value. Each of these ideas has been appropriated and refined by one or another subsequent thinker of note. All figure prominently in the free speech tradition. That said, I consider the following four ideas to constitute the core of the *Areopagitica*'s accomplishment going forward.

A. THE DERACINATION OF HERESY

Milton's most important contribution to the modern understanding of the freedom of speech is the way his argument in *Areopagitica* lays the groundwork for the eventual discrediting of the concept of heresy, an idea that historically has played a prominent, mischievous role in both religious and civil discourse. Some persons are comfortable with belief systems that treat all propositions claiming truth value as contingent and perspectival, but many persons—probably most—are not. There is a powerful impulse to treat at least some ideas as constitutive of a regime or a faith, such that denials of their truth are seen as subversive and disqualifying for membership in the community. Milton demonstrates that one can hold certain ideas to be fundamental and essential yet still need to hear them challenged. He achieves this with four different but related arguments.

First, he asserts over and over again how important it is not simply to hold true ideas but to hold them in the correct way. Preserving a "fugitive and cloistered virtue" will not do.[100] To understand truth and virtue fully, one must "scout into the regions of sin and falsity."[101] Doing so helps the holder of a truth "to discover, to confute, to forewarn, and to illustrate."[102] A person who takes his beliefs on faith or authority can be "a heretic in the truth" says Milton, even when his received opinions are in fact true: "if he believes things only because his pastor says so, or the Assembly so determines, without knowing other reason, though his belief be true, yet the very truth he holds

---

[100] Id at 728.

[101] Milton, *Areopagitica* at 729 (cited in note 12).

[102] Id at 727.

becomes his heresy."[103] Notice that in this key passage he does not renounce the concept of heresy but rather redefines it. In his view, the transgression that separates a person from the community is not believing a proposition that is forbidden but rather coming to and retaining a belief by means of a forbidden process of unthinking deference to authority or custom.[104]

Milton was by no means the first important thinker to emphasize the "how" over the "what" in matters of fundamental belief. The distinguished Milton scholar Nigel Smith traces this priority to the concept of *proairesis*—the practice of informed, reasoned choice—in ancient Greek philosophy. The contrary privileging of "what" over "how" derives, he explains, from the "Augustinian understanding of heresy as that which is forbidden and to be expunged from believers, making them if need be the object of persecution." According to Smith, the *Areopagitica* makes "a forceful plea" for embracing the Greek rather than Augustinian ideal.[105] One might even speculate that Milton's choice of title for his tract may have had something to do with his admiration for the Greek ideal of *proairesis*.[106]

Second, "in the field of this world" good and evil are not as easily separated as the traditional conception of heresy assumes. They "grow up together almost inseparably." The knowledge of good is "involved and interwoven with the knowledge of evil, and in so many cunning resemblances is hardly to be discerned."[107] Attempting to purge books of their heretical ideas would result in "the fall of learning." False appearances and precipitant judgment compound the cost of trying to eradicate ideas that are considered to be heretical in themselves.

Third, his critique of excessive attention to form at the expense of spirit and character, manifested throughout *Areopagitica* in imagery

---

[103] Id at 739.

[104] See Tobias Gregory, *How Milton Defined Heresy and Why*, 45 Religion & Literature 148, 151 (2013).

[105] See Nigel Smith, *Paradise Lost and Heresy*, in Nicholas McDowell and Nigel Smith, eds, *The Oxford Handbook of Milton* 508 (2009). For a detailed argument that *Areopagitica*'s notion of "knowing good by evil" represents a pronounced rejection of Augustine's restrictive conception of human agency in the postlapsarian condition, see Dennis Richard Danielson, *Milton's Good God* 164–77 (Cambridge, 1982).

[106] Regarding Milton's affinity for the notion of *proairesis*, see Janel Mueller, *Milton on Heresy*, in Stephen B. Dobranski and John P. Rumrich, eds, *Milton and Heresy* (Cambridge, 1998).

[107] Milton, *Areopagitica* at 728 (cited in note 12).

exalting the inner over the outer, the essential over the superficial, helps to explain why the conventional understanding of heresy is a regulatory concept that cannot serve a worthy end. Punishment for heresy in the traditional sense seeks only a false order—"the forced and outward union of cold and neutral and inwardly divided minds"[108]—and thereby thwarts the construction of a true kind of order based on trust, commitment, and mutual responsibility. Because the regulation of printing typically is imbued with imprecision and futility, the act of licensing has the character of a formal gesture, a regulatory show. Central to Milton's thought in several domains—religion, poetry, politics, education, marriage—is his objection to reliance on forms as a substitute for having to choose wisely. Those who would regulate writings judge them superficially for several reasons, but important among them is the fact that most of the time the censorship of ideas is not really meant to be a discriminating gesture. It is intended rather to be a formal discharge of regulatory responsibility or a public affirmation of conventional forms of authority and thought. No justification for regulating speech embodies this formalism so much as the claim that certain beliefs as such may not be entertained no matter how worthy is the process by which the believer has come to hold them.

Fourth, Milton is able to discredit the conventional understanding of heresy even while basing his argument on the need to facilitate a supremely important and ambitious truth-seeking process that assumes the existence of genuine moral and religious knowledge. He does this by embracing one kind of skepticism but not another. He is not the least bit skeptical about the existence of enduring truths, political as well as divine, that are accessible to human inquiry. But he is impressed by how difficult and error-ridden is the process by which fallible human beings in a fallen world go about trying to discover and live those truths. In such a world of partial understanding, the attempt to classify beliefs in themselves as grounds for punishment is misconceived. Persons who err while undertaking a sincere effort to understand in the light of scripture, reason, and spirit working together deserve both charity and membership in the community of inquirers.

Milton makes strong, controversial claims about the nature of truth and the best way to attain meaningful understanding. Many of his

---

[108] Id at 742.

particular prescriptions are a product of his unique situation and do not translate well to other times and places. But in demonstrating how one can believe in genuine community-defining truths and still have no use for the traditional conception of heresy, Milton advances the case for toleration immeasurably.[109] As his treatment of Catholic idolatry and unspecified non-Catholic practices that are "evil absolutely" indicates, in theory Milton's analysis could justify punishment for excessive passivity and conformity in the realm of belief or, at the other end of the spectrum, impulsive, fanciful, provocative religious assertion that flouts the Protestant duty of earnest, informed, patient, disciplined, independent spiritual inquiry. But given the Pauline imperative of charity that he invokes ("provided first that all charitable and compassionate means be used to regain the weak and the misled")[110] and the practical difficulty of judging transgressions of method and spirit rather than content, Milton's redefinition of heresy implies its demise as an operational matter, his stated exclusions for popery and impiety notwithstanding.

Many of the arguments that he advances to undercut the claim that the traditional conception of heresy is a defining feature of a faith community also have purchase in pluralistic regimes, such as modern Western democracies. For his insistence that there are better and worse ways of holding beliefs and positive value to confronting suspect, even offensive and dangerous, ideas—"knowing good by evil"[111]—does much to justify what may be the essential commitment in any broad-based ethic of toleration: the assumption that the benefits of free inquiry and respect for sincere belief are such important goods that the harms they can cause must be endured, except in rare, narrowly defined circumstances. Milton demonstrates how even persons who are committed to certain beliefs, whether on grounds of knowledge or experience or faith or attachment or identity, have good reasons to learn, consider, and respond to what others are thinking. Even if there are severe limits to human understanding and (contrary to Milton's view) no transcendent sources of value and duty, what he observes about the individual and collective processes of inquiry and judgment provides reasons to attend to the thought of others, if only

---

[109] See Benjamin Myers, *"Following the Way Which Is Called Heresy": Milton and the Heretical Imperative*, 69 J History of Ideas 375, 392–93 (2008).

[110] Milton, *Areopagitica* at 747 (cited in note 12).

[111] Id.

for purposes of scavenging and testing. One need not exalt truth-seeking in the way that Milton does to acknowledge that in a pluralistic regime designed to govern a theologically and philosophically diverse population, the ways that persons and groups develop and defend their conflicting understandings can matter. Milton's memorable accounts of deceiving appearances, incremental enlightenment, energizing effects, layers of understanding, overreaction to small differences, and the dynamic character of belief can be appropriated in service of the proposition that free speech is an activity of particular importance in such regimes.

The greatest achievement of modern First Amendment law is its hard-won abolition of the concepts of heresy and its cousin sedition. Today, would-be regulators of speech have to demonstrate the risk of material harm. As a matter of principle, proving error or incompatibility with fundamental tenets is never enough. From a historical perspective, that is a remarkable development, and Milton deserves some of the credit.

B. FREE SPEECH ENVIRONMENTALISM

Milton's argument for free printing is distinctive even among audience-centered arguments in the degree to which it emphasizes the impact of regulation on the overall environment of public disputation. He cares fervently that what he takes to be the relevant community maintain a vibrant discursive spirit bursting with inquisitive energy. He argues that licensing saps that spirit by virtue of the disrespect to authors and audiences it embodies, the delays and opportunities for corruption and incompetent exercise of authority it creates, and the false order it imposes. One might say that he cares about what modern doctrine labels the "chilling effect." This is true and important, and something contemporary First Amendment thinkers can build on without having to share his religious premises. Many of Milton's multifarious, imaginative arguments relating to intellectual independence pitted against conventional understanding have a general thrust. They address ways that unsettling ideas of *various* sorts can germinate, penetrate defenses, sustain themselves, and proliferate, as well as how such salutary ferment can be threatened by predictable dynamics of regulatory rigidity and abuse.

One might even think that Milton's emphasis in this respect is a precursor of the modern Court's reigning doctrinal shibboleth, first articulated in *New York Times v Sullivan*, "that debate on public issues should be uninhibited, robust, and wide-open."[112] The Justices have invoked this ideal in a range of cases, both to expand the scope of activities considered to be within the domain of First Amendment coverage and to disallow various forms of regulation designed to make public debate more balanced, civil, transparent, or factually accurate. Across a broad spectrum of problems, "more speech is always better" has become the clinching argument in First Amendment adjudication.[113]

Milton, however, issues no such call for unbounded verbal insouciance. He has nothing to say about the value of speech for its own sake or as a means of letting off steam or being provocative in order to irritate, intimidate, or fuel resentment. He does not address the role that speech plays in the competition for power and influence. Learning, not self-expression, is what he takes to be the benefit of free printing. Milton is all about discipline and duty. He does not claim about all speech that "more is always better," rather that more informed, pious, even if bold and unsettling *inquiry* is always better. Harms caused by "uninhibited" speakers not engaged in such inquiry are beyond the scope of his argument.

Although Milton does not believe that more speech is always better among ill-motivated or impious speakers, he does claim that more exposure to sin and falsehood can be highly beneficial to the serious thinkers he is most concerned about, and not only because such exposure requires them as individuals to exercise the discipline and commitment to resist temptation and refute specious arguments. He regards the vanquishing of sin and falsity as a collective project, symbolized by his vision of England as the "mansion house of liberty"[114] inhabited by armies of energetic, bold thinkers with their pens and lamps continually engaged in "the reforming of Reformation itself."[115] He maintains that the acquisition and active maintenance of knowledge depends on both courageous individuals and a supportive environment, and he argues that licensing not only thwarts the former but enervates the latter.

---

[112] 376 US 254, 270 (1964).

[113] See, e.g., *United States v Alvarez*, 132 S Ct 2537, 2550 (2012); *Sorrell v IMS Health, Inc.*, 131 S Ct 2653, 2675 (2011); *Citizens United v FEC*, 558 US 310, 355, 361 (2010).

[114] Milton, *Areopagitica* at 743 (cited in note 12).

[115] Id.

Milton's "free speech environmentalism" can be seen as a contribution that is not confined to the way it serves his own uncommonly ambitious argument. A regime that understands the principle of freedom of speech to have a different rationale, a wider scope, and less exalted objectives than what he urges nevertheless can draw on his environmentalism. The discursive environment can be important in a speaker-centered view of the freedom of speech as well as in Milton's duty-driven, audience-centered understanding. Even autonomy-based accounts of the freedom of speech sometimes stress the central role of the surrounding environment in facilitating the speaker's development, dignity, and choice.[116] Regarding the indiscriminate "more is always better" presumption, a supportive environment, especially one that energizes its participants, can be a significant factor in stimulating speech designed to advance the narrow objectives of the speaker no less than the speech of disciplined inquiry in the service of the common good or the divine plan.

His claim that true freedom requires a spirit of boldness in the air that can be dissipated by distrustful, prescriptive regulatory ordering might be considered to apply across a wide range of activities. Even though different arguments from those that Milton offers are needed to establish that communicative self-assertion as such is an activity worthy of special regard in its own right,[117] such self-assertion could have instrumental value by virtue of its contribution to the overall energy level that he prizes. In this way, his insights regarding what is needed for valuable freedoms to flourish might help to justify a far broader understanding of the freedom of speech than Milton himself ever would have embraced.

Actually, he was relatively capacious among the free speech advocates of his day in the breadth of the principle he defended. Although he did not extend his principle of protection to "popery," "open superstition," or that which is "evil absolutely,"[118] neither did most of his peers.[119] Where Milton's notion of coverage was broad for

---

[116] See Joseph Raz, *Free Expression and Personal Identification*, 11 Oxford J Legal Studies 303 (1991); Seana Valentine Shiffrin, *A Thinker-Based Approach to Freedom of Speech*, 27 Const Comm 283 (2011).

[117] Dean Post is critical of modern doctrine for treating as self-evident the proposition that the First Amendment protects "speech as such" independent of the function served. See Robert Post, *Recuperating First Amendment Doctrine*, 47 Stan L Rev 1249, 1279 (1995).

[118] Milton, *Areopagitica* at 747 (cited in note 12).

[119] See Arthur Barker, *Milton and the Puritan Dilemma* 93–94 (Toronto, 1942). The most notable exception was Milton's friend, Roger Williams. See Thomas N. Corns, *John Milton*,

its time was in the instrumental value he found in the speech of the radical sectaries, whose ideas were viewed by most observers as blasphemous and irresponsible. He respected the sectaries not out of compassion or because their humanity required it. Rather, he thought their strange ideas might have something to contribute to his own understanding and that of others, and not only by serving as a foil. For "if it comes to prohibiting, there is not aught more likely to be prohibited than truth itself, whose first appearances to our eyes, bleared and dimmed with prejudice and custom, is more unsightly and implausible than many errors, even as the person is of many a great man slight and contemptuous to see to."[120] Furthermore, apart from the possibility that genuine truths might be lurking in their provocative ideas, Milton valued the radical sectaries for their example of intellectual independence and courage, as well as their contribution to collective energy.

So why didn't he apply such reasoning to the speech of Catholics? This question is worth an article in its own right, but one might begin by noting that he denied even the possibility that genuine truths might be lurking in Catholic theology. God might "deal out by degrees his beam"[121] but the falsity of Catholicism was, to Milton's mind, a divine judgment already dealt out. Even if true, however, there remains the objection that an argument urging readers to "scout into the regions of sin and falsity"[122] so as to facilitate "knowing good by evil"[123] would seem to be served by the availability of Catholic writings.[124] If Milton's exclusion of Catholicism can be defended at all within the terms of his overall argument, his concern for free speech environmentalism offers the best prospect. Catholic ecclesiastic hierarchy, seductive ritual, and systematic persecution of heretics constituted, in his view, the supreme threat to sustaining an environment of intellectual independence and inquisitive energy. In no way did he consider Catholic theology and practice to be a possible source of

---

Roger Williams, and the Limits of Toleration, in Sharon Achinstein and Elizabeth Sauer, eds, *Milton and Toleration* 72–85 (Oxford, 2007). See generally Norah Carlin, *Toleration for Catholics in the Puritan Revolution*, in Ole Peter Grell and Bob Scribner, eds, *Tolerance and Intolerance in the European Reformation* 216 (Cambridge, 1996).

[120] Milton, *Areopagitica* at 748 (cited in note 12).

[121] Id.

[122] Id at 729.

[123] Id at 728.

[124] See Thomas N. Corns, *John Milton: The Prose Works* 59 (Twayne, 1998).

those invaluable public goods.[125] In that regard, the speech of the sectaries was very different.

C. THE CENTRE CANNOT HOLD

Milton's consistent attention to the practical realities of speech regulation is one of his important legacies. In his case, astonishing creativity was not a substitute for, but rather a product of, shrewd observation and demanding appraisal. He was a close student and admirer of Machiavelli, hence his emphasis on political energy. The *Areopagitica* is couched in the argot of political realism: "to sequester out of the world in Atlantic and Utopian polities which can never be drawn into use will not mend our condition," Milton states. Instead, he urges his readers to "ordain wisely . . . in this world of evil."[126] In Book VIII of *Paradise Lost*, the angel Raphael counsels Adam: "be lowly wise. . . . Dream not of other worlds."[127]

The lowly wisdom of *Areopagitica* is considerable. Milton insists, for example, that the policy of licensing cannot be assessed without taking into account the capacities, working conditions, loyalties, and temperaments of the persons who will serve as licensers. In a way, he anticipates the modern attention to institutional incentives as a key factor in First Amendment analysis. Still another practical feature of licensing he identifies is how responsibility for the censorial decision is often divided and accountability thereby evaded. His image of "five Imprimaturs . . . seen together dialoguewise in the piazza of one titlepage, complimenting and ducking each to other"[128] captures this phenomenon—a problem, we might believe, that also plagues the modern administrative state.

In recounting the history of licensing, he observes that the authority to regulate speech was routinely abused. Licensers did not "stay in matters heretical" but rather asserted control over "any subject that was not to their palate."[129] Much of modern free speech doctrine is

---

[125] For a comprehensive account of Milton's treatment of Catholics in his polemics, see Andrew Hadfield, *Milton and Catholicism*, in Achinstein and Sauer, *Milton and Toleration* 186 (cited in note 119).

[126] Id at 732–33.

[127] John Milton, *Paradise Lost*, Book VIII, lines 173–75 (1674), in *John Milton, Complete Poems and Major Prose* 211, 367 (cited in note 1).

[128] Milton, *Areopagitica* at 724 (cited in note 12).

[129] Id.

founded upon generalized distrust of regulatory motives, even as adjudication of such motives in individual cases is deemed impractical for the most part. In the *Areopagitica* Milton mercilessly harnesses his formidable satiric talent to urge such distrust.

Milton's most interesting practical argument is an observation about the cumulative effect of several of his discrete points regarding corruption, futility, unintended consequences, mediocrity, frustration, and the true sources of order. In essence, he argues that, as a practical matter, there can be no such thing as a measured, disciplined, rational censorship. Inevitably, licensing "will prove the most unlicensed book itself."[130] The choice, he maintains, is between the regime of free printing that he advocates and the severe Counter-Reformation "model of Trent and Seville."[131] There is no middle ground.

Even if in modern times the choice is not so stark, Milton makes a lasting contribution by deploying piercing ridicule to discredit the notion of speech regulation ever being conducted with a light touch. His compelling images of administrative arrogance, corruption, and mindless rigidity should always be part of the equation as each new threat or outrage generates well-meaning proposals for limited, carefully confined restrictions on speech.

D. THE CLAIMS OF POSTERITY

Another enduring contribution of Milton's is his insistence that the value of free thinking and writing be assessed with due regard for its possible long-range benefits. In discussing the suppression of ideas, he laments that "revolutions of ages do not oft recover the loss of a rejected truth, for the want of which whole nations fare the worse."[132] Necessarily, the net effects of free thinking over time must be highly speculative. Because truth is dynamic and experiential, something to be lived rather than possessed, its long-term benefits cannot be computed objectively or precisely. For Milton, that is not a sufficient reason to ignore or discount them. Despite his keen interest in the burgeoning scientific discoveries of his age,[133] Milton never succumbed to the scientistic fallacy of wanting to accord significance in his quest

---

[130] Id at 749.

[131] Id at 734.

[132] Milton, *Areopagitica* at 720 (cited in note 12).

[133] See John Rogers, *The Matter of Revolution: Science, Poetry, and Politics in the Age of Milton* 146–47 (Cornell, 1996). During his only visit to the European continent, Milton secured an

for understanding only to matters that can be rigorously observed and measured.[134] The long term is what mattered most in his mature intellectual universe, notwithstanding the need to rely heavily on unprovable teachings of history and suppositions about character, behavior, and tendency that such a priority entails.

In taking the long view, and refusing to be paralyzed by the obvious difficulty of predicting future consequences, Milton addresses a structural difficulty of the case for protecting free speech. The harms that unpopular speech—the kind that generates regulatory responses—can cause are often salient in the short run, the benefits less so. That is especially true of the benefits from speech that relate to character development, necessarily a slow process. Similarly, giving due regard to benefits that take the form of providing ideas or observations that future inquirers can put to better use than can their originators requires both a long-term perspective and an appreciation of how this dynamic has virtually defined the course of learning throughout history. Even the more specific benefit of correcting error by means of refutation is seldom realized directly, expeditiously, and without relapse. One-on-one persuasion usually is a matter of creating doubt that leads over time to a change of mind. Moving the needle of public opinion by means of reasoned argument or empirical demonstration rather than demagoguery typically is an even more drawn-out phenomenon.

Milton was well equipped to focus on the future and the arc of history. Almost every day of his life was devoted to scriptural study (in the original languages of Hebrew, Greek, and Aramaic), including of course the prophecies that dominate the Old Testament. We think of Milton primarily as a poet but he was also a historian, having written a lengthy history of England and even a short history of Russia.[135] His considerable interest in Machiavelli was mainly in the Florentine's historiographic theories. It is no accident that the form of poetry that from an early age Milton aspired to write was epic poetry, modeled on his hero Virgil. Characteristically, Milton begins his multifaceted

---

introduction to Galileo, a meeting he mentions in *Areopagitica*. Milton, *Areopagitica* at 737–38 (cited in note 12).

[134] Apart from disdain for simple-minded scientism, Milton experienced "ambivalence about the new science" on account of what he took to be its adverse impact on sophisticated metaphysical inquiry, whether due to the exaltation of the mechanistic in the manner of Hobbes or the categorical separation of the material and the spiritual in the manner of Descartes. See Stephen M. Fallon, *Milton Among the Philosophers* 135 (Cornell, 1991).

[135] See Barbara K. Lewalski, *The Life of John Milton* 198 (Blackwell, 2000).

argument in *Areopagitica* with an effort to distill the lessons of history regarding the regulation of speech. He ends *Paradise Lost* with an extended conversation in which the angel Michael narrates to Adam two thousand years of the history to come in order that the progenitor of the human race, about to be expelled from Eden, may "[g]ood with bad expect to hear, supernal grace contending with the sinfulness of man, thereby to learn true patience. . . ."[136]

The *Areopagitica* is vulnerable to modern criticism in that it does not say much about the immediate and short-run harms that speech can cause. This omission, if such it be, may well be due to Milton's assumption that what matters most is the long-term ledger. On the subject of the supposed long-term costs of free printing, no less than the long-term benefits, he has a great deal to say. The most feared long-term cost in his day—and quite possibly even in ours—was the specter of incremental anarchy, the gradual unraveling of the achievements of civilization. It is no exaggeration to say that Milton's addressing of that concern takes up fully half of his tract. The *Areopagitica* is at pains on almost every page to prove that the "bonds and ligaments"[137] that hold a political community together consist much more of mutual trust and education in history and duty than in coercive measures. His many paeans to dynamism are about how order depends on continual adaptation, renewal, and active "closing up truth to truth." The regulators who seek to stamp out the "much arguing, much writing, many opinions" that grow out of those endeavors are the real "dividers of unity," he maintains.[138]

Besides disorder, the long-term cost that most concerned supporters of the Licensing Order was error. Here I mean something different from heresy, which has connotations of separation and disobedience. Quite apart from those perceived moral and membership failings, error was seen as a serious matter on account of its practical consequences. Clearly Milton believed, and argued fervently in *Areopagitica*, that error is more likely to follow from the silencing of independent thinkers and the entrenchment of received wisdom than from any misleading that bold, subversive ideas might accomplish. His reasons for holding that view are many, but most have in com-

---

[136] John Milton, *Paradise Lost*, Book XI, lines 358–61, in *John Milton, Complete Poems and Major Prose* 441 (cited in note 1).

[137] Milton, *Areopagitica* at 733 (cited in note 12).

[138] Id at 742–43.

mon the quality of taking into account phenomena such as character effects and corrective responses that play out over time. For example, he says:

> And though all the winds of doctrine were let loose to play upon the earth, so truth be in the field, we do injuriously by licensing and prohibiting, to misdoubt her strength. Let her and Falsehood grapple; who ever knew Truth put to the worse, in a free and open encounter.[139]

Many commentators, Alexander Meiklejohn among them,[140] have cited this passage to discredit Milton, accusing him of ungrounded optimism or reliance on a divine providence that many modern readers do not believe in. Both charges are plausible, the second in fact irrefutable. But Milton's claim about the strength of truth is more defensible regarding long-term patterns of understanding than it is for short-run effects. Admittedly, over time error can be entrenched by "the grip of custom"[141] or compounded by misbegotten extrapolation. Nevertheless, in an energetic, inquisitive society of the sort Milton envisioned, were licensing to be lifted much weeding out of false beliefs would very likely occur by means of both critical challenge and experiences of inefficacy. Both correctives, however, take time.

My point here is not that Milton is necessarily right in his optimism about the strength of truth, rather that his taking the long view is a distinctive contribution to the case for the freedom of speech because it makes available a more defensible argument grounded in the self-correcting dynamic of speech answering speech. Notice that the plausibility of effective if delayed correction is much greater when the harm that needs countering is the *persuasive* effect of false *ideas*. Not all error resulting from speech is caused by ideas. Not all speech harms derive from persuasion. Demagogic triggering of primordial, correction-proof anxieties and prejudices, intrusive or disruptive acts of communication, and costly methods of generating speech (such as child pornography, political fundraising, and animal torture) cause much of the harm that is traceable to speech. Milton's long view does not improve the assessment of communications that cause harm in these ways. Accordingly, *Areopagitica* tells us little about whether and how his understanding of the freedom of speech extends to disputes

---

[139] Id at 746.

[140] See Alexander Meiklejohn, *The First Amendment Is an Absolute*, 1961 Supreme Court Review 245, 263 (1961).

[141] Milton, *Areopagitica* at 747 (cited in note 12).

over such matters. His argument is about ideas and his claim is that truth has an advantage over the long haul in the wars of persuasion.

X. Expiring and Reviving Liberty

In none of his writings does Milton better express his belief in the power of persuasion over time than in the closing words of *The Ready and Easy Way to Establish a Free Commonwealth*, a pamphlet written in anguish in 1660 to protest the headlong rush of the strife-weary English people to restore the Stuart monarchy. Blind, betrayed by his countrymen and even by his erstwhile hero Cromwell,[142] eligible for execution on account of his polemics in defense of the regicide, he remained unbowed. Risking his freedom and possibly his life, he challenged the ascendant royalists by issuing an uncompromising indictment of monarchical government. As other republicans were busy trimming to protect their positions against the impending Restoration, he defiantly reaffirmed his commitment to the Good Old Cause, finding succor in the prospect of eventual political renewal:

> Thus much I should perhaps have said though I were sure I should have spoken only to trees and stones, and had none to cry to, but with the prophet, "O earth, earth, earth!" to tell the very soil itself what her perverse inhabitants are deaf to. Nay, though what I have spoke should happen . . . to be the last words of our expiring liberty. But I trust I shall have spoken persuasion to abundance of sensible and ingenuous men, to some perhaps, whom God may raise of these stones to become children of reviving liberty.[143]

Probably due to the intervention of friends in high places, when the Stuart monarchy returned to rule England three months later, Milton somehow escaped the executioner's axe.[144] Then he resumed work on his half-completed, most ambitious project of persuasion ever: an epic poem, addressed to his disillusioned, vanquished compatriots but also to posterity, designed amid defeat "to assert eternal providence and justify the ways of God to men."[145]

---

[142] See Blair Worden, *Literature and Politics in Cromwellian England: John Milton, Andrew Marvell, Marchamont Nedham* 245–46, 258–61 (Oxford, 2007).

[143] John Milton, *The Ready and Easy Way to Establish a Free Commonwealth* (1660), in *John Milton, Complete Poems and Major Prose* 880, 898 (cited in note 1).

[144] See Anna Beer, *Milton: Poet, Pamphleteer, and Patriot* 286–87 (Bloomsbury, 2008).

[145] John Milton, *Paradise Lost*, Book I, lines 25–26, in *John Milton, Complete Poems and Major Prose* 212 (cited in note 1).

RANDALL KENNEDY

WALKER v CITY OF BIRMINGHAM REVISITED

The Supreme Court of the United State has received high praise for its handling of civil liberties controversies arising from the racial conflicts of the Second Reconstruction. The story, Professor Harry Kalven, Jr., remarked, "is a happy and encouraging one," featuring a black protest movement blessed by "extraordinary tact and sure instinct" and "a gallant and sensitive Supreme Court." The two collaborated in producing, he maintained, "an appropriate and exciting reworking of First Amendment doctrine."[1] It is significant that Kalven wrote his encomium in 1965. Supporting his assessment are rulings in which the Court shielded the organizational privacy of the National Association for the Advancement of Colored People (NAACP), acknowledged litigation as a form of protected political expression, inhibited the squelching of massed dissent, and furnished journalists with new layers of insulation against potentially ruinous libel actions as they sought to inform the country about Jim Crow

---

Randall Kennedy is the Michael R. Klein Professor of Law, Harvard Law School.

AUTHOR'S NOTE: I thank Justin Driver, Richard Fallon, Owen Fiss, and the participants at a workshop at the Vanderbilt Law School for comments on an earlier draft. I am pleased to acknowledge as well the research and editorial assistance of Aabid Allibhai, Harvard Law School, JD 2018.

[1] Harry Kalven, Jr., *The Negro and the First Amendment* viii (Ohio State, 1965). See also Burt Neuborne, *The Gravitational Pull of Race on the Warren Court*, 2010 Supreme Court Review 59 (2010).

racial oppression in the Deep South.[2] As the sixties wore on, however, there emerged good reason to be less impressed by the Court's performance as a guardian of constitutional freedoms menaced by hostile officials. A striking instance of failure is *Walker v City of Birmingham.*[3]

The case arose from events that transpired in the spring of 1963, as movement activists focused as much pressure as they could muster against racist practices in Birmingham, Alabama. They confronted a formidable challenge.[4] White supremacist dogma and practices demanded and enforced preference for whites over blacks in virtually every social domain. A rigid racial bar subordinated blacks to whites at workplaces. Eating establishments were racially segregated, as were drinking fountains, dressing rooms, bathrooms, elevators, taxis, ambulances, and hotels. It was a crime for blacks and whites to play cards, checkers, or dice with one another. When a court ordered the desegregation of the city's recreation facilities, the municipal government closed them all—sixty-eight parks, thirty-eight playgrounds, six swimming pools, and four golf courses. Noting that in Birmingham a book depicting black rabbits associating with white rabbits had been banned, a correspondent for the *New York Times* observed that "every channel of communication, every medium of mutual interest, every reasoned approach, every inch of middle ground has been fragmented by the emotional dynamite of racism, reinforced by the whip, the ra-

---

[2] See *NAACP v Alabama*, 357 US 449 (1958); *NAACP v Button*, 371 US 415 (1963); *Edwards v South Carolina*, 372 US 229 (1963); *New York Times v Sullivan*, 376 US 254 (1964).

[3] 388 US 307 (1967). Commentaries on *Walker* that I have found to be particularly instructive include Patrick O. Gudridge, *Emergency, Legality, Sovereignty: Birmingham, 1963*, in Austin Sarat, ed, *Sovereignty, Emergency, Legality* (Cambridge, 2010); Owen Fiss, *The Civilizing Hand of the Law? Birmingham, 1963*, 89 Yale Rev 1 (2001); Martha Minow, *Politics and Procedure*, in David Kairys, ed, *The Politics of Law: A Progressive Critique* (Basic Books, 3d ed 1998); David Benjamin Oppenheimer, *Martin Luther King, Walker v. City of Birmingham, and the "Letter from Birmingham Jail*," 26 UC Davis L Rev 791 (1993); David Luban, *Difference Made Legal: The Court and Dr. King*, 87 Mich L Rev 2152 (1989); Alan F. Westin and Barry Mahoney, *The Trial of Martin Luther King* (Crowell, 1974); William H. Rodgers, Jr., *The Elusive Search for the Void Injunction: Res Judicata Principles in Criminal Contempt Proceedings*, 49 BU L Rev 251 (1969); Sheldon Tefft, *Neither Above the Law nor Below It: A Note on Walker v Birmingham*, 1967 Supreme Court Review 181 (1967).

[4] Martin Luther King, Jr. maintained that "Birmingham is probably the most thoroughly segregated city in the United States. Its ugly record of police brutality is known in every section of this country. Its unjust treatment of Negroes in the courts is a notorious reality. There have been more unsolved bombings of Negro homes and churches in Birmingham than any city in this nation." *Letter from Birmingham City Jail*, in James M. Washington, ed, *A Testament of Hope: The Essential Writings and Speeches of Martin Luther King, Jr.* 290 (Harper Collins, 1986).

zor, the gun, the bomb, the torch, the club, the knife, the mob, the police, and many branches of the state's apparatus."[5]

The most influential politicians in the state and city were white supremacists devoted to pigmentocracy. When Alabama's governor, George Corley Wallace, was inaugurated in January 1963, he vowed to fight for "segregation now, segregation tomorrow, and segregation forever."[6] Similarly fervent was Theophilus Eugene "Bull" Connor, the long-serving Commissioner of Public Safety in Birmingham, and a key figure in the *Walker* litigation. Disdaining due process rights that got in the way of repressing adversaries, Connor once ordered the arrest of three visiting Negro ministers simply because they had the temerity to meet with the city's leading civil rights crusader, Reverend Fred Shuttlesworth.[7] "We don't give a damn about the law," Connor confessed when questioned about the legality of the arrests. "Down here we make our own law. . . ."[8] Connor was also known for rhetoric shot through with malapropisms: "We're not going to have white folks and nigras segregatin' together in this man's town."[9]

In the spring of 1963, activists accelerated their efforts to challenge the Jim Crow regime, targeting businesses that discriminated against blacks as employees and customers. African Americans, for example, were no longer willing to shop for merchandise while being excluded from eating facilities reserved for whites. To protest, activists organized boycotts, marches, and sit-ins.

City officials responded initially by simply arresting protestors. Then, on the evening of Wednesday, April 10, 1963, officials deployed a different weapon. They applied for a temporary injunction

[5] See Oppenheimer, 26 UC Davis L Rev at 794–801 (cited in note 3); Westin and Mahoney, *Trial of Martin Luther King* at 8–22 (cited in note 3); Harrison E. Salisbury, *Fear and Hatred Grip Birmingham*, NY Times 1 (Apr 12, 1960); *Shuttlesworth v Gaylord*, 202 F Supp 59 (ND Ala 1961), aff'd *Hanes v Shuttlesworth*, 310 F2d 303 (5th Cir 1962). See also Diane McWhorter, *Carry Me Home: Birmingham, Alabama—The Climactic Battle of the Civil Rights Revolution* (Simon & Schuster, 2001).

[6] See Dan T. Carter, *The Politics of Rage: George Wallace, The Origins of the New Conservatism and the Transformation of American Politics* 109 (Louisiana State, 2d ed 2000).

[7] On the remarkable career of Frederick Lee Shuttlesworth, see Andrew Manis, *A Fire You Can't Put Out: The Civil Rights Life of Birmingham's Reverend Fred Shuttlesworth* (Alabama, 1999).

[8] Quoted in Westin and Mahoney, *Trial of Martin Luther King* at 18–19 (cited in note 3). Continuing, Connor said, "We're not going to have outsiders coming in and stirring up trouble. If they come here and do the wrong type of talking, they'll see the inside of our jail." See generally William A. Nunnelley, *Bull Connor* (Alabama, 1991).

[9] Quoted in Westin and Mahoney, *Trial of Martin Luther King* at 15 (cited in note 3).

to restrain two organizations, the Alabama Christian Movement for Human Rights (ACMHR) and the Southern Christian Leadership Conference (SCLC), and 139 individuals, including Shuttlesworth, Wyatt Tee Walker, and the movement's leading figure, Martin Luther King, Jr. The application alleged that those named had sponsored or encouraged unlawful sit-ins, kneel-ins, and picketing. The city's lawyers charged that these actions were "calculated to provoke breaches of the peace," "threaten[ed] the safety, peace and tranquility," and placed "an undue burden and strain upon the manpower of the Police Department." They asserted that inasmuch as these and similar actions were expected to continue and would "lead to further imminent danger to the lives, safety, peace, tranquility and general welfare of the people of the City of Birmingham," equitable relief was necessary immediately. In an *ex parte* proceeding, Circuit Judge William A. Jenkins, Jr., responded favorably. He enjoined King and company from participating in or encouraging "mass processions or like demonstrations" without a permit as required by a city ordinance.[10]

In the predawn hours of Thursday, April 11, King and several colleagues were served with the injunction. They were not surprised. Years before, during the epochal fight against segregation on the busses of Montgomery, Alabama, a state court had enjoined King and associates from operating a private car pool that transported boycotters. That injunction was issued the very day that the federal Supreme Court, in *Browder v Gayle*,[11] affirmed a lower court that had invalidated the state law requiring segregation on the busses. In the absence of *Browder* the injunction might well have unraveled the boycott, the beginning of King's meteoric rise as a civil rights leader,

---

[10] The Birmingham parade ordinance, § 1159 of the Birmingham City Codes, provided that:

> It shall be unlawful to organize or hold, to assist in organizing or holding, or to take part or participate in, any parade or procession or other public demonstration on the streets or other public ways of the city, unless a permit therefor has been secured from the commission.
>
> To secure such permit, written application shall be made to the commission.... The commission shall grant a written permit for such parade, procession or other public demonstrations, prescribing the streets or other public ways which may be used therefor, unless in its judgment the public welfare, peace, safety, health, decency, good order, morals or convenience require that it be refused....

Walker, 338 US at 309.

[11] 352 US 903 (1956).

and one of the key triumphs of the Second Reconstruction.[12] Six years later, in Albany, Georgia, just as a protest was gaining traction, a federal district court promulgated an injunction ordering King to cease demonstrating. Some partners in King's coalition, mainly those associated with the Student Non-Violent Coordinating Committee (SNCC), urged him to disobey the injunction. They feared that waiting to have it dissolved upon appeal to a higher court would deflate the protest. Others implored King to proceed with demonstrating only after the order had been lifted by higher judicial authority. Among those who urged King to follow the latter course was United States Attorney General Robert F. Kennedy. King did wait, and his lawyers eventually succeeded in having the injunction dissolved. But the attendant delay was one of the ingredients that doomed the protest in Albany, a setback that constituted one of the worse defeats in King's career.[13]

Facing the injunction in Birmingham, King was again beset by conflicting advice. His father and other associates recommended obeying the injunction. Others urged disobedience notwithstanding the likelihood of being held in contempt of court. With the bitter memory of Albany in mind, the knowledge that more militant activists were questioning his toughness, and keenly aware of the deep religious symbolism involved in defying authority at Eastertime, King resolved to protest despite the injunction. His lawyers apprised him of the risk of doing so. They explained again that defying an injunction was different than defying a statute. Upon being prosecuted for disobeying the latter, one was allowed to challenge the constitutionality of the law in question. Upon prevailing, one was free because the statute was deemed to be a nullity to which no obedience was owed. With injuctions, however, the rules were different. Upon disobeying a standing injunction, one was, with certain exceptions, precluded from challenging the injunction's legality as a defense to a contempt citation. In other words, if the target of an injunction declined to seek its modification or dissolution and instead defied it, the target lost his right to contest the injunction's legality in subsequent proceedings—

---

[12] See Randall Kennedy, *Martin Luther King's Constitution: A Legal History of the Montgomery Bus Boycott*, 98 Yale L J 999 (1989).

[13] See David J. Garrow, *Bearing the Cross: Martin Luther King, Jr., and the Southern Christian Leadership Conference* 173–230 (William Morrow, 1986); Westin and Mahoney, *Trial of Martin Luther King* at 44–47 (cited in note 3).

even if the injunction was unconstitutional. This is known as the collateral bar rule.[14]

The collateral bar rule is largely an application of *res judicata*, the idea that once a party has had an opportunity to litigate a matter, he ought not be permitted to relitigate the issue in a collateral proceeding. Precluding litigation in circumstances in which a party has already had an opportunity to make his case is justified as a means of promoting efficiency, finality, and fairness. Like any rule, however, the collateral bar rule can be turned into a destructive weapon. By issuing in bad faith a speech-restrictive injunction in circumstances in which a target has insufficient time to seek review of the order, a judge can pin a target into an excruciating position. Facing the injunction, the target may, on the one hand, desist from engaging in his protest until he can obtain a judicial resolution of his challenge to the injunction—a choice that might cost him irreparably in terms of momentum, prestige, or the other intangibles that sometimes make all the difference to a political struggle. On the other hand, the target may disobey the injunction before it is subjected to review—a choice that might allow him to engage in the prohibited conduct but at the cost of inviting punishment for contempt of court even if the injunction is indeed unlawful.

Aware of this dilemma, King acted decisively. "If we obey this injunction," he remarked, "we are out of business."[15] Preferring the likelihood of jail to the likelihood of another thwarted protest, King and his associates donned clothing that could withstand the rigors of incarceration, prepared to march, and explained publicly why they were prepared to disobey the court order. They said that in the past they had "abided by Federal injunctions out of respect for the forth-

---

[14]

The collateral bar rule limits the grounds on which a person who has disobeyed a court order can challenge that order to avoid being punished for criminal contempt.... [T]he rule generally prevents such a person from challenging the merits of the order, even if the order infringed on constitutional rights.... The rule thus forces people to obey erroneous and invalid court orders and to challenge them directly (if at all), unless they are willing to incur the cost of punishment.

John R. B. Palmer, *Collateral Bar and Contempt: Challenging a Court Order after Disobeying It*, 88 Cornell L Rev 215, 216 (2012).

[15] Quoted in Taylor Branch, *Parting the Waters: America in the King Years, 1954–63* 728 (Simon & Schuster, 1988).

right and consistent leadership that the Federal judiciary has given in establishing the principle of integration as the law of the land." They contended, however, that in this case they confronted "recalcitrant forces in the Deep South that will use the courts to perpetuate the unjust and illegal system of racial separation." They maintained that the injunction was "raw tyranny under the guise of maintaining law and order" and "an unjust, undemocratic and unconstitutional misuse of the judicial process." Stating their position without equivocation, King and company averred that "[j]ust as in all good conscience we cannot obey unjust laws, neither can we respect the unjust use of the courts." Undaunted by their legal jeopardy, they asserted that they risked taking "this critical move with an awareness of the possible consequences involved."[16]

The next day, Good Friday, April 12, 1963, King and company, numbering around fifty, started out from the Sixteenth Street Baptist Church[17] while a crowd of about 1,000 to 1,500 looked on. After proceeding a few blocks the marchers were arrested and jailed for violating the city's parade ordinance.[18] A reporter for the *New York Times* described the march as the "most spectacular" up to that point in the campaign against segregation in Birmingham.[19] On Easter Sunday more demonstrations and arrests transpired, albeit without King who, detained for the next several days, penned his iconic defense of civil disobedience, "Letter from Birmingham City Jail."

On Monday, April 15, city attorneys sought from Judge Jenkins citations for criminal contempt of court against those who knowingly disobeyed the injunction. Protesters replied by challenging the constitutionality of the injunction and the municipal ordinance on which it was based. Judge Jenkins refused, however, to consider their argument. He noted that they had failed either to comply with the injunction or to seek to have it dissolved prior to disobeying it. Invoking

---

[16] *Walker*, 388 US at 323–24.

[17] The Sixteenth Street Baptist Church is a holy site in the iconography of the Second Reconstruction. On Sunday, September 15, 1963, four young girls were killed there by bombs planted by white supremacists. See McWhorter, *Carry Me Home* (cited in note 5); Frank Sikora, *Until Justice Rolls Down: The Birmingham Church Bombing Case* (Alabama, 1991).

[18] Alabama courts upheld the conviction of a co-marcher, Reverend Fred Shuttlesworth, who was arrested alongside King for violating the Birmingham parade ordinance. The Supreme Court, however, reversed the Alabama courts. See *Shuttlesworth v Birmingham*, 394 US 147 (1969).

[19] See Foster Hailey, *Dr. King Arrested at Birmingham*, NY Times 1 (Apr 13, 1963).

the collateral bar rule, he maintained that by disregarding the injunction the respondents had forfeited their right to test its legitimacy. The only issues he was willing to consider were whether he had jurisdiction to issue the injunction and whether the protesters before him knowingly disobeyed it. He ruled against them, handing down punishments of five-day jail terms and $50 fines. The Supreme Court of Alabama affirmed most of the convictions.[20]

A closely divided (5–4) U.S. Supreme Court affirmed the decision of the Alabama court.[21] Writing for the majority, Justice Potter Stewart stressed two points. First, the petitioners did nothing to contest the lawfulness of the injunction before violating it. Second, the collateral bar rule was firmly established in Alabama law. In one previous case, for example, the Alabama courts had refused to entertain constitutional challenges brought by a "White Supremacy" organization after it had disobeyed an injunction. King and the other petitioners were thus clearly "on notice that they could not bypass orderly judicial review of the injunction before disobeying it."[22] In conclusion, the Court lauded the Alabama judiciary, declaring that "the rule of law that Alabama followed in this case reflects a belief that in the fair administration of justice no man can be judge in his own case."[23]

Four justices—Earl Warren, William O. Douglas, William Brennan, and Abe Fortas—dissented sharply, sometimes vociferously.[24] They maintained that the petitioners should have been permitted to question the lawfulness of the injunction and that the injunction was unconstitutional. Chief Justice Warren accused local officials of engaging in "a gross misuse of the judicial process."[25] Justice Douglas charged

---

[20] The Alabama Supreme Court vacated the conviction of one defendant because of insufficient proof that he knew of the injunction before engaging in conduct it prohibited and vacated the convictions of two others because of an absence of proof that they had disobeyed the court order. See *Walker v City of Birmingham*, 181 S2d 493, 503–04 (Ala 1965).

[21] The majority consisted of Justices Hugo Black, John Marshall Harlan, Byron White, Tom Clark, and Potter Stewart. The dissenters were Chief Justice Earl Warren, William O. Douglas, William Brennan, and Abe Fortas.

[22] *Walker*, 388 US at 320.

[23] Id at 321.

[24] For reasons that are unclear Douglas did not join Warren's dissenting opinion, though otherwise the dissenters joined one another's opinions.

[25] *Walker*, 388 US at 330.

that "the Alabama courts have flouted the First Amendment."[26] Justice Brennan called the injunction "a blatantly unconstitutional restraining order."[27]

The Supreme Court's resolution of *Walker* remains "good law" and has garnered considerable praise. Supporting the judgment, the *New York Times* editorialized that the doctrine the Court upheld was "absolutely basic to a democratic society."[28] In these very pages fifty years ago Professor Sheldon Teft maintained that the decision "seems eminently sound" and averred that with respect to Justice Stewart's opinion "there is little to fault."[29]

Professor Teft, however, was wrong. The decision was unsound and there is much fault to be found in the opinion. It evinced a regrettable amnesia regarding both the troublesome history of the collateral bar rule and the racial facts of the life obtaining in Birmingham in 1963. In the first half of the twentieth century, business interests and cooperative federal and (especially) state judges repeatedly used the collateral bar rule as a bludgeon against organized labor. In an all too frequent scenario, a business would obtain an injunction forbidding a strike just before a planned work stoppage. If union leaders obeyed the injunction, the momentum of the workers' campaign would be disrupted. Even if the union leaders succeeded in having the injunction dissolved, the attendant delay would often doom the union's efforts. On the other hand, if union leadership disobeyed an injunction, they would be fined or even jailed and lose the right to challenge subsequently the legality of the injunction. In his dissent, Chief Justice Warren makes much of the "long and odious history" of the *ex parte* temporary injunction:

> As a weapon against strikes, it proved so effective in the hands of judges friendly to employers that Congress was forced to take the drastic step of

---

[26] Id at 334.

[27] Id at 341.

[28] See ... *and Dr. King to Jail*, NY Times (June 14, 1967).

[29] Teft, 1967 Supreme Court Review at 192, 186 (cited in note 3). Judge John Minor Wisdom, a stalwart advocate of racial justice and civil liberties, referred to the collateral bar rule as "the sine qua non of orderly government," though he did so in a ruling that absolved a newspaper of disobeying an injunction before seeking to dissolve it. *Appeal of Providence Journal*, 820 F2d 1342, 1344 (1st Cir 1986). See also the commentary of the enlightened and deeply informed court watcher Anthony Lewis, *The Civilizing Hand*, NY Times A27 (Apr 7, 1986) ("if it becomes the practice to ignore court orders in the belief that they will later be found invalid, the system would not work").

removing from federal district courts the jurisdiction to issue injunctions for labor disputes.[30]

Such injunctions, Chief Justice Warren lamented, "so long discredited as weapons against concerted labor activities, have now [in *Walker*] been given new life by the Court as weapons against the exercise of First Amendment freedoms."[31] Justice Stewart's opinion says nothing about the collateral bar rule's role in the "long and odious" record to which Chief Justice Warren alluded.

Justice Stewart's *Walker* opinion also leaves readers insufficiently aware that the defiance of the injunction arose from one of the bitterest of all the battles of the Second Reconstruction. Justice Stewart acknowledges that Commissioner Connor "rudely rebuffed" a request for a permit prior to the issuance of the injunction, reportedly saying, "No, you will not get a permit in Birmingham, Alabama, to picket. I will picket you over to the City jail."[32] Otherwise, however, there is nothing in the Court's opinion that tells a reader about Connor's egregious conduct and reputation as a conspicuously cruel and lawless segregationist. Chief Justice Warren's dissent usefully informs or reminds readers that Connor was a "self-proclaimed white supremacist," that he "made no secret of his personal attitude towards the rights of Negroes and the decisions of [the Supreme] Court," that he vowed that racial integration would never come to Birmingham," and that he "wore a button inscribed 'Never' to advertise that vow."[33] These facts constitute more than interesting background material; they are pertinent to a proper handling of the legal issues in dispute. The Court misportrays the Birmingham authorities as having proceeded in good faith while the protestors, in disobeying the injunction, succumbed to an impetuous disrespect for the judicial process. Chief Justice Warren makes clear, by contrast, that there was "no doubt that [the protestors] were not going to be issued a permit under any circumstances."[34] In his depiction, Birmingham's officialdom had forfeited any reasonable expectation that they should be given any benefit

---

[30] See Norris-Laguardia Act, Pub L No 72-65, 47 Stat 70 (1932), codified at 29 USC §§ 101–15.

[31] *Walker*, 388 US at 330–31. See also Westin and Mahoney, *Trial of Martin Luther King* at 54–59 (cited in note 3); Luban, 87 Mich L Rev at 2170–71 (cited in note 3).

[32] *Walker*, 388 US at 317.

[33] Id at 325.

[34] Id.

of the doubt regarding racial matters.[35] It was naïve, if not foolish, Chief Justice Warren suggests, for the Court to "indulge [ ] in speculation that these civil rights protestors might have obtained a permit from this city . . . had they made enough repeated applications."[36] Directly impugning motives, including those of Judge Jenkins, the Chief Justice charged harshly but rightly that there was "only one apparent reason why the city sought this injunction and why the [circuit] court issued it: to make it possible to punish petitioners for contempt rather than for violating the ordinance, and thus to immunize the unconstitutional statute and its unconstitutional application from any attack."[37]

According to Justice Stewart:

> This case would arise in quite a different constitutional posture if the petitioners, before disobeying the injunction, had challenged it in the Alabama courts, and had been met with delay or frustration of their constitutional claims. But there is no showing that such would have been the fate of a timely motion to modify or dissolve the injunction.[38]

The petitioners, he complains, give "absolutely no explanation" of why they made no effort to modify or dissolve the injunction before demonstrating on Good Friday.[39]

In seizing upon the absence of any effort to modify or dissolve the injunction before disobeying it, Justice Stewart highlighted a real weakness in the petitioners' case. They were well aware of the collateral bar rule and the dilemma that it thrust upon them. Recollections vary, however, regarding their response. Wyatt Tee Walker, one of King's principal deputies (and the lead defendant), recalls rejecting the prospect of challenging the injunction in court:

> One option we eliminated was going to court to try to get the injunction dissolved. We knew this would tie us up in court at least ten days or two

---

[35] Turning facetious, Chief Justice Warren writes that the record "hardly suggests that Commissioner Connor and the other city officials were motivated in prohibiting civil rights picketing only by their overwhelming concern for particular traffic problems." Id at 329.

[36] Id at 325 n 1.

[37] Id at 334.

[38] Id at 318.

[39] Id at 319. Although Solicitor General Thurgood Marshall entered the case on the side of the petitioners, he believed that King's lawyers had erred in failing to make any filing aimed at modifying or dissolving the injunction before the Good Friday march. Westin and Mahoney, *Trial of Martin Luther King* at 221 (cited in note 3).

weeks, and even then we might not get it dissolved. We would have a lengthy lawsuit to appeal but no Birmingham campaign.[40]

Norman Amaker, one of King's attorneys, recalls, on the other hand, that he and local counsel "might have decided to file some kind of action ... if there had been enough time to prepare it, and if the movement leaders had approved, but everything was happening so quickly that [the lawyers] simply didn't consider that a practical possibility."[41]

It is understandable why King was so attentive to the threat of delay. Good Friday and Easter come along only once a year. He surely wanted to avoid depriving his followers of the emotional uplift that would come from witnessing protest on those specific holy days. And the alchemy of dissent that enables long-oppressed people to throw off habits of subordination may present itself only once in a lifetime. King was simply unwilling to allow in Birmingham a replication of the deflation that defeated him in Albany. Waiting, moreover, had become intolerable for him and other activists who chafed at being told to accommodate themselves to the slow requisition of rights to which they long been entitled. "For years now," he declared in "Letter from Birmingham City Jail," "I have heard the word 'Wait!' It rings in the ear of every Negro with piercing familiarity. This 'Wait' has almost always meant 'Never.'"[42]

Whatever lay behind the omission, the absence of a filing of some sort manifested a lapse of capacity or judgment. It would have been prudent to have filed a petition for review immediately contesting the injunction and requesting expedited review. King and company could have done so and continued to prepare to demonstrate according to their own timetable of protest. They might have been held in contempt anyway had they sought review of the injunction but marched before a definitive judicial resolution of the dispute. But filing *something* before marching would have strengthened the protestors' legal position. It would at least have obviated the charge that King and associates wholly disregarded the injunction before

---

[40] Id at 76.

[41] Id at 82. In the Brief for Petitioners there is a fleeting mention of King saying that the lawyer would attempt to dissolve the injunction. Brief for Petitioner 15. But obviously that thought never was acted upon.

[42] King, Jr., *Letter from Birmingham City Jail* at 292 (cited in note 4).

violating it. King was the recipient of inspired lawyering on some occasions, but this time his attorneys let him down.

To be sure, it is unlikely that a filing alone would have satisfied either the Alabama courts or the Supreme Court.[43] Alabama precedent quoted by Justice Stewart declared that an injunction must be obeyed on pain of contempt of court "until its unconstitutionality has been judicially declared in appropriate proceedings."[44] Another case he cited declared that an issuing tribunal's order must be obeyed "until its decision is reversed for error by orderly review, either by itself or by a higher court."[45] Justice Stewart wrote that things might have been different had the petitioners challenged the injunction directly and shown that they "met with delay or frustration of their constitutional claims," a standard that would seem to entail waiting for a judicial response for at least some appreciable amount of time. By failing, however, to seek any sort of reconsideration, modification, or dissolution, King's attorneys let the Alabama authorities off the hook. It is difficult to imagine the Alabama courts responding to a plea for expedited proceedings in good faith with celerity.[46] But we cannot know for sure given the absence of a request.

Still, the mistake on the part of King's camp does not justify *Walker*. Avenues for an alternative holding were available. One would have entailed abandoning the collateral bar rule at least with respect to certain categories of dispute. The American Federation of Labor and Congress of Industrial Organizations (AFL-CIO) submitted an *amicus curiae* brief urging that the Court rehear *Walker*. Noting that it had never before made such a request, the AFL-CIO did so now, it declared, because the organization was "concerned that [*Walker*] may furnish local officials and judges with a means of destroying rights of free speech and assembly generally, and the right of workers to orga-

---

[43] Cf Zechariah Chafee, Jr., *Some Problems of Equity* 362–63 (Michigan, 1950) ("The consequences would be terrific if any defendant who did not like being enjoined could get out from under a judge's order by merely filing some pieces of paper in the clerk's office.... All injunctions ought to continue until stayed or modified by some court.").

[44] *Walker*, 388 US at 320, quoting *Fields v City of Fairfield*, 273 Ala 588, 590 (1963), rev'd 375 US 248 (1963).

[45] *Walker*, 388 US at 314, quoting *Howat v Kansas*, 258 US 181, 189–90 (1922).

[46] "Surely it is a flight of fancy to think that counsel for the petitioners in *Walker* could have filed a notice of appeal, obtained permission ... to expedite the appeal, filed a record and brief, argued orally, and obtained a decision all in a day and a half. It took the Alabama Supreme Court 31 months to decide *Walker*...." Doug Rendleman, *More on Void Orders*, 7 Ga L Rev 246, 264 n 88.

nize in particular."[47] To avoid this risk, the AFL-CIO proposed abandoning the collateral bar rule in the context of labor disputes and, by implication, more widely:

> Unless the right to organize is to be completely destroyed over wide areas of the country, a union which is conducting or organizing a campaign or strike must have the right to ignore, though at its peril, an injunction against picketing or striking which it believes to be illegal. If the injunction is ultimately adjudged to be lawful, the union can be punished for contempt, but if the injunction is ultimately adjuged to be unlawful there is no reason why the union should be subject to punishment for having refused to surrender the most basic rights of workers in deference to an illegal decree.[48]

Another alternative was posited by the office of the Solicitor General. In a Memorandum for the United States as Amicus Curiae, Thurgood Marshall, John Doar, and Louis F. Claiborne[49] argued that the undiluted version of the collateral bar rule ought not be applied in the circumstances involved in *Walker*. They contended that disobedience to an injunction should not preclude a testing of its validity when the order "broadly suppresses the exercise of First Amendment rights, in a context that permits no effective alternative means of expression and no timely opportunity to obtain relief from the ban."[50] They maintained that in *Walker* and like cases "an appropriate ac-

---

[47] Motion for Leave to File a Brief as Amicus Curiae and Brief for the American Federation of Labor and Congress of Industrial Organizations as Amicus Curiae, *Walker v City of Birmingham*, No 249, *ii (US filed July 10, 1867) (available on Westlaw at 1967 WL 113908).

[48] Id at *11. See also Hal Scott Shapiro, *The Collateral Bar Rule—Transparently Invalid: A Theoretical and Historical Perspective*, 24 Colum J L & Soc Probs 561 (1991).

[49] This was a particularly distinguished array of attorneys. Thurgood Marshall, "Mr. Civil Rights," had been the preeminent advocate for the protection and enhancement of African American rights during the 1940s and 1950s. That he was appointed Solicitor General in 1965, the first black to hold that position, was in part a testament to the effectiveness of his contribution to the advancement of African Americans. The argument he made on behalf of the United States in *Walker* was in keeping with the activist liberalism that characterized his career. Less than three months after *Walker* was announced, Marshall joined the Supreme Court, becoming the first African American Justice. See Mark V. Tushnet, *Making Civil Rights Law: Thurgood Marshall and the Supreme Court, 1936–1961* (Oxford 1994); *Making Constitutional Law: Thurgood Marshall and the Supreme Court, 1961–1991* (Oxford, 1997).

John Doar was widely respected for his punctilious, pragmatic, and brave efforts as a leading figure in the Civil Rights Division of the United States Department of Justice. See Owen Fiss, *Pillars of Justice: Lawyers and the Liberal Tradition* 49–62 (Harvard, 2017).

Louis Claiborne was an experienced and talented deputy solicitor general. See Irvin Molotsky, *Louis Claiborne, 72, Deputy Solicitor General*, NY Times B13 (Oct 12, 1999).

[50] Memorandum for the United States as Amicus Curiae at 9 (available in The Making of Modern Law: U.S. Supreme Court Records and Briefs, 1832–1978 (Gale)).

commodation of the important policy of requiring respect for court orders with the constitutional prohibition against undue abridgement of the rights secured by the First Amendment must permit the violator to defend his contempt on the ground that the judicial order is invalid."[51]

Justice Stewart's opinion also hints at an alternative outcome. *Walker*, he insisted, was "not a case where the injunction was transparently invalid or had only a frivolous pretense to validity," implying that the presence of those features would have led to a different conclusion. But there was good reason to believe that the order was "transparently invalid." It was issued *ex parte* without justification. The targets of the injunction were well known and clearly available; no valid interest would have been compromised by granting the protestors notice and a hearing before possibly prohibiting them from marching and engaging in other acts of dissent. There was also strong evidence that invidious racial discrimination infected the process by which city authorities denied issuing a permit to the protestors. Furthermore, the city ordinance regulating demonstrations was obviously vague and overbroad, constitutional vices that were transmitted to the injunction when Judge Jenkins used the ordinance as the model for his injunction. The Solicitor General's assessment of the injunction was unequivocal; he deemed it to be "plainly void."[52] Chief Justice Warren called the injunction "a gross abuse of the judicial process" while Justice Brennan called it a "blatantly unconstitutional restraining order."

Although illegitimacy was written all over the injunction, the Court saw it differently. Conditioning the right of the petitioners to challenge the injunction collaterally on a thin distinction between mere invalidity and transparent invalidity, the Court ruled that the injunction was not transparently invalid. The Court acknowledged that because of its evident flaws the injunction would "unquestionably be subject to substantial constitutional question."[53] But the Court maintained that the injunction was not so flawed as to be transparently invalid because it at least touched upon a governmental interest in regulating streets and other public places.

---

[51] Id at 11.

[52] Id at 16.

[53] *Walker*, 388 US at 317.

In previous times, in previous cases, the Court had bestowed upon civil rights protestors a conspicuous solicitude. Here, however, the Court's line drawing went against them, though a strong, indeed compelling, argument militated in favor of the proposition that the injunction in question was transparently, blatantly, conspicuously invalid.[54] Why? I suspect that two unspoken but powerful sentiments played major, perhaps decisive, roles. One was a cooling toward the black liberation movement. In prior cases, when more of the Justices were more sympathetically disposed toward the movement, the Court read the facts of disputes in a fashion that consistently and sometimes dramatically aided protestors. By the time it adjudicated *Walker*, however, the Court was no longer disposed to being so generous to movement litigants.[55] The Court states, for example, that "[t]here was an interim of two days between the issuance of the injunction and the Good Friday march."[56] Actually, the protest leaders received copies of the injunction at 1:00 am on Thursday, April 11, *one* day before the Good Friday demonstration. The Court complains repeatedly that the protestors omitted pursuing the established procedures for obtaining a permit. Twice, though, representatives of the

---

54

  Walker was a particularly strong case for allowing the defendants to raise questions going to the validity of the Birmingham ordinance and the ensuing injunction proceedings for violation of the court's order. On the basis of all prior decisions the Birmingham ordinance was invalid on its face as vague and overbroad, beyond the possibility of redemption by judicial interpretation. Charges were made, clearly not unfounded, that the ordinance had been administered on a discriminatory basis. The temporary injunction had been issued *ex parte*. Defendants had only one day in which to move for judicial reconsideration before the scheduled demonstration on the strategic day, Good Friday. The injunction served no purpose except to transpose proceedings for violation of the ordinance from criminal to contempt procedures, and to immunize the ordinance from constitutional attack. The entire context of the affair made it plain that the officials, led by Police Commissioner Eugene (Bull) Connor, were engaged in a determined attempt to prevent the Negro groups from exercising their rights of assembly and petition. If, as the majority conceded, there are some occasions when the respect owed the courts is outweighed by other circumstances, this would seem to be such a case.

Thomas I. Emerson, *The System of Freedom of Expression* 383 (Random House, 1970).

[55] "If the Birmingham contempt case had reached the U.S. Supreme Court in 1964 or 1965, when memories of Bull Connor's police dogs were still fresh and national support for civil rights groups was at an all-time high, it is hard to resist the conclusion that the justices would have found a way to void the convictions of the Birmingham leaders." Westin and Mahoney, *Trial of Martin Luther King* at 161 (cited in note 3).

[56] *Walker*, 388 US at 318–19.

protestors had attempted to secure a permit. The Court discounts the significance of these efforts because they were undertaken *before* the injunction was handed down. More empathy might have led the Court to credit the protestors' argument that they had reasonably believed it to be futile to try any further to obtain a permit.

The reservoir of good will nourishing previous interventions by the Court on behalf of civil rights protestors had appreciably receded. The change was not wholesale; the vote in *Walker*, remember, was extremely close. But because of the closeness of the vote, small changes in the attitude of a Justice or two mattered greatly. Apprehension about the movement had been growing for a while. Judicial angst is seen best in the writings of Justice Black, the dominant figure in the wing of the Court that prevailed in *Walker*.[57] In 1964, in *Bell v Maryland*,[58] Justice Black, joined by Justices Harlan and White, dissented from the Court's vacation of trespass convictions imposed upon Negro students who had engaged in a sit-in. Justice Black remarked that

> the Constitution does not confer upon any group the right to substitute rule by force for rule by law. Force leads to violence, violence to mob conflicts, and these to rule by the strongest groups with control of the most deadly weapons. . . . At times the rule of law seems too slow to some for the settlement of their grievances. But it is the plan our Nation has chosen to preserve both "Liberty" and equality for all. On that plan we have put our trust and staked our future.[59]

In 1965, in *Cox v Louisiana*,[60] Justice Black, joined by Justices Clark, Harlan, and White, dissented from the reversal of a demonstrator's conviction for violating a statute that prohibited anyone from picketing or parading near premises occupied by judges, jurors, and other court officers with the intent of influencing them. Justice Black averred that "[t]hose who encourage minority groups to believe that the United States Constitution and federal laws give them the right to patrol and picket in the streets whenever they choose, in order to

[57] See A. E. Dick Howard, *Mr. Justice Black: The Negro Protest Movement and the Rule of Law*, 53 Va L Rev 1030 (1967); Charles E. Rice, *Justice Black, the Demonstrators and a Constitutional Rule of Law*, 14 UCLA L Rev 454 (1967).

[58] 378 US 226 (1964).

[59] Id at 346.

[60] 379 US 559 (1965).

advance what they think to be a just and noble end, do no service to those minority groups, their cause, or their country."[61]

In 1966, in *Brown v Louisiana*,[62] Justice Black, joined by Justices Clark, Harlan, and Stewart, dissented from the Court's reversal of convictions for breach of the peace at a public library that allegedly engaged in racial discrimination. "It is an unhappy circumstance," he declared, "that the group, which more than any other had needed a government of equal laws and equal justice, is now encouraged to believe that the best way for it to advance its cause, which is a worthy one, is by taking the law into its own hands...."[63]

By 1967 the Court had typically (albeit not invariably)[64] ruled in favor of dissidents in the civil rights protest cases it decided to review. That the Court adjudicated so many of these cases was itself remarkable in that most were fact-bound disputes that did not involve major doctrinal conflicts of the sort that typically elicit resolution by the Justices. These repeated interventions constituted a notable, perhaps unprecedented, instance of the Court providing protection to a protest movement that had won the high regard, if not the admiration, of most of the Justices.[65] The Court's reversal of 187 convictions for breach of the peace in *Edwards v South Carolina* is indicative of that sympathy.[66] Writing for the Court, Justice Stewart did not merely conclude that the state had encroached unconstitutionally on activities protected by the First and Fourteenth Amendments; he declared, with evident feeling, that the exercise of those

---

[61] Id at 583–84.

[62] 383 US 131 (1966).

[63] Id at 167–68.

[64] But see *Adderley v Florida*, 385 US 39 (1966).

[65] Commenting on the Supreme Court's repeated reversal of convictions of protestors in seemingly ordinary cases of disorderly conduct or trespass, Jack Greenberg observed:

> The pattern of decision is highly unusual if the cases are viewed in isolation as so many trespass, breach of the peace, disorderly conduct and weight of evidence cases. It is unheard of for the Supreme Court, which can decide only a relatively small number of cases each term, to repeatedly take up such apparently minor matters. Viewed in the context of race relations in the United States, however, the Court's constant involvement can be understood as reflecting concern that a nonviolent movement, struggling toward the same goals that the Court itself had urged more abstractly on the nation in the early school desegregation decisions, should not be worn down by petty prosecutions.

The Supreme Court, Civil Rights and Civil Dissonance, 77 Yale L J 1520, 1528 (1968).

[66] 372 US 229 (1963).

rights had been effectuated in "their most pristine and classic form by the student dissidents."[67]

By the time of *Walker* much had changed. The Supreme Court had extended the reach of *Brown v Board of Education* to domain after domain. The same day that *Walker* was announced the Court handed down *Loving v Virginia*,[68] invalidating the oldest form of government-mandated racial segregation—the laws prohibiting marriage across the race line. Congresses and presidents had also been active, enacting the Civil Rights Act of 1964 and the Voting Rights Act of 1965. By 1967, civil rights fatigue had started to emerge. Emergent, too, was a feeling that the mission of deploying law against racism had proceeded about as far as it could prudently be pushed. At the same time, alarming disorder, provocative tactics, and extravagant rhetoric alienated many onlookers who feared that seeds of lawlessness were now blossoming under the ministrations of fearsome militants who made a point of abjuring any continued commitment to nonviolence. In 1965, rioting erupted in the Watts section of Los Angeles. In 1966, Stokely Carmichael electrified the black liberation movement with the slogan "Black Power!" During this same period, protests against the Vietnam War escalated, elevating fears of mayhem to new levels of intensity. Birmingham's attorneys sought to focus the Court's attention onto the prevalence of disorder, joining a chorus that included leading advocates such as Lewis F. Powell, Jr., president of the American Bar Association in 1964–65 (who would join the Court in 1971). In a widely noted law review article, "A Lawyer Looks at Civil Disobedience," Powell denounced King's distinction between laws warranting obedience and compelling disobedience. According to Powell, the "disobedience movement" of segregationists and antisegregationists, as well as the antiwar movement and the New Left, had been tolerated excessively.[69]

Given Justice Black's passionate dissents prior to *Walker*, it is somewhat surprising that he declined to write the opinion of the

---

[67] Id at 235.

[68] 388 US 1 (1967).

[69] See Brief for Respondent, *Walker v City of Birmingham*, No 249, *46 (US filed Feb 2, 1967) (available on Westlaw at 1967 WL 113909). See also Lewis F. Powell, Jr., *A Lawyer Looks at Civil Disobedience*, 23 Wash & Lee L Rev 205 (1966); Charles E. Whittaker, *Will Civil Disobedience Lead to Chaos in Our Society?*, Trial 10 (Dec/Jan 1965); Morris I. Leibman, *Civil Disobedience: A Threat to Our Law Society*, 51 ABA J 645 (1965); Louis Waldman, *Civil Rights—Yes; Civil Disobedience—No*, 37 NY State Bar J 331 (1965).

Court when he finally commanded a majority. With the Chief Justice in the minority, Black as the senior Justice exercised the prerogative of assigning the Court's opinion. Why didn't he assign it to himself? One speculation is that Justice Black assigned it to someone else because he was an Alabamian and thought perhaps that there might be some awkwardness in *his* delivering the Court's judgment in a dispute arising from Birmingham.[70] Another speculation is that Black was intent upon choosing someone in the middle of the prevailing faction who would write an opinion that would retain the needed five votes.[71]

Justice Stewart's opinion offers no direct comment on the discord that had engulfed much of the country. It is almost certain, however, that anxiety over unrest affected the Court's judgment. Supportive evidence is found in Justice Brennan's dissent where he declared plaintively: "we cannot permit fears of 'riots' and 'civil disobedience' generated by slogans like 'Black Power' to divert our attention from what is here at stake. . . ."[72] Notwithstanding Justice Brennan's plea, fears of riots and Black Power did, alas, influence the Court, facilitating the issuance of a regrettable decision.

I suspect that a second sentiment, unacknowledged by the Court, helped to reinforce its unwillingness in *Walker* to modify the collateral bar rule even in circumstances that vividly highlighted the rule's potential for repressive mischief. That sentiment is judicial exceptionalism—a belief that judges are better stewards of ordered liberty than other types of officials and that therefore judges are entitled to more deference than their so-called "political" peers. Justice Frankfurter gave voice to this intuition in a concurring opinion in *United States v United Mine Workers*.[73] Although Justice Stewart never quotes from *United Mine Workers*, noting it only glancingly in a long string citation, that decision, particularly Justice Frankfurter's justification of it, presages the attitude and rhetoric of *Walker*.[74] Uninhibitedly lauding judicial exceptionalism, at least with respect to federal judges, Justice Frankfurter maintained that the Founding Fathers:

---

[70] Fiss, 89 Yale Rev at 11 (cited in note 3).

[71] Westin and Mahoney, *Trial of Martin Luther King* at 341 (cited in note 3).

[72] 388 US at 349.

[73] 330 US 258 (1947).

[74] Id at 308–09.

set aside a body of men, who were to be the depositories of law, who by their disciplined training and character and by withdrawal from the usual temptations of private interest may reasonably be expected to be "as free, impartial, and independent as the lot of humanity will admit." So strong were the framers of the Constitution bent of securing a reign of law that they endowed the judicial office with extraordinary safeguards and prestige. No one, no matter how exalted his public office or how righteous his private motive, can be judge in his own case. That is what courts are for.

Justice Frankfurter further declared that the Supreme Court "beyond any other organ of society, is the trustee of law and charged with the duty of securing obedience to it."[75] A little over a decade later, the Supreme Court echoed Frankfurter's assertion of judicial primacy in *Cooper v Aaron*.[76] In its opinion famously signed by all of the Justices, the Court averred "that the federal judiciary is supreme in the exposition of the law of the Constitution."[77] In *Cooper* the Court was specifically asserting that it had greater authority as an interpreter of the Constitution than state governors and legislators, though they, too, swear oaths to support the federal Constitution and necessarily engage in interpreting it. In *Walker* the Court was focused not so much on promoting the supremacy of federal over state authority as in asserting, albeit only inferentially, the supremacy of judges over other lawgivers. In *Walker* a bare majority of the Justices echoed Frankfurter in suggesting that courts "beyond any other organ of society" are the trustees of law and that therefore their orders, even when unlawful, warrant more deference than directives from other officials.

Chastising the petitioners, Justice Stewart declared in the most oft-cited passage from *Walker* that

> [N]o man can be judge in his own case, however exalted his station, however righteous his motives, and irrespective of his race, color, politics, or religion. This Court cannot hold that the petitioners were constitutionally free to ignore all of the procedures of the law and carry their battle to the streets. One may sympathize with the petitioners' impatient commitment to their cause. But respect for judicial process is a small price to pay for the civilizing hand of law, which alone can give abiding meaning to constitutional freedom.[78]

---

[75] Id at 312.

[76] 358 US 1 (1958).

[77] Id at 18.

[78] 388 US at 321.

This peroration, though celebrated, does not fare well under close scrutiny. A call for humility, it evinces a judicial conceit that is misleading. The petitioners were not seeking to judge their own case and did not claim to be free to ignore lawful procedures. They simply argued that, under the trying circumstances they confronted, encountering bad faith on the part of local officials, federal constitutional law, rightly understood, entitled them to act in disregard of the injunction and to challenge it later in defense to charges of criminal contempt of court.

A distinguished jurist has insisted that the collateral bar rule "is not the product of self-protection or arrogance of Judges."[79] That is true, at least to a large extent. As we have seen, the collateral bar rule, appropriately limited, serves valid ends. But any rule can become subject to human vices and fashioned into an abusive weapon. The collateral bar rule was cagily put to that use in *Walker*, and the federal Supreme Court wrongly sanctioned that malign deployment, swayed in part by a sentimental complacency about judges.[80]

Some solace can be gleaned from recalling that *Walker* was decided by the narrowest of margins. Indeed, notes written by Justices Douglas and Brennan indicate that, initially, there were five votes the other way, with Justice Harlan agreeing to vacate the Alabama Supreme Court decision and remand it with instructions to determine whether the Birmingham Commission had engaged in illicit discrimination in the allocation of permits for demonstrations.[81] Then Justice Harlan changed his mind and the "law of the land" became the opinion by Justice Stewart instead of the opinion by Chief Justice Warren. The numerical strength of the dissenting bloc did not matter in terms of the authority behind *Walker*; five votes create a

---

[79] Chief Judge John R. Brown in *United States v Dickinson*, 465 F2d 496, 510 (5th Cir 1972).

[80] Justice Antonin Scalia offers a useful warning about speech-restricting injunctions. Arguing that these powerful judicial implements should be subjected to "strict scrutiny," he remarks that "[t]he right to free speech should not lightly be placed within the control of a single man or woman." He goes on to observe that "persons subject to a speech-restricting injunction who have not the money or not the time to lodge an immediate appeal face a Hobson's choice: They must remain silent, since if they speak their First Amendment rights are no defense in subsequent contempt proceedings. This is a good reason to require the strictest standard for issuance of such orders." *Madsen v Women's Health Center, Inc.*, 512 US 753, 793–94 (1994) (Scalia, J, concurring and dissenting).

[81] See Del Dickson, ed, *The Supreme Court in Conference (1940–1985): The Private Discussions Behind Nearly 300 Supreme Court Decisions* 327–29 (Oxford, 2001).

ruling of "the Court."[82] But the dissenting bloc did matter insofar
as it contained minds attentive to opportunities to dilute *Walker*'s
toxicity. Opportunities to do just that subsequently arose. In *Carroll v President and Commissioners at Princess Anne*,[83] the Court invalidated an *ex parte* injunction that, with little time for appellate review, prohibited the white supremacist National States Rights Party
(NSRP) from holding rallies for ten days. The result in *Carroll* is
consistent with the outcome of *Walker*. The NSRP did not disregard
the injunction as did King and company. Instead, the NSRP obeyed
the order but challenged the legitimacy of the injunction through direct appeal—the procedure that, according to the Court, King should
have followed. The reasons given for invalidating the injunction in
Carroll, however, are in tension with the Court's toleration of the injunction in *Walker*. In *Carroll*, in an opinion by Justice Fortas (who
dissented in *Walker*), the Court maintained that while there is a place
for *ex parte* issuance, without notice, of temporary restraining orders,
"there is no place within the area of basic freedoms guaranteed by the
First Amendment for such orders where no showing is made that it is
impossible to serve or to notify the opposing parties and give them an
opportunity to participate."[84] In *Walker* only the dissenters complained about deficiencies in the process that led to the issuance of the
injunction—the unexplained need to issue an injunction at night, *ex
parte*, without notice, to parties whose identities and whereabouts
were well known. In *Carroll* all of the members of the Court paid heed
to the need for enhanced attentiveness when reviewing a governmental effort, absent notice and a hearing, to mute, even if only temporarily, political expression.

In *Shuttlesworth v City of Birmingham*,[85] in another opinion by Justice Stewart, the Court, without dissent, invalidated the conviction
of Reverend Fred Shuttlesworth, who was arrested alongside King,
for violating the city ordinance that had been incorporated into the
injunction at issue in *Walker*. All of the Justices agreed to what only
the dissenters had asserted in *Walker*: that the administration of the

---

[82] Sometimes much is made over the vote count behind a decision. It has long been taken
for granted, for example, that unanimity was key in the single most important Supreme Court
decision of the twentieth century: *Brown v Board of Education*. I would be happy to be in-
structed by findings that either substantiated or questioned that widespread belief.

[83] 393 US 175 (1968).

[84] Id at 180.

[85] 394 US 147 (1969).

permit system in Birmingham was unconstitutional. Voicing a salutary hostility toward unguided governmental authority, the Court in *Shuttlesworth* declared:

> Even when the use of its public streets and sidewalks is involved ... a municipality may not empower its licensing officials to roam essentially at will, dispensing or withholding permission to speak, assemble, picket, or parade, according to their own opinions regarding the potential effect of the activity in question or the "welfare," "decency," or "morals" of the community.[86]

In *Walker* the Court refused to be moved by pleas regarding the essentiality of timing to protest. In *Shuttlesworth* it was moved, with Justice Harlan remarking that "it is often necessary to have one's voice heard promptly, if it is to be heard at all."[87] In *Walker* the Court's opinion is an exercise in formalism, seemingly devoid of knowledge about the racial facts of life obtaining in Birmingham, Alabama, in April 1963. In *Shuttlesworth* the Court is more realistic, expressly taking account of "surrounding relevant circumstances."[88]

Still, *Walker v City of Birmingham* should prompt sober reflection. That people were compelled to resort to political protest to challenge widespread and blatant racial discrimination in mid-twentieth-century America was disgraceful. That they were arrested and jailed by local authorities intent upon suppressing their message is outrageous. That this persecution was then blessed by the United States Supreme Court was tragic—with a bit of absurdity thrown in for good measure.[89] Of all the places to proclaim the civilizing hand of law, the Supreme Court chose a case that absolved judicial white supremacists and relegated to jail Martin Luther King, Jr.[90]

---

[86] Id at 153.

[87] 388 US at 163.

[88] 394 US at 158.

[89] See Martin Edelman, *The Absurd Remnant: Walker v. Birmingham Two Years Later*, 34 Albany L Rev 523 (1970).

[90] At the end of his life, in his final civil rights campaign in Memphis, Tennessee, in April 1968, King again faced the dilemma posed by the collateral bar rule. After violence erupted at a march led by King, Memphis officials succeeded in convincing a federal judge to issue a temporary restraining order prohibiting King and his associates from staging any mass protests for ten days. King's attorneys sought a modification of the order and were told informally that the judge would indeed modify it permitting a march of some sort to proceed. King told colleagues that he planned to protest whether or not the judge modified the injunction. King's murder mooted the issue. See Garrow, *Bearing the Cross* at 619 (cited in note 13); Michael K. Honey, *Going Down Jericho Road: The Memphis Strike, Martin Luther King's Last Campaign* 410–18 (W.W. Norton, 2007).

MICHAEL COLLINS AND
ANN WOOLHANDLER

JUDICIAL FEDERALISM UNDER
MARSHALL AND TANEY

The Supreme Court during the Chief Justiceship of John Marshall (1801–35) is associated with endorsement of broad regulatory powers in Congress and broad federal question jurisdiction in the federal courts under Article III.[1] By contrast, the successor Court under Chief Justice Roger Taney (1836–64) remains tied to its determination in *Dred Scott* that Congress lacked powers to enact the Missouri

Michael Collins is Joseph M. Hartfield Professor, University of Virginia School of Law. Ann Woolhandler is William Minor Lile Professor and Class of 1966 Research Professor, University of Virginia School of Law.

AUTHORS' NOTE: Our thanks to Aditya Bamzai, Barry Cushman, John Harrison, Gordon Hylton, Michael Klarman, Chuck McCurdy, Jonathan Nash, Caleb Nelson, Cynthia Nicoletti, George Rutherglen, and Ted White. Thanks to Virginia Adamson for research assistance.

[1] See, for example, *McCulloch v Maryland*, 17 US (4 Wheat) 316 (1819); *Osborn v Bank of the United States*, 22 US (9 Wheat) 738 (1824); George Lee Haskins, *History of the Supreme Court of the United States 1801–1815* at 14 (Cambridge, 2010) (stating that by the close of 1835, the Marshall Court "had extended the compass of its jurisdiction into areas hardly envisaged in 1800, including . . . corporations law, maritime law, and interstate commerce"); Alison L. LaCroix, *Federalists, Federalism, and Federal Jurisdiction*, 30 L and Hist Rev 205, 210 (Feb 2012) (seeing the Marshall Court as engaged in an extended attempt "to use judicial interpretation of the Constitution and congressional statutes as a means of expanding the inferior federal courts' power to hear cases arising under federal law"); cf. Michael J. Klarman, *How Great Were the "Great" Marshall Court Decisions?*, 87 Va L Rev 1111, 1133–34 (2001) (although taking issue with such assessments, citing authority for viewing Marshall Court decisions, such as *McCulloch*, and *Gibbons v Ogden*, 22 US (9 Wheat) 1 (1824), as educating Americans in nationalism).

Compromise prohibiting slavery in certain of the territories acquired after promulgation of the Constitution,[2] and to Taney's opinion that descendants of African slaves could never be citizens who could invoke the federal courts' diversity of citizenship jurisdiction.[3]

An earlier generation of scholars believed the differences between the two courts at a more general level amounted to a revolution. Then-Professor Felix Frankfurter—while disagreeing with that overall assessment—acknowledged that "even the most sober historians have conveyed Taney as the leader of a band of militant 'agrarian,' 'localist,' 'pro-slavery' judges, in a strategy of reaction against Marshall's doctrines. They stage a dramatic conflict between Darkness and Light."[4] Modern scholars perceive the conflict in less dramatic terms, particularly noting a rough continuity in the Taney Court's defense of the Court's role in the constitutional structure and the institution of judicial review.[5]

Still, the identification of the Taney Court with its narrow views of congressional power and of constitutional citizenship in *Dred Scott* may obscure the fact that as to the powers of the federal courts, and particularly the lower federal courts, the Taney Court was in many ways "even more national than Marshall himself."[6] We address the ways in which the Taney Court outdid the Marshall Court in terms of a nationalist approach to judicial federalism, and the reasons for

---

[2] *Scott v Sandford*, 60 US (19 How) 393 (1857); see also Mark A. Graber, *Dred Scott and the Problem of Constitutional Evil* 15–16 (Cambridge, 2006) (collecting scholars' negative views of *Dred Scott*); James Blacksher and Lani Guinier, *Free at Last: Rejecting Equal Sovereignty and Restoring the Constitutional Right to Vote, Shelby County v. Holder*, 8 Harv L & Policy Rev 39 (2014) (criticizing *Shelby County v Holder*, 570 US 529 (2013), for using an equality-of-the-states argument that the authors trace to *Dred Scott*).

[3] 60 US (19 How) at 419–23.

[4] Felix Frankfurter, *The Commerce Clause under Marshall, Taney, and Waite* 48 (1937); cf. Edward S. Corwin, *The Passing of Dual Federalism*, 36 Va L Rev 1, 15–16 (1950) (viewing the Taney Court as treating states as more on an equal footing with the federal government).

[5] See, for example, Bernard Schwartz, *A History of the Supreme Court* 92 (Oxford, 1993) (saying that "almost three decades as Chief Justice gave ample proof of [Taney's] full adherence to the notion of judicial power expounded by the Marshall Court"); Carl B. Swisher, *History of the Supreme Court of the United States: The Taney Period 1836–64* at 974 (Macmillan, 1974) ("The Taney Court and the Marshall Court, for all the seeming difference in emphasis, proved to be very much the same."); Mark A. Graber, *The Jacksonian Makings of the Taney Court* 14 (Univ of Md School of Law Legal Studies Research Paper No 2005-63), http://ssrn.com/abstract=842184 ("Jacksonians in power exhibited no general hostility to judicial power.").

[6] Charles Evans Hughes, *Roger Brooke Taney*, 17 ABA J 785, 787 (1931) (internal quotation marks omitted) (referring to the admiralty jurisdiction).

the difference. Both Courts expanded federal judicial power, but with the significant difference that the Marshall Court tied its expansions to broad views of congressional power, whereas the Taney Court did not.

The Marshall Court faced a political environment hostile to the Federalist-dominated federal courts,[7] including concerns that it would sanction common law jurisdiction in excess of constitutional and statutory limits.[8] In reaction, the Marshall Court repeatedly expressed respect for congressional power over its jurisdiction,[9] and tied its expansions of federal judicial power closely to expansive views of congressional power.[10] The Taney Court, by contrast, did not face similar political-branch threats,[11] and it expanded federal judicial power in ways that might have been congenial to the Marshall Court had the political environment been different.[12] The Taney Court, however, did not merely do what the Marshall Court might have done in similar circumstances. Rather, Taney Court jurisdictional opinions were less deferential to Congress than Marshall Court opinions and traced congressional power to narrower constitutional sources. And while the Marshall Court tied its expansions of judicial power

---

[7] See, for example, Klarman, 87 Va L Rev at 1154 (cited in note 1), and sources cited in notes 19–31 below; Gerard N. Magliocca, *Andrew Jackson and the Constitution: The Rise and Fall of Generational Regimes* 7–11 (Kansas, 2007) (indicating that the Marshall Court had reached an era of good feeling in 1819, but that the Court's decision in *McCulloch v Maryland*, 17 US (4 Wheat) 316 (1819), and economic circumstances led to a backlash).

[8] See G. Edward White, *Recovering Coterminous Power Theory: A Lost Dimension of the Marshall Court Sovereignty Cases*, in Maeva Marcus, ed, *Origins of the Federal Judiciary: Essays on the Judiciary Act of 1789* at 66, 69–70, 84–85 (Oxford, 1992) (discussing how the Marshall Court operated amid concerns that the federal judiciary's using a common law of the United States would expand the power of Congress). While lower federal courts' recognition of common law crimes was a particular concern, see notes 18–19, Professor White has shown that the concerns encompassed the idea that recognition of English common law generally as federal common law would expand congressional power. See note 20 and accompanying text.

[9] A notable exception was *Marbury v Madison*, 5 US (1 Cranch) 137, 180 (1803), in which the Court held that Congress had exceeded the limits of Article III by granting original mandamus jurisdiction to the Supreme Court.

[10] Cf. White, *Recovering Coterminous Power Theory* at 85–89 (cited in note 8) (seeing coterminous power theory, which saw legislative and judicial power as coextensive, as having informed Marshall Court decisions).

[11] See, for example, Klarman, 87 Va L Rev at 1131 (cited in note 1) (indicating that states' rights Democrats controlled either the Senate or the presidency from the late 1820s through 1860).

[12] See R. Kent Newmyer, *The Supreme Court under Marshall and Taney* 112 (Thomas Y. Crowell, 1968) (indicating Marshall would have approved of the Taney Court's extension of admiralty jurisdiction).

to broad views of congressional power, the Taney Court's expansions of judicial power operated to limit any concomitant expansion of congressional power.[13]

The Taney Court accomplished this by expanding diversity of citizenship jurisdiction beyond what the Marshall Court had done and by explicitly adopting the use of a uniform judge-made general common law in diversity cases. It also expanded admiralty jurisdiction by an interpretation of Article III's admiralty provision that was contrary to Marshall Court precedent, and rejected a proffered Commerce Clause justification that would have entailed broader congressional powers. And when it channeled certain matters away from the state courts to the federal courts based on exclusive federal powers, the Taney Court relied on implied federal powers whose enforcement could be limited by stricter notions of necessity, as distinguished from the Marshall Court's looser version of necessary and proper.[14]

I. THE MARSHALL COURT

A. EARLY CHALLENGES

The years preceding Marshall's Chief Justiceship saw rising Republican discontent with the Federalist-dominated judiciary.[15] The federal courts had enforced the Alien and Sedition Acts[16]—primarily against Republicans and likely Republican voters[17]—and many saw the acts as exceeding congressional power. Republicans also voiced

---

[13] See G. Edward White, *History of the Supreme Court: The Marshall Court and Cultural Change, 1815–35* at 594 (Cambridge, 2010) (noting that in 1835, "there was no national bank, no national system of bankruptcy. . . . One might suggest that an implicit constitutional compromise had been arrived at in the 1830s, that compromise consisting of a retention of the extensive Article III powers claimed by the Marshall Court and a circumscription of the equally extensive Article I power claimed for Congress.").

[14] We consider all the cases decided while Taney was Chief Justice to be Taney Court decisions, irrespective of whether the majority included Chief Justice Taney. See, for example, note 116 and accompanying text.

[15] Many scholars have described the problems faced by the Supreme Court when John Marshall became Chief Justice in early 1801. This section provides an overview.

[16] Haskins, *History of the Supreme Court* at 126 (cited in note 1); see also id (also attributing hostility to incursions on states' rights and to Federalist-oriented jury charges, as well as to anti-French sentiments attributed to Federalists); id at 156–57 (noting hostility to enforcement of debts). An early sign of trouble was the reaction to the pre-Marshall Court's holding states liable to suit in *Chisholm v Georgia*, 2 US (2 Dall) 419 (1793). See Haskins, *History of the Supreme Court* at 140, 312 (cited in note 1).

[17] See Alfred H. Kelly, Winfred A. Harbison, and Herman Belz, 1 *The American Constitution: Its Origins and Development* 131–32 (7th ed 1991).

opposition to federal courts' imposing liability for common law crimes—that is, for crimes that Congress had not specifically defined.[18] This complaint was sometimes expressed as an objection to the federal courts' assuming a "common law jurisdiction."[19]

A related objection, as illuminated by Professor G. Edward White, was that the expansion of judicial power could serve as a constitutional justification for expanding federal legislative power, based on conterminous power theory. Under this theory, federal judicial and legislative power were coextensive. A relatively unexceptionable version of coterminous power theory—one the Marshall Court would in fact espouse—was that if Congress has power to legislate as to a matter, it may also provide federal court jurisdiction with respect to cases that arise under that legislation. Under a more questionable version, the expansion of power could run from the judiciary to the legislature. If the federal courts treated the English common law as federal law, then Congress might possess implied power to legislate as to the same unenumerated subjects.[20]

---

[18] See, for example, *United States v Worrall*, 2 Dall 384, 394 (CCD Pa 1798) (opinion of Chase, Cir J) (arguing for dismissal of an indictment for attempted bribery of a revenue officer, and discussing the need for Congress to define the offense and punishment); *Henfield's Case*, 11 F Cas 1099, 1120 (CCD Pa 1793) (in response to counsel's inquiry as to what laws of the United States Henfield had violated, charging the jury that Henfield had violated the treaty with the Netherlands, Great Britain, and Prussia); *United States v Ravara*, 2 Dall 297, 299* (CCD Pa 1793) (indicating that the consul's sending threatening letters to the British minister and others with a view to extort money was indictable at common law).

[19] See notes 38–39 and accompanying text. In the 1789 Judiciary Act, Congress had provided the federal courts with jurisdiction over "all crimes and offenses cognizable under the authority of United States." Judiciary Act of 1789, ch 20, §§ 9, 11, 1 Stat 73, 76–77, 78–79. Commentators, however, tended to treat the common law crimes issue as one of the federal courts' expanding their own jurisdiction. See David P. Currie, *The Constitution in the Supreme Court 1789–1888*, 94–95 n 30 (1985) (questioning whether the common law crimes issue should have been treated as jurisdictional in light of the 1789 Judiciary Act); see also Haskins, *History of the Supreme Court* at 158 (cited in note 1) (noting hostility to use of English criminal law precedents); Morton J. Horwitz, *The Transformation of American Law* 10 (Oxford, 1992) (stating that the objection to common law crimes "boiled down to the assertion that if the federal judiciary possessed jurisdiction to impose criminal sanctions without a statute it would be able to obliterate all constitutional limitations on the federal government").

[20] See White, *Recovering Coterminous Power Theory* at 69 (cited in note 8) ("[St. George] Tucker argued that if there were a federal common law of the United States, not only would the jurisdiction of the federal courts extend to every 'legal' subject, but the jurisdiction of Congress would likewise thus extend."); id at 70 ("Tucker's belief that for every extension of federal judicial power there would be a corresponding extension of federal legislative power, and vice versa, was premised on a cluster of assumptions that amounted to a widely held proposition of political theory at the time of the framing of the Judiciary Act of 1789 and during the early and middle years of the Marshall Court."); id at 84 (attributing similar beliefs to Thomas Jefferson); White, *The Marshall Court and Cultural Change* at 122–27, 969 (cited in note 13) (discussing such concerns); cf. Wythe Holt, *The First Federal Question Case*, 3 L &

Thomas Jefferson was elected President in 1800, along with Republican majorities in the House and Senate. Appointed by outgoing (Federalist) President John Adams, John Marshall became the Chief Justice on February 4, 1801, a month before Jefferson assumed the presidency.[21] On February 13, the departing Congress enacted the 1801 Judiciary Act,[22] providing for federal question jurisdiction in the lower federal courts, for new federal judgeships, and for an end to circuit riding for the Supreme Court Justices. And in a February 27 act for the government of the District of Columbia,[23] Congress provided for new justices of the peace,[24] some of whose commissions had not been delivered when Jefferson became President.[25]

By an Act of March 8, 1802, the new Republican Congress repealed the 1801 Judiciary Act. Congress also canceled the June and December 1802 terms of the Court, in order to delay the possibility of the Supreme Court's holding the 1802 repeal statute unconstitutional.[26] Also figuring in the congressional debates was the pending but as-yet-undecided case of *Marbury v Madison*, in which William Marbury sought his undelivered District of Columbia justice of the peace commission from Secretary of State James Madison. The case raised the specter of judicial control of the executive by issuance of a writ of mandamus.[27]

Hist Rev 169, 178–82 (1985) (uncovering a lower court case under the 1801 Judiciary Act which the author reads as suggesting that common law actions might have been treated as arising under federal law).

[21] See, for example, Richard H. Fallon, Jr., et al, *Hart and Wechsler's The Federal Courts and the Federal System* 68 (Foundation, 7th ed 2015); Haskins, *History of the Supreme Court* at 183 (cited in note 1).

[22] Fallon et al, *Hart and Wechsler's The Federal Courts and the Federal System* at 68 (cited in note 21).

[23] Act of Feb 27, 1801, 2 Stat 103.

[24] Id.

[25] Fallon et al, *Hart and Wechsler's The Federal Courts and the Federal System* at 68 (cited in note 21).

[26] Id (indicating that a single February term was substituted); Haskins, *History of the Supreme Court* at 167 (cited in note 1); Klarman, 87 Va L Rev at 1154 (cited in note 1) ("When Marshall became Chief Justice in 1801, the Jeffersonians were about to assume control of Congress and the presidency, and some form of retribution against Supreme Court Justices was widely predicted." (footnote omitted)). The argument that the repeal was unconstitutional was based on Article III, § 1's provision, "The Judges, both of the supreme and inferior Courts, shall hold their Offices during good Behaviour." See Currie, *The Constitution in the Supreme Court 1789–1888* at 75 (cited in note 19).

[27] Haskins, *History of the Supreme Court* at 164 (cited in note 1) (discussing debates over the 1802 repeal, including references to the *Marbury* case).

After the Court reconvened in 1803, it decided *Marbury*, in which the Court indicated that high level executive officers were subject to judicial process,[28] but at the same time avoided issuing such process by holding that Congress's apparent grant of original mandamus jurisdiction to the Court exceeded Article III's provision of limited original jurisdiction to the Supreme Court.[29] A few days later in *Stuart v Laird*,[30] the Court rejected a constitutional challenge to certain aspects of the 1802 act.[31]

B. CONTINUED DEFERENCE TO CONGRESS; MANDAMUS

The Marshall Court's prudent handling of these early challenges to the federal judicial power is well known. The Court, however, continued to avoid conflict with Congress well after *Stuart v Laird*.[32] Apparently reacting to the concerns that the federal courts would attempt to claim a common law jurisdiction over crimes and perhaps

---

[28] Klarman, 87 Va L Rev at 1116 (cited in note 1).

[29] 5 US (1 Cranch) 137 (1803); see also Klarman, 87 Va L Rev at 1123–24 (cited in note 1) (discussing that *Marbury* reflected the weakness of the Marshall Court). *Marbury* involved § 13 of the 1789 Judiciary Act, ch 20, 1 Stat 73, 81, which provided that the Supreme Court had jurisdiction to issue "writs of *mandamus*, in cases warranted by the principles and usages of law, to any courts appointed, or persons holding office, under the authority of the United States." Cf. William W. Van Alstyne, *A Critical Guide to Marbury v. Madison*, 1969 Duke L J 1, 15–16 (arguing that Marshall easily might have read § 13 to grant mandamus only as part of the Supreme Court's otherwise existing jurisdiction). Opposition to the Federalist judiciary continued after *Marbury*, with attempts to remove some judges. See, for example, Haskins, *History of the Supreme Court* at 205–45 (cited in note 1) (discussing the impeachment and conviction of John Pickering, and the impeachment and acquittal of Justice Samuel Chase); Klarman, 87 Va L Rev at 1167–68 (cited in note 1) (discussing the impeachment effort against Justice Samuel Chase).

[30] 5 US (1 Cranch) 299, 308 (1803); Klarman, 87 Va L Rev at 1124–25 (cited in note 1) (indicating that Justice Samuel Chase and Chief Justice Marshall believed the 1802 law unconstitutional, but apparently thought that its invalidation would "guarantee Jeffersonian political retaliation against the court," and citing authority).

[31] The Court did not address the difficult issue of whether Congress could remove Article III judges by abolishing courts. See Currie, *The Constitution in the Supreme Court 1789–1888* at 75 (cited in note 19); Klarman, 87 Va L Rev at 1163 (cited in note 1) (treating *Stuart v Laird* as an instance when Marshall "knew when to duck"). Rather, the Court addressed whether jurisdiction could be transferred from a court created under the 1801 act to another federal court, 5 US (1 Cranch) at 308–9, and whether Supreme Court Justices could be assigned circuit duties without a separate appointment. Id at 309.

[32] See Herbert A. Johnson, *History of the Supreme Court of the United States, 1801–1815* at 646 (Cambridge, 2010) (indicating that at least for its early years the Marshall court "avoided direct conflict" with the political branches by taking a "narrow and restrictive view of the constitutional and statutory foundations of judicial power"); cf. White, *The Marshall Court and Cultural Change* at 883 (cited in note 13) (noting that the Marshall Court took care not to be overly expansive in decisions that might be seen as usurping state prerogatives).

other matters, the Court repeatedly emphasized that the federal courts could only exercise the power that Congress had granted by statute, even if jurisdiction was otherwise within the Article III judicial power.[33] Some of these cases primarily involved issues of federal judicial control of federal executive officers,[34] although the Marshall Court's caution in interpreting the scope of federal jurisdiction would also be manifest in diversity and admiralty cases.

For example, in *Ex parte Bollman*, the Marshall Court found both statutory and constitutional authorization for its issuance of writs of habeas corpus to determine the legality of detention by federal officials,[35] but disclaimed any common law jurisdiction to do so. "Courts which originate in the common law possess a jurisdiction which must be regulated by their common law," said Marshall, "but courts which are created by written law, and whose jurisdiction is defined by written law, cannot transcend that jurisdiction."[36] Marshall seemed to suggest, moreover, that habeas corpus addressing allegedly unlawful federal executive detention would be unavailable had Congress failed to provide habeas jurisdiction to the federal courts:

---

[33] See, for example, *Durousseau v United States*, 10 US (6 Cranch) 307 (1810) (stating that Congress, by providing less than the full appellate power described in Article III, had effectively made exceptions to the Supreme Court's appellate jurisdiction); Johnson, *History of the Supreme Court of the United States, 1801–1815* at 398–99, 404 (cited in note 32) (indicating that the Marshall Court showed reluctance to extend jurisdiction beyond that provided by statute); id at 403 (indicating that the Marshall Court tended to uphold congressional legislation). In *Martin v Hunter's Lessee*, 14 US (1 Wheat) 304, 331 (1816), Justice Story aired a mandatory vesting idea that suggested less congressional discretion, but the Marshall opinions overall helped to enshrine the notion of near-plenary congressional power over lower federal court jurisdiction.

[34] *McClung v Silliman*, 19 US (6 Wheat) 598 (1821), discussed in note 43, also involves issues of state court control of federal officers.

[35] 8 US (4 Cranch) 75 (1807); see Judiciary Act of 1789, ch 20, § 14, 1 Stat 73, 81–82. In *Bollman*, two prisoners challenged their detention on charges of treason by seeking habeas in the Supreme Court after the District of Columbia circuit court entered an order of commitment. 8 US (4 Cranch) at 75 (statement of the case). The prisoners were associated with Aaron Burr's western adventures, for which Burr would later be charged with, but not convicted of, treason. See Haskins, *History of the Supreme Court* at 248–62, 277, 285, 289 (cited in note 1). The Court held that the grant of habeas jurisdiction to the federal courts was not limited to granting the writ in aid of other jurisdiction, 8 US at 95–96, and that the federal courts could grant habeas although the grants of power were to "judges of the district courts" and "justices of the supreme court." Id at 96. It also held that its own habeas jurisdiction was "clearly appellate. It is the revision of a decision of an inferior court, by which a citizen has been committed to jail." Id at 101.

[36] 8 US (4 Cranch) at 93; see also note 204 (discussing *Bollman* as suggesting that state courts lacked jurisdiction to issue habeas with respect to federal executive detention).

> It may be worthy of remark that this [Judiciary] act was passed by the first congress of the United States, sitting under a constitution which had declared "that the privilege of the writ of *habeas corpus* should not be suspended. . . ." Acting under the immediate influence of this injunction, they must have felt, with peculiar force, the obligation of providing efficient means by which this great constitutional privilege should receive life and activity; for if the means be not in existence, the privilege itself would be lost, although no law for its suspension should be enacted.[37]

In the later case of *United States v Hudson & Goodwin*,[38] moreover, the Court held that the lower federal courts could not "exercise a common law jurisdiction in criminal cases," given that the jurisdiction of the inferior federal courts depended on statutory grants.[39]

In addition, mandamus continued to be an area of Marshall Court wariness. The Supreme Court in *Marbury* had lessened political fallout by holding that it lacked original jurisdiction under Article III to grant mandamus directed to a federal executive officer. In *McIntire v Wood*, claimants sought a writ of mandamus—but this time from a federal circuit court[40]—to compel the register of the federal land office to issue a certificate of purchase that the plaintiffs claimed they were entitled to under a federal statute. The Supreme Court held that Congress in the 1789 Judiciary Act had only granted the circuit courts power to issue mandamus in aid of otherwise existing statutory jurisdiction,[41] which was lacking in *McIntire* because Congress had not provided the circuit courts with jurisdiction over cases arising under the laws of the United States except in specified cases.[42] The Court subsequently indicated that Congress had also not authorized the issuance of original writs of mandamus to federal executive officers in

---

[37] Id at 95.

[38] 11 US (7 Cranch) 32, 33 (1812). See generally Haskins, *History of the Supreme Court* at 309–10 (cited in note 1) (discussing Marshall's ambivalence on common law crimes); id at 355 (indicating that both political parties seemed to disfavor common law crimes by the time of *Hudson*); White, *The Marshall Court and Cultural Change* at 458–59, 865 (cited in note 13) (indicating that Marshall had thought that crimes on the high seas could be punished without congressional statute, but that he retreated, and was aware of "concerns about the apparently necessary relationship between extensive judicial power in the federal courts and extensive legislative power in Congress" (footnote omitted)).

[39] 11 US (7 Cranch) at 32, 33.

[40] The circuit courts operated as trial courts, although they also exercised appellate jurisdiction over federal district court cases. See Judiciary Act of 1789, ch 20, § 11, 1 Stat 73, 78–79.

[41] 11 US (7 Cranch) 504, 506 (1813); see also Judiciary Act of 1789, ch 20, § 14, 1 Stat 73, 81.

[42] 11 US (7 Cranch) at 506.

diversity cases, even though the circuit courts' diversity jurisdiction under § 11 of the 1789 Judiciary Act arguably provided an existing basis of jurisdiction.[43] The implication seemed to be that Congress would explicitly have to grant the lower federal courts original mandamus jurisdiction with respect to federal officers.[44]

In *Marbury*, the Court had avoided implementing its dictum that the federal courts potentially could issue mandamus to federal officers by holding that Article III did not allow Congress to confer original mandamus jurisdiction on the Supreme Court. In *McIntire*, the Court similarly avoided issuing mandamus to a federal officer, but this time by determining that Congress had not conferred such power on the lower federal courts, and by deferring to congressional control over federal court jurisdiction.[45]

---

[43] In *McClung v Silliman*, 19 US (6 Wheat) 598 (1821), the Court held that state courts could not issue mandamus to an officer in the federal land office, in part because Congress had not given lower federal courts such power. Id at 604. Although *McClung* was a case of direct review, the petitioner argued in support of jurisdiction that *McIntire* could be distinguished because in *McClung* the parties were citizens of different states. See id at 601. The argument seemed to be that the federal courts would have had jurisdiction in *McIntire* had diversity existed, which would undermine the argument that the state court could not exercise a mandamus power that Congress had withheld from the lower federal courts. The Court, however, indicated that Congress had not granted power to the lower federal courts to issue original mandamus to federal officers, even where diversity existed. See *McClung*, 19 US (6 Wheat) at 601–2; see also *Kendall v United States ex rel. Stokes*, 37 US (12 Pet) 524, 615 (1838) ("It is admitted that those cases [*McIntire* and *McClung*] have decided that the circuit courts of the United States, in the several states, have not authority to issue a mandamus against an officer of the United States"); Paul M. Bator et al, *Hart and Wechsler's Federal Courts and the Federal System* 1378 (2d ed 1973) (indicating *McClung* "made plain that diversity of citizenship did not give such an independent jurisdiction").

[44] The Court thus treated the absence of an explicit congressional grant of original mandamus power with respect to federal officers as an absence of jurisdiction. Cf. *McClung*, 19 US (6 Wheat) at 601–2. This resembles its treatment of the absence of a statutory definition of a crime as indicating that federal courts lacked jurisdiction. See note 19; cf. *Kendall*, 37 US (12 Pet) at 628 (Taney, CJ, dissenting) (in disagreeing with the Court's holding that the circuit court for the District of Columbia could exercise original mandamus jurisdiction, stating that "[t]he power is certainly no where given in direct and positive terms"). Indeed, with the exception of *Kendall*'s holding that the Circuit Court for the District of Columbia had original mandamus jurisdiction, the requirement of an explicit grant continued. See Henry M. Hart, Jr. and Herbert Wechsler, *The Federal Courts and the Federal System* 1181 (1953) (hereafter *Hart & Wechsler I*) (indicating that *McIntire* had survived in spite of the 1875 general grant of federal question jurisdiction, and that original mandamus in federal courts outside of the District of Columbia was only under specific statutory grants); Clark Byse and Joseph V. Fiocca, *Section 1361 of the Mandamus and Venue Act of 1962 and "Nonstatutory" Judicial Review of Federal Administrative Action*, 81 Harv L Rev 308 (1967) (discussing legislation extending mandamus jurisdiction to federal district courts generally, Act of Oct 5, 1962, 76 Stat 744 (codified at 28 USC § 1361)).

[45] Cf. Richard H. Fallon, Jr., *Marbury and the Constitutional Mind: A Bicentennial Essay on the Wages of Doctrinal Tension*, 91 Cal L Rev 1, 52 n 271 (2003) (opining that in "the politically

C. DIVERSITY, FEDERAL QUESTIONS, AND CORPORATIONS

A wariness of expansive interpretation of federal judicial powers was also evident in diversity of citizenship jurisdiction. To be sure, some decisions allowed for rather easy manufacturing of diversity,[46] through certain transfers of interests and by reliance on the face of the pleadings to establish jurisdiction.[47] On the other hand, the Marshall Court in *Strawbridge v Curtiss*[48] read the statutory grant of diversity[49] to require complete diversity as between all plaintiffs and all defendants—a significant limit on the ability to invoke diversity jurisdiction. In addition, amid arguments against extending federal judicial power,[50] the Court held in *Bank of the United States v Deveaux* that corporations were not citizens for diversity purposes, seemingly as both a constitutional and statutory matter.[51] The Court stated, "The duties of this court, to exercise jurisdiction where it is conferred, and not to usurp it where it is not conferred, are of equal obligation."[52] It also held that Congress's giving the Bank of the

---

charged atmosphere" when the Court decided *Marbury*, "it seems highly doubtful that the Court . . . would have upheld the authority of the D.C. courts to order mandamus relief," as the Taney Court would later do in *Kendall*).

[46] See White, *The Marshall Court and Cultural Change* at 837–38 (cited in note 13) (characterizing the Marshall Court as "cautious" with respect to its direct review and admiralty jurisdiction, but expansive as to diversity); id at 843–45 (giving examples where diversity was sustained by holding that citizenship was determined at the commencement of litigation, giving a narrow interpretation to the Assignee Clause, Judiciary Act of 1789, ch 20, § 11, 1 Stat 73, 78–79, and treating as irrelevant a motive to create diversity by conveying land); Johnson, *History of the Supreme Court of the United States, 1801–1815* at 618 n 26 (cited in note 32) (citing *Browne v Strode*, 9 US (5 Cranch) 303 (1809) (holding that citizenship of nominal parties suing for an alien could be ignored, and upholding jurisdiction), and *Chappedelaine v Dechenaux*, 8 US (4 Cranch) 306, 307–8 (1808) (looking to citizenship of executor rather than testator, and sustaining diversity)).

[47] Michael G. Collins, *Jurisdictional Exceptionalism*, 93 Va L Rev 1829, 1838–43 (2007) (discussing that pleading good diversity often sufficed to establish subject matter jurisdiction, and that disincentives existed to challenging jurisdiction by a plea in abatement).

[48] 7 US (3 Cranch) 267, 267 (1806).

[49] See Judiciary Act of 1789, ch 20, § 11, 1 Stat 73, 78, granting jurisdiction where "an alien is a party, or the suit is between a citizen of the state where the suit is brought, and a citizen of another state."

[50] *Bank of the United States v Deveaux*, 9 US (5 Cranch) 61, 72–74 (1809) (argument of counsel).

[51] 9 US (5 Cranch) at 86–87; see also *Hope Insur. Co. v Boardman*, 9 US (5 Cranch) 57, 61 (1809) (stating that the Court in *Deveaux* "decided that the right of a corporation to litigate in the courts of the United States depended upon the character (as to citizenship) of the members which compose the body corporate, and that a body corporate as such cannot be a citizen, within the meaning of the constitution.").

[52] 9 US (5 Cranch) at 87.

United States the power "to sue and be sued . . . in courts of record, or any other place whatsoever" did not constitute a congressional grant of federal court jurisdiction, but only granted party capacity to the bank in cases where a court's jurisdiction otherwise existed.[53]

Deveaux involved the First Bank of the United States' challenge to a Georgia tax, thus presenting issues similar to the Second Bank's later challenge to an Ohio tax in *Osborn v Bank of the United States*.[54] The Court in *Deveaux* found a way around its own restrictive jurisdictional holding that corporations were not citizens by looking through the corporate form "to the character of the individuals who compose the corporation."[55] The Court then relied on the bank's untraversed pleadings that the members of the corporation all resided in Pennsylvania, while the defendants were all from Georgia; it thus upheld jurisdiction after all. This maneuver, however, would fail if the opposing party were prepared to traverse untrue allegations of citizenship of the members of the corporation, but that did not happen in *Deveaux*.[56] The Court, moreover, apparently treated all shareholders rather than just officers as constituents of the corporation, thus making complete diversity harder to establish.[57]

Of course, the Marshall Court later[58] gave expansive interpretations of federal question jurisdiction in *Osborn* and its companion

---

[53] Id at 84–86; see also LaCroix, 30 L and Hist Rev at 22 (cited in note 1) (characterizing *Deveaux* as Marshall's rejecting the Court's ability to clothe itself with broad "arising under" power; such power would need to come from Congress).

[54] 22 US (9 Wheat) 738 (1824).

[55] 9 US (5 Cranch) at 91–92; see also Swisher, *History of the Supreme Court* at 459 (cited in note 5) (indicating that *Deveaux*'s finding jurisdiction was "to take a considerable step" given the Jeffersonian hostility to "the federal courts and to large-scale business enterprise"); cf. White, *The Marshall Court and Cultural Change* at 749 (cited in note 13) (indicating there were only eighteen cases concerning partnerships or corporations on the Supreme Court's nonconstitutional docket from 1816 through 1835).

[56] In addition, interpretations of the 1789 diversity statute's language apparently limited jurisdiction to cases in which "all the corporators were citizens of the state in which the suit was brought." See *Louisville, Cincinnati, and Charleston Railroad Co. v Letson*, 43 US (2 How) 497, 555 (1844) (referring to this as the practice, and changing it); see note 133.

[57] See *Bank of the United States v Planters' Bank*, 22 US (9 Wheat) 904, 909–10 (1824); cf. *Breithaupt v Georgia*, 26 US (1 Pet) 238, 240 (1828) (indicating the federal court lacked jurisdiction in a suit brought by South Carolinians, because the pleadings did not show that the defendant corporate officials of a Georgia corporation "were citizens of Georgia, nor are there any distinct allegations . . . that the same was the fact, as to the stockholders in the bank"), discussed in White, *The Marshall Court and Cultural Change* at 836 (cited in note 13); see also id at 847 (summarizing various limitations on federal court jurisdiction discussed in an 1842 treatise).

[58] Some attribute nationalist cases such as *McCulloch* to the Court's enjoying greater latitude due to the rise of nationalism with the War of 1812. See Klarman, 87 Va L Rev at 1135–

case, *Bank of the United States v Planters' Bank.*[59] The Court held that Congress conferred jurisdiction on the federal courts whenever the bank was a party by the language in the Second Bank's charter that the bank could "sue and be sued . . . in any Circuit Court of the United States,"[60] distinguishing the First Bank's charter which had conferred power to "sue and be sued . . . in Courts of record, or any other place whatsoever."[61] In upholding federal jurisdiction in *Osborn* for cases in which the bank was a party, the Court tied its decision not only to the wording of the congressional charter, but also to the breadth of congressional power.

> In support of this clause, it is said, that the legislative, executive, and judicial powers, of every well constructed government, are co-extensive with each other; that is, they are potentially coextensive. The executive department may constitutionally execute every law which the Legislature may constitutionally make, and the judicial department may receive from the Legislature the power of construing every such law.[62]

Osborn was thus the jurisdictional counterpart to *McCulloch v Maryland*, where the Court had held on direct review that Congress had power to create the bank as necessary and proper to various enumerated powers granted to Congress in Article I.[63] In *Osborn*, the federal courts could exercise power because Congress had properly legislated under its broad Article I powers and had provided for commensurate jurisdiction that the Court held to be within the Ar-

---

36 (cited in note 1). Few constitutionally-based objections arose, moreover, when Congress chartered the Second Bank in 1816. See id at 1129; cf. Gerald Leonard, *Party as a "Political Safeguard of Federalism": Martin Van Buren and the Constitutional Theory of Party Politics*, 54 Rutgers L Rev 221, 242 (2001) (indicating that the Marshall Court did "little to irk the Jeffersonians after the *Marbury* case of 1803 until after the close of the War of 1812" (footnotes omitted)). On the other hand, *McCulloch* and other nationalist decisions evoked states' rights–based criticism, which Professor Klarman attributes partially to backlash against those decisions. Klarman, 87 Va L Rev at 1138 (cited in note 1); cf. Newmyer, *The Supreme Court under Marshall and Taney* at 82 (cited in note 12) ("For its last decade (1825–1835), the [Marshall] Court faced a hostile political and economic environment. . . .").

[59] 22 US (9 Wheat) 904 (1824).

[60] *Osborn*, 22 US (9 Wheat) at 817 ("sue and be sued, plead and be impleaded, answer and be answered, defend and be defended, in all state courts having competent jurisdiction, and in any Circuit Court of the United States").

[61] Id at 817.

[62] 22 US (9 Wheat) at 818; White, *The Marshall Court and Cultural Change* at 527–28 (cited in note 13) ("The linchpin of Marshall's *Osborn* opinion was once again conterminous power theory.").

[63] 17 US (4 Wheat) 316 (1819).

ticle III arising under grant.[64] The Marshall Court, however, would not employ the more radical version of coterminous powers so reprobated by Jeffersonians whereby the federal courts might treat English common law as federal law, which in turn could be read to expand congressional power over common law subjects, in derogation of the limitations on congressional powers in the Constitution.[65]

While *Osborn* and *Planters'* provided perhaps the broadest ever interpretation of Article III "arising under" jurisdiction, the decisions at the time helped only one corporation—the Second Bank of the United States.[66] Most corporations were chartered by state legislatures rather than Congress, meaning that there was no federal charter language that might be read as supporting federal court jurisdiction. Nor could state-chartered corporations often take advantage of diversity jurisdiction in the federal courts, given the Court's requirements of complete diversity and its treating all shareholders as parties.

Indeed, the Court's broad reading of the Second Bank's charter and of Article III federal question jurisdiction provided a means for the bank to get around the Court's prior narrow interpretation of corporate diversity jurisdiction. The *Planters' Bank* decision noted the near impossibility of the bank's satisfying the requirements of diversity jurisdiction given that the bank had investors in all commercial states.[67] The Court in *Deveaux* had managed to uphold diversity jurisdiction for the First Bank, but only because the bank's

---

[64] See also *Cohens v Virginia*, 19 US (6 Wheat) 264, 384 (1821).

[65] See note 20 and accompanying text; cf. White, *Recovering Coterminous Power Theory* at 98 (cited in note 8) (indicating that the concerns as to coterminous powers faded over time, particularly the concern that federal court jurisdiction might imply congressional regulatory power); id (seeing the Marshall Court as allowing for more concurrent state power in commerce cases after *McCulloch*).

[66] See LaCroix, 30 L and Hist Rev at 234 (cited in note 1) (noting that *Osborn's* return to 1801 act's views of "arising under" jurisdiction only applied to cases involving the bank). The bank's charter, moreover, expired in 1836, President Jackson having vetoed renewal of the charter in 1832. See Carl Brent Swisher, *Roger B. Taney* 197, 250 (Macmillan, 1935). The bank reincorporated as a Pennsylvania corporation and dissolved in 1841. See Swisher, *History of the Supreme Court* at 123–24 (cited in note 5).

[67] *Bank of the United States v Planters' Bank*, 22 US (9 Wheat) 904, 909–10 (1824) ("There is, probably, not a commercial State in the Union, some of whose citizens are not members of the Bank of the United States. There is, consequently, scarcely a debt due to the Bank, for which a suit could be maintained in a federal Court, did the jurisdiction of the Court depend on [diversity of] citizenship."); see also *Osborn*, 22 US (9 Wheat) at 813 (argument of counsel) (arguing against jurisdiction in *Planters'* that no averment of diversity could have honestly been made).

allegations of Pennsylvania citizenship of its members were untraversed. The defendant in *Planters' Bank*, however, had contested citizenship.[68] The Court's holding in *Osborn* and *Planters'* that the federal charter conferred federal question jurisdiction[69] thus gave the Second Bank jurisdiction similar to what it would have had if it had been able to invoke diversity jurisdiction with respect to either the Ohio auditor in *Osborn*, or the Georgia bank in *Planters'*—that is, jurisdiction encompassing federal issues and ordinary nonfederal questions alike.[70] But again, the expansive view of federal judicial power was in service of the bank, which was a creation of Congress.

D. ADMIRALTY

The Marshall Court's narrow interpretations of diversity jurisdiction were paralleled in admiralty. In *The Thomas Jefferson*, a worker brought a libel in admiralty for "subtraction of wages" as to a river voyage from Kentucky to Missouri and back. The Court affirmed the dismissal of the case because the wage claim did not relate to employment on the sea nor on waters within the ebb and flow of the tide.[71] Justice Story seemed to treat this limit on the admiralty jurisdiction as a constitutional one that Congress could not exceed, at least as a matter of Article III's admiralty provision.[72] Story him-

---

[68] 22 US (9 Wheat) at 905.

[69] *Osborn*, 22 US (9 Wheat) at 823 ("It is not only itself the mere creature of a law, but all its actions and all its rights are dependent on the same law. Can a being, thus constituted, have a case which does not arise literally, as well as substantially, under the law?").

[70] Id at 824 (indicating that the right of the bank to sue once decided "is decided for ever" but reasoning that defendants might at will revive capacity issues). Indeed, the traditional concern about *Osborn* and *Planters'* is the Court's effectively allowing for a protective jurisdiction similar to diversity. See Fallon et al, *Hart and Wechsler's The Federal Courts and the Federal System* at 785, 792 (cited in note 21) (suggesting that *Osborn* and *Planters'* were instances of protective jurisdiction); see also *The Pacific Railroad Removal Cases*, 115 US 1 (1885) (effectively providing similar protections to federally-chartered railroads based on *Osborn*); 28 USC § 1348 (treating national banks as citizens of "the States in which they are respectively located"); *Wachovia Bank v Schmidt*, 546 US 303, 307 (2006) (interpreting this citizenship to be only in the state where the bank has its main office, as set forth in its articles of association).

[71] *The Steam-Boat Thomas Jefferson*, 23 US (10 Wheat) 428 (1825).

[72] 23 US (10 Wheat) at 429 ("This is the prescribed limit which [the admiralty] was not at liberty to transcend."); see also Johnson, *History of the Supreme Court of the United States, 1801–1815* at 632 (cited in note 32) (stating that "the Marshall Court in this early period was extremely cautious in expanding admiralty jurisdiction beyond its traditional English limits."); see also White, *The Marshall Court and Cultural Change* at 471–74 (cited in note 13) (discussing evidence that Marshall may have been strategic in his acquiescence in *Thomas*

self favored broad federal jurisdiction, as manifested in his Circuit Court decision in *DeLovio v Boit* extending the admiralty jurisdiction to all maritime contracts.[73] He suggested in *The Thomas Jefferson* that Congress should take the lead on extending jurisdiction over cases involving navigation on inland waters,[74] perhaps under the Commerce Clause rather than by legislation to enforce the admiralty provision of Article III.[75] And Story would later help to draft legislation to extend federal trial court jurisdiction to the Great Lakes, thus leaving this expansion of jurisdiction to Congress.[76]

E. DIRECT REVIEW OF STATE COURTS

Under standard accounts of the Madisonian Compromise—the agreement at the Constitutional Convention to empower Congress to create lower federal courts rather than mandating them—it was lower federal court jurisdiction and not direct review of state court decisions in the Supreme Court that was the main source of disputes among the Framers. Aggressive assertions of lower federal court powers during the Federalist era, such as in some judges' recognition of common law crimes, did nothing to shake the anti-Federalists' (later, Jeffersonians') preference for the direct review model in which the Supreme Court sat atop the state courts. The Marshall Court's early exercise of direct review of state courts under § 25 of the 1789 Judi-

---

Jefferson); Newmyer, *The Supreme Court under Marshall and Taney* at 84–85 (cited in note 12) (seeing *The Thomas Jefferson* as at least partly a response to the "strategic vulnerability" of the Court).

[73] *DeLovio v Boit*, 7 F Cas 418, 441 (CCD Mass 1815) (Story, J) (indicating that all maritime contracts including insurance contracts, as well as all torts, injuries, and offenses on high seas, and in ports as far as the ebb and flow of the tide, were within the admiralty jurisdiction). This contract jurisdiction was broader than that exercised in England. See id at 441, 443.

[74] In *The Thomas Jefferson*, the Court also declined to interpret certain other statutes as intended to extend the jurisdiction. 23 US (10 Wheat) at 430.

[75] Id ("Whether, under the power to regulate commerce between the States, Congress may not extend the remedy, by the summary process of Admiralty, to the case of voyages on the western waters, it is unnecessary for us to consider."); see also Swisher, *History of the Supreme Court* at 323, 429 (cited in note 5) (indicating that around 1842, Story submitted a draft bill for extension of admiralty to the Great Lakes). The idea seems to have been that interstate traffic on inland waters was within the commerce power, although not within Article III's and the 1789 Judiciary Act's grant of admiralty. There would still be a constitutional question of whether Congress could grant federal court jurisdiction without having also regulated substantively. See text accompanying note 171. But cf. *Textile Workers Union v Lincoln Mills*, 353 US 448 (1957) (treating the grant of jurisdiction to the federal courts over certain union contracts as conferring power to make federal common law).

[76] See text accompanying notes 156–60.

ciary Act[77] raised little opposition.[78] For the most part, moreover, the Marshall Court was careful to respect congressional limits on direct review in § 25, which excluded certain claims of state overvindication of federal rights, and which required that federal issues appear on the face of the record.[79] Consistent with its decisions respecting congressional power over lower federal court jurisdiction, the Court said that it could only exercise such appellate jurisdiction as Congress had provided for.[80] And although the Court's appellate power was arguably granted by the Constitution "with such Exceptions . . . as the Congress shall make,"[81] the Court held that the limited statutory grant under the 1789 Judiciary Act operated as an exception of all remaining appellate jurisdiction.[82]

Supreme Court reversals of politically sensitive state court decisions, however, eventually occasioned opposition to the Court's exercise of its § 25 jurisdiction. "Compact theory," which had surfaced

---

[77] Judiciary Act of 1789, ch 20, § 25, 1 Stat 73, 85–87 (providing, with various limitations, appellate review of federal questions arising in final judgments from the state courts).

[78] Johnson, *History of the Supreme Court of the United States, 1801–1815* at 626 (cited in note 32) (indicating that the early Marshall Court's work under § 25 was not of great political concern, but that *Martin v Hunter's Lessee*, 14 US (1 Wheat) 304 (1816), led to a more direct confrontation); Charles Warren, *Legislative and Judicial Attacks on the Supreme Court of the United States— A History of the Twenty-Fifth Section of the Judiciary Act*, 47 Am L Rev 1, 6 & n 12 (1913) (noting some state court objections to federal jurisdiction generally, but that otherwise, prior to 1816, the "Supreme Court had, without serious opposition of counsel or of State courts, taken jurisdiction of writs of error to such courts in sixteen cases," listing those cases, and indicating that the Judiciary Act was held inapplicable in two such cases). Warren notes that "the apparent acquiescence in the power of the Supreme Court" was evidently due to the fact that "of these sixteen writs of error only two had involved the direct question of the repugnancy between the Federal Constitution and a State statute." Id at 6; see, for example, *New Jersey v Wilson*, 11 US (7 Cranch) 164 (1812) (holding violative of the Contract Clause the state's repeal of a statutory tax exemption for lands purchased by the Delaware Indians); cf. *Smith v Maryland*, 10 US (6 Cranch) 286, 306–7 (1810) (holding that under state law a confiscation of land of a British subject occurred before the 1783 treaty forbidding further confiscation); *Palmer v Allen*, 11 US (7 Cranch) 550 (1813) (reversing a damages judgment against a deputy US marshal).

[79] Judiciary Act of 1789, ch 20, § 25, 1 Stat 73, 85–87.

[80] *Clarke v Bazadone*, 5 US (1 Cranch) 212, 214 (1803) (quashing a writ of error from a territorial court, because an "act of congress had not authorized an appeal or writ of error"); see also *Gordon v Caldcleugh*, 7 US (3 Cranch) 268, 270 (1806) (determining that a writ of error from the state court's allowing removal was unavailable because the decision "was not *against* the privilege claimed under the statute; and, therefore, this court has no jurisdiction in the case"); *Williams v Norris*, 25 US (12 Wheat) 117, 118 (1827) (stating that the Court "can exercise no other jurisdiction in the case than is given by the 25th Section of the Judiciary Act"). But cf. *Fairfax's Devisee v Hunter's Lessee*, 11 US (7 Cranch) 603 (1813) (reviewing state law issues that bore on the treaty claim).

[81] US Const, Art III, § 2, cl 2.

[82] *Durousseau v United States*, 10 US (6 Cranch) 307, 314 (1810).

in the Virginia and Kentucky Resolutions opposing the Alien and Sedition laws and that was later enlisted to support secession, bolstered arguments against direct review.[83] Compact theorists treated the Constitution as an agreement among the states, which implied that individual states could reject assertions of federal power that the state deemed clearly to violate the compact.[84] For example, in *Fairfax's Devisee v Hunter's Lessee*, the Supreme Court held that Virginia's confiscation of Lord Fairfax's land violated the 1783 Treaty of Peace between the United States and Great Britain.[85] On remand, the Virginia Court of Appeals held that § 25 violated the Constitution, and refused to enter the decree,[86] thus necessitating the Supreme Court's reaffirmation of its power to review state court judgments when the case returned as *Martin v Hunter's Lessee*.

Opponents of Supreme Court review in *Martin* argued that the states—as constituents of a compact—could not be conclusively bound by a decision of the United States through the federal courts, and that the Constitution had not explicitly granted Supreme Court review of state court judgments.[87] To arguments that the lack of Supreme Court review of state court judgments would undermine the enforcement and uniformity of federal law, the compact theorists responded that problems as to enforcing federal law and uniformity

[83] See White, *The Marshall Court and Cultural Change* at 126 (cited in note 13) (discussing support for compact theory and the view that the federal government should not be able to review the activities of states courts and legislatures).

[84] Virginia Resolutions, Dec 21, 1798, in *The Virginia Report of 1799–1800* at 22 (Lawbook Exchange, 2004) ("That this Assembly doth explicitly . . . declare, that it views the powers of the Federal Government as resulting from the compact, to which the States are parties, as limited by the plain sense and intention of the instrument constituting that compact; as no further valid than they are authorized by the grants enumerated in that compact; and that in case of a deliberate, palpable, and dangerous exercise of other powers not granted by the said compact, the States, who are the parties thereto, have the right, and are in duty bound, to interpose for arresting the progress of the evil, and for maintaining, within their respective limits, the authorities, rights, and liberties appertaining to them.").

[85] 11 US (7 Cranch) 603 (1813).

[86] See *Hunter v Martin*, 18 Va 1, 15 (1815), rev'd sub nom *Martin v Hunter's Lessee*, 14 US (1 Wheat) 304, 323 (1816); Klarman, 87 Va L Rev at 1142–42 (cited in note 1) (noting widespread opposition in Virginia to *Martin*, *Cohens v Virginia*, 19 US (6 Wheat) 264 (1821), and *McCulloch v Maryland*, 17 US (4 Wheat) 316 (1819)).

[87] See *Hunter*, 18 Va at 52–53 (opinion of Roane, J) (discussing with approval a Pennsylvania opinion, to the effect "that when two nations differ, about the construction of a league or treaty, existing between them, neither has the exclusive right to decide it; and that, if one of the states should differ with the United States, as to the extent of the grant made to them, there is no common umpire between them, but the people, by an amendment of the constitution"); id at 14 (opinion of Cabell, J) (arguing that the Constitution did not expressly give the Supreme Court the power to review state court judgments, and that such power should not be implied).

could be resolved by providing lower federal courts to which parties could resort if they chose.[88] At least for purposes of these arguments against the Supreme Court's appellate jurisdiction over state courts, then, lower federal court jurisdiction was preferable to direct review.[89] This seemed to mark something of a reversal of the position of the Anti-Federalists who once had championed the absence of lower federal courts altogether.[90] Similar arguments surfaced with respect to Supreme Court review in *McCulloch v Maryland*[91] and *Cohens v Virginia*.[92] Some members of Congress piled on by threatening to repeal § 25.[93]

The Marshall Court famously rebuffed state-court challenges to direct review. The Court responded to compact-theory arguments that the Union was the creation of the people, not a compact among

---

[88] *Martin*, 14 US (1 Wheat) at 319–20 (argument of counsel) (arguing that Supreme Court appellate jurisdiction extended only to lower federal courts); *Hunter v Martin*, 18 Va 1, 15 (1815) (opinion of Cabell, J) ("All the purposes of the constitution of the United States will be answered by the erection of Federal Courts, into which any party, plaintiff or defendant, concerned in a case of federal cognizance, *may* carry it for adjudication. . . ."); id at 22 (opinion of Brooke, J) (indicating that he did not foresee dangerous consequences of his interpretation, because the "power which is given to congress to ordain and establish inferior courts, was evidently intended to enable the national government to institute, in each state or district of the United States, a tribunal competent to the determination of all matters of national jurisdiction within its limits, whenever deemed necessary by congress").

In addition, state courts increasingly took the position that they would not enforce various federal civil actions for fines and penalties brought by the United States. Instead, state courts began to assert that Congress would be obliged to supply lower federal courts to enforce such provisions. See Michael G. Collins and Jonathan Remy Nash, *Prosecuting Federal Crimes in State Courts*, 97 Va L Rev 243, 266–70 (2011); Michael G. Collins, *Article III Cases, State Court Duties, and the Madisonian Compromise*, 1995 Wis L Rev 39, 146–47.

[89] See Graber, *Jacksonian Makings* at 21 (cited in note 5) (indicating that opponents of judicial review in the 1820s focused on § 25); White, *The Marshall Court and Cultural Change* at 843 (cited in note 13) (indicating the states were less sensitive to the potential creation by the lower federal courts of an alternative jurisprudence than they were of direct review).

[90] See Collins and Nash, 97 Va L Rev at 269 n 100 (cited in note 88).

[91] See Spencer Roane writing as Hampden in the *Richmond Enquirer* (June 22, 1819), reprinted in Gerald Gunther, ed, *John Marshall's Defense of McCulloch v. Maryland* 138, 152 (Stanford, 1969) (in discussing his "objection to the jurisdiction of the court," stating, "When a right is claimed by one of the contracting parties to pass finally upon the rights or powers of another, we ought at least to expect to see an *express* provision for it."); LaCroix, 30 L and Hist Rev at 239 (cited in note 1) (noting that Roane suggested that Supreme Court review was more of a problem than lower federal courts).

[92] 19 US (6 Wheat) 264, 315 (1821) (argument of counsel) ("The appellate jurisdiction conferred by the constitution on the Supreme Court, is merely authority to revise the decisions of inferior Courts of the United States."); White, *The Marshall Court and Cultural Change* at 508 (cited in note 13) (discussing Virginia's arguments).

[93] See, for example, Charles Warren, *The Supreme Court in United States History 1789–1835* at 663 (Little, Brown, 1926) (discussing proposals to repeal § 25 beginning in 1822); Graber, *Jacksonian Makings* at 17 (cited in note 5) (noting an 1831 effort to repeal § 25 that was defeated by a wide margin).

the states.[94] The federal government, although of limited powers, was "supreme within its sphere of action,"[95] such that states could not interpose their power to refuse to enforce Supreme Court judgments.[96] And while the federal courts could only exercise the jurisdiction given by Congress and within the Constitution, they were obligated to entertain such jurisdiction when properly invoked.[97] The mantra against exercising unprovided-for jurisdiction could therefore be flipped to justify mandatorily exercising jurisdiction that Congress had provided for.

In summary, the Marshall Court faced Republican opposition to expanding federal court power. In response, the Marshall Court tied its own powers to the recognition of broad congressional legislative powers. The Court's Congress-centric approach to jurisdiction lessened conflict with Congress, while also giving play to the Court's capacious view of national power. It repeatedly referred to congressional control of its jurisdiction and abjured common law jurisdiction and common law crimes. In addition, it often gave restrained interpretations to the existing statutory grants of mandamus, diversity, and admiralty jurisdiction. On the other hand, in keeping with its broad view of congressional powers to provide for a Bank of the United States in *McCulloch*, it gave a broad view to Article III arising under jurisdiction in *Osborn* such that the federal courts could take jurisdiction over matters, such as cases involving the bank, as to which Congress could and did legislate.

II. The Taney Court

The Taney Court had more latitude than the Marshall Court to expand federal judicial power without necessarily evoking accusations that it was concomitantly expanding congressional power. After

---

[94] *Martin*, 14 US (1 Wheat) at 332 (stating that the Confederation was a compact between the states, but the Constitution was the act of the people); *McCulloch*, 17 US (4 Wheat) at 429 (stating that sovereignty of the states does not extend to the means employed by Congress, and that the people of a single state cannot confer a sovereignty which will extend over the people of the United States).

[95] *McCulloch*, 17 US (4 Wheat) at 405; see also *Cohens*, 19 US (6 Wheat) at 381.

[96] *Cohens*, 19 US (6 Wheat) at 389 (stating that the people made the Constitution and could unmake it, but that power resides only in the whole body and not a subdivision); see also Warren, *The Supreme Court in United States History 1789–1835* at 547–50 (cited in note 93) (discussing Virginia's opposition to the Supreme Court's jurisdiction in *Cohens*).

[97] *Cohens*, 19 US (6 Wheat) at 404.

all, the Jacksonian agenda shared by Taney and many of his fellow Justices[98] was characterized by opposition to the Bank of the United States,[99] by opposition to the expansive version of congressional power by which the Marshall Court in *McCulloch v Maryland* had upheld it,[100] and by opposition to *McCulloch*'s deference to congressional judgments as to the scope of Congress's own powers.[101] For Jacksonians, moreover, broad powers under the Commerce Clause or other constitutional provisions raised the specter that Congress might not only charter banks[102] and more widely fund internal improvements,[103] but

---

[98] Schwartz, *A History of the Supreme Court* at 71 (cited in note 5) (indicating Jackson appointed six Justices); see also Klarman, 87 Va L Rev at 1131 (cited in note 1) ("So long as states' rights Democrats controlled either the Senate or the presidency—which they did without interruption from the late 1820s through 1860—the nationalist followers of Henry Clay and Daniel Webster were powerless to capitalize on the [Marshall] Court's generous understanding of congressional power." (footnote omitted)).

[99] As President Jackson's Attorney General, Taney helped to draft Jackson's 1832 message accompanying veto of the bank's reincorporation, and as Secretary of the Treasury, Taney withdrew government deposits from the Second Bank. See Swisher, *History of the Supreme Court* at 100–104 (cited in note 5). Jackson's Farewell Address, which Taney helped to write, also spoke against the bank, federally-funded internal improvements, and too broad a view of federal government powers. Andrew Jackson's Farewell Address, March 4, 1837, in James D. Richardson, ed, 3 *Messages and Papers of the Presidents 1789–1897* at 298–300, 303 (Government Printing Office, 1896); Swisher, *Roger B. Taney* at 335–36 (cited in note 66) (indicating that Taney helped to draft the address).

[100] The debate about the extent of congressional powers continued to play out in the political branches. See, for example, Klarman, 87 Va L Rev at 1130–31 (cited in note 1) (discussing presidential vetoes of internal improvements bills); Graber, *Dred Scott and the Problem of Constitutional Evil* at 71–72 (cited in note 2) ("*McCulloch* survived the Taney Court only because Jacksonian presidents vetoed on constitutional grounds every measure that might have given the justices an opportunity to overrule or narrow Marshall's broad conception of national power." (footnote omitted)).

[101] Jackson's Bank Veto Message argued that some of the bank's powers "are unauthorized by the Constitution." Veto Message, July 10, 1832, in James D. Richardson, ed, 2 *Messages and Papers of the Presidents 1789–1897* at 576 (Government Printing Office, 1896). The message cleverly relied on Marshall's statements that the degree of necessity was a matter for legislative consideration, by arguing that the President acting in his legislative capacity could also make such determinations. Id at 582–83. "Without commenting on the general principle affirmed by the Supreme Court," Jackson proceeded to state that many of the powers and privileges conferred on the bank were unnecessary "and consequently not justified by the Constitution." Id at 583; id at 588 (questioning the Supreme Court's implication that the "power over means is so absolute that the Supreme Court will not call in question the constitutionality of an act of Congress"); see also Magliocca, *Andrew Jackson and the Constitution* at 54–55 (cited in note 7) (discussing Daniel Webster's concern that the Veto Message did not respect legislative precedent).

[102] Cf. Leonard, 54 Rutgers L Rev at 275 (cited in note 58) (discussing Martin Van Buren as a theorist for the Democratic party, and his opposition to restoration of a national bank).

[103] See Graber, *Jacksonian Makings* at 8 (cited in note 5) (noting Jacksonian opposition to internal improvements); id at 29 (noting that Democratic platforms from 1840 to 1860 fa-

also regulate slavery.[104] Indeed, debates as to whether Congress could prohibit slavery in the federal territories surfaced contemporaneously with *McCulloch*, occasioned by Missouri's seeking admission to the Union as a slave state.[105] And many saw preventing Congress from limiting the spread of slavery as necessary to preserve the Union.[106]

---

vored limited federal powers, and opposed a national bank and federally-financed internal improvements); id at 3 (noting success of Jackson at appointing jurists committed to narrow federal powers); Leonard, 54 Rutgers L Rev at 267 (cited in note 58) (indicating that Jackson and Van Buren believed that some national projects might be within the scope of congressional powers, but that funding local projects was beyond federal power); Kelly, Harbison, and Belz, *The American Constitution: Its Origins and Development* at 202 (cited in note 17) (indicating Jackson approved some internal improvements).

[104] See, for example, Klarman, 87 Va L Rev at 1141 & n 156 (cited in note 1) (stating that for southerners from 1819 on, "the scope of congressional power could not be divorced from the slavery issue," thus explaining the "ferocity of the Virginians' attack on *McCulloch*"). The Justices seemed to agree that Congress could not regulate slavery under the Commerce Clause. See *Groves v Slaughter*, 40 US (15 Pet) 449 (1841) (holding in a suit to collect on a contract for payment for a sale of slaves, that the Mississippi constitution's prohibition on bringing slaves into the state for sale required state legislation to be effective, and not reaching the plaintiff's claim that the state prohibition violated the Commerce Clause); id at 507 (McLean, J, concurring) (indicating that Congress could not regulate sales of slaves as commerce, but rather the matter was one for the states); id at 508 (Taney, CJ, concurring) (stating that power over whether to allow slaves to be brought into the state from another state and their treatment within the state was exclusively within the power of the several states and "cannot be controlled by Congress, either by virtue of its power to regulate commerce, or by virtue of any other power conferred by the Constitution of the United States"); id at 510 ("Mr. Justice Story, Mr. Justice Thompson, Mr. Justice Wayne, and Mr. Justice M'Kinley concurred with the majority of the Court in opinion" that the power of Congress over commerce "did not interfere with the provision of the constitution of the state of Mississippi, which relates to the introduction of slaves as merchandise, or for sale"); cf. id at 515 (Baldwin, J) (indicating that in states that recognized slavery, slaves were property, and if the state allowed trafficking in them among their own citizens, the Privileges and Immunities Clause would require that out of staters could trade on the same footing); id (indicating that Congress has no power to determine whether slaves could be held as property in each state).

[105] See Klarman, 87 Va L Rev at 1140–41 (cited in note 1). Professor Klarman states that "just three weeks before *McCulloch* was decided, Congress began debating the admission of Missouri to the Union." He describes the issues that arose in the Missouri Compromise debates:

> First, did Congress have the power to condition the admission of new states into the Union on their forbidding slavery in their constitutions? Second, did Congress have the power to bar slavery from national territories. . . . The Constitution does not clearly answer either of these questions. Both turn on the scope of Congress's implied powers, which, of course, was precisely the same issue adjudicated in *McCulloch*.

[106] See Kelly, Harbison, and Belz, *The American Constitution: Its Origins and Development* at 280 (cited in note 17) (stating that before the election of 1860, "state sovereignty was intended to serve the southern constitutional purpose of preserving the Union on the basis of proslavery principles").

While the Taney Court overall had a relatively narrow view of congressional powers including the commerce power,[107] it nevertheless favored preserving the Union[108] and promoting national commerce.[109] The Court resolved any seeming tension between this nationalism on the one hand, and distrust of congressional power on the other, by expanding federal judicial power while minimizing concomitant expansions of federal legislative power.[110]

---

[107] Scholars tend to see the Taney Court as generally having a less expansive view of the commerce power than the Marshall Court, and as less favorable to suggestions that exercised or unexercised commerce power excluded state regulation. See generally Schwartz, *A History of the Supreme Court* at 79–88 (cited in note 5) (discussing police power and commerce cases). Professor Schwartz has said that neither the Marshall nor the Taney Court was a proponent of exclusive federal commerce power, but where "Marshall and Taney differed was in their conception of just how much power over commerce remained in the states." Id at 82; see also Swisher, *History of the Supreme Court* at 357 (cited in note 5) (indicating that most Commerce Clause cases involved whether states could exercise power in light of federal statutes or dormant commerce power). Schwartz points to *Mayor of New York v Miln*, 36 US (11 Pet) 102 (1837), as a case that the Marshall Court would have decided differently. Schwartz, *A History of the Supreme Court* at 77 (cited in note 5). The Taney Court in *Miln* allowed as within the state's police power a requirement that ship masters provide a record of landing passengers and post a bond to cover costs if the passengers became public charges; the Marshall Court presumably would have found the law impinged on the federal government's power over foreign commerce. Id at 78–79. Justice Curtis's opinion for the Taney Court in *Cooley v Board of Wardens of the Port of Philadelphia*, 53 US (12 How) 299 (1851), is generally seen as providing a template for concurrency of state and federal powers with some areas necessarily exclusive to the federal government. Schwartz, *A History of the Supreme Court* at 84–86 (cited in note 5). The Taney Court is also seen as having a less expansive view of the Contract Clause than the Marshall Court. Cf. Currie, *The Constitution in the Supreme Court 1789–1888* at 209 (cited in note 19) (discussing *Charles River Bridge v Warren Bridge*, 36 US (11 Pet) 420 (1837)).

[108] Cf. Kelly, Harbison, and Belz, *The American Constitution: Its Origins and Development* at 201–2 (cited in note 17) (discussing that the Jacksonians at once rejected centralization, but also saw union as essential). Given the states-rights bent of the Democrats, obviously not all were staunch unionists. See, for example, id at 201 (indicating that southern planters and John C. Calhoun joined the Jackson movement).

[109] See Newmyer, *The Supreme Court under Marshall and Taney* at 110–12 (cited in note 12) (describing the Taney Court as favorable to the sanctity of private property, corporate capitalism, and national commerce, and discussing, inter alia, *Louisville, Cincinnati & Charleston Railroad v Letson*, 43 US (2 How) 497 (1844), *Swift v Tyson*, 41 US (16 Pet) 1 (1842), and *The Propeller Genesee Chief v Fitzhugh*, 53 US (12 How) 443 (1851)); id at 113 ("The [Taney] Court showed no doubt . . . that economic enterprise and social progress went hand-in-hand. . . ."); Swisher, *History of the Supreme Court* at 154 (cited in note 5) (indicating that the Taney Court provided a substantial bulwark against the breakdown of contractual relations); id at 328 (noting that Story and other Justices were interested in protecting the commercial community's use of bills of exchange).

[110] See Herbert Hovenkamp, *Enterprise and American Law 1836–1937* at 83 (Harvard, 1991) ("[Story's] great treatises on commercial law were generally hostile toward statutory regulation, unless it merely codified rules created by custom. Story practically worshipped the *lex mercatoris*. . . ."); cf. White, *Recovering Coterminous Power Theory* at 98 (cited in note 8) (suggesting that the Marshall Court cut back on expansive interpretations of the Commerce

A. REDUCED DEFERENCE TO CONGRESS; MANDAMUS

An early example of the Taney Court's reduced deference to Congress was its determination that the District of Columbia Circuit Court could issue writs of mandamus directed against federal officers. As discussed above, the Marshall Court in *Marbury* had avoided issuing mandamus to a federal executive official by finding no original Supreme Court mandamus jurisdiction under Article III, and later reached a similar result with respect to the lower federal courts in *McIntire* by holding that Congress had failed to confer such jurisdiction. In *Kendall v United States ex rel. Stokes*,[111] however, the Taney Court affirmed the District of Columbia Circuit Court's issuing mandamus to compel the Postmaster General to credit the plaintiffs' accounts as Congress had directed in a special bill.[112]

To be sure, the particular order implemented a specific congressional directive to the Postmaster,[113] and thus was unlikely unduly to upset Congress—even if the executive branch objected.[114] Still, the Court had to do some fancy footwork to find that mandamus juris-

---

Clause to preserve Article III power); LaCroix, 30 L and Hist Rev at 206 (cited in note 1) (saying that Marshall and Story were committed to a judiciary-centric federalism).

State legislative overspending on internal improvements, attributed in part to cronyism, reinforced a less favorable view of legislatures relative to judiciaries. See Jed Handelsman Shugarman, *Economic Crisis and the Rise of Judicial Elections and Judicial Review*, 123 Harv L Rev 1061, 1067 (2010) (attributing the rise of elected judiciaries to 1840s revulsion from state legislatures' accumulation of debt for internal improvements, partly attributed to corruption); id at 1080 (tying antidebt sentiment to Republican and Jacksonian resistance to a national bank); see also Kermit L. Hall, *The Judiciary on Trial: State Constitutional Reform and the Rise of an Elected Judiciary, 1846–1860*, 45 Historian 337 (1983) (seeing elections as meant to enhance the prestige of the judiciary). But cf. Caleb Nelson, *A Re-Evaluation of Scholarly Explanations for the Rise of the Elective Judiciary in Antebellum America*, 37 Am J Legal Hist 190, 203, 206, 224 (1993) (seeing the elective judiciary as a means to strengthen judiciaries relative to legislatures, but also aimed at weakening officialdom as a whole).

[111] 37 US (12 Pet) 524 (1838).

[112] Id at 610.

[113] Id at 611 (indicating Congress had passed a special bill and "[t]he terms of the submission [to the solicitor of the Treasury] was a matter resting entirely in the discretion of congress.").

[114] See, for example, id at 535 (argument of counsel) ("The judiciary has assumed a power which the executive department resists."); John G. Roberts, Jr., *What Makes the D.C. Circuit Different? A Historical View*, 92 Va L Rev 375, 382 (2006) (indicating that in his 1838 State of the Union address, President Van Buren urged Congress to remove the mandamus authority from the D.C. Circuit Court, and that the Senate passed a proposal that failed in the House). But cf. *Kendall*, 37 US (12 Pet) at 613 (stating that the President "did not forbid or advise the postmaster general to abstain from executing the law, and giving the credit thereby required").

diction existed in the District of Columbia Circuit Court, given that the Marshall Court had held that Congress had not provided for such jurisdiction in the federal circuit courts under the 1789 Judiciary Act,[115] and seemed to require that Congress make an explicit grant.[116] The Taney Court resorted to the February 27, 1801, act with respect to the District of Columbia that established the circuit court for the district (the "Organic Act"),[117] and which was enacted shortly after Congress passed the short-lived February 13, 1801, Judiciary Act. The Organic Act provided that then-existing law of Maryland should continue in force in the Maryland-ceded part of the district,[118] and the Court determined that the Maryland courts had common law mandamus jurisdiction.[119] The Organic Act also gave the D.C. Circuit Court all powers that the other circuit courts possessed,[120] which included arising under jurisdiction under the 1801 Judiciary Act.[121] Although Congress repealed the 1801 Judiciary Act the next year, the Supreme Court in *Kendall* held that the D.C. Circuit Court's jurisdiction over cases arising under federal law was unaffected by the repeal.[122] Theoretically, then, this previously undiscovered mandamus jurisdiction in the D.C. Circuit Court would have existed during the Marshall era.[123] Original mandamus directed to federal officers,

---

[115] See *Kendall*, 37 US (12 Pet) at 615 (acknowledging that the circuit courts in the several states had no authority to issue mandamus to federal officials).

[116] See id at 628 (Taney, CJ, dissenting) (arguing that "[t]he power is certainly no where given in direct and positive terms").

[117] Act of Feb 27, 1801, ch 15, 2 Stat 103.

[118] Act of Feb 27, 1801, ch 15, § 1, 2 Stat 103, 103–5 ("that the laws of the state of Maryland, as they now exist, shall be and continue in force in that part of the said district, which was ceded by that state to the United States").

[119] 37 US (12 Pet) at 619–20, 624–25. The Circuit Court was sitting in the Maryland-ceded portion of the district. Id at 620.

[120] Act of Feb 27, 1801, § 3, 2 Stat 105 ("and the said court and the judges thereof shall have all the powers by law vested in the circuit courts and the judges of the circuit courts of the United States").

[121] In addition, the Court relied on § 5: that the court "shall have cognizance of all cases, in law and equity between parties, both or either of which shall be resident or be found within said district." 37 US (12 Pet) at 622–23 (citing Act of Feb 27, 1801, § 5, 2 Stat 106).

[122] Id at 625.

[123] See Susan Low Bloch, *The Marbury Mystery: Why Did William Marbury Sue in the Supreme Court?*, 18 Const Comm 607, 607, 617–18, 620, 626 (2001) (arguing that *Marbury* could have brought his claim in the Circuit Court for the District of Columbia); cf. Fallon, 91 Cal L Rev at 52 n 271 (cited in note 45) (indicating it was unlikely the Marshall Court would have found such jurisdiction in the D.C. Court given the political atmosphere in 1803).

although of limited utility due to the Taney Court's holding that the writ was only available with respect to strictly ministerial duties,[124] remained in the arsenal of the District of Columbia courts from *Kendall* onward.[125]

B. DIVERSITY

As suggested above, the Taney Court accommodated its narrow view of the commerce power with its desire to promote national commerce by expanding federal jurisdiction while limiting any accompanying expansion of congressional power.[126] One aspect of this judicial-but-not-congressional expansion was the Taney Court's explicit adoption in diversity cases of the general common law as the rule of decision for commercial transactions, in *Swift v Tyson*.[127] The Court would subsequently extend this uniform, federal-court-centered regulatory law into other areas.[128] The Court's general common law, more-

---

[124] See *Decatur v Paulding*, 39 US (14 Pet) 497 (1840); Aditya Bamzai, *The Origins of Judicial Deference to Executive Interpretation*, 126 Yale L J 908, 953 (2017) (indicating that after *Decatur*, the Supreme Court did not approve a grant of mandamus to a federal officer until 1880); *Hart & Wechsler I* at 1185 n 2 (cited in note 44) (giving examples of Supreme Court cases in which mandamus was and was not granted); Byse and Fiocca, 81 Harv L Rev at 308–9, 312–13 (cited in note 44) (discussing persistent problems with obtaining mandatory as opposed to negative injunctions).

[125] See *Hart & Wechsler I* at 1181 (cited in note 44) ("The holding in Kendall survives to this day."); Roberts, 92 Va L Rev at 381 (cited in note 114) ("For the next 125 years, the Circuit Court for the District of Columbia would be the only court that could issue writs of mandamus challenging official conduct by the new national government.").

[126] See text accompanying note 110.

[127] 41 US (16 Pet) 1 (1842). The Marshall Court sometimes used general common law, particularly in equity. See Horwitz, *The Transformation of American Law* at 221–23 (cited in note 19) (discussing the Court's assertion of a power in equity to recognize negotiability in *Riddle v Mandeville*, 9 US (5 Cranch) 322, 331 (1809)); see also Johnson, *History of the Supreme Court of the United States, 1801–1815* at 562–64 (cited in note 32) (discussing *Riddle* and other cases that ignored state law in equity); cf. id at 566 (seeing the Marshall Court's District of Columbia negotiable instruments cases as precursors to *Swift*); White, *The Marshall Court and Cultural Change* at 445–46 (cited in note 13) (indicating that there were less clear divisions between state and federal law and that the Marshall Court sometimes followed local law and sometimes general common law in diversity); William A. Fletcher, *The General Common Law and Section 34 of the Judiciary Act of 1789: The Example of Marine Insurance*, 97 Harv L Rev 1513, 1515 (1984) (indicating that the federal courts developed a uniform general common law of marine insurance well before *Swift*).

[128] See Tony Freyer, *Harmony & Dissonance: The Swift and Erie Cases in American Federalism* 46–51 (NYU, 1981) (discussing the antebellum decisions applying general common law to insurance contracts, to construction of a will, and to certain other contract issues); cf. Swisher, *History of the Supreme Court* at 331–34 (cited in note 5) (discussing the Taney Court's continued expansion of general law); id at 323–24 (noting land cases in which the Taney Court followed federal equity).

over, included a general constitutional law that it employed to restrict state and local governmental authority in diversity cases. In such cases, federal courts might supply their own interpretations of general constitutional limitations, sometimes explicit in state constitutions, with respect to such matters as public purpose limitations on legislation, takings of property, and due process. And as under the general commercial law associated with *Swift*, federal courts sometimes ignored state decisional law to the contrary.[129]

Taney Court expansions of the availability of diversity jurisdiction, moreover, increased the occasions for use of a federal-judge-administered law—whether general law, state law, or federal law. The Taney Court particularly expanded jurisdiction for cases involving corporate parties, whose economic importance was ever increasing.[130] As noted above, the Marshall Court had held in *Deveaux* that a corporation could not itself be a citizen for purposes of diversity, seemingly as both a constitutional and statutory matter. In *Louisville, Cincinnati, and Charleston Railroad Co. v Letson*,[131] however, the Taney Court apparently treated the corporation itself as a citizen for purposes of diversity jurisdiction.[132] To the extent the Court hedged as to whether the citizenship of members of the corporation counted, moreover, the Court rejected an existing interpretation of the 1789 Judiciary Act that all members of the corporation had to be from the state where suit was brought, even if complete diversity existed be-

---

[129] See, for example, *Groves v Slaughter*, 40 US (15 Pet) 449 (1841) (holding in a diversity action that a Mississippi constitutional provision barring importation of slaves into the states after a particular date required implementing legislation, such that a promissory note given for a sale of slaves was enforceable); *Gelpcke v Dubuque*, 68 US (1 Wall) 175 (1863) (holding in a diversity suit to enforce payment on the bonds that the city's issuance of the bonds was valid as a matter of nonfederal law, despite the Iowa Supreme Court's recent contrary conclusion); Michael G. Collins, *Before Lochner—Diversity Jurisdiction and the Development of General Constitutional Law*, 74 Tulane L Rev 1263 (2000) (detailing the federal courts' development of a uniform but nonfederal constitutional law in diversity that limited the scope of governmental action); cf. *Terrett v Taylor*, 13 US (9 Cranch) 43, 52 (1815) (holding that the state could not, under "the fundamental laws of every free government" take title to property owned by a private corporation).

[130] See Hovenkamp, *Enterprise and American Law 1836–1937* at 2 (cited in note 110) (treating the modern business corporation as a Jacksonian product, manifesting the value placed on economic growth and the disfavoring of artificial constraints).

[131] 43 US (2 How) 497 (1844).

[132] Id at 555 ("A corporation created by a state to perform its functions under the authority of that state and only suable there, though it may have members out of the state, seems to us to be a person, though an artificial one, inhabiting and belonging to that state, and therefore entitled, for the purpose of suing and being sued, to be deemed a citizen of that state.").

tween all members and the opposing parties.[133] The Court reiterated the *Letson* result in *Marshall v Baltimore & Ohio Railroad*, but this time, the Court relied on a conclusive presumption that all shareholders were citizens of the state of incorporation.[134] Under either the theory of corporate citizenship or a presumption of shareholder citizenship, the Court supplied antidotes to the Marshall Court's diversity-killing combination of *Deveaux* and *Strawbridge*.

In addition, the Taney Court made it easier for corporations to use diversity as an avenue for raising issues of federal law, in an era before there was general federal question jurisdiction in the lower federal courts. In *Dodge v Woolsey*, the Court allowed a Connecticut shareholder to sue an Ohio-incorporated bank and an Ohio taxing official in diversity to enjoin the enforcement of a state tax that the shareholder and bank claimed violated the Contract Clause.[135] Had the corporation sued in its own name, it would not have been diverse from the taxing official. In addition, the Court's presumption in *Marshall v B. & O. Railroad* that all members of a corporation resided in the state of incorporation suggested that the plaintiff shareholder too would have been treated as having Ohio citizenship. The Court nevertheless

---

[133] The first argument for the plaintiff in error in *Letson* was that a "citizen of one state cannot sue a corporation in the Circuit Court of the United States in another state, unless all the members of the corporation sued are citizens of the state in which the suit is brought," and indicated that this was a separate argument from any absence of complete diversity. 43 US (2 How) at 499 (argument of counsel). Justice Wayne in *Letson* said, "The practice has been, since [*Strawbridge* and *Deveaux*] were decided, that if there be two or more plaintiffs and two or more joint-defendants, each of the plaintiffs must be capable of suing each of the defendants in the courts of the United States in order to support the jurisdiction, and in cases of corporation [*sic*] to limit jurisdiction to cases in which all the corporators were citizens of the state in which the suit was brought." Id at 554–55. This seems to have been an interpretation of § 11 of the 1789 Judiciary Act giving the circuit courts jurisdiction, when over $500 was in controversy, when "the suit is between a citizen of the state where the suit is brought, and a citizen of another state." See *Letson*, 43 US (2 How) at 552–53; cf. *Breithaupt v Georgia*, 26 US (1 Pet) 238, 240 (1828) (seeming to indicate jurisdiction was lacking for failure to allege that the officers and shareholders were citizens of Georgia).

[134] 57 US (16 How) 314, 327–28 (1853); id at 328–29 ("The persons who act under these faculties, and use this corporate name, may be justly presumed to be resident in the State which is the necessary *habitat* of the corporation, and where alone they can be made subject to suit . . . ."); *Lafayette Insur. Co. v French*, 59 US (18 How) 404, 405 (1856) (indicating that while the allegation that the defendant insurance company was "a citizen of the State of Indiana" was insufficient to show diversity, the plaintiff's replication—confessed by demurrer— that the defendant was incorporated and had its principal place of business in Indiana, sufficed under *B. & O.*); cf. Swisher, *History of the Supreme Court* at 468, 470 (cited in note 5) (indicating there was remaining unclarity in *B. & O.* as to whether the Court was looking at the citizenship of the directors).

[135] 59 US (18 How) 331 (1856).

allowed the out-of-state shareholder to use his real, Connecticut citizenship, to sue the Ohio corporation and the Ohio tax official as defendants.[136]

In thus expanding diversity, the Taney Court apparently entertained less concern than the Marshall Court that increasing federal jurisdiction might evoke political branch backlash.[137] The Court in *Letson* noted the general dissatisfaction of the bar with the *Strawbridge* and *Deveaux* decisions.[138] It also saw its decision as consistent with 1839 legislation providing that the federal courts could generally proceed based on jurisdiction over the parties before them, which the Court saw as passed "with an intent to rid the courts of the decision in the case of Strawbridge and Curtiss."[139]

Although relying in part on congressional sentiment in *Letson*,[140] the Taney Court—unlike the Marshall Court—did not advert to Congress's plenary powers.[141] Such a bow to Congress in all events might have been out of place, given that the Court itself was taking the lead in broadening the meaning of diversity with respect to corporations for purposes of Article III and the 1789 Judiciary Act. Perhaps, too, the Taney Court was generally less inclined to talk about plenary congressional powers, even in areas of acknowledged legislative compe-

---

[136] Id at 346 (stating that Woolsey as a citizen of Connecticut had a right to invoke diversity).

[137] This is not to say that the extensions went unopposed. See, for example, *Deshler v Dodge*, 57 US (16 How) 622, 632 (1854) (Taney, CJ, and, Catron, Daniel, and Campbell, JJ, dissenting); id at 633–34 (Catron, J, dissenting) (arguing that the replevin action for property distrained for taxes was not proper under Ohio law, and that the assignment to an out-of-stater was improper).

[138] 43 US (2 How) 497, 555 (1844).

[139] Id at 556. That law provided "where in any suit at law, or in equity, commenced in any court of the United States, there shall be several defendants, any one or more of whom shall not be inhabitants of, or found within the district where the suit is brought, or shall not voluntarily appear thereto, it shall be lawful for the court to entertain jurisdiction, and proceed to the trial and adjudication of such suit between the parties who may be properly before it, but the judgment or decree rendered therein shall not conclude or prejudice other parties not regularly served with process or, or not voluntarily appearing to answer." See 43 US (2 How) at 502 (quoting the statute); id at 503 (argument of plaintiff in error as to the meaning of this statute not affecting corporations).

[140] 43 US (2 How) at 556 ("But if in all we have said upon jurisdiction we are mistaken, we say that the act of 28th of February, 1839, enlarges the jurisdiction of the courts, comprehends the case before us, and embraces the entire result of the opinion which we shall now give.").

[141] Cf. *Dodge v Woolsey*, 59 US (18 How) 331, 349 (1856) (discussing limits on congressional power).

tence such as in providing for federal court jurisdiction.[142] The Taney Court decisions in *Letson*, in *B. & O.*, and in *Woolsey* thus relied on constitutional purposes and treated the diversity jurisdiction, at least when implemented by statute, as having constitutional overtones—a crucial way to protect the rights of out-of-state litigants.[143]

At times the Court focused on the rights of those who sued corporations. The *Letson* opinion noted that prior opinions allowed shareholders to "exempt themselves from their constitutional liability to be sued" in the federal courts.[144] Justice Grier in *B. & O.* similarly opined that providing diversity jurisdiction was necessary to keep state incorporation laws from depriving out-of-state citizens of their rights to sue those corporations in the federal courts;[145] the federal constitutional right to diversity could not be so limited by state law.[146]

---

[142] Id at 354 (stating that the mode of exercising judicial power is to be provided legislatively); *Sheldon v Sill*, 49 US (8 How) 441 (1850) (upholding the constitutionality of the limitation of diversity jurisdiction under the Assignee Clause, Judiciary Act of 1789, ch 20, § 11, 1 Stat 73, 78–79). The Taney Court, as did the Marshall Court, respected the limits on direct review in § 25 review. See, for example, *Commonwealth Bank of Kentucky v Griffith*, 39 US (14 Pet) 56 (1840) (holding that review was unavailable when the state Supreme Court held that the bank had issued constitutionally forbidden bills of credit); *Walker v Taylor*, 46 US (5 How) 64 (1847) (review was unavailable when the party claiming a constitutional right had won in the state court).

[143] See notes 144–49 and accompanying text. This is not to say that a litigant had a right to a federal diversity forum absent a congressional statute. Still, the Court treated a diversity forum, at least when there was a congressional grant, as a constitutionally-tinged entitlement. Cf. Hovenkamp, *Enterprise and American Law 1836–1937* at 89–90 (cited in note 110) (concluding that in *Watson v Tarpley*, 59 US (18 How) 517, 519–20 (1855), the Court held it was error for the federal court to consider a state statute only allowing a suit on a bill of exchange after maturity, and that the Court treated use of the general common law in a bill of exchange case as in the nature of a constitutional choice of law rule); id at 90 ("*Watson* established that a federal court was constitutionally required to ignore a state's statute designed to protect is own debtor citizens from out-of-state creditors, if the statute was inconsistent with the general commercial law."); Horwitz, *Transformation* at 225–26 (cited in note 19) (discussing negotiability cases in which the Court ignored state statutes). This is not to suggest that the Court treated the general common law as controlling in the state courts.

[144] 43 US (2 How) at 552–53 ("Constitutional rights and liabilities cannot be so taken away, or be so avoided."); *Marshall v B. & O.*, 57 US (16 How) at 328–29 ("If it were otherwise it would be in the power of every corporation, by electing a single director residing in a different State, to deprive citizens of other States with whom they have controversies, of this constitutional privilege, and compel them to resort to State tribunals in cases in which, of all others, such privilege may be considered most valuable."); cf. Swisher, *History of the Supreme Court* at 470 (cited in note 5) ("For the most part during this period corporations seem to have tried as hard to escape that jurisdiction as to have it confirmed.").

[145] 57 US (16 How) at 326.

[146] Id ("Now, if this be a right, or privilege guaranteed by the Constitution of citizens of one State in their controversies with citizens of another, it is plain that it cannot be taken away from the plaintiff by any legislation of the State in which the defendant resides."); see also id at 327 (quoting Justice Catron in *The Rundle v Del. and Raritan Canal Co.*, 55 US (14

At other times, the Court focused on the rights of investors in the corporation.[147] In *Woolsey*, allowing the derivative action to challenge an Ohio tax on Contract Clause grounds, the Court stated that the case was brought by a "citizen of the United States, residing in Connecticut, having a large pecuniary interest in a bank in Ohio," and would affect the citizens of all states who had had an interest in banking capital.[148] The Court also discussed at length the need for federal judicial supremacy as to matters of federal law,[149] thus indicating that its diversity expansion was a way to bring federal constitutional questions, such as the Contract Clause issue in *Woolsey*, before the lower federal courts prior to the advent of general federal question jurisdiction.

The Taney Court's corporate diversity decisions had similar results as did the Marshall Court's federal question decision in *Osborn* and *Planters'*: cases involving corporate parties gained greater access to federal trial courts for both federal and nonfederal issues. The *Letson* opinion noted that Marshall had expressed dissatisfaction with *Strawbridge* and *Deveaux*, and that the restrictions on diversity in those cases were inconsistent with the Marshall Court's later decision in *Planters' Bank*.[150] The Taney Court here saw itself as expanding federal jurisdiction in ways one can imagine the Marshall Court would

---

How) 80 (1853): "if the United States courts could be ousted of jurisdiction, and citizens of other States be forced into the State courts, without the power of election, they would often be deprived, in great cases, of all benefit contemplated by the Constitution; and in many cases be compelled to submit their rights to judges and juries who are inhabitants of the cities where the suit must be tried, and to contend with powerful corporations, where the chances of impartial justice would be greatly against them. . . . State laws, by combining large masses of men under a corporate name, cannot repeal the Constitution."); cf. *Deshler v Dodge*, 57 US (16 How) 622 (1854) (allowing a diversity replevin action that likely would not have been allowed under state law to challenge a seizure under an Ohio tax alleged to violate the Contract Clause), discussed in Ann Woolhandler, *The Common Law Origins of Constitutionally Compelled Remedies*, 107 Yale L J 77, 108 (1997).

[147] See *Dodge v Woolsey*, 59 US (18 How) 331, 346 (1856); cf. *Marshall v B. & O.*, 57 US (16 How) at 353 (Campbell, J, dissenting) (discussing the value to corporations of being treated as citizens); id at 354 ("I am not willing to strengthen or to enlarge the connections between the courts of the United States and these litigants."); Newmyer, *The Supreme Court under Marshall and Taney* at 111–12 (cited in note 12) (indicating that the Taney Court "came to the rescue of corporations" in cases such as *Letson*).

[148] *Woolsey*, 59 US (18 How) at 346 ("Mr. Woolsey's right, as a citizen of the State of Connecticut, to sue citizens of the State of Ohio in the courts of the United States, for that State, cannot be questioned.").

[149] Id at 349–50; see also *Wright v Sill*, 67 US (2 Black) 544 (1862) (affirming decree in a federal equity action enjoining collection of the Ohio bank tax).

[150] 43 US (2 How) at 555.

have approved.[151] The Taney Court helped to provide all corporations, under the rubric of diversity jurisdiction, what the Marshall Court had provided for a single corporation under the rubric of federal question jurisdiction.[152]

What is more, shareholder suits and related actions by bond trustees would become a standard vehicle for challenges to state, local, and federal legislation on both federal and nonfederal law grounds. This was true even after the 1875 advent of general federal question jurisdiction, and diversity remained a primary avenue for raising federal challenges to legislation well into the twentieth century. After *Ex parte Young*, federal question actions for challenging the constitutionality of laws gradually gained ascendance.[153] But because diversity actions had helped to maintain the central role of the lower federal courts in deciding constitutional issues, the move to arising under jurisdiction did not signal a dramatic change in the role of the lower federal courts in policing state action.

Nor would the law that developed under the Fourteenth Amendment in the latter part of the nineteenth century mark a dramatic change in the federal courts' role. Many of the norms developed by the Court as general constitutional law (as noted above) under diversity—for example, as to public use, takings, and rate reasonableness—would be forerunners to Fourteenth Amendment claims even when diversity did not exist.[154]

C. ADMIRALTY

As noted above, the Marshall Court in *The Thomas Jefferson* limited Article III and statutory admiralty jurisdiction to the high seas

---

[151] Perhaps, too, the Marshall Court was reluctant to overturn its own long-established precedents.

[152] Later, other federally chartered corporations took advantage of the decision. See, for example, *Pacific Railroad Removal Cases*, 115 US 1 (1885).

[153] 209 US 123 (1908). See generally Woolhandler, 107 Yale L J at 97–99 & nn 100–11, 127–30 (cited in note 146).

[154] See, for example, *Pumpelly v Green Bay Co.*, 80 US (13 Wall) 166, 176–78, 180 (1871) (requiring just compensation under the state constitution for flooding the plaintiff's land to build a dam, notwithstanding state court precedent); Collins, 74 Tulane L Rev at 1284–93 (cited in note 129) (giving examples of diversity actions addressing as a matter of general law issues of public purpose, just compensation, and rate reasonableness); id at 1308 (stating that "the transition from general to federal constitutional law was quite smooth as a substantive matter, the main difference being that the relevant state-limiting norms had now become federalized"); id at 1311 (indicating that this transition did not occur immediately upon the provision of general federal question jurisdiction, given that diversity was often available).

and waters within the ebb and flow of the tide. Congress could not therefore use the Necessary and Proper Clause to implement Article III by legislating to expand admiralty jurisdiction itself beyond these limits. But in *The Thomas Jefferson*, Justice Story suggested that Congress might use commerce powers to extend federal jurisdiction to inland waters that were not subject to the ebb and flow of the tide.[155] Indeed, Story helped to draft the 1845 Great Lakes Act.[156] The act provided that district courts of the United States would have the same jurisdiction on the lakes[157] as to "vessels of twenty tons burden and upwards . . . and at the time employed in business of commerce and navigation between ports and places in different States and Territories" as those courts had as to like vessels under the admiralty jurisdiction.[158] The act also provided that the federal courts would apply the same rules of decision as in admiralty cases.[159] Justice Story as well as congressional proponents seemed to rely on a Commerce Clause justification for the expansion of the federal courts' jurisdiction beyond the ebb-and-flow limits of *The Thomas Jefferson*.[160]

The act's validity came before the Taney Court when owners of a vessel libeled the propeller *Genesee Chief* for allegedly causing a collision on Lake Ontario.[161] The owners of the *Genesee Chief* sought to

---

[155] See text accompanying notes 74–75; *The Propeller Genesee Chief v Fitzhugh*, 53 US (12 How) 443, 451 (1851) (indicating that the view that admiralty had been too narrowly defined grew "with the growing commerce on the lakes and navigable rivers of the western States"); Swisher, *History of the Supreme Court* at 427–28 (cited in note 5) (noting that "businessmen making use of Western lakes and rivers felt aggrieved at their disadvantage by contrast with those engaged in interstate commerce on the Atlantic Ocean who had the right of resort to admiralty").

[156] Act of Feb 26, 1845, ch 20, 5 Stat 726; Swisher, *History of the Supreme Court* at 430 (cited in note 5) (stating that the bill "was passed almost or entirely without debate").

[157] "and navigable waters connecting said lakes." Ch 20, 5 Stat 726.

[158] Id.

[159] Id ("[A]nd in all suits brought in such courts in all such matters of contract or tort, the remedies, and the forms of process, and the modes of proceeding, shall be the same as are or may be used by such courts in cases of admiralty and maritime jurisdiction; and the maritime law of the United States, so far as the same is or may be applicable thereto, shall constitute the rule of decision in such suits. . . .").

[160] Swisher, *History of the Supreme Court* at 430–31 (cited in note 5) (saying Story did not specify the power, and that he may have favored commerce, but left room for others to use admiralty); see also id at 431, 440 (indicating that Webster thought admiralty jurisdiction was limited and would have favored a commerce justification at the time of drafting the 1845 act).

[161] 53 US (12 How) at 443–44; see Schwartz, *A History of the Supreme Court* at 103 (cited in note 5) (noting the nationalism of the Taney Court's *Genesee Chief* decision, and quoting Chief Justice Hughes); text accompanying note 6.

dismiss the case for lack of jurisdiction. They argued that the Great Lakes Act could not be upheld as appropriate to implement Article III admiralty jurisdiction, because the collision occurred outside the ebb and flow of the tide.[162] Nor, they argued, could the jurisdiction be upheld as a regulation of commerce.[163] The Court nevertheless upheld the extension of jurisdiction, and interpreted the constitutional admiralty jurisdiction to extend to all navigable waters of the United States—not just to the high seas and those waters subject to the ebb and flow of the tide as the Marshall Court had held.[164]

According to Taney, the English tidal rule was really a rule of navigability, because there were no navigable English waters that were not subject to the tide.[165] The Court would not then "follow an erroneous decision into which the court fell," which had been made at a time when "the commerce on the rivers of the west and on the lakes was in its infancy."[166] "[A]t this day," Taney continued, limiting the jurisdiction to tidal waters would produce "serious public as well as private inconvenience."[167]

While *The Genesee Chief* manifests the pro-commerce stance of the Taney Court, it arguably also illustrates a difference in approach to the relationship of congressional to judicial power between the Marshall and Taney Courts. One could imagine the Marshall Court's upholding the Great Lakes Act by relying at least in part on Congress's control of federal jurisdiction, and deferring to Congress's

---

[162] 53 US (12 How) at 444 (also indicating that the collision was entirely within New York).

[163] Id at 448.

[164] Id at 454–57. While the case upheld the jurisdiction under the Great Lakes Act, the Court indicated that the 1789 grant of maritime jurisdiction was coextensive with the constitutional grant. Id at 457 (saying this was obviously the view of Congress in § 9 of the 1789 Judiciary Act, which provided for the admiralty jurisdiction to include "all seizures under the laws of impost, navigation, or trade of the United States, where the seizures are made on waters which are navigable from the sea by vessels of ten or more tons burden, within their respective districts, as well as upon the high seas"); see also *Jackson v Steamboat Magnolia*, 61 US (20 How) 296 (1858) (holding that the admiralty jurisdiction included river commerce not covered by the Great Lakes Act); cf. *The Propeller Commerce*, 66 US (1 Black) 574, 578–79 (1862) (holding it was unnecessary to show that either boat that had collided was engaged in interstate or foreign commerce); Swisher, *History of the Supreme Court* at 454–55 (cited in note 5) (indicating that postwar, the Court abandoned an interstate commerce requirement for Great Lakes traffic, although the Great Lakes Act had an interstate commerce limitation).

[165] 53 US (12 How) at 454.

[166] Id at 456.

[167] Id at 457, 459.

interpretation of what was necessary and proper to implement the Commerce Clause.[168] Chief Justice Taney, however, flatly stated that the Great Lakes Act would be unconstitutional if its validity depended on congressional power to regulate commerce.[169] Rather than defer to congressional power to judge the scope of the commerce power, the Court upheld jurisdiction by interpreting the constitutional grant of admiralty jurisdiction more broadly than had the Marshall Court. And similar to its treatment of diversity, the Court treated access to admiralty jurisdiction as partly a constitutional right—a right that should not be denied to the inland states and parties:

> The union is formed upon the basis of equal rights among all the States. . . . And it would be contrary to the first principles on which the Union was formed to confine these rights to the States bordering on the Atlantic, and to the tide-water rivers connected with it, and to deny them to the citizens who border on the lakes, and the great navigable streams which flow through the western States.[170]

While *The Genesee Chief* opinion upheld congressional power to enact the Great Lakes Act, the Court's reliance on the Article III's grant of admiralty jurisdiction made any accession of congressional power much narrower than it would have been under the commerce power. A mere jurisdictional statute, Taney concluded, was not an appropriate exercise of the commerce power.[171] Taney reasoned that if the commerce power were the basis for jurisdiction, Congress might, by extension, expand federal jurisdiction to inland torts and contracts affecting commerce even when diversity was lacking.[172]

The Genesee Chief thus fits the pattern of diversity jurisdiction, where the Taney Court increased federal judicial power while limiting any attendant expansion of congressional power. The expansion

---

[168] On the other hand, Marshall had never gone so far as to say that a jurisdictional statute could itself supply the federal question that gave jurisdiction without the possibility of a federal issue. And Marshall favored a more expansive interpretation of the admiralty jurisdiction. See White, *The Marshall Court and Cultural Change* at 472–82 (cited in note 13) (discussing Marshall's views on admiralty and citing an 1833 letter written by Story stating that Marshall favored extending the admiralty jurisdiction "to all waters, rivers, etc navigable from the sea at the head of waters of such navigation"); see also note 12.

[169] 53 US (12 How) at 453; see also White, *The Marshall Court and Cultural Change* at 468–69, 471 (cited in note 13) (discussing the relationship of the commerce power and admiralty).

[170] 53 US (12 How) at 454.

[171] Id at 451–52.

[172] Id at 452; see also id at 448 (argument of counsel).

of both diversity and admiralty jurisdiction, moreover, allowed more play for uniform federal judge-made law.[173]

D. DIRECT REVIEW OF STATE COURTS

As discussed above, the Marshall Court faced compact-theory-driven arguments that it lacked the power to review state court judgments involving federal issues, to which the Court responded that the people, not the states, formed the Constitution, and that the federal courts were supreme within their sphere. Taney Court decisions on direct review also met with periodic compact-theory eruptions, and the Taney Court responded similarly to the Marshall Court.

The response comported with the Unionist stance of the Jacksonians. The Nullification Crisis during Jackson's presidency solidified the Jacksonian rebuff of extreme versions of compact theory[174] and acceptance of federal supremacy within its sphere.[175] An 1832 South Carolina ordinance declared that the federal tariffs of 1828 and 1832 were "null, void, and no law, nor binding upon this State, its officers or citizens"; that "all judicial proceedings which shall be hereafter had in affirmance thereof . . . shall be held utterly null and void";[176] and that the use of force by the federal government to enforce the laws would be "inconsistent with the longer continuance of South Caro-

---

[173] Cf. David W. Robertson, Steven F. Friedell, and Michael F. Sturley, *Admiralty and Maritime Law in the United States* 106 (Carolina Academic, 3d ed 2015) (noting that while the Court has generally upheld congressional maritime legislation, "some of the opinions have been grudging in tone, carrying the implication that Congress ought to be diffident when venturing into territory that the Court regards primarily as its own domain," and citing, inter alia, *The Genesee Chief*).

[174] See Graber, *Jacksonian Makings* at 7 (cited in note 5) ("Jacksonian judicial nominees before joining the federal bench had uniformly demonstrated strong public support for Jackson's militantly nationalistic, anti-states rights positions and proposals during the nullification crisis."); Kelly, Harbison, and Belz, *The American Constitution: Its Origins and Development* at 202 (cited in note 17) (describing Jacksonian "dual federalism," which saw the state and federal powers as operating within "mutually exclusive and reciprocally limiting spheres"); cf. Tara Leigh Grove, *The Origins (and Fragility) of Judicial Independence*, 71 Vand L Rev (forthcoming 2018) (William & Mary Law School Research Paper No 09-357, at 19, 22) (available at http://ssrn.com/abstract=2963683) (discussing Jackson's resistance to some judicial orders); Klarman, 87 Va L Rev at 1174–80 (cited in note 1) (discussing how the Nullification Crisis of 1832–33 helped to dissipate the conflict between Jackson and the Court as to Cherokee removal in Georgia in the late 1820s and early 1830s).

[175] The Democrats of course included many who approved of some version of compact theory, as well as the possibility of secession. See note 108.

[176] *South Carolina Ordinance of Nullification, 1832*, reprinted in Paul Leicester Ford, ed, *The Federalist* 690 (Henry Holt, 1898).

lina in the Union."[177] Jackson's proclamation against the South Carolina actions stated that the nation was not a league of states,[178] and that the states therefore had neither the power to nullify the federal revenue laws nor the right to secede from the Union.[179] He invoked implied as well as express national powers to preserve the Union by force if necessary.[180] And in Jackson's Farewell Address, which Taney helped to draft, Jackson spoke of the need for obedience to federal law until invalidated by the courts or repealed.[181]

Compact theory flared up again in several cases in which the Taney Court held that Ohio's tax on certain state-chartered banks violated the Contract Clause, as discussed above with respect to *Dodge v Woolsey*.[182] The first case in which the Court so held, *Piqua Branch Bank v Ohio*, came up on direct review.[183] On remand, the Ohio Supreme Court delayed implementing the Supreme Court's decision for over two years,[184] thus reprising the Virginia Court of Appeals's refusal to

---

[177] Id at 692.

[178] Jackson's Proclamation, Dec 10, 1832, in *2 Messages and Papers of the Presidents* at 648 (cited in note 101). Professor Klarman says Jackson "did not reject compact theory entirely." See Klarman, 87 Va L Rev at 1179 & n 363 (cited in note 1). Jackson sometimes used the word "compact" to describe the Union, but he believed that the nullifiers were abusing the term by treating it "as synonymous with league, although the true term is not employed, because it would at once show the fallacy of the reasoning." Jackson's Proclamation at 650.

[179] See Jackson's Proclamation, Dec 10, 1832 at 648 (cited in note 178) ("But each State, having expressly parted with so many powers as to constitute, jointly with the other States, a single nation, can not, from that period, possess any right to secede, because such secession does not break a league, but destroys the unity of a nation"); see also id at 649–50 (denying that the states reserved an undivided sovereignty, and that the United States was a league).

[180] Id at 649 ("A government [as distinguished from a league] always has a sanction, express or implied; in our case it is both necessarily implied and expressly given."); see also id at 654–55 (stating that those claiming that preventing execution of federal law can be achieved peacefully "know that a forcible opposition could alone prevent the execution of the laws, and they know that such opposition must be repelled").

[181] Andrew Jackson's Farewell Address, Mar 4, 1837 at 296–97 (cited in note 99). Jackson also spoke, inter alia, against interference with the rights of states to regulate their internal concerns, id at 298, and of the need for the general government to stay within "the sphere of its appropriate duties." Id at 298–99, 301.

[182] 59 US (18 How) 331 (1856); see text accompanying notes 135–36, 143.

[183] 57 US (16 How) 369, 376 (1854); see also Swisher, *History of the Supreme Court* at 475–77 (cited in note 5) (discussing *Piqua*); Charles Warren, *The Supreme Court in United States History 1836–1918* at 250–56 (Little, Brown, 1926) (discussing the Ohio bank tax cases).

[184] In *Piqua*, the U.S. Supreme Court reversed the Ohio Supreme Court judgment and remanded for proceedings in conformity with the U.S. Supreme Court's opinion. 57 US (16 How) at 415. The U.S. Supreme Court later entered a special mandate ordering the Ohio court to carry its judgment into execution. See *Piqua Branch of the State Bank of Ohio v Knoup*, 6 Ohio St 342, 406 (Dec Term 1856) (Bartley dissenting). When the Ohio court finally entered the mandate, the dissenting judge argued that the Supreme Court could not be the

enter the Marshall Court's decree in *Fairfax's Devisee v Hunter's Lessee*. Although it eventually entered the mandate in *Piqua*, the Ohio Supreme Court continued to treat the bank taxes as valid, and the U.S. Supreme Court continued to reverse the Ohio court's decrees and to reaffirm that its prior decisions were controlling.[185]

Similarly the Wisconsin Supreme Court approved lower state court decisions ordering the release from federal custody of abolitionist Sherman Booth, both before and after his federal court conviction for violating the 1850 Fugitive Slave Act.[186] The three justices of the Wisconsin Supreme Court held the federal statute unconstitutional,[187] with one justice explicitly refusing to treat as binding the Supreme Court's earlier decision in *Prigg v Pennsylvania*, which had upheld congressional power to legislate to implement the Fugitive Slave Clause.[188] The Wisconsin court subsequently ordered its clerk not to make a return to the U.S. Supreme Court's writ of error in the postconviction case, on the ground that the U.S. Supreme Court could not review its determination because § 25 of the 1789 Judiciary Act was unconstitutional.[189]

The Supreme Court reviewed the Wisconsin courts' grant of both pre- and postconviction habeas in *Ableman v Booth*. Chief Justice Taney for a unanimous Court wrote that the state courts lacked power to

---

final arbiter of the respective powers of the state and federal governments. 6 Ohio St at 406 (Bartley dissenting); Warren, *The Supreme Court in United States History 1836–1918* at 256 (cited in note 183) (indicating that three judges of the state supreme court decided to enter the decree late in 1856 and said that they were "not prepared to adopt the theory" denying U.S. Supreme Court jurisdiction); see 6 Ohio St at 343.

[185] See, for example, *Jefferson Branch Bank v Skelly*, 66 US (1 Black) 436, 448 (1862) ("It has been decided three times by this court, that the 60th section of the charter of the State Bank of Ohio was a contract between the State and the bank, within the meaning . . . of the Constitution. . . ."); *Franklin Branch Bank v Ohio*, 66 US (1 Black) 474 (1862) ("In all of these cases this court held, that the 60th section was a contract, and that the various State laws, which attempted to change the rule of taxation fixed by such contract, were void.").

[186] *In re Booth*, 3 Wis 1 (1854) (pretrial); *In re Booth and Rycraft*, 3 Wis 157 (1854) (postconviction).

[187] Two of the three Wisconsin Supreme Court justices held the act unconstitutional because of its use of non–Article III commissioners and the absence of jury trials for fugitive slaves. See Ann Woolhandler and Michael G. Collins, *The Story of Tarble's Case: State Habeas and Federal Detention*, in Vicki C. Jackson and Judith Resnick, eds, *Federal Courts Stories* 147 (Foundation, 2010).

[188] 41 US (16 Pet) 539 (1842).

[189] See *Ableman v Booth*, 62 US (21 How) 506, 514 (1859). The clerk had complied with the writ of error in the pretrial detention case. See Warren, *The Supreme Court in United States History 1836–1918* at 336 n 2 (cited in note 183).

issue habeas with respect to detention by a federal officer.[190] He am-
plified Marshall-style arguments of the supremacy of the federal government within its sphere, stating that "the sphere of action appropriated to the United States is as far beyond the reach of the judicial
process issued by a State judge or a State court, as if the line of division
was traced by landmarks and monuments visible to the eye."[191]

The Taney Court arguably outdid the Marshall Court in using
state court resistance to direct review as the occasion for channeling
contentious cases to lower federal courts—thereby reducing opportunities for state-court recalcitrance.[192] One avenue to divert cases
from state to federal courts was to expand diversity jurisdiction; another was to treat certain aspects of existing federal jurisdiction as
more or less exclusive of state jurisdiction. For example, the Supreme
Court's decision in *Dodge v Woolsey* allowed a diversity shareholder
derivative action to challenge the Ohio bank tax. *Woolsey* was decided
two years after the Court had first held the Ohio tax violative of the
Contract Clause in *Piqua*[193]—the two years during which the Ohio
Supreme Court had failed to enter the U.S. Supreme Court mandate

---

[190] State courts had previously granted habeas with respect to detention by federal officers.
See Marc M. Arkin, *The Ghost at the Banquet: Slavery, Federalism, and Habeas Corpus for State
Prisoners*, 70 Tulane L Rev 1, 14–22 (1995) (indicating state courts had granted habeas with
respect to federal officer custody as to military enlistment); id at 49–56 (describing Ohio state
cases ordering release of fugitive slaves from federal custody, which were resisted by federal
officials and courts); Todd E. Pettys, *State Habeas Relief for Federal Extrajudicial Detainees*,
92 Minn L Rev 265, 268 (2007) (stating that "the state courts routinely granted habeas relief
to federal extrajudicial detainees for half a century" (footnote omitted)); id at 276 (citing cases
involving military enlistments). State-court habeas as to military enlistment persisted to some
extent until *Tarble's Case*, 80 US 397 (1872). See Pettys, 92 Minn L Rev at 285–88.

[191] 62 US (21 How) at 516.

[192] Of course perceived infirmities of the state courts generally have provided a spur to
increasing lower federal court powers. Presumably the Marshall Court's expansive view of
federal question jurisdiction in *Osborn*, 22 US (9 Wheat) 738 (1824), resulted from concerns
about state court fairness, as well as the resistance to the direct review decision in *McCulloch*.
See generally Collins, 1995 Wis L Rev at 146–47 (cited in note 88) (quoting Marshall's
reasoning in *Osborn*, 22 US (9 Wheat) at 821, that Congress should not be forced to rely on
state courts, "tribunals over which the government of the Union has no adequate control, and
which may be closed to any claim asserted under a law of the United States").

[193] *Piqua* was decided on May 24, 1854, *Woolsey* on April 8, 1856. In *Piqua*, the banks' tax
exemption had been repealed by statute. After *Piqua*, Ohio amended its constitution to effect
the repeal. See Warren, *The Supreme Court in United States History 1836–1918* at 254 (cited
in note 183). The state apparently hoped the constitutional change would get around the
Contract Clause provision that "No State shall . . . pass any . . . Law impairing the Obligation
of Contracts." US Const, Art I, § 10, cl 1; see also *Dodge*, 59 US (18 How) at 334 (argument
of counsel) (arguing that the tax immunity had been accepted by the banks "with a tacit
understanding that its efficacy might be impaired by the sovereignty of the State").

in *Piqua*.[194] Even though *Woolsey* was a diversity case, the opinion defended Supreme Court review of state court decisions as necessary to federal supremacy: "Without the supreme court . . . neither the constitution nor the laws of congress passed in pursuance of it, nor treaties, would be in practice or in fact the supreme law of the land, and the injunction that the judges in every State should be bound thereby . . . would be useless."[195] So, too, allowing lower federal court jurisdiction would implement the supremacy of federal law: "Without a judicial department, just such as it is, neither the powers of the constitution nor the purposes for which they were given could have been attained. We do not know a case more appropriate to show the necessity for such a jurisdiction than that before us."[196]

Northern state resistance to the federal fugitive slave laws also seemed to inspire the Taney Court to hold federal powers in that area to be exclusive of state powers. In *Prigg v Pennsylvania*, the Court held that Congress had power to enact legislation to enforce Article IV's Fugitive Slave Clause, despite the absence of any explicit provision for congressional implementation.[197] The case came to the Supreme Court on direct review of Prigg's conviction under a state personal liberty law for removing a fugitive slave from the state without complying fully with its requirements for removal. Prigg had obtained a warrant from a Pennsylvania justice of the peace to arrest the fugitive and returned to the justice of the peace to seek a certificate of removal after capturing him. The justice of the peace refused further cognizance of the case; Prigg then removed the fugitive from the state without obtaining a certificate.[198] Justice Story's opinion not only up-

---

[194] The Ohio court finally entered the mandate in *Piqua* in its December term, 1856. *Piqua Branch of the State Bank of Ohio v Knoup*, 6 Ohio St 342, 343 (Dec Term 1856).

[195] 59 US (18 How) at 355; see also id at 350, 353–54. *Deshler v Dodge* was an Ohio bank case that came to the Court contemporaneously with *Piqua* and allowed diversity through an assignment of a claim. 57 US (16 How) 622, 631 (1854) (holding the Assignee Clause, Judiciary Act of 1789, ch 20, § 11, 1 Stat 73, 78–79, inapplicable to an action for wrongful detention of bank notes).

[196] See 59 US (18 How) at 356 (discussing that the case raised an issue as to the "constitutional validity" of the tax).

[197] 41 US (16 Pet) 539 (1842).

[198] Id at 556–57 (statement of the case). The state courts later convicted Prigg on an agreed set of facts based on the jury findings, with a view to bringing the case before the U.S. Supreme Court. Id at 557–58 (statement of the case). *Prigg* was thus not a case of state supreme court resistance to U.S. Supreme Court review, as were *Piqua* and *Ableman*, but rather involved more general resistance to federal requirements for the return of fugitive slaves.

held congressional power to enact the 1793 Fugitive Slave Act[199] but also held that the states lacked power to legislate as to the subject—whether the legislation obstructed or supplemented the enforcement of federal law—thus invalidating Prigg's conviction.[200] His opinion further stated that the participation of state magistrates in enforcement of the 1793 act, as provided in the act itself,[201] was optional and could not be compelled by the federal government, apparently as a constitutional matter.[202] The 1850 Fugitive Slave Act, enacted after *Prigg*, removed provisions for participation of state magistrates, and made federal personnel and judges the exclusive enforcers of the act.[203] And the Court took an additional step to remove state courts from fugitive slave issues in *Ableman v Booth*, in which the Court on direct review held that the state courts had no power to issue habeas with respect to federal detention.[204]

---

[199] Act of Feb 12, 1793, ch 7, 1 Stat 302, 302–5.

[200] The opinion stated that the federal statute covered the whole subject, 41 US (16 Pet) at 617, and also that this federal power was exclusive even absent congressional legislation. Id at 622; see also id at 625 (indicating there were police power exceptions). At least three Justices disagreed as to the exclusivity ruling. See 41 US (16 Pet), at 627–33 (Taney, CJ, concurring) (arguing that states had power to enact laws that in good faith were intended to assist the owner and that did not conflict with federal law); id at 634 (Thompson, J, concurring) (while legislation "belongs more appropriately to congress . . . but there is nothing in the subject-matter that renders state legislation unfit"); id at 652 (Daniel, J, concurring) (arguing against exclusivity); see also id at 636 (Baldwin, J, concurring) (although concurring in the result saying he "dissented from the principles laid down by the court as the grounds of their opinion"). The Court would later countenance some state laws that in effect aided in enforcement. See *Moore v Illinois*, 55 US (14 How) 13, 17, 19–20 (1852) (upholding a state conviction for "harboring and secreting" a slave).

[201] Act of Feb 12, 1793, ch 7, § 3, 1 Stat 302–5.

[202] 41 US (16 Pet) at 616, 622 (stating that all the leading provisions of the act were free from reasonable doubt as to their constitutionality "with the exception of that part which confers authority upon state magistrates"); see also Newmyer, *The Supreme Court under Marshall and Taney* at 125 (cited in note 12) (indicating that Story lacked a majority on this point). The elective nature of state enforcement was at least temporarily a setback for enforcement, which led to the 1850 act's bolstering federal enforcement. See id (noting that this part of the decision undercut enforcement of the 1793 act).

[203] Act of Sept 18, 1850, ch 60, 9 Stat 462. The Taney Court also tended to enforce exclusivity of foreign affairs powers. See Swisher, *History of the Supreme Court* at 175, 202 (cited in note 5).

[204] 60 US (21 How) at 516. The Marshall Court seemed inclined to hold certain coercive powers with respect to federal officers exclusive to the federal courts. In *Ex parte Bollman*, Marshall implied that absent the congressional grant of habeas jurisdiction to the federal courts, the right would have remained inactive, see text accompanying notes 35–37, thus arguably suggesting state courts lacked power to grant habeas as to those in federal custody. See 8 US (4 Cranch) 75, 94 (1807). In *McClung v Silliman*, the Court held that state courts could not issue mandamus to an officer in the federal land office. 19 US (6 Wheat) 598 (1821); see note 43. Justice Johnson said that the conduct of a federal land officer in disposing

Reliance on implied powers in Congress to pass legislation to enforce the Fugitive Slave Clause may seem out of step with the Taney Court's tendency to avoid broad interpretations of congressional power. Article IV's Fugitive Slave Clause had no provision for congressional implementation; nor did the clause seem to vest a "power" in the United States that Congress could implement under the necessary and proper provision in Article I, § 8, clause 18. On the other hand, as indicated by Jackson's claiming an implied power of self-defense in the Union in response to the Nullification Crisis, Jacksonians did not oppose implication of powers they saw as truly necessary, as distinguished from merely "appropriate."[205] Justice Story's opinion for the Court in *Prigg* treated implied congressional power to implement the Fugitive Slave Clause as a matter of necessity; otherwise the slaveowners' right to retrieve the fugitive would effectively be nullified in many states.[206] The necessity rationale also implied that Congress would be more or less limited to facilitating the return of the slave, rather than undermining it.[207]

III. Evaluating the Marshall and Taney Courts, and the Shadow of Dred Scott

Both the Marshall and Taney Courts promoted a strong federal judiciary, as shown by their direct review decisions under § 25, but the Taney Court outdid the Marshall Court in expanding lower federal court jurisdiction in mandamus, diversity, and admiralty. It also channeled Fugitive Slave Act enforcement and habeas addressing federal detention from the state courts to the lower federal courts. Part of the reason for the underappreciation of the Taney Court's expansion of federal judicial power, relative to the Marshall Court's, is that the Taney Court's expansions of lower federal court jurisdic-

---

of federal property "can only be controlled by the power that created him." 19 US (6 Wheat) at 605. The Court in *McClung*, however, also relied on Congress's not having given power even to the federal courts to issue mandamus in such cases. Id at 604.

[205] Cf. Jackson's Bank Veto Message at 589 (cited in note 101) ("That a bank of the United States, competent to all the duties which may be required by Government, might be so organized as not to infringe on our own delegated powers or the reserved rights of the States I do not entertain a doubt.").

[206] 41 US (16 Pet) at 614–15.

[207] Cf. id at 627–33 (Taney, CJ, concurring) (indicating states could enact laws that would assist in retrieving fugitive slaves).

tion were in diversity and admiralty as distinguished from federal question jurisdiction, which over the course of the twentieth century became the focal point for evaluating the role of the federal courts.[208] In addition, the Marshall Court tied a broad view of federal court jurisdiction to a broad view of congressional powers, while the Taney Court expanded federal court jurisdiction while maintaining a more restricted view of congressional powers.[209] The Marshall Court's views coincide with the modern acceptance of broad federal legislative competency.[210]

And of course the Taney Court's reputation is forever linked to the *Dred Scott* decision.[211] As Professor Bernard Schwartz has stated, "Until the *Dred Scott* case, the stature of the Supreme Court compared favorably with what it had been under Marshall, and, if anything, its decisions were more generally accepted."[212] No doubt had

---

[208] See LaCroix, 30 L and Hist Rev at 225–26, 238 (cited in note 1) (discussing the "talismanic power" of "arising under" jurisdiction to the Federalists); id at 238 (treating the Marshall Court as engaged in a continued attempt to create an approximation of the federal question jurisdiction that was lost in the 1801 Judiciary Act); id at 238 ("[T]he federalist justices continued to chivy away at creating an approximation of that lost jurisdictional grant.").

[209] See Klarman, 87 Va L Rev at 1126–28 (cited in note 1) (discussing scholarly emphasis on Marshall's decisions in *Gibbons v Ogden*, 22 US (9 Wheat) 1 (1824), and *McCulloch v Maryland*, 17 US (4 Wheat) 316 (1819)).

[210] See Newmyer, *The Supreme Court under Marshall and Taney* at 148 (cited in note 12) (stating that "American history has favored" the nationalist principles that Marshall worked for); Klarman, 87 Va L Rev at 1128 (cited in note 1) ("Twentieth-century advocates of expansive national power have insisted that Marshall's capacious understandings of the Necessary and Proper Clause and the Commerce Clause were sufficient to accommodate the modern regulatory state." (footnote omitted)); Magliocca, *Andrew Jackson and the Constitution* at 100 (cited in note 7) (comparing *Dred Scott* to Marshall's decision in *Worcester v Georgia*, 31 US (6 Pet) 515 (1832), and stating "The only difference between *Worcester* and *Dred Scott* is that one comports with modern concepts of federal power and civil rights while the other does not."). In *Worcester*, the Court indicated that relations with the Indian tribes were exclusively federal. 31 US (6 Pet) at 561.

[211] *Scott v Sandford*, 60 US (19 How) 393 (1857); Newmyer, *The Supreme Court under Marshall and Taney* at 89–90 (cited in note 12) ("The *Dred Scott* decision of 1857 obliterated twenty-one years of effective judicial government and left the Court burdened with the moral obloquy of slavery, as well as a heavy share of war guilt.").

[212] See Schwartz, *A History of the Supreme Court* at 91 (cited in note 5); Newmyer, *The Supreme Court under Marshall and Taney* at 118 (cited in note 12) (stating that "by 1850, the national prestige of the Court was as great as in the golden days of Marshall"). Although the result in *Dred Scott* may have been "consistent with the policy preferences of the dominant national coalition before the Civil War," Graber, *Dred Scott and the Problem of Constitutional Evil* at 30 (cited in note 2), scholars suggest that the decision evoked extensive contemporary criticism. See Swisher, *History of the Supreme Court* at 631–52 (cited in note 5) (discussing aftermath of *Dred Scott*); Walker Lewis, *Without Fear or Favor* 420–29 (Houghton Mifflin, 1965) (same); Warren,

Dred Scott come out differently, there might have been greater appreciation of the Taney Court's jurisdictional nationalism. On the other hand, the *Dred Scott* opinion manifests reasoning similar to that in the Taney Court's other jurisdictional opinions.

Dred Scott held that Congress lacked power to enact the Missouri Compromise,[213] by which Congress had prohibited slavery in the Louisiana Purchase territories above Missouri's southern border, excepting Missouri itself. Six of seven Justices in the majority joined this conclusion, although with variations in their reasoning.[214] *Dred Scott* is also known for Chief Justice Taney's conclusion—although clearly joined by only two other Justices[215]—that descendants of African slaves could not be citizens of a state for federal constitutional

---

The Supreme Court in United States History 1836–1918 at 207, 213 (cited in note 183) (noting the "crash of the Court's reputation" and "the storm of odium which the Court brought upon its own head" by the *Dred Scott* opinion); id at 316–17 (saying that "the loss of confidence in the Court was due not merely to the Court's decision but to the false and malignant criticisms" by influential northern newspapers). And jurists and historians have subsequently vilified the decision. See, for example, *Planned Parenthood of Southeastern Pennsylvania v Casey*, 505 US 833, 998 (1992) (Scalia, J, dissenting in part) ("In my history book, the Court was covered with dishonor and deprived of legitimacy by *Dred Scott v Sandford*. . . ."); Graber, *Dred Scott and the Problem of Constitutional Evil* at 15–16 (cited in note 2).

[213] The Compromise had prohibited slavery in Louisiana Purchase territories above 36° 30′, excepting Missouri itself. Act of Mar 6, 1820, ch 22, § 8, 3 Stat 545, 548. The Kansas-Nebraska Act of 1854 replaced the Missouri Compromise. See Act of May 30, 1854, ch 59, 10 Stat 277; Newmyer, *The Supreme Court under Marshall and Taney* at 130 (cited in note 12). Scott claimed he was free by virtue, inter alia, of his then-master's taking him into territory where slavery was forbidden under the Missouri Compromise. Scott sued in diversity in a Missouri federal court, alleging he was a Missouri citizen, and that his current owner was a New York citizen. See Currie, *The Constitution in the Supreme Court 1789–1888* at 264 (cited in note 19). The determination on the merits that Scott remained enslaved also indicated that Scott could not be a citizen for diversity, at least for those Justices in the majority who believed the jurisdictional issue was properly before the Court. See 60 US (19 How) at 452, 454 (Taney, CJ); see Collins, 93 Va L Rev at 1852–53 (cited in note 47) (discussing disagreement among the Justices as to whether the jurisdictional issue was before the Court). Had a majority agreed with Taney's reasoning that descendants of African slaves could never be citizens, a decision on congressional power to enact the Missouri Compromise would have been unnecessary. See Currie, *The Constitution in the Supreme Court 1789–1888* at 267 (cited in note 19) (indicating that Grier and Daniel's determination that Scott remained a slave was necessary to the decision against jurisdiction).

[214] Justice Nelson was a seventh vote with the majority, but decided only that Scott remained a slave under Missouri law. See 60 US (19 How) at 461, 465, discussed in Currie, *The Constitution in the Supreme Court 1789–1888* at 267 (cited in note 19).

[215] See 60 US (19 How) at 476–77 (Daniel, J, concurring); id at 454 (Wayne, J, concurring); cf. id at 469 (Grier, J, concurring) (unclear as to this point); Graber, *Dred Scott and the Problem of Constitutional Evil* at 19 (cited in note 2) (treating Taney's opinion on citizenship as joined by three other Justices).

purposes,[216] and neither the states[217] nor Congress could provide otherwise.[218] At a high level of generality these determinations reflect the Taney Court's tendencies to limit congressional powers, as well as the Court's reliance on its own views of the Constitution in determining the scope of Article III jurisdiction.[219]

In addition, one finds more specific parallels in Taney's reasoning as to why Congress lacked power to enact the Missouri Compromise. The most obvious source of congressional power to regulate slavery in the territories was Article IV, § 3, clause 2's territorial clause: "The Congress shall have Power to dispose of and make all needful Rules and Regulations respecting the Territory . . . belonging to the United States." But sourcing congressional power in the territorial clause might imply that Congress had power to limit slavery in all territories—both those within the United States in 1787 and those subsequently acquired—due to the precedent of the Northwest Ordinance, which had forbidden slavery in the Northwest Territory. While initially enacted by the Confederation Congress in 1787, Congress reenacted the ordinance in 1789, presumably under the territorial clause.[220] Taney, with two other Justices who joined his reasoning on this score,[221] got around this problem by concluding that

---

[216] See 60 US (19 How) at 419–22, 425, 427. State citizenship for purposes of Article III diversity jurisdiction requires U.S. citizenship, which Taney held descendants of African slaves could not attain. Id at 421–23, 425; see also Currie, *The Constitution in the Supreme Court 1789–1888* at 266 (cited in note 19).

[217] 60 US (19 How) at 405; see also id at 482 (Daniel, J, concurring) (indicating states lacked power to give national citizenship to descendants of African slaves). Taney indicated states could determine state citizenship for their own purposes. Id at 405 (Taney, CJ).

[218] See 60 US (19 How) at 420.

[219] See Magliocca, *Andrew Jackson and the Constitution* at 108 (cited in note 7) ("*Dred Scott* repudiated *McCulloch*'s admonition that courts should defer to legislative judgments about the appropriate means for exercising its authority."). Taney's opinion also reiterates the strand of the Taney Court's corporate diversity cases that the states could not conclusively determine citizenship for diversity. See notes 145–46 and accompanying text.

[220] See 60 US (19 How) at 440–42 (Taney, CJ). According to Taney, the plenary power of the Confederation Congress to forbid slavery in the territories resulted from the fact that the confederated states as independent sovereigns could unanimously agree on measures even if not specifically within powers granted to the Confederation Congress. Id at 434–35. Congress under the Constitution could reenact the Northwest Ordinance acted under the territorial clause, because that clause allowed Congress to confirm existing arrangements as to territories possessed at the time the Constitution went into effect. Id at 438–39.

[221] See Currie, *The Constitution in the Supreme Court 1789–1888* at 268 (cited in note 19) (saying Taney's reasoning on this point was only joined by Wayne and Grier).

the territorial clause referred only to territories held by the United States when the Constitution was ratified.[222]

Rather than deriving congressional power over territory such as that acquired in the Louisiana Purchase from the explicit grant in the territorial clause, Taney determined that congressional power over newly acquired territories was implied from Article IV, § 3, clause 1's provision that "[n]ew States may be admitted by Congress into this Union."[223] The implied power to regulate the territories thereunder, however, gave no power to forbid property in slaves of those who might move to the territories pending statehood.[224] Taney traced this protection in part to the Fifth Amendment's Due Process Clause[225] and also to the entitlement of new states to enter the union on equal terms as other states[226]—that is, as free or slave states as their inhab-

---

[222] 60 US (19 How) at 436. Three other Justices who joined in holding that the Missouri Compromise was beyond congressional power viewed the territorial clause as applicable, but determined that Congress lacked power thereunder to forbid slavery. See 60 US (19 How) at 489–90 (Daniel, J, concurring) (arguing that the territorial clause could not be read to destroy "the civil and political rights of the citizens of the United States" and "to exclude or to disenfranchise a portion of them because they are the owners of slaves"); id at 491 (arguing that the Northwest Ordinance never was legitimate or binding); id at 512, 516–17 (Campbell, concurring) (opining that the territorial clause did not contain plenary powers and that Congress generally lacked power to regulate slavery, but that the Northwest Ordinance was valid); id at 519–20, 524, 528–29 (Catron, J, concurring) (not rejecting the territorial clause as the source of congressional power and also determining that the Northwest Ordinance was constitutional due to the cession of Virginia to the Confederation providing no slavery; also holding the conditions of the French treaty of 1803 protecting property as well as the Constitution's Privileges and Immunities Clause did not allow Congress to forbid slavery in the territories at issue in *Scott*).

[223] 60 US (19 How) at 447 (saying there was no express power).

[224] 60 US (19 How) at 452 (referring to the Constitution generally with respect to property in slaves, stating, "The only power conferred is the power coupled with the duty of guarding and protecting the owner in his rights."); see also id at 488 (Daniel, J, concurring) (arguing that an attempt was being made to give Congress a power of forfeiture of property for no offense).

[225] Id at 450.

[226] Id at 448 (stating that because the territory when acquired from France was not ready for states to be formed "it therefore was absolutely necessary to hold possession of it, as a Territory belonging to the United States, until it was settled and inhabited by a civilized community capable of self-government, and in a condition to be admitted on equal terms with the other States as a member of the Union"); see also id at 450–51 (Congress's not being able to forbid property in slavery "places the citizens of a Territory, so far as these rights are concerned, on the same footing with citizens of the States, and guards them as firmly and plainly against any inroads which the General Government might attempt, under the plea of implied or incidental powers"); cf. *Strader v Graham*, 51 US (10 How) 82, 95–96 (1850) (stating that the Northwest Ordinance was no longer in force in states formed from it, because if it were, it would place states formed from the territory "in an inferior condition as compared with the other States, and subject their domestic institutions and municipal regulations to the constant supervision and control of this court").

itants determined upon statehood. The limitations on Congress's implied powers under the admission-of-states clause meant Congress had no power to prohibit slavery in the new territories.[227]

Taney's reasoning resembled that in *The Genesee Chief*, in which the Court upheld the extension of admiralty jurisdiction into the Great Lakes under the more limited, and Court-controlled, Article III admiralty power, not under the potentially broader Commerce Clause. In *Dred Scott*, Taney used a narrower power of the admission-of-states clause because use of the territorial clause could have indicated there was a broader congressional power to limit slavery in the territories. The implied power under the admission-of-states clause, moreover, was similar to the implied power under the Fugitive Slave Clause in *Prigg*; in both instances, there was implied congressional authority to protect but not undermine slavery. And the implied power was limited not only by owners' property rights in enslaved persons, but by an entitlement of the states to enter the union on equal terms—echoing Taney's *Genesee Chief* reasoning that western states should have the same access to admiralty jurisdiction as coastal states.

IV. Conclusion

The Marshall Court faced hostility to federal judicial power, and it shied from broad interpretations of federal court jurisdiction for mandamus, diversity, and admiralty. The Taney Court faced fewer political-branch threats than its predecessor, and it enlarged the availability of jurisdiction in those three areas. In addition, it channeled matters involving the Fugitive Slave Acts and habeas corpus to address federal detention away from the state courts and into the federal courts.

The Taney Court's enlargement of corporate diversity and admiralty, moreover, helped to consolidate the federal courts' role in

---

[227] 60 US (19 How) at 448 (indicating there was no power in the "General Government to obtain and hold colonies and dependent territories, over which they might legislate without restriction"); id at 449 (indicating that when the general government acquired territory, "It enters upon it with its powers over the citizen strictly defined, and limited by the Constitution"). Congress would be obliged to provide the same protections for property in slaves as for other property. Id at 451 ("And if the Constitution recognizes the right of property of the master in a slave, and makes no distinction between that description of property and other property . . . no tribunal acting under the authority of the United States, whether it be legislative, executive, or judicial, has a right to . . . deny to it the benefit of the provisions and guarantees which have been provided for the protection of private property against the encroachments of the Government.").

providing a uniform commerce- and contract-friendly law. And more than the Marshall Court's broad view of arising under jurisdiction with respect to the Bank of the United States in *Osborn*, the Taney Court's expansions of diversity made the lower federal courts available for challenges to state and local action, whether under federal, state, or general constitutional law.

One might easily imagine the Marshall Court's reaching results similar to those of the Taney Court, had its political environment been more favorable. But the two Courts' opinions reveal important differences in approach. Chief Justice Marshall repeatedly spoke of the plenary powers of Congress over federal jurisdiction within the limits of Article III, and the Court tied its expansive view of arising under jurisdiction to broad powers in Congress. The Taney Court, by contrast, tended to use its own constitutional interpretations in determining federal court jurisdiction, and to minimize accretions of congressional power—features that appear in *Dred Scott*.

The modern focus on arising under jurisdiction rather than diversity and admiralty has obscured the relative contributions of the Taney Court and the Marshall Court to judicial federalism. The Taney Court's restrictive view of congressional powers, moreover, is less in line with modern political realities than Marshall's broad views. And *Dred Scott* casts a deserved shadow on the Taney Court's more nationalist jurisdictional decisions. But the relationship between the two Courts is not one of revolutionary discontinuity, as was once thought, or straightforward continuity. Rather the discontinuity reflected the link between judicial federalism and congressional power.